THE INDIVIDUAL
AND THE
POLITICAL ORDER

Do Rawls!
Friday at 1:0

THE INDIVIDUAL AND THE POLITICAL ORDER

AN INTRODUCTION TO SOCIAL AND POLITICAL PHILOSOPHY

FOURTH EDITION

Norman E. Bowie and Robert L. Simon

ROWMAN & LITTLEFIELD PUBLISHERS, INC.
Lanham • Boulder • New York • Toronto • Plymouth, UK

ROWMAN & LITTLEFIELD PUBLISHERS, INC.

Published in the United States of America
by Rowman & Littlefield Publishers, Inc.
A wholly owned subsidiary of The Rowman & Littlefield Publishing Group, Inc.
4501 Forbes Boulevard, Suite 200, Lanham, Maryland 20706
www.rowmanlittlefield.com

Estover Road
Plymouth PL6 7PY
United Kingdom

British Library Cataloguing in Publication Information Available

Library of Congress Cataloging-in-Publication Data:
Bowie, Norman E., 1942–
   The individual and the political order : an introduction to social and political
philosophy / Norman E. Bowie and Robert L. Simon. — 4th ed.
       p. cm.
   Includes bibliographical references and index.
   ISBN-13: 978-0-7425-5005-6 (pbk. : alk. paper)
   ISBN-10: 0-7425-5005-2 (pbk. : alk. paper)
   1. Liberty. 2. Equality. 3. Justice. I. Simon, Robert L., 1941– II. Title.
   JC571.B675 2008
   323.01—dc22   2007007687

Printed in the United States of America

To our wives and children.

And to our grandchildren:

Alec, Kealyn, and Ainsley Bowie

Chika, Maya, Kayla, Jake, Zakary, and Travis Simon

CONTENTS

PREFACE AND ACKNOWLEDGMENTS

The Individual and the Political Order is now in its fourth edition, the second with Rowman & Littlefield. We appreciate the encouragement of our editors, Eve DeVaro and Ross Miller, and editorial assistant Ruth Gilbert, whose interest in this project encouraged us to take it on and pursue it with enthusiasm.

In this edition, we attempt to retain the style of earlier editions, which we hope has been both accessible to students and fair to opposing positions. We continue to defend a version of liberal political theory but also have devoted more space to consideration of critiques of liberalism from postmodern, feminist, and Marxist perspectives. Some chapters from the earlier versions, such as our discussions of different philosophies of law and of affirmative action, have been replaced by extended examinations of such central concepts of political thought as liberty and democracy, including a fuller discussion of deliberative democracy. In addition, we have paid greater attention than in earlier editions to the role of religion in democratic discourse and its relation to liberal neutrality. We also delve much further into the realm of international affairs, especially issues of morality and war, which are covered for the first time in *The Individual and the Political Order* in chapter 9.

We owe a large debt to all who have helped us prepare the manuscript, especially the editing and copyediting staff at Rowman & Littlefield. We also want to thank the reviewers for Rowman & Littlefield who read the third edition and made many suggestions for change, especially the proposal that we should expand our treatment of alternatives to and criticisms of liberal thought. Robert L. Simon is grateful to Hamilton College for award of a Faculty Fellowship for the fall of 2006 that made it possible to finish this project in a timely manner, and to Deans David Paris and Joe Urgo for their support. Above all, we appreciate the assistance of our wives, Maureen and Joy, whose patience and support, tolerance of excessive abstraction during the final stages of preparation of the manuscript, and assistance in preparing the final draft was absolutely invaluable. All errors and lapses in arguments are our own responsibility, but if these have been kept to a minimum, it is because of the help of others, for which we are most grateful.

INTRODUCTION

Although the twenty-first century has scarcely begun, its first decade has been filled with political and social crises. In 2006 in the United States alone, 45 million Americans lacked health insurance. Many nursing homes and other facilities for the elderly were substandard. Inequality in income and wealth was increasing, and many commentators saw the country divided into "red" and "blue" states with little willingness to compromise among politicians who seemed to many to cater more to their political "base" than to the national interest. Concerns about global warming and other environmental threats continued to grow. The United States was involved in a controversial war in Iraq, and the sense of nearly global support and sympathy for America after the 9/11 attacks seemingly had eroded. Poverty and starvation abounded in less developed countries, and AIDS was expected to cause untold numbers of deaths throughout Africa and other parts of the world.

Of course there is much more to the lives of those of us who are fortunate enough to live in more affluent liberal democracies than one crisis after another, but there is no denying that these political and social problems affect us all—some in ways more devastating than others.

Consideration of crucial issues, such as the fairness of the distribution of resources within a country or the justice of a war in which it is engaged, can lead us to examine and evaluate underlying social and political arrangements and institutions, and the moral principles they presuppose. For example, does the state have a moral right—or even a moral obligation or duty—to take resources from the affluent and redistribute them to eliminate or reduce poverty or to provide decent medical care to all? Would such a redistributive state, favored by some liberals, violate the property rights of those who are taxed by unjustly confiscating their property? Would the government bureaucracy needed to implement antipoverty programs actually create more poverty than it would eliminate, perhaps by creating incentives for the poor to become dependent on handouts, as some conservatives claim? Whether or not there is a general entitlement to some form of welfare support or safety net, does government have a special duty to eliminate burdens that fall disproportionately on minority racial groups, perhaps because of the legacy of past racial injustice?

Ethical questions involving political and social issues do not necessarily stop at the borders of a nation. Do ethical principles apply to international affairs, and, if so, do the principles that apply resemble those that apply domestically? For example, if social justice within the state requires some redistribution of wealth from the more affluent to the poor, does international justice similarly require redistribution from the rich nations to the impoverished of the globe? What about ethics and war? Are there moral limits on the behavior of warring parties, and, if so, how stringent are they? Is modern war even permissible given its destructiveness and the dangers to noncombatants? Is a just war possible? Does the need to combat terrorism justify limitations on basic civil liberties that are protected in liberal democracies?

These and a whole host of related issues are hotly debated, not only in the press and by political leaders, but by ordinary citizens as well. Very often, however, the important philosophical questions underlying such debates, rather than being clarified or examined, are obscured in the heat and simplistic rhetoric of political argument.

Political arguments of the kind in question rest on philosophical presuppositions that need to be clarified and evaluated. The price of failure to do so is that the heat of rhetoric replaces the clarity of analysis, and our real problems are shrouded rather than being understood and squarely faced. For example, consider the following dialogues.

> Citizen A: The idea that I should pay taxes to cover the medical care of others is wrong. It is unjust to tax me, in effect seizing my earnings through the threat of force, to care for others. Why don't they just buy their own health insurance? For that matter, why should I have to pay taxes to cover provision of food for others, or even for the education of other people's children? Why shouldn't people have to pay for those things themselves?

> Citizen B: But proper medical care is a necessity. (So, for that matter, are food and basic education for our community's children.) Moreover, medical care in particular is expensive, and people often can't afford to pay for it themselves. Is it fair, for example, for children of poorer people not to get medical care (or food, or education) because their parents can't afford it? One of the obligations of living in a society and enjoying its benefits is paying back so that all citizens can enjoy its basic benefits.

> Citizen A: But it's not the community's job to provide everything that people need. What about the responsibility of individuals to provide for themselves? After all, just because I may need exercise, should other people be forced to provide me with exercise equipment or a good gym? Your view just leads to "tax and spend" liberalism, which discourages individual initiative and creates a big and inefficient government.

> Citizen B: But health care is a basic right. If we don't tax to provide basic necessities, people, through no fault of their own, will lead impoverished lives and even die. I thought you conservatives were compassionate, not heartless!

Citizen A: How do you know there is a right to medical care? And even if I conceded such a right, where does the list of such rights end? What about my right to do what I want with what I earn? How do you decide what is a right and which rights we have? Compassion can be expressed through charity, not through the state taxing and taxing what we have worked so hard to earn.

Citizen C: How can you advocate keeping God out of the public schools? We ought to open the school day with prayer. That would express the religious orientation of our country and remind students of basic moral principles and duties.

Citizen D: But whose prayer is the official one? Do we want the state determining which religious views are official and sanctioned by the government? We have separation of church and state to protect a vast variety of religions from state-enforced worship. Like Citizen A above, you claim to be against big government, but then you go ahead and say you want the government determining how we should pray, and forcing school kids to pray in the official manner.

Citizen C: Who said anything about forcing anyone? Of course, prayers in schools should be voluntary. Our country is religious and there are common elements of prayer that members of virtually all religions would agree upon.

Citizen D: I doubt if there is a common prayer that is not totally vacuous or insignificant. Moreover, don't atheists, agnostics, and adherents of non-traditional religions have rights? Moreover, we don't want the state telling us what is common to all; that is giving too much power to government. Even if there is not outright coercion at work (and I don't concede that point at all) the state should be neutral on religious matters. It's up to individuals to choose for themselves what kind of life they want to lead, to pick their own account of the good life, whether it is religious or not.

Citizen C: Your neutrality is a sham. By keeping silent on large moral issues, the state abandons the idea of an American community in favor of individualism run wild. Your so-called neutral state really is endorsing a superficial, even harmful, ideal: that nothing is more sacred than individual choice, no matter how bad the choices some individuals will make. We need to stand as a society for wholesome values, not collapse, as you advocate, into moral relativism and nihilism.

Debates such as these raise the kinds of issues that this book will address. In each exchange, fundamental philosophical issues are being discussed. But in each exchange, there also is the danger that the fundamental issues will be ignored as each side resorts to name-calling and "mud-slinging" against the other. For example, in the first exchange, Citizen A holds that there are moral limits to the domain within which government may exercise power over its citizens. These limits are set by the entitlements or rights of citizens, including the right to control the fruits of their labors. Citizen B seems to agree that the rights of citizens are basic, but believes in a wider set of rights than Citizen A. According to B, these rights include entitlements to necessary benefits, and these entitlements do impose obligations on the more affluent to help provide necessities to others. It is all too easy in the actual political arena, where winning elections becomes paramount, or in the press, which often does not delve into such issues in depth, to fail to adequately examine the justifications that might be offered on behalf of different views. It is easier to just skim the surface, or to call opponents names, such as "tax and spend liberal" or "heartless conservative," than to explore whether one side is supported by better arguments than the other. Each citizen seems to appeal to an underlying conception of justice or fairness, but neither makes explicit what that conception is or how it is to be defended against other conceptions. Similarly, in the second dialogue, each citizen seems to have a different set of underlying assumptions about the proper limits of state activity and how intrusive the state should be with respect to the choices of individual citizens.

Political and social philosophy grapples with issues such as these by clarifying different points of view on complex social and political issues, identifying and formulating arguments on different sides, and by evaluating such arguments themselves. It is primarily an exercise in *moral* evaluation of political and social issues, although political and social philosophers employ analysis and logic in their explorations. Thus, it is important to understand not only how the political order *does* work but also how it *should* work. Without such critical normative analysis, criticisms and defenses of current institutions may lack rational support, and discourse within the political arena runs the all too evident danger of becoming debased, amounting to little more than emotional rhetorical appeals that may only contribute to, rather than help resolve, the very real political and social problems we all face.

There are at least two related ways in which political philosophy can contribute to evaluation of the political and social order. First, it can help clarify the concepts and arguments that are employed in political discourse. Unless such notions as "authority," "rights," justice," and "liberty" are analyzed, it is far from clear that the parties to disputes such as those in our sample dialogues understand just what it is they are arguing about. Moreover, even agreement on terms of discourse can obscure fundamental disagreement. Thus, Citizen A and Citizen B might both be in favor of "equality" but one might understand equality in terms of fair opportunities to compete, taking individual responsibility for the outcome, while the other might understand it as requiring provision of basic necessities so that all have a roughly equal or at least fair start to the competition.

This does not mean that philosophers clarify terms simply by reporting ordinary usage (although that may be relevant to their inquiries) or looking up words in dictionaries. Most often, terms like "equality," "fairness," "rights," and "liberty" are understood very differently by different people because they are embedded in different political theories. In effect, there are different conceptions or theories of how equality, fairness, rights, or liberty should best be understood. People who understand equality in terms of open access to fair competition alone have a very different normative conception of the political order than those who understand it in terms of fair representation of major ethnic groups and genders in our institutions. One of the tasks of political philosophy is to clarify and explicate the different theoretical meanings of the major concepts of political thought.

While it is important to be clear about what we or others are saying, it surely is crucial to say something that is not only clear but also defensible or justified. Surely we want to know not only what is meant by liberty in a particular context, but also how much liberty people are entitled to have. For example, is a law that regulates the sale of pornographic material morally defensible or is it an unjustified restriction on personal freedom? Are regulations prohibiting and calling for punishment of so-called hate speech on college campuses necessary protections for minorities or unwarranted and dangerously vague intrusions on free speech and the uninhibited exchange of ideas in an academic setting? Political philosophy can contribute to the justification of political and social decisions, rules, policies, and institutions by formulating and critically assessing arguments of proponents and opponents alike.

Some readers may be skeptical about the second enterprise and ask, "Who is to say which views are morally justified and which are not?" Unfortunately, this attitude leads to the kind of moral paralysis revealed by one of our students who wrote in an essay, "Of course I don't like the Nazis, but who am I to say they are morally wrong?" Surely each of us can make reasonable moral judgments by assessing the arguments for and against particular positions under consideration.

But isn't claiming that some positions are right and others wrong showing disrespect for others, perhaps by failing to recognize the cultural differences that may lead to moral disagreement? Isn't it demonstrating intolerance for the views of others? Those who ask such questions may fail to notice that the claims "We ought to respect the views of others" and "We ought not to be intolerant" are themselves moral judgments with which some other people may disagree. We also point out that taking moral positions does not require one to do so in a self-righteous or uncritical way, and that perhaps the best way of coming to a reasoned moral view is through dialogue with those with whom one disagrees. Such moral disagreement, mediated by dialogue, can be among the highest forms of showing respect for others since it recognizes the status of those with whom we disagree as thinking, rational persons who have the same opportunity to change our minds through argument as we do to change theirs. At the very least, such dialogue, even if it does not result in consensus, can lead to a better understanding of how reasonable people of good will can disagree on serious matters without either party being evil, although of course in some extreme cases, such as that of the Nazis, dialogue might also expose the irrationality and moral evil that sometimes infect the political order.

As it sometimes is helpful to know where one is going before one sets out, the following guide to subsequent chapters of this book should prove useful. Our first task will be to evaluate the different accounts of the proper role of government and the proper limits to its authority over the individual. Suspicion of government is growing in contemporary America, and some Americans, such as the so-called militia groups, go so far as to view their own government as their enemy. Does government have a legitimate function? If so, should it be limited to providing self-defense and ensuring fair competition on the free market, as libertarians claim, or is a more extensive government, such as the modern welfare state, not only desirable but just and fair as well? Do modern liberal and libertarian theories overemphasize the rights of the individual and ignore the role of community and family values?

More specifically, in chapter 1 we will consider whether ceding authority to the state is compatible with respecting our own personal autonomy and freedom of choice. In chapters 2 and 3 we will consider two important theories of the proper role of the state (the state as an instrument to maximize social utility and the state as a protector of fundamental human rights) and in chapter 4 we will examine the notion of social justice and resolving conflicts that arise when individual rights conflict. As a result of our discussions, we will propose a perspective of our own which maintains that the government ought to be regarded primarily as the protector of individual rights and implementer of certain broad principles of justice and fairness that can be applied to concrete policy issues.

The middle chapters of the book apply our general conception of the role of the state to more concrete issues of policy. Many of the questions in these chapters concern the conflict between individual behavior and institutions within the political order, such as the legal system. For example, what is the domain of individual liberty and how is liberty to be reconciled with other values, such as security and respect? For example, should speech that insults or offends others be regulated? Should "hate speech" be permitted at colleges and universities? Under what conditions does democracy exist, and how should it be implemented? For example, is democracy simply a mechanism for resolving the clashes that arise among competing interest groups, so-called special interests, or should it be conceived differently, say as a forum of reasonable civil discourse through which citizens develop as social and political beings?

Finally, in the last two chapters of the book, we will examine two issues that arise in international affairs: on one hand, the issue of international obligations (including the obligation to relieve poverty and suffering in other lands) and on the other the question of whether morality applies to war, and if it does, in what way. Do we have a duty to alleviate starvation in other countries? Do we act wrongly by not giving to famine relief, or is giving a form of charity which it is good to do but not wrong to fail to do? Do ethical principles apply to war, or is any behavior against the enemy permissible in times of war? What are our duties to civilians or innocents? Is just war even possible given the destructiveness of modern warfare?

Throughout our discussion, we will sometimes try to defend particular positions, but above all we will try to be fair to opposing viewpoints by presenting them in their strongest possible form. All too often in the actual political arena, views are caricatured by their opponents in a way that demonizes the opposition. "She's a heartless conservative" or "He's a 'tax and spend' liberal" function as epithets rather than arguments. (For example, what sane person would want to tax and spend for no purpose?) We hope, through fair consideration of contrary stances, to enable readers to see what is good in opposing positions as well as understand the weaknesses of different viewpoints. As a result, actual political dialogue between opposing viewpoints can be rational and informed. Perhaps, we can even move beyond the kind of preaching to the converted, where each side talks only to those who already agree, that seems so prevalent not only in America generally but on college campuses in particular.

We also hope to defend a position that reflects and applies the principle so eloquently stated by John Rawls that "Each person possesses an inviolability . . . that even the welfare of society cannot override . . ."[1] Accordingly, while we mean to provide an introduction to a wide range of views in political philosophy, our work also defends a perspective of its own. We hope, of course, that readers find that perspective plausible, but we hope also that we provide a fair enough account of other views so that the major objections to our own views are available for assessment. Whichever political position turns out to be most defensible, perhaps the study of political philosophy itself is of the highest value, for it can lead to critical and reflective evaluation of that great leviathan, the political order, which so significantly affects our lives, those of our fellow citizens, and those of our fellow inhabitants of the globe.

NOTE

1. John Rawls, *A Theory of Justice* (Cambridge, MA: Harvard University Press, 1971), 3–4.

LOVE IT OR LEAVE IT? INDIVIDUAL CONSCIENCE AND POLITICAL AUTHORITY

We live in an age of great political conflict. Internationally, although the balance of nuclear terror between the superpowers has abated due to major changes in what used to be the Soviet Union, famines, poverty in the Third World, wars, and international terrorism continue to threaten stability and disrupt the lives of millions. Domestically, controversies rage over the proper role of government in such areas as providing benefits for its citizens or promoting important moral values. Is it the responsibility of the state to provide some degree of welfare, including food, shelter, medical care, and education for its citizens and, if so, how much? Indeed, there is little consensus on how major social problems are to be solved. How can we best deal with crime in the streets or in the executive suites? Should the "war on drugs" be stepped up or should use of certain drugs by competent adults be legalized? Does government have an obligation to promote "family values" or should it be neutral with respect to such matters as personal lifestyle and sexual orientation?

In the international arena, the problems are perhaps especially acute. What are the obligations of people living in affluent countries to the millions of sick, starving, and otherwise suffering people throughout the world? What is the best way to deal with terrorism? Is war justified only in response to aggression or are there other grounds for a "just" war? What about preventive war—that is, war launched against a country that might attack us in the future?

How such major social and political issues are dealt with will profoundly affect us all. The wise use of political power can benefit millions of people, while the unwise or immoral use of such power can seriously harm millions more. It is important, then, not only to describe how government does work but also to consider how it *should* work. One of the principal tasks of social and political philosophy is to formulate, clarify, and examine criteria for evaluating political institutions, such as government. Accordingly, political philosophy is a critical activity in at least the sense that it subjects political and social institutions and practices to intensive moral scrutiny.

It is characteristic of such institutions that they claim to have authority over individuals who stand in certain relationships to them. For example, a college or its faculty may claim the authority to establish requirements for graduation. A coach of a sports team may claim to have the authority to decide the lineup and determine who plays during games. To have authority in the sense in question is to have the *right* to make decisions in areas to which one's authority applies. Thus, authority differs from mere power in that authority is normative; the authority is not simply claiming to have more power than others but rather is claiming a right to decide, a right to exercise power.

The nation or state is perhaps the dominant political institution, although some observers believe that multinational corporations have come to rival the state in some areas of influence. States claim to have authority over their citizens in the sense of having a right to be obeyed. If states required obedience to law simply on the grounds that they are sufficiently powerful to make their subjects obey, they would differ only in scope from the biggest bully in the neighborhood. Their commands would lack moral legitimacy and would be based only on force. Normally, states do not claim merely to be the biggest bully of them all. The U.S. government, for example, does not say its citizen should obey the law simply because they will be punished if they disobey. Rather, the government claims that since its status is morally legitimate, citizens have a moral duty to follow the law. This strong sense of authority in which the state's supposed right to command generates an alleged obligation to obey generates a major problem. The problem arises when the claims of the state to obedience clash with the consciences of its citizens.

The clash between conscience and authority can arise in a variety of contexts. Suppose, for example, that in a high school basketball team, the home team's worst foul shooter is fouled at a crucial point in the game. The coach notices that the referee is confused as to who was fouled and tells her best foul shooter to go to the line. The player is shocked and replies that she can't do that because it is cheating. The coach replies, "I'm the coach and I decide what you do during the game." The coach is asserting a claim to authority. The player is responding that her conscience doesn't allow her to follow such directions. Thus, the kind of conflict we want to focus upon is at issue.

In many cases of conflict between individual conscience and authority, it may not be so clear which side ought to prevail. Consider, for example, the problem of a hospital's ethics committee faced with the task of deciding which of two terminally ill patients will receive the one organ available for transplant. According to the rules of the hospital, which have been accepted by the staff, cases that raise tough ethical issues are sent to the committee, whose decision is binding. In this particular case, each patient will die without a transplant, but not enough compatible organs are available to save both.

The first patient, A, must have the transplant almost immediately because his situation is very unstable. However, A would not have needed the transplant so quickly had he followed his physician's instructions about diet, medication, and exercise. Because of his own behavior, he needs treatment right now. The second patient, B, has been highly responsible and has postponed the need for treatment through good health habits. Furthermore, because B can be relied on to follow instructions, he could wait at least a short time in the hope that another organ will become available. While the odds are against another compatible organ becoming available, there is some chance that one will be found. Should the doctors give the organ to A, who will die imminently without a transplant, and hope that another organ will be found in time to save B, or should they save B on the grounds that A's predicament is his own fault for which B should not suffer?

Suppose the committee decides that B should get the transplant because its members find A's behavior irresponsible, and further suppose that the physician who will perform the transplant believes that he cannot just stand by and let A die, especially when there is some chance another organ will become available in time to save B.

One issue raised by this case concerns the justification of the decision by the ethics committee. Was its decision warranted?[1] A second issue concerns what the physician should do. Should he follow the directive of the committee and operate on B, or should he follow his own conscience and reject the committee's directive? It might not be easy to decide what the best resolution is to either issue.

In this chapter, we will focus primarily on the second issue, the apparent clash between the claims of authority and the claims of conscience, as well as on some of the broader questions of political philosophy to which our examination leads. The twentieth century has seen horrible deeds committed by followers of charismatic leaders claiming authority. But at the same time, if we were never able to put aside our individual viewpoints and accede to the decisions of an authority, the result might well be chaotic. Is there such a thing as legitimate authority? What is its moral basis or justification? Is it possible to somehow reconcile the claims of both authority and conscience, so that the twin evils of social chaos and blind subservience might each be avoided?

In the political arena, many are inclined to give absolute authority to the commands of the state. Particularly in times of crisis, it is often felt that criticism of our leaders, let alone protests or disobedience of their commands, is disloyal, dangerous, and subversive. Thus, in the 1960s at the start of the antiwar movement, many Americans regarded those who vigorously protested the Vietnam War, especially those who avoided military service, as having deserted or even as having betrayed their country in time of need. Similar criticism was sometimes made initially against those who doubted the wisdom of President George W. Bush's decision to invade Iraq. The slogan "Love it or leave it," which was so frequently directed at protesters against the Vietnam War, quite clearly expresses the attitude that criticism of the political order, particularly in time of crisis after a decision by authorities has been made, is incompatible with allegiance to it.

But while some persons are disposed to give absolute weight to the claims of authority, others are equally disposed to go the other way. Consider, for example,

Henry David Thoreau's reaction to what he considered an unjust war. Rather than pay taxes that would have supported the Mexican War effort, he refused to pay and was subsequently imprisoned. Thoreau denied that his legal obligation to pay his taxes was a sufficient moral reason for obedience. In defense of his disobedience, Thoreau declares that

> Laws never made men a whit more just: and, by means of the respect for it, even the well disposed are daily made instruments of injustice. A common and natural result of an undue respect for law is, that you might see a file of soldiers . . . marching in admirable order over hill and dale to the wars, against their wills, ay, against their common sense and consciences . . .[2]

It appears as if there is great tension between the claims to authority over citizens made by political and social institutions, particularly the state, and the claims of individual conscience and autonomy. As one contemporary writer puts it,

> The defining mark of the state is authority, the right to rule. The primary obligation of man is autonomy, the refusal to be ruled. It would seem, then, that there can be no resolution of the conflict between autonomy . . . and the putative authority of the state.[3]

The implications of this apparent conflict are enormous. If the conflict is indeed genuine, we are faced with a momentous choice. If, on one hand, we are overly impressed by the need for order and stability that can be promoted by allegiance to a common authority, we may be led to stifle the exercise of independent critical judgment. But, as a result, we are in danger of ending up with the abhorrent picture of "good Germans" engaging in genocide under the commands of the Nazis. If, on the other hand, we assign absolute weight to individual autonomy, we may end up with the community in chaos, as individuals go their own way with no conception of the common good or common rules recognized as binding.

A major goal of political philosophy is to formulate defensible criteria for assessing the political order, particularly as embodied in the state. However, as the preceding discussion suggests, it is imperative to consider what is involved in accepting political authority in the first place. Perhaps the costs of acceptance are prohibitive. For example, does acceptance of authority require us to abandon autonomy and disregard conscience? Under what circumstances, if any, are claims to political authority morally legitimate or justified? Is the only alternative to acceptance of absolute authority a kind of anarchy of individual conscience?

We will begin by considering a classic and highly influential defense of the necessity of absolute political authority provided by Thomas Hobbes. In particular, we will consider the kind of justification offered by Hobbes for recognizing the authority of the state. Then we will consider the claim that our obligation to exercise our own critical judgment and be autonomous overrides any possible obligation to the state. Finally, we will suggest a strategy for evaluating the state, for distinguishing good states from bad ones, and for determining under what conditions the former might legitimately claim some form of authority over its citizens. That strategy will be developed and contrasted with alternate approaches throughout the book.

THE GROUNDS OF POLITICAL AUTHORITY

Thomas Hobbes (1588–1679): The Case for Absolute Authority

Hobbes's political philosophy reflects his horror of war, particularly civil war. This is not surprising in view of the tumultuous times in which Hobbes lived. He was born as the Spanish Armada was approaching England. He joked that "Fear and I were born twins," and he actually was born prematurely, perhaps because of his mother's fear of an invasion. The England of his time was filled with domestic political strife as Parliament and the monarchy struggled for power, and civil war between factions was a real danger. The reigns of Elizabeth I and James I, the Civil War, the rule of Cromwell and the Puritans, and the Restoration of the monarchy all occurred within his lifetime.

Educated at Oxford, with the scholastic tradition that he later repudiated, Hobbes spent much of his life as a tutor and later adviser to the children of the aristocratic Cavendish family. His employment provided time for reading, writing, and thinking. Moreover, through the Cavendish family and later through other leading families who also employed him in various capacities, he was able to meet many of the great thinkers of his own time.

Politically, he was in favor of a strong central government, and his sympathies in the struggles between Parliament and the monarchy were with the latter. Because of his political views, he feared enemies in Parliament and the outcome of the looming Civil War and so, before the outbreak of the conflict, left England for Paris. There, he tutored the Prince of Wales, who was later to become King Charles II. However, the ideas expressed in his major work, *Leviathan* (1651), made him unpopular with some factions in France, including the Church, because of its naturalistic, scientific, and rationalistic approach to political thought. Consequently, he made his peace with Parliament and with Cromwell, the leader of the Puritans, and returned to England. The Puritans believed that government had a responsibility to enforce a kind of pietistic Christian way of life and scorned such activities as the theatre as frivolous. (Although Hobbes favored the monarchy, he believed, as we will see, that any strong existing central government, such as that of Cromwell and the Puritans, was legitimately sovereign.) When Charles II assumed the throne after the fall of Cromwell's government and the restoration of the monarchy he remembered Hobbes with affection. The last years of Hobbes's life were spent in philosophical reflection and conversation, with financial support provided by the throne.

Hobbes's Political Philosophy

In political philosophy, Hobbes's goal was to explain and justify a form of that great leviathan, the state, solely by reference to its elements, the individuals of whom it was composed. For Hobbes, human action was either largely or entirely egoistic, aimed ultimately at satisfying the desires of the agent or avoiding their frustration.[4] Agents normally are, and always have the potential to be, efficient rational calculators. They can select the most efficient means to their goals, which ultimately involve their own self-interest.

Hobbes's starting point is an account of human nature. It is a conception of how human nature would be, in its pristine state, apart from the influence of the political order. The proper function of the state is to remedy the defects of the state of nature. The state is justified by appeal to the nature of life among the individual people that would exist if human nature were left as it is apart from political and related institutional structures. Since the life of such individuals would be horrible, and the state can remedy the defects that cause such horror, the existence of the state is warranted.

Hobbes is often criticized for exaggerating the extent of human egoism and for postulating an egoistic view of human nature without appropriate empirical evidence. We agree that these criticisms have great force, but it is important to note that they do not discredit Hobbes's approach to political philosophy. Thus, we doubt if psychological egoism—the view that human action, always and everywhere, is basically selfish—can be sustained in the face of counterexamples such as heroism, the often unconditional love of parents for their children, and the countless acts that show concern for others that almost all of us engage in every day.[5]

However, a Hobbesian could reply that at least some such acts are engaged in because we have institutions in place, such as the legal and educational systems, which protect us if our altruism makes us vulnerable and which tend to promote reciprocal altruism on the part of others. Without such institutions, even if much human action was not egoistic, agents would have little assurance, in advance of extensive contact with others, concerning who would behave as an amoral egoist and who would not. Thus, even if not all human behavior was naturally selfish, prudent persons in the state of nature would have to take precautions against victimization simply because they would have no fully reliable method of distinguishing those who would exploit them from others.

Given Hobbes's assumptions, which include not only a tendency toward egoism, but also a not unreasonable postulate about the scarcity of things we most want, what would life be like without the state? According to Hobbes, life in this state of nature would be "solitary, poor, nasty, brutish, and short."[6] If there were no state to preserve law and order, then given human selfishness, or at least the presumption of it, scarcity of resources, and approximate equality in strength, cunning, and personal resources, the result would be a war of all against all. If there were not enough to go around, and everyone, whether through strength or cunning, was a potential threat to everyone else, and if it would be prudent to assume the worst about the intentions of others, competition for the objects of common desire would be constant and often bloody.

More precisely, each person would reason that others are either dangerous threats to their safety or else relatively harmless. If the other is a threat, it is best to strike preemptively. But if the other is not a threat, one can gain an advantage by striking preemptively. Since everyone reasons the same way, all persons in the state of nature would regard preemptive strikes as their best strategy. Hence, the war of all against all is a necessary consequence of Hobbes's starting points and assumptions.

If this was Hobbes's reasoning, he anticipated the famous "prisoner's dilemma" of modern game theory. The prisoner's dilemma concerns two suspects who are questioned separately by the police. If neither confesses, they will each get a relatively light sentence, but if only one confesses and the other does not, the holdout will get a maximally long sentence and the one who cooperates with the police will get off lightly. If both confess, they will get a longer sentence than if neither confesses. Just as in the state of nature, each prisoner reasons that self-interest requires confession. (Prisoner A reasons as follows: "If B does not confess and I do, I'll get off lightly, while if he does confess, I'd better confess to avoid getting the maximally long sentence. So whatever B does, I'd better confess." B, in the exact similar situation, reasons the same way.) As a result, they both confess and both get longer sentences than if they had cooperated with each other by remaining silent.[7]

Consequently, given Hobbes's postulates—that humans are or must be reasonably assumed to be selfish, that not all selfish desires can be satisfied, and that humans are approximately equal in their capacities to harm one another—the conclusion that the state of nature would be one of anxiety, violence, and constant danger would seem to follow. Humans would reason as in the case of the prisoner's dilemma and conclude that preemptive aggression is their best strategy.

Human beings, however, need not be stuck in the state of nature. On the contrary, Hobbes has described human beings as rational, as efficient calculators about how to reach their goals. Thus, people in the state of nature would realize that the war of all against all was contrary to their interests, particularly their overriding concern with self-preservation. For whatever else people want, and surely different individuals want diverse things, they all need personal security and continued existence as prerequisites for their enjoyment of anything else. "The passions that incline men to peace are fear of death, desire of such things as are necessary to commodious living, and a hope by their industry to obtain them. And reason suggesteth convenient articles of peace . . . which otherwise are called Laws of Nature."[8]

According to Hobbes, "A law of nature . . . is a precept or general rule, found out by reason, by which a man is forbidden to do that which is destructive of his life, or taketh away the means of preserving the same. And consequently, that every man ought to endeavor peace, as far as he has hope of obtaining it; and when he cannot obtain it, then he may seek . . . all help and advantages of war."[9] In other words, since the state of nature, being a state of war of all against all, is a disaster for all concerned, it is in the rational self-interest of the inhabitants to end the war by forming a state with the authority and power to limit conflict. Thus, the first law of nature, which enjoins everyone to seek peace, implies the second; namely, that when others are willing, all parties to the state of war contract together, or create a covenant, to set up a supreme authority over them all. By doing so and (given the postulates about human motivation and scarcity) *only* by doing so can the evils of the state of nature be avoided. The state, then, is an instrument to keep the evils of the unregulated pursuit of self-interest in check.

In fact, given his view of human nature, Hobbes concludes that only a state with absolute power over its citizens can provide security for them. For "covenants without the sword are but words, and of no strength to secure a man at all . . . if there be no power . . . every man will rely on his own strength and art . . . against all other men."[10] That is, if citizens are given some freedoms against the state, then given the initial assumptions about the pursuit of self-interest, they will use that freedom to advance their own ends and defeat the opposing plans of others. The state of nature will just reappear in a new guise. Since only an absolute power can prevent the reversion of the war of all against all, that is exactly the kind of state rational parties to the original covenant would create.

Hobbes's argument, as reconstructed here, does not presuppose there ever actually was a state of nature. Hobbes can best be understood as presenting a hypothetical argument. *If* the political state did not exist, look how bad things would be. If the state did not exist, we would need to create it.[11]

Hobbes believes, then, that the authority of the state cannot coexist with the individual autonomy of the citizens. Although rational inhabitants of the state of nature may autonomously agree to the covenant that creates the sovereign, the absolute state that enforces the peace, by creating that leviathan they surrender their own power of decisionmaking. Little if any room is left in the Hobbesian state for the kind of individual rights valued in liberal democracies.[12] To Hobbes, the constant struggles between interest groups in the liberal state and the degeneration of political discourse into insult and invective are simply evidence of the inherent instability of liberal democracy and of the thin blue line that stands between such degenerate forms of the state and the war of all against all.

In spite of these gloomy conclusions, however, Hobbes's approach to political philosophy is of the greatest value. First, it is an attempt to explain not only the need for the political order but the necessity for all rational individuals to assent to it on the basis of minimal assumptions about human altruism or human kindness. The state is an instrument of mutual advantage. The political order is explained and justified in naturalistic terms without recourse to controversial moral assumptions or such metaphysical doctrines as the divine right of rulers or the special fitness of one group of humans to rule all the others. Rather, what Hobbes has done is to isolate what he takes to be the basic unit of political and social analysis—the individual person—and ground his account of the political order upon it. According to his argument, rational individuals under conditions of scarcity would be under constant threat in a brutal natural state and would unanimously consent to the absolute state in order to escape their predicament.

Evaluation of Hobbes's Political Theory

Hobbes views the state as an instrument for providing those basic primary goods without which a minimally satisfactory human life is impossible. These basic goods, according to Hobbes, are peace and security. In his view, only a state with absolute authority can provide them.

If we are to avoid Hobbes's defense of the absolute state, we must either reject his premises or his reasoning from premises to conclusion. For if we accept his starting points and concede that he has reasoned cogently from them, his conclusion that an absolute sovereign, not liberal democracy, is a rational necessity would be inescapable. Critics might begin by questioning Hobbes's pessimistic view of human nature. Even if it is true, as Hobbes seems to maintain, that humans always act to satisfy their desires, it does not follow that their desires always are selfish ones. Parents who act for the benefit of their children, soldiers who sacrifice themselves for their comrades, and teachers who give up their own time to help their students all count as examples of individuals who sometimes act for unselfish reasons. Of course, one could reply that the parents really act for the personal satisfaction they get from helping their children, the soldier really wants to be remembered as a hero, and the teachers are trying to avoid the pain of guilt they would experience if they did not help their students. But these replies are implausible. Why, for example, would the teachers even feel guilt unless they cared about their students and thought the students ought to get help?[13] It is difficult to believe that all apparently unselfish acts really are selfish ones, especially when one sees that the goals of avoiding guilt and receiving satisfaction presuppose that the agent thinks some ways of treating others are right and wrong independently of any personal benefit the agent receives.

Of course, it is always possible to discount any data that conflicts with one's pet theory, but the same can be done for any theory. For example, one might argue that all human actions are really altruistic and that apparently selfish acts are really done to benefit the agent in the long run. "That mugger was really trying to toughen you up and show you not to be so trusting." If such armchair psychology is implausible when arguing that all acts really are unselfish, it must be equally implausible when used to show that all acts are selfish. Consequently, Hobbes's apparent defense of psychological egoism—the view that all human behavior is selfish—seems altogether too extreme to withstand examination.

However, as suggested above, Hobbes might not need such an extreme view to make his point. Perhaps he could argue more modestly that (1) a good deal of human behavior is selfish; (2) selfish behavior is more likely to occur in the state of nature than in the state where political institutions control selfishness; and (3) in the state of nature, where any mistake could be deadly, it is simply prudent for each agent to assume that all other agents are acting only for their own good, even if each agent knows that is not always true. That is because one is more likely to be harmed or killed by mistaking an egoist for an altruist than by mistrusting everyone. Indeed, if the parties reason according to the logic of the prisoner's dilemma previously outlined, prudential rationality will lead to the war of all against all even if we do not presume that every single human action is motivated by self-interest.

Perhaps also of importance, Hobbes may not be making claims about human nature in a straightforward empirical way. Rather, he may be suggesting that we ought to start our political philosophy not with optimistic assumptions about how nice we naturally would be to one another—for given an assumption of universal niceness many of the problems of political philosophy would not even arise—but with some more pessimistic assumptions whose implications we should examine. If we can solve many of our conflicts by finding points of agreement that even largely self-interested parties would agree upon, the solutions would rest on a much more powerful basis than solutions based on a kind of "sweetness and light" view of human nature which, if true, makes it difficult to see how the problems ever got started in the first place.

Let us suppose that Hobbes can make his argument work with this revised assumption about what it is rational to assume in the state of nature.[14] His view still faces serious difficulties. The problem we have in mind can be seen most clearly, perhaps, by thinking of the court of a king or queen. If we think of the king or queen as the sovereign, all of the problems of court intrigue come to the fore. Different courtiers and aristocrats, given Hobbes's assumptions about human nature, will be pursuing their own interests, which frequently may clash with that of the ruler. The state of nature simply will reappear in the form of struggles for power within the court.

This problem can be generalized given the following points. First, if we assume a general tendency toward selfishness, Hobbes's version of the state would itself seem to be an impossibility. For the state to have the kind of absolute power Hobbes thinks is necessary to keep the peace, it must have a powerful coercive apparatus under its control, for example, a strong police force or army. But given Hobbes's assumptions about human psychology, who will coerce the coercers? The police and soldiers, like the courtiers conspiring against the king or queen, will have a tendency to act in their own interest where it conflicts with that of the sovereign. That is, the sovereign and its agents will be in a state of nature with respect to one another. As a result, breakdown of the very coercive order that is supposed to preserve the peace is always a real threat. Even if we assume that many individual members of the sovereign's force have a disposition to do their duty and put aside self-interest, each may find it prudent to suspect the others. How could the kind of trust needed to preserve the state be generated? Hobbes's psychology, then, tends to undermine his political theory.[15]

A second problem is even more important, however. As the seventeenth-century philosopher John Locke argued, individuals in Hobbes's state of nature would be irrational to set up an absolute sovereign state in the first place.

> Though men when they enter society give up the equality, liberty and executive power they had in the state of nature into the hands of society . . . yet it [is] only with an intention in every one the better to preserve himself, his liberty and property—for no rational creature can be supposed to change his condition with an intention to be worse.[16]

Locke's point is that it would be irrational to leave the approximate equality of the state of nature simply to create a sovereign more powerful than any of one's previous enemies. Given Hobbes's psychology of human nature, rational individuals would be prudent to assume that the sovereign and its agents will act for their own selfish purposes. If so, Hobbes's deduction of the absolute authority of the state over the individual seems invalid since the Hobbesian covenant not only makes individuals no better off than they were in the state of nature but also makes them liable to a new and powerful threat, more dangerous than their enemies of old.

For Hobbes, at least as we have read him, power relations are central. The state is a mechanism for preventing the disastrous use of power by unconstrained individuals, each following their own self-interest at the expense of others. It is mutually advantageous for each individual in the state of nature to set up an absolute sovereign to end the war of all against all. However, Hobbes's argument as so understood may undermine itself since, for one thing, it is hard to see how the different agents of the state could ever trust one another sufficiently to keep the state going, and, for another, it is hard to see why the parties in the state of nature would ever find it rational to sign the social contract or covenant to begin with.

But we should not abandon what surely is one of Hobbes's major insights—namely, that the state is an instrument to secure some benefit to its citizens or to protect them from some evil. It should not be viewed as a private preserve divinely assigned to a ruler (the theory of the divine right of kings) or a resource to be exploited by the few at the expense of the many. Hobbes's insistence on mutual consent and mutual advantage suggests the state's claims of authority could be justified if reasons were provided for accepting it that would or could be made acceptable to everyone. Thus, we may want to follow Locke, whose views we will explore in chapter 3, in denying Hobbes's claim that absolute authority and power must be ceded to the state but accepting at least some of Hobbes's assumptions about the need to provide an argument for state authority that should be found acceptable or reasonable by all.

Thus, Hobbes's approach to political philosophy reveals both the dangers of submitting to an absolute authority, whose will would dominate the autonomy of individuals, and the possible benefits of grounding the authority of the state on considerations mutually acceptable to all. The first road, if we are not careful, may lead down the path to dictatorship and tyranny, but the second may help ground the liberal democratic state. If so, in spite of the weaknesses of Hobbes's approach to political philosophy some of his insights, suitably revised, might prove part of an acceptable approach to justifying the political order.

Robert Paul Wolff: The Supremacy of Individual Autonomy

If one rejects the idea of an absolute and unquestionable authority, does it follow that one is thereby committed to rejecting political authority altogether? According to contemporary philosopher Robert Paul Wolff, there is an irreconcilable conflict between the claim that we ought to submit to authority and our duty to think for ourselves and exercise personal autonomy over our actions. As Wolff puts it in a passage quoted earlier, "The defining mark of the state is authority, the right to rule. The primary obligation of man is autonomy, the refusal to be ruled. It would seem, then, that there can be no resolution of the conflict between autonomy . . . and the putative authority of the state."[17]

Wolff's point should be familiar to those who have studied the catalogs of many of the best liberal arts colleges and universities in the United States. Such institutions claim to help students learn to think critically and develop and test their own systems of values. But how can we both think for ourselves and judge the positions of others critically, and at the same time simply obey the commands of an authority, especially the state? Wolff's claim is that it is impossible to do both. As a result, he concludes that "it would seem that anarchism is the only political doctrine consistent with the virtue of autonomy."[18]

Wolff performs a valuable task in emphasizing the importance of individual judgment, conscience, and autonomy—features that Hobbes's defense of the absolute sovereign state would require us to ignore. In fact, both Hobbes and Wolff accept the very same assumption: that autonomy and authority necessarily conflict. Hobbes, fearful of the state of nature, argues that the autonomy of individuals must be ceded to the sovereign while Wolff, fearful that power corrupts and absolute power corrupts absolutely, argues for the retention of autonomy and the rejection of authority. Again, both accept the same assumption—the incompatibility of autonomy and authority. However, it is exactly this assumption that we believe should be rejected.

Criticism of that assumption might start with the point that authority itself can be accepted by autonomous decision. That is, autonomous individuals might decide for themselves that living under an authority entitled to make decisions might be better for everyone than living in the kind of chaos that might result if there was no way of coordinating individual decisionmaking or adjudicating conflicts among individuals. However, this point by itself is not enough. Wolff might reply that just as one can freely decide to sell oneself into slavery, one can autonomously decide to accept the authority of the state. But, once the sale into slavery has been completed, freedom has been lost. Similarly, once the state's authority has been accepted, individual autonomy has been lost. From the fact that one can decide for oneself to regard the state's commands as authoritative, it does not follow that one can remain autonomous once such a decision has been made.

However, there appears to be a crucial difference between selling oneself into slavery and accepting the authority of certain kinds of political decisionmaking procedures. Once one is a slave, one has no say in formulating the commands of the master. But a political decisionmaking procedure can itself be based on autonomous decisionmaking by citizens. Thus, in the democratic state, the citizens determine the policies of the whole. Rather than abandoning their autonomy to the state, they express it through democratic procedures that determine state policy in the first place.

If this suggestion has force, then perhaps the major mistake on Wolff's part is his too narrow conception of what it is to accept authority. Wolff seems to view obedience as a kind of blind subservience, a total surrender of one's capacity to think and decide independently. On this view of obedience, we can see why Wolff regards authority with such distaste. Obedience does require individuals to simply let their own judgment be overridden by the commands of the authority. What this account leaves out, however, is first that there may be good reasons for accepting the authority that individuals themselves autonomously affirm and, second, that the individual's own values may be given a fair and equitable voice in determining the policies of the authority. Advocates of the liberal democratic state claim that it satisfies these two requirements and hence avoids Wolff's argument, at least in principle.

Wolff, however, might remain unconvinced and reply that even if one has some voice in democratic decisionmaking, that voice is often very minimal. In particular, in today's representative mass democracies, the voice of the individual, particularly if he or she is not wealthy or influential, may be thought to count for very little. Moreover, the decision of the majority in the mass democratic state may run counter to the conscience of the individual. For example, the majority, or its representatives, may vote to send you to fight in a war you think is morally wrong. Even if you had a voice, a vote, in the decisionmaking, it would seem that obedience to the authority of the majority means rejecting the dictates of your own conscience and forfeiting your autonomy to decide for yourself what to do.[19]

This rejoinder has force, and we will try to discuss it more thoroughly in our chapter on democracy. For now, we suggest that two points need to be considered. First, in a democratic state, one does not have to defer blindly to the majority when one thinks it is wrong. Rather, one can attempt to change the minds of others, support organizations that favor one's own point of view, and try to bring about change through democratic institutions. Second, in extreme cases, one might practice principled civil disobedience against laws or policies one regards as seriously unjust, as advocated by thinkers such as Gandhi and Martin Luther King Jr. That is, allegiance to a democratic authority does not require blind, unquestioning obedience to its commands, and it does not necessarily require obedience no matter how seriously unjust the commands of the authority may be thought to be. However, as we will argue later, it does create a presumption in favor of obedience, based in part on the moral reasons for supporting the liberal democratic state, that cannot be easily overridden.

Of course, all of this requires fuller development than we have given it in this chapter. In fact, much of the book will be devoted to examining principles for evaluating the political order. One of our major tasks will be to identify conditions under which the state and other political institutions justifiably can call for our commitment and within which we retain a significant degree of autonomy and decisionmaking power. What we do want to suggest for now, however, is that we need not be forced to embrace either absolute authority, and the danger of tyranny it carries with it, or total rejection of authority, with its loss of the advantages of the political order. These two extremes might not be the only possibilities open to us.

Of course, the mere possibility that there may be other alternatives does not show specifically what they are, let alone that any actual state can justifiably claim authority over us.[20] However, it does indicate that an inquiry into the conditions under which the state can justifiably claim authority is not necessarily pointless.

AUTHORITY AND THE NEUTRAL STATE

Suppose we are able to develop a plausible argument justifying the claims to authority of certain kinds of states, for example, democratic ones. Issues would still remain about the extent or proper domain of the authority that such states would wield. For example, should a state have the authority to promote certain religious views, to redistribute wealth, to promote "family values," or to prohibit behavior that it regards as immoral but that does not necessarily harm other individuals, such as same-sex marriages?

One important view central to liberal democracy is that the authority of the state should be limited by the freedom of the individual. But how much freedom should the individual have? The liberal tradition in Western thought has tended to defend two very important principles in this area. The first is that the freedom of the individual is limited only (or mainly) by the threat of harm to others. The mere fact that my behavior might offend others, or violate their moral principles, is no reason for restricting my liberty as long as my behavior is not harmful to others. Second, liberals often argue that the state should be neutral with respect to different theories of the good or proper life. That is, it may be the state's role to protect individuals from harm, or safeguard their rights, or provide a fair and just framework for individual choice and development. But is it not the state's business, on this view, to tell individuals how they should live or what choices they should make, so long as no harm to others or threat to their rights is involved.

But is this liberal view sustainable? Does the kind of liberty and individualism it defends turn into license? Doesn't the state have a role in promoting values and in trying to produce individuals who will be good citizens rather than indifferent louts? As the great nineteenth-century conservative thinker Edmund Burke mused, "The effect of liberty to individuals is, that they may do what they please; we ought to see what it will please them to do, before we risk congratulations."[21]

Thus, contemporary critics of liberalism argue that the neutral state, if neutrality is really possible at all, gives its citizens no guidance on what choices to make and ends up with the bonds of community split asunder as individuals pursue their own goods in independent and often mutually antagonistic directions. For example, are pornography and misogynist forms of rap music demeaning to women just goods to be pursued in the individual's search for private pleasure while the quality of public life and civic values degenerate? As political commentator George Will once argued, "an aim of government—indeed, a prerequisite of popular government—must be a sense of community rooted in a substantial range of shared values and aims." In Will's view, "matters touching the generation of life and the quality of life should not be matters of indifference to the community."[22] Indeed, as we will see, philosophers who argue from a more communitarian-oriented perspective than many liberals would find amenable maintain that the whole dichotomy between the individual and institutions like the state has been overemphasized or distorted by thinkers such as Hobbes and by the liberal tradition, including John Locke and contemporary liberal theorists, whose works will be considered in subsequent chapters. According to communitarian critics of individualistic liberal approaches to political theory, the individual is in significant part a product of cultural, social, and political practices and so these institutions cannot be regarded from a neutral perspective without putting the very nature of society in danger.

On the other hand, do we want the state telling us what values we should hold or how we should behave, even in the privacy of our own homes? Clearly, the debate over the proper domain of state authority is not something that concerned only Hobbes's contemporaries. While few thinkers in today's Western liberal democracies favor Hobbes's view of absolute authority, many would reject the liberal ideal of the neutral state and suggest instead that the authority of the state should be used in morally acceptable ways to promote important ethical values and civic virtues.

Clearly, the debate between liberalism and its critics on the proper domain of state authority is sophisticated and important. This debate will be pursued in later chapters and, as we will see, whether it is ultimately defensible or not, liberalism is a far more sophisticated and resourceful doctrine than the simplistic insults about "tax and spend liberals" that are found in the political arena would ever lead people to believe.

EVALUATING THE POLITICAL ORDER

Even if acceptance of political authority does not entail commitment to authoritarian rule, it does not follow that any actual political institutions can justifiably claim authority over individuals. Consider, for example, that all too many great evils, including the practices of genocide and slavery, have been carried out with the direct support of the state. Democracy itself is not immune to the grave misuse of power, either through the manipulation of the citizenry by unscrupulous leaders or through the ignorance or immorality of the majority. Accordingly, it is crucial that the state and its claims to authority be subject to critical scrutiny.

JUSTIFYING THE STATE

As we noted above, one strategy for justifying the state and its claims to authority over individuals is to consider what the state is for, what functions it can serve, or what individuals might get from belonging to a state that they would lack without it. Then we can consider whether it is morally permissible for the state to serve such a function, and whether the means it might need to do so are morally permissible as well.

In our own time, much of the debate in the United States over the function of the state has centered on its role in providing minimal material prerequisites of well-being for its citizens. The extent of poverty in an affluent society has aroused considerable concern. Moreover, African Americans, Native Americans, and members of other minority groups have borne a disproportionate share of the burdens of poverty, unemployment, and ill health. In response, many liberal advocates of the welfare state have supported "Great Society" programs as part of a war on poverty. On this liberal view, although government should be neutral concerning what sort of life people should choose to lead, it does have the obligation to provide a fair framework within which people can develop their abilities and talents. Thus, under the influence of this form of welfare liberalism, the United States government has sponsored food stamp programs, welfare, unemployment compensation, and Medicaid, to name just a few of the campaigns in the assault on poverty.

Others have objected to what they regard as big government, a dangerous threat to individual freedom. These critics, including libertarians as well as many conservatives, may share the liberal belief in the neutral state (although, as we will see, other conservatives such as those on the religious right pursue an agenda of values that they wish the government to support), but they unite in regarding many government programs not only as in violation of individual liberty but as wasteful and inefficient. Many of these critics argue that welfare provides incentives for poor individuals to remain in poverty and so, on their view, the program perpetuates the very conditions it was designed to overcome.

Thus, in our own society as well as in others, there is considerable disagreement over what the purposes of government should be and how fit government is to carry them out. Our first task, then, is to ask what purposes the state should serve. Moreover, if good states are those that perform their functions well, good states may have the strongest claims to authority over their citizens, at least under certain conditions. It also seems plausible to think, at least at the start, that the limits of the authority of the state are set in great part by its function. In all other areas, individuals would be free of obligations to the state. Accordingly, we propose to begin by investigating what the proper function(s) or goal(s) of the state might be.

In the course of examining this question, we hope to shed light both on the contemporary debate over big government and on the claim that the state should be neutral among rival conceptions of the good life found among its citizens. Thus, if one set of questions concerns the ground or justification for the state's claims to authority, a second set concerns the domain or limits to that authority.[23]

A third set of questions, which receives particular attention in chapter 4, concerns how the state should exercise its authority when its citizens disagree about basic values or when different principles of governance conflict. For example, if the role of the state is to protect the rights of its citizens, what happens when rights clash, as when some claim it is necessary to limit some basic liberties in order to better protect national security?

In this section, three distinct lines of inquiry concerning the authority of the state have been identified, as expressed in the following questions:

1. Under what conditions, if any, is the state's claim to authority justified?
2. How far does that authority extend?
3. How are conflicts of values among citizens or conflicts among basic principles of governance to be reconciled, given a proper account of the limits of state authority?

These questions should be considered in depth not only because of their own importance but also because they lead to examinations of other equally significant issues, such as an inquiry into the nature of justice, a question just as important as the one with which we started. Indeed, an inquiry into justification of the authority of the state can be expected to broaden into an examination of most of the major questions of political and social philosophy.

In the next few chapters, we examine various criteria for evaluating the state. One criterion often appealed to is social utility. The good state is one whose actions or policies produce as good or better consequences than those of alternate acts or policies available to it. It is to the ethical theory of utilitarianism and its application to political philosophy that we now turn.

NOTES

1. Similar issues are raised in other areas of medicine whenever goods or services available are insufficient to meet crucial needs. There is an extensive discussion of such issues of allocation in the literature on medical ethics. A selection of articles relevant to the issue can be found in John D. Arras and Bonnie Steinbock, *Ethical Issues in Modern Medicine* (Mountain View, CA: Mayfield, 1999), 652–99, as well as in other widely used anthologies on medical ethics.

2. Henry David Thoreau, "Civil Disobedience," in Thoreau's *A Yankee in Canada* (Boston: Ticknor and Fields, 1866), 125. Thoreau's essay is widely reprinted and is available, for example, in *Civil Disobedience: Theory and Practice*, ed. Hugo A. Bedau (New York: Pegasus, 1969).

3. Robert Paul Wolff, *In Defense of Anarchism* (New York: Harper & Row, 1970), 18.

4. The issue of whether Hobbes believed that all human action was selfish is complex. For discussion, see Jean Hampton, *Hobbes and the Social Contract* (New York: Cambridge, 1986), especially 19–24.

5. Often, egoists reply that such apparently unselfish acts are really selfish after all, since they are done to avoid the pain of guilt that the agent would otherwise have felt. But as a philosophical tradition going back at least to Bishop Joseph Butler (1692–1752) replies, a truly unselfish agent would not feel guilt in the first place. The fact that we often feel guilty for harming others shows that rather than being selfish we are concerned for others and sometimes count their interests as equal to or even more important than our own. After all, if we didn't feel we had done something wrong in harming others, why would we feel guilty to begin with?

6. Thomas Hobbes, *Leviathan* [1651] reprinted in *Hobbes: Selections*, ed. Fredrick J. E. Woodbridge (New York: Scribners, 1930), 253.

7. For discussion of the prisoner's dilemma and its relation to evolutionary advantages of a strategy of reciprocal altruism, see Robert Axelrod, *The Evolution of Cooperation* (New York: Basic Books, 1984).

8. Hobbes, *Leviathan*, 257.

9. Hobbes, *Leviathan*, 269–70.

10. Hobbes, *Leviathan*, 335–36.

11. Hobbes, though, does suggest that the nations of the world are in fact in a state of nature with respect to each other, since there is no common power above them.

12. Hobbes does make an exception for self-preservation. If the life of a citizen is threatened by the sovereign, then that citizen may resist. Indeed, if the sovereign fails in its function of keeping the peace, so that civil war threatens, citizens may no longer have a duty to obey. See *Leviathan*, chapter 21, especially 376–81.

13. As pointed out in an earlier citation, this line of argument goes back at least to Bishop Butler (1692–1752).

14. An alternate and perhaps equally plausible assumption is that all humans have an innate tendency toward reciprocal altruism. That is, people might conform to minimal guidelines of fair behavior toward those who obeyed such guidelines toward them. Some sociobiologists have argued that genes promoting such reciprocal altruism might confer survival advantages on their bearers, since any sacrifices required would benefit a greater number of bearers of the genes than would egoism. Whether the genetic argument is plau-

sible or not, parties to the state of nature who tried to behave ethically toward those who would respond by behaving ethically toward them might actually do better under some conditions than those who presumed that no one else ever was to be trusted. Of course, such an assumption might not work in single encounters where a failed experiment might mean death, but the assumption could lead to the development of ties of trust under circumstances where encounters could be repeated over time. For discussion, see Axelrod, *The Evolution of Cooperation.*

15. Moreover, any attempt to minimize the influence of egoism among the rulers also casts doubt about the extreme effects of egoism in the state of nature postulated by Hobbes.

16. John Locke, *Second Treatise of Government* (1690), chapter 9, section 13 (9, 13).

17. Wolff, *In Defense of Anarchism*, 18.

18. Wolff, *In Defense of Anarchism*, 18.

19. Wolff does agree that authority and autonomy can coexist in a direct democracy in which unanimous votes are required for decisionmaking but denies that any other kind of democracy, particularly indirect representative democracy, reconciles authority with autonomy for the reasons given in the text. See *In Defense of Anarchism*, 22ff.

20. For a recent discussion of political obligation, authority, and consent that acknowledges that in principle political authority can be legitimatized but questions whether any state has passed the moral threshold of legitimacy in practice, see A. John Simmons, "Political Obligation and Authority," in *The Blackwell Guide to Social and Political Philosophy*, ed. Robert L. Simon (Malden, MA: Blackwell Publishers, 2002), 17–37.

21. Edmund Burke, *Reflections on the Revolution in France* [1790], reprint edited by Conner Cruise O'Brian (Harmondsworth, England: Penguin, 1969), 91.

22. George Will, *Statecraft as Soulcraft: What Government Does* (New York: Simon and Shuster, 1983), 149, 151.

23. There also is the issue of how the state should deal with injustice and violation of law. Injustice, of course, can be by the state itself. The United States, for example, once enforced laws mandating slavery and racial segregation. Racial segregation in the public schools was not found to be unconstitutional until the *Brown* decision by the Supreme Court in 1954. In the case of individuals such as Martin Luther King Jr. who violate the law not for criminal purposes and personal profit but to protest injustice, how should the state react? What should the state's position be toward civil disobedience?

QUESTIONS FOR FURTHER STUDY

1. Explain the difference between the normative analysis of political institutions and descriptive and explanatory analyses of them.
2. Explain the alleged conflict between authority and autonomy. Why do some theorists, such as Robert Paul Wolff, think that an autonomous individual cannot recognize the claims of authority?
3. Hobbes appeals to the idea of the state of nature. Do you think the state of nature, as described by Hobbes, ever existed? How would you defend your view? Do you think Hobbes's argument can have force even if the state of nature never existed? Why or why not?

4. Why does Hobbes believe that it is individually rational for each person in the state of nature to strike first at others, given his assumptions about human nature? How does this lead to the war of all against all? Explain how this situation is structurally similar to the prisoner's dilemma of game theory.

5. Why does Hobbes believe we must accept a virtually absolute authority rather than retain our autonomy? How would you reconstruct his argument?

6. Explain and evaluate at least two criticisms of Hobbes's approach. Are these objections successful? Defend your view.

7. Explain and evaluate at least one major criticism of Wolff's view that authority and autonomy are incompatible. Is the criticism successful? Defend your view.

8. Do you agree that anarchism is the only form of social organization compatible with human autonomy and respect for the conscience of the individual? Defend your view.

9. How would you explain the idea of state neutrality toward conceptions of the good? In what way might a neutral state be compatible with individual autonomy?

SUGGESTED READINGS

Axelrod, Robert. *The Evolution of Cooperation.* New York: Basic Books, 1984.

Edmundson, W. A., ed. *The Duty to Obey the Law.* Lanham, MD: Rowman & Littlefield, 1999.

Hobbes, Thomas. *Leviathan* (1651); found in many editions.

Raz, J., ed. *Authority.* New York: New York University Press, 1990.

Simmons, A. John. "Political Obligation and Authority," in *The Blackwell Guide to Social and Political Philosophy*, ed. Robert L. Simon. Malden, MA: Blackwell Publishers, 2002.

Wolff, Robert Paul. *In Defense of Anarchism.* New York: Harper & Row, 1970.

2

UTILITARIANISM

Suppose one asked the following question of a cross section of American society: "What should the U.S. government be doing for its citizens?" Many people would answer in specific terms. For example, some would say that the U.S. government should do more to protect the environment. Others would say that the government should lower taxes. Many of those who respond in more general terms, however, will say that the government should act in the general interest, the public interest, or that it should do what will benefit all Americans, not just the interests of business or labor, for example. Americans often talk as if they want their elected leaders to serve all constituencies. A leader too closely identified with one faction or "special interest" risks defeat at the polls. Many Americans, then, would argue that the purpose of government is to promote the general welfare or serve the public good.

Terms like "public interest" and "general good" have rich positive emotional associations, but just what they mean is often unclear. Although everyone seems to be in favor of the general good or the public interest, it is very difficult to get everyone to agree on what the public interest or general good really is, let alone on what policies actually promote such values. There is a tendency for each particular interest to claim that an activity or program that benefits its particular goal is really in the public interest while the activity or program that benefits a competing particular interest is not in the public interest but serves only a "special interest." Each interest group has its own version of "What's good for business is good for America." Few, if any, interest groups have much of an idea of how to determine the public interest.

However, there is a well-developed philosophical theory called *utilitarianism,* which does have a carefully worked out program for defining the public interest. The public interest is defined as the sum of individual interests. By examining this theory in some detail, we will see some of the advantages and disadvantages of a theory that views the function of the state as a means for providing the aggregate welfare or public good, conceived of as the greatest good for the greatest number.

HISTORICAL BACKGROUND

Jeremy Bentham (1748–1832): A Version of Classical Utilitarianism

Jeremy Bentham was born in London and raised by a family with strict monarchical views. He studied law at Lincoln's Inn, and during the course of his studies he was introduced to the contract theory of natural rights and obligations (which will be examined in later chapters). However, he was also introduced to the legal works of the Italian writer Beccaria, the philosophical treatises of David Hume, and the economic writings of Adam Smith. As a result of these influences, he became skeptical of a social contract theory as the basis for the legitimacy of the state because there was no empirical justification for asserting that any social contract ever existed. In addition he came to recognize that tradition, custom, and instinct had no foundation in reason. Indeed, Bentham concluded, blind adherence to tradition had created significant problems. Hence, Bentham saw his task as one of reform. Individualistic utilitarianism, he believed, was an appropriate tool for the reformation of the major political institutions of his society.

Perhaps we can best understand utilitarianism if we consider a question that a legislator might well ask. "From among these competing policies, how can I choose the best one?" Bentham's answer was clear. The legislator ought to choose the policy that leads to the greatest good for the greatest number. Indeed the test of the greatest good for the greatest number became Bentham's test for all social institutions. Upon applying his test, Bentham found that many nineteenth-century English laws and institutions failed it. It is for this reason that Bentham's utilitarian principle was viewed as a principle of reform.

Bentham's earliest work, *Fragment on Government* (1776), provided a utilitarian critique of the British legal system and of its chief intellectual champion, the English jurist Sir William Blackstone. In the criminal law, for example, Bentham believed that the traditional and formal classification of crimes and punishments should be given up. Crimes should be classified according to the amount of unhappiness they bring about. Punishments must be similarly classified to fit the crime. The basic rule is that the punishment must exceed the advantage gained by committing the offense. Penal institutions should make it likely that indeed crime does not pay. Legal punishment is defended by Bentham as a socially useful practice designed to prevent the harms resulting from criminal behavior by deterring it.

Bentham's concern in punishment was not to set the moral order right, nor did he believe the infliction of punishment to be valuable because in some way criminals were made to pay for their crimes by getting what they deserved. Rather, Bentham argued that the infliction of pain was always an evil and hence was to be avoided unless it could bring about more good. One calculates the benefits of rehabilitation and deterrence that punishment creates and subtracts the pain that punishment causes. Punishment is justifiable only when the benefits exceed the pain. One should only punish up to that point where the infliction of pain brings about the greatest benefits in rehabilitation and deterrence. Only in this way does punishment provide for the greatest good of the greatest number.

In order to apply utilitarianism, one must have an account of what is most valuable or intrinsically good. Bentham's view was based on his account of human psychology. He believed that human action was motivated by the desire for pleasure and for the avoidance of pain. He then concluded that individual happiness was the supreme good:

> Nature has placed mankind under the governance of two sovereign masters, pain and pleasure. It is for them alone to point out what we ought to do, as well as to determine what we shall do. . . . The principle of utility recognizes this subjection, and assumes it for the foundation of that system, the object of which is to rear the fabric of felicity by the hands of reason and of law. . . . By the principle of utility is meant that principle which approves or disapproves of every action whatsoever, according to the tendency which it appears to have to augment or diminish the happiness of the party whose interest is in question.[1]

By claiming that only pleasure is intrinsically good and only pain is intrinsically bad, Bentham meant that these were the only things good or bad *in themselves*. For example, pain may be good as a means (extrinsically good) as when the pain of an injury influences us to go to the doctor for treatment. Such pain considered in itself is bad, but it has value as a means since the doctor's treatment may cause us to have less pain or more pleasure in the future.

Having decided on what was most valuable, it was easy enough to formulate a utilitarian moral principle that stated that the right thing to do was to maximize that which was most valuable, namely happiness (or a highly positive balance of pleasure over pain). On utilitarian morality, one ought to act so as to produce the most happiness—the greatest good for the greatest number.

If one is to act on utilitarian morality, however, one has to have some way of measuring happiness so that the individual happiness or unhappiness created by any given act can be compared and summed up. Bentham is committed to a quantitative measurement of happiness whereby one computes the greatest total happiness by adding the quantitative units of individual happiness and by subtracting the units of individual unhappiness in order that one might arrive at a measure of total happiness. Bentham developed a device he called the hedonic calculus for measuring pleasure. The quantitative figure for any pleasurable experience is reached by considering its intensity, duration, certainty or uncertainty, propinquity or remoteness, fecundity, purity, and extent. Perhaps it is worth quoting Bentham's six-step process for evaluating any proposed action or event:

> To take an exact account then of the general tendency of any act, by which the interests of a community are affected, proceed as follows. Begin with any one person

of those whose interests seem most immediately to be affected by it: and take an account,

1. Of the value of each distinguishable pleasure which appears to be produced by it in the first instance.
2. Of the value of each pain which appears to be produced by it in the first instance.
3. Of the value of each pleasure which appears to be produced by it after the first. This constitutes the fecundity of the first pleasure and the impurity of the first pain.
4. Of the value of each pain which appears to be produced by it after the first. This constitutes the fecundity of the first pain, and the impurity of the first pleasure.
5. Sum up all the values of all the pleasures on the one side, and those of all the pains on the other. The balance, if it be on the side of pleasure, will give the good tendency of the act upon the whole, with respect to the interests of that individual person; if on the side of pain, the bad tendency of it upon the whole.
6. Take an account of the number of persons whose interests appear to be concerned; and repeat the above process with respect to each. Sum up the numbers expressive of the degrees of good tendency, which the act has, with respect to each individual, in regard to whom the tendency of it is good upon the whole: do this again with respect to each individual, in regard to whom the tendency of it is bad upon the whole. Take the balance; which, if on the side of pleasure, will give the general good tendency of the act with respect to the total number or community of individuals concerned; if on the side of pain, the general evil tendency, with respect to the same community.[2]

We now have a means for evaluating matters of policy and legislation. In facing a problem of what to do, for example, staying with your sick mother or joining the Peace Corps to fight global poverty, make your decision on the basis of the greatest happiness. Use the hedonic calculus to get a quantitative figure for the happiness of all relevant individuals affected by your act. Then, after adding the happiness and subtracting the unhappiness for each alternative act, perform the act that produces the most happiness.

Criticism of Bentham's Utilitarianism

Bentham's theory has been the target of vigorous and sustained criticism. We limit our discussion to three traditional lines of criticism of Bentham's utilitarian political philosophy: a critique of its hedonism, a critique of its quantitative methodology, and a critique of utilitarianism as a normative test of state actions.

Bentham's hedonistic view that individual happiness was best understood in terms of pleasure soon came under ridicule. In fact, his philosophy was sometimes referred to as the "pig philosophy." The difficulty concerns a conflict between the logic of hedonism and some commonly held beliefs on matters of value. In point of logic, under hedonism the pleasures of artistic creation may be no better than, or even inferior to, the pleasures of wine, sex, and song so long as the happiness of the latter is equal to or more than the former. It is charged that on hedonistic grounds it is better to be a satisfied pig than a dissatisfied Socrates. To see the force of this criticism, readers should ask themselves whether they would willingly become a pig even with an ironclad guarantee that the life of the pig would be happier. Those who are still with us can see that hedonism conflicts with our strong convictions, that in fact some activities are better than others even if they are not more pleasurable.

A second objection is that experiences of pleasure are not capable of quantitative measurement, that Bentham's hedonic calculus is really a useless device. How could one use the seven measuring devices of the calculus to compare quantitatively the pleasure of solving a difficult philosophical problem with the pleasures of a cool swim on a hot summer's day? Certainly Bentham's calculating tools are inadequate.

Even more serious are the moral objections that can be raised against utilitarianism. On moral grounds, utilitarianism, unless modified, provides neither necessary nor sufficient conditions for justifying either state action or any of the institutions of government.

Thus, utilitarianism cannot provide sufficient justification because some governmental decisions cannot be made on utilitarian grounds alone. For example, suppose a government could choose between two possible programs.

	Program One	Program Two
Citizen One	3 units of pleasure	4 units of pleasure
Citizen Two	3 units of pleasure	5 units of pleasure
Citizen Three	3 units of pleasure	0 units of pleasure
	9 total units	9 total units

Since the greatest total happiness is identical for both programs, there is no basis on utilitarian grounds for choosing between them. However, other things being equal, most everyone would prefer Program One on egalitarian grounds. Equality provides an additional condition for evaluation.

Suppose it were replied that utilitarianism has a built-in concern for equality captured by the slogan "the greatest good for *the greatest number*." However, the traditional utilitarian formula "the greatest happiness for the greatest number" can provide conflicting results. Consider the following two government programs.[3]

	Program A	Program B
Citizen One	5 units of happiness	3 units of happiness
Citizen Two	4 units of happiness	3 units of happiness
Citizen Three	0 units of happiness	4 units of happiness
	9 total units	10 total units

Program A has more citizens happier than program B, but program B provides the greatest total happiness. Which program should the government provide?

Another important problem can be raised when one considers questions of population control. Consider the following situation, which reflects problems in the real world. If the government takes no steps to control population, a million residents can be supported at a minimum standard of living. Let us say that such a minimum standard of living has a hedonic value of 10. Total utility for a population of one million would be ten million, with the average utility for each person equal to 10. Suppose the population were limited by government action to three quarters of a million. This policy would enable each person to live a more comfortable life with an average utility value of 13. Total utility for the society would equal 9,950,000 utility units. Is it better to have a large population at a minimum standard of living or a small population that has a smaller total of happiness but where nonetheless each person is happier on the average? Utilitarianism seems to have nothing to say here or, at the very least, it is unclear which version of utilitarianism is most acceptable. Is it the greatest happiness we should aim for, which might encourage a large but only minimally happy population, or a higher average utility with a smaller population?

The reason for these difficulties is clear. In providing his account of utilitarianism, Bentham did not indicate whether total or average happiness was to be used as the criterion for determining what should be done. Neither did he recognize that an appeal to equality or some other distributive principle might be necessary when two or more potential distributions of some goods yielded identical or similar totals of utility. Most contemporary utilitarians have adopted the average utility criterion, although there is controversy among utilitarians over which approach is best.

Some have also argued that utilitarianism is too demanding as a moral theory or, in other words, that it asks too much of us. It seems as if Bentham would require us to consider all of the alternatives to any act that we undertake in order to determine which one of the alternatives leads to the greatest good. But surely that would be too demanding. In fact, common sense, as well as much nonutilitarian moral theory, regards many of our acts as morally neutral or without significant moral import. Surely when we are brushing our teeth we need not consider whether there is an alternative action that would bring about a greater good.

Utilitarians could respond to this criticism by saying that experience has taught us that many actions lack consequences of moral significance, and that in many circumstances alternative acts of significance are not open to us. Therefore, the greatest good is done simply through ordinary acts. Normally, we should just brush our teeth without worrying about whether an alternative action would bring about the greatest good. Indeed, ordinarily, spending all our time worrying about whether there is such a significantly better alternative actually may be harmful since little will get done. However, a utilitarian also would insist that sometimes an ordinary act does have moral import. If a person were just beginning to brush her teeth and she hears a cry for help from next door, the utilitarian would say that she should investigate and try to help if aid is required.

From our point of view, one of the most important values omitted from Bentham's utilitarianism is the value of individual rights. Indeed, failure to consider individual rights is one of the chief criticisms of utilitarianism today. We can illustrate this point with one of the most common and most persuasive objections against utilitarian analysis: the so-called punishment-of-the-innocent example. Consider the following: a small city has been plagued by a number of particularly vicious unsolved crimes. The citizenry is near panic. All homeowners have guns; doors and windows are locked. The local police officer goes to the freight yards and arrests a homeless person who has taken shelter in an abandoned railway car. Investigation shows that although the accused is innocent, he can be made to appear guilty. Without family or friends, utility, both total and average, could be increased if he were punished and the rest of the population were calmed. Real criminals might be deterred by the example of punishment, having been led to believe that the police are more efficient than actually is the case. On utilitarian grounds, the innocent man should be punished. But should he?

The point of this example can be generalized. None of our rights are safe from the measuring rod of utility. On the whole, our rights to freedom of the press, freedom of speech, and a trial by jury are consistent with utilitarian considerations, but on occasion they are all subject to surrender. Indeed, under utilitarianism there is nothing inconsistent in saying that a slave society is the best society. All one would need to show is that the happiness (total or average) of the slave society exceeds that of the society without slavery. Most of us, however, would deny that the slave society is morally superior even if it is happier. The utilitarians' lack of concern with rights offends some of our more firmly grounded moral insights.

Supporters of utilitarian theory denied that their theory had these undesirable consequences, or claimed at least that Bentham's theory could be repaired so as to avoid them. These repairs began almost immediately and continue in the work of contemporary utilitarians discussed later in this chapter.

John Stuart Mill (1806–1873): A Modified Form of Utilitarianism

John Stuart Mill was stung by the barbs calling utilitarianism a "pig philosophy." One of his intellectual projects was to reformulate Bentham's utilitarianism so that it avoided the objections of its critics.

Quality of Pleasure and the Panel of Experts

Mill abandoned quantitative utilitarianism and the hedonic calculus that accompanied it for a qualitative utilitarianism. Mill vigorously maintained that some pleasures really are better than others. Pushpin, a parlor game popular during Mill's lifetime, is not as good as poetry. A dissatisfied Socrates' life is qualitatively better than the life of a satisfied pig. As Mill maintained, "It is quite compatible with the principle of utility to recognize the fact that some kinds of pleasure are more desirable and more valuable than others. It would be absurd that, while in estimating all other things quality is considered as well as quantity, the estimation of pleasure should be supposed to depend on quantity alone."[4]

Having introduced qualitative distinctions and having abandoned the hedonic calculus, Mill needed some other means for comparing and qualitatively ranking experiences. Mill claimed that we know that one experience is better than another by consulting a panel of experts. Mill was not entirely clear as to how this panel of experts was to be composed, but one condition was that the members have had both of the experiences in question. Having experienced both, they have met at least one of the conditions for making a qualified comparison:

> Of two pleasures, if there be one to which all or almost all who have experience of both give a decided preference, irrespective of any feeling of moral obligation to prefer it, that is the more desirable pleasure. If one of the two is, by those who are competently acquainted with both, placed so far above the other that they prefer it, even though knowing it to be attended with a greater amount of discontent, and would not resign it for any quantity of the other pleasure which their nature is capable of, we are justified in ascribing to the preferred enjoyment a superiority in quality so far outweighing quantity as to render it, in comparison, of small account.[5]

To those who might retort that such a panel of experts could not take the perspective of the pig, Mill argued that humans were qualitatively different from animals. Humans have a higher capacity that prevents them from desiring a lower grade of existence even if they would be happier. Mill refers to this capacity as man's sense of dignity. This sense of dignity provides the ground for qualitative distinctions among pleasures.

This reference to a human capacity might well provide the clue to Mill's answer to the moral objections to utilitarianism. It may well be that there are a number of human practices that if followed would lead to the greatest happiness, understood qualitatively as well as quantitatively. By protecting these precious practices and by ensuring everyone's right to participate and benefit, the general welfare can best be achieved. Perhaps, following this line of thought, we can regard fundamental or basic rights as protections entitling each of us to participate in social practices that help us develop our human capacities and give us the opportunity to flourish. In other words, human rights are norms that are adopted because of their utilitarian value. It may well be that Mill was working toward a distinction that split utilitarianism into two camps. Today, these two types of utilitarianism are most frequently referred to as act utilitarianism and rule utilitarianism.

Act Utilitarianism and Rule Utilitarianism

Act utilitarians, such as Bentham, argue that one ought to do those particular acts that produce the greatest good for the greatest number. In an act utilitarian view, rules are mere shorthand devices that are suitable as rules of thumb and are to be abandoned on those occasions where following them would not lead to the greatest good for the greatest number:

> Does the utilitarian formula leave any place for moral maxims like "Keep your promises" and "Always tell the truth"? Yes, these maxims can be regarded as directives that for the most part point out what is a person's duty. They are rules of thumb. They are properly taught to children and used by everybody as a rough timesaving guide for ordinary decisions. . . . However, we are not to be enslaved to them. When there is good ground for thinking the maximum net expectable utility will be produced by an act that violates them, then we should depart from them. Such a rule is to be disregarded without hesitation, when it clearly conflicts with the general welfare.[6]

Under rule utilitarianism, however, rules have a very different status. On rule utilitarianism, the appropriate answer to the question "What ought I to do?" is, "You ought to follow the appropriate rule for that type of situation." However, the appropriate answer to the question, "What rules should one adopt?" is "One should adopt those rules that lead to the greatest good for the greatest number."

Perhaps the difference between the two types of utilitarianism can be illustrated by an example. Consider the practice of grading college students for course work. Suppose that one of the rules for assigning a grade of A in Mathematics II requires obtaining a 90 average or better on quizzes and examinations. An act utilitarian would treat the rule of 90 for an A as a rule of thumb. In circumstances where utility would be maximized, one could give an A for less than 90, say if that would make the recipient unusually happy, or one could give a B for a grade of 90 or better if one thought the student in question needed encouragement to work harder and that would produce more happiness in the long run. What determines each act of grading is the consequences of giving a certain grade in that particular case. The rule of A for 90 is a guide, but it is not authoritative. For the rule utilitarian, things are different. A student with an 85 could not argue for an A on the basis of the special circumstances of his or her case alone. Rather, he or she would have to show that the grading rule of A for 90 does not provide the greatest good for the greatest number.

The task of the moral philosopher, in the rule-utilitarian account, is to formulate those rules that pass the utilitarian test. For example, perhaps the rule for giving an A that has the most utility should allow some exceptions for test performances that were affected by serious illness.[7] The rule utilitarian does not necessarily endorse following popular or fashionable rules but believes that we should follow the rules that would maximize utility if they were generally complied with. Thus, rule utilitarians can be critics of existing rules or practices if they believe that the existing rules could be replaced with ones that work better.

If Mill is interpreted as a rule utilitarian, individual rights can be construed as rules that protect individuals. These rights, however, are grounded on utilitarian considerations. Individual rights should be recognized only if by recognition of such rights the happiness of the greatest good for the greatest number can be secured. Whether or not Mill actually was a rule utilitarian is a matter of scholarly debate. However, interpreting him as a rule utilitarian enables us to see how Mill could construct a reply to those who criticized Bentham for ignoring moral rules, particularly rules for the distribution of happiness, and rules that protect individual rights. A society has such rules because they pass the utilitarian test.

Indeed, one can more readily understand some of Mill's remarks on liberty, representative government, and laissez-faire capitalism from this rule utilitarian perspective. Mill saw the political philosopher's task as one of describing the procedures and institutions that make the realization of the greatest good for the greatest number most likely. In his writings on liberty, he attempted to describe the social and political conditions that must exist if individual liberty is to flourish. In his economic writings, he attempted to describe what social and political conditions are necessary to overcome the evils of industrialization, that is, to increase the public good. For example, Mill's *On Liberty* discusses various institutional arrangements that support the free exchange of ideas. Mill was greatly concerned about the tyranny of public opinion, especially the tyranny of the opinions of the uneducated. Hence, one institutional safeguard he recommended in *Considerations on Representative Government*[8] was weighted voting. The votes of the educated would count more than the votes of the uneducated (a proposal we reject later in our discussion of democracy).

In summary, one could argue that Mill strengthened utilitarianism by making qualitative distinctions among pleasures, by abandoning Bentham's simplistic hedonic calculus, and by finding a place for justice and individual rights within a utilitarian framework.

Criticism of Mill's Utilitarianism

Mill's efforts, however, did not put an end to the critical commentary. Mill's critics argued that the attempt to make qualitative distinctions among pleasures was to concede that utilitarianism was inadequate. If the pleasure of listening to rock music is quantitatively greater than the pleasure of listening to Beethoven, even though Beethoven is better, what does the music of Beethoven have that rock does not have? Mill would say that Beethoven's music provides a higher pleasure. But surely Mill's response is deceptive. After all, how can pleasures differ except quantitatively? Beethoven's music must have some quality other than pleasure that makes us rate Beethoven's music higher than rock music. Mill's appeal to higher pleasures is not an appeal to pleasure at all. Rather, by implication Mill concedes that there are some qualities that have value in addition to pleasure. In other words, there are a number of goods, in addition to pleasure, that are valuable, perhaps including the beauty of certain music.

In the late nineteenth and early twentieth centuries some utilitarians, such as G. E. Moore, accepted this critique of Mill and formulated a new version of utilitarianism called ideal utilitarianism. Ideal utilitarianism asserts that there are many goods besides pleasure; for example, beauty, achievement, and knowledge might be plausible candidates for such status. What one ought to do is maximize the greatest goods for the greatest number. Ideal utilitarianism is not hedonistic, but it still subscribes to the principle of maximizing benefits and minimizing harm, using a pluralistic view of what counts as an intrinsic good (or intrinsic evil). In this view the function of the state is to maximize the total good, understood pluralistically.

Mill's substitution of the panel of experts for Bentham's hedonic calculus came under attack as well. Some argued that we could not say the life of a dissatisfied Socrates is better than the life of a satisfied pig since we could not get the opinion of the pig. At this level, the objection misses the point since Mill stipulates that the panel of experts must have had both experiences. Of course, the panel could not literally live the life of the pig, but, following Aristotle, the panel could contrast animal-like pleasures with the pleasure of rationality.

This interpretation does not remove all of the difficulties, however. Mill either assumes that the panel of experts will approach unanimity in their comparative judgments or that a majority opinion is sufficient to decide the question. Neither assumption would seem justified. Lifestyles are notoriously diverse even among the well-traveled and well-educated. There is no reason to think that a consensus would develop on anything but the most general value judgments. Most people probably would say that the life of a dissatisfied Socrates is better than the life of a satisfied pig, but unanimity on much else is fairly unlikely. For example, would there be unanimous agreement that the pleasure of reading great literature is higher than that of playing sports or watching popular TV series or fantasy movies? Moreover, it is not self-evident that the device of majority voting is the correct device for deciding questions of this type. Finally, many objected to the elitism of Mill's panel of experts. Heavily influenced by the discipline of economics, which counted each person's desire as equal to every other, most utilitarians returned to a more refined hedonic calculus to measure and compare happiness. The economic theory of utility provided one such basis.

However, the most complicated and arguably the most important exchange of ideas concerned whether or not Mill succeeded in finding a legitimate place for rights and justice. Indeed, contemporary utilitarians have spent so much time discussing this issue that we should turn to their accounts of the matter. After a thorough analysis of these discussions we will decide whether utilitarianism is able to provide the test for the justifiability of state actions.

UTILITARIANISM AND THE ECONOMISTS: CONTEMPORARY DISCUSSIONS OF UTILITARIANISM

Despite the shortcomings of both Bentham's and Mill's formulations of utilitarianism, the theory remains attractive to many people and perhaps especially to economists. If utility were to refer to preferences expressed by consumer choice in the marketplace, utilitarians could avoid the issues involved in the measurement of such psychological states as pleasure and pain. Utility would be maximized when everyone made choices in a free competitive market. The competitive market assures that the highest average of personal preference satisfaction is obtained. Preference utilitarianism also seems capable of quantification that gives it the appearance of rigor, a quality not often seen in ethical theories. In fact, John Harsanyi derived a rule utilitarianism that maximized satisfaction of personal preferences from the postulates of an important (Bayesian) account of rational choice theory.[9]

However, in spite of its attractive features, the difficulties facing preference utilitarianism are at least somewhat analogous to those that plagued Bentham. Since all preferences are taken as given, there is nothing in the theory that allows us to distinguish rational, refined, socially responsible preferences from irrational, crude, or antisocial preferences. The preferences of an unbiased social worker would count the same as those of a racist.[10]

In utilitarianism, the satisfaction of any desire has some value in itself that must be taken into account in deciding what is right. In calculating the greatest balance of satisfaction, it does not matter, except indirectly, what the desires are for. We are to arrange institutions so as to obtain the greatest sum of satisfactions; we ask no questions about their source or quality but only how their satisfaction would affect the total of well-being. Social welfare depends directly and solely upon the levels of satisfaction or dissatisfaction of individuals. Thus, if schoolyard bullies take a certain pleasure in tormenting a younger child, or a racist group enjoys subjecting a racial minority to a lesser liberty as a means of enhancing their own self-respect, then the satisfaction of these desires must be weighed in our deliberations according to their intensity, or other qualities, along with other desires.[11]

Although economists have tended to accept this idea of preference neutrality, many moral philosophers, including Harsanyi, have not. Harsanyi, like most preference utilitarians, insists that only *rational* preferences should count. To avoid the problem presented by immoral preferences such as that of the bully or those of racists, he also has stipulated that antisocial preferences should not count either.

Although these stipulations seem morally correct, in making them Harsanyi and other preference utilitarians may have moved beyond utilitarianism in a way analogous to Mill. Mill claimed to find a special quality in some pleasures, which enabled him to say that the life of a satisfied pig could not be better than the life of a dissatisfied Socrates. But what could this quality be if Mill was to remain a hedonistic utilitarian? Similarly, Harsanyi argues for the principle of preference autonomy and yet eliminates "irrational" or "antisocial" preferences from utilitarian calculations. But mustn't this involve the use of some other criterion of value or some other theory of the good than preference satisfaction and, if so, how is this consistent with the kind of preference autonomy required by utilitarianism?

Contemporary utilitarians have not only discussed utilitarian theories of the good, such as the idea of preference satisfaction, but have also continued the debate between rule and act utilitarianism.[12] One of the challenges to contemporary utilitarianism that has engaged defenders of both act and rule versions of the theory is to avoid counterexamples like the following:

> It [utilitarianism] implies that if you have employed a boy to mow your lawn and he has finished the job and asks for his pay, you should pay him what you promised only if you cannot find a better use for your money. It implies that when you bring home your monthly paycheck you should use it to support your family and yourself only if it cannot be used more effectively to supply the needs of others. It implies that if your father is ill and has no prospect of good in his life, and maintaining him is a drain on the energy and enjoyment of others, then, if you can end his life without provoking any public scandal or setting a bad example, it is your positive duty to take matters into your own hands and bring his life to a close.[13]

Many act utilitarians respond by claiming that alleged counterexamples like these are based on totally unrealistic situations. For example, it often is claimed that utilitarianism would justify convicting a friendless and homeless person of a crime, even though authorities knew him to be innocent, in order to deter criminals and reassure citizens, thereby maximizing utility but treating the victim unjustly. The act utilitarian might reply, however, that it is extremely implausible to think that the decision to consciously punish an innocent person could remain secret. In addition, long-term consequences, such as the erosion of the sense of justice of the prosecutors, would work against the public interest in the long run. Similarly, the counterexample requiring us to kill ill parents normally runs against emotions of love and ignores the insecurity we would all feel if we could be killed just to prevent bad consequences for others. Hence, it is extremely unlikely that killing a parent in the situation described would promote utility, although of course the issue becomes more complex if we consider requests for voluntary euthanasia from terminally ill patients who are experiencing intense pain.

A careful act utilitarian, moreover, would not only be sensitive to the likely consequences of actions but also would take account of rules of justice and equity, and the dangers that result from breaking them. *Normally* justice should be promoted, and well-entrenched moral rules should not be broken. Rules that have proved to promote utility over time should be treated, as we noted above, as useful but not perfect guides to conduct—as rules-of-thumb. Normally they should be followed, but sometimes they should be broken, namely, in those rare cases where utility is maximized by breaking them and all the consequences of breaking the rules have been factored in.

Is such a response on behalf of act utilitarianism satisfactory? Consider that it may be extremely difficult to predict the consequences of acts, particularly those undertaken under pressure. Under pressure, it may seem efficient to ignore equity, fairness, justice, and rights and maximize utility, even though judgment about such factors is likely to be distorted by the pressure of the situation itself. At the very least, it seems to us that act utilitarianism does not offer sufficient protection for the innocent; the innocent are protected only insofar as complex calculations about consequences tend to come out the right way. And the very circumstances where the innocent, or unpopular individuals and minorities, need protection the most are exactly those where utilitarian calculations are likely to be done carelessly or under the influence of pressure or bias.

Considerations like these have encouraged other contemporary utilitarians to reformulate the rule utilitarianism of Mill. Richard Brandt's book *A Theory of the Good and the Right*, published in 1979, remains a leading defense of a contemporary version of rule utilitarianism. Brandt argues that utilitarians should advocate the adoption of a welfare-maximizing moral system (or code of moral conduct). The rules in such a system would be suited to the nature of human beings and would take into account the intellectual capacities of the average person as well as the negative qualities the average human being possesses—negative qualities such as selfishness and impulsiveness. The code of moral conduct must be simple enough to be teachable and should have fairly concrete rules for frequent situations.[14]

Brandt thinks that utilitarianism is the principle that should serve as the guide for deciding what moral rules should be included in a moral system. The rules that should be included are those that would maximize utility if they are generally or universally complied with. This version of rule utilitarianism also urges us to consider psychological facts about human beings as various rules are proposed. Thus, we should not include rules that human beings, given their psychology, are extremely unlikely or unable to follow. Only in this way can a welfare-maximizing moral system be ensured.

A similar argument can be made for the accommodation of individual rights within a rule utilitarian framework. Such an argument is found, for example, in David Braybrooke's *Three Tests for Democracy*. Indeed, Braybrooke refers to rights as rule utilitarian devices. The chief purpose of rights in Braybrooke's view is to forestall some of the difficulties that attend act utilitarianism:

> However, one of the basic principles behind the practice of asserting and heeding rights is precisely to forestall general considerations of happiness or well-being and the like from being freely invoked to decide the particular cases embraced by rights. Neither the person asserting the right nor the agent or agents called upon to respect it would normally be able in a particular case to review the alternative possibilities and their consequences really thoroughly. It would be dangerous to empower agents to act on such reviews: . . . dangerous not only because the agents are liable to bias in their own interests, . . . but dangerous also because the agents involved are out of communication with one another and do not have the information necessary to coordinate their actions.[15]

In this view, rights are institutional safeguards to protect us from our own short-sightedness and bias in considering individual cases; rights protect us from the frailty of human nature. Thus, in a world with no human frailty, that is, in a world of perfectly rational and knowledgeable impartial observers, rule utilitarians would acknowledge that there need be no rights at all. In the real world, they also might admit that rare circumstances could arise in which we would want to say that rights should be given up since in those circumstances failure to give up such rights would lead to disastrous consequences. However, for a few rights, the probability of disastrous consequences arising that would nullify the right is virtually zero. These rights, in Braybrooke's analysis, are inalienable and inextinguishable:

> Men may regard certain rights as inalienable, considering that the rights in question have emerged from profound social processes worth continuing respect. . . . There is, furthermore, an impressive empirical consideration that offers a strong defense, indefinitely continuing, for the inalienability of certain rights. Mindful of the weaknesses of human nature and aware of the imperfections of provisions for legislation, people believe that they will be safer if certain rights are kept out of reach. . . . Some rights, it might be said, are inalienable and inextinguishable for reasons that no empirical evidence could upset. Could the alienation or extinction of the right to a fair trial be accepted under any social conditions? . . . If a society makes any use of the concept of rights to regulate its affairs then in that society there must be a right to a fair trial.[16]

Inalienable and inextinguishable rights are like other rights in being grounded in utilitarian considerations; however, they differ from other rights in that empirical circumstances that would enable us to give up the practice are not a realistic possibility. In this respect, inalienable rights are like basic laws of nature; falsification by empirical events is not to be expected.

The thrust of points of view like Brandt's and Braybrooke's is to find a place for our commonsense convictions about rights and justice within the structure of utilitarianism itself. Indeed, the convictions and corresponding rights structure arise because adherence to justice and individual rights does work for the greatest good for the greatest number. If a system of rights did not work for the greatest good of the public it would soon be abandoned. Hence, the rights theorists are correct in emphasizing the importance of rights but they are incorrect in making them independent. We do not use rights to constrain utilitarianism; rather, utilitarianism is the justification for having rights in the first place.

Criticism of Contemporary Utilitarianism

Perhaps the place to begin this aspect of the debate is with a hypothetical but very dramatic example described by Bernard Williams. In the example, an American tourist, Jim, finds himself by accident in a small South American village.

Tied up against the wall are a row of twenty Indians, most terrified, a few defiant, in front of them several armed men in uniform. A heavy man in a sweat-stained khaki shirt turns out to be the captain in charge and, after a good deal of questioning of Jim which establishes that he got there by accident while on a botanical expedition, explains that the Indians are a random group of the inhabitants who, after recent acts of protest against the government, are just about to be killed to remind other possible protesters of the advantages of not protesting. However, since Jim is an honored visitor from another land, the captain is happy to offer him a guest's privilege of killing one of the Indians himself. If Jim accepts, then as a special mark of the occasion, the other Indians will be let off. Of course, if Jim refuses, then there is no special occasion, and Pedro here will do what he was about to do when Jim arrived, and kill them all. . . . The men against the wall, and the other villagers, understand the situation, and are obviously begging him to accept. What should he do?[17]

Before discussing this example, it should be pointed out, as noted above, that many contemporary utilitarians argue that it is not fair to use what R. M. Hare has called "fantastic examples."[18] After all, any ethical theory can be criticized by creating some far-fetched story that makes the theory look ridiculous but which resembles fantasy rather than reality. Ethical theories are designed to guide human conduct in the real world and they should be tested against realistic rather than fantastic examples. Thus, many utilitarians would argue that the story about Jim and the Indians never could happen and so does not constitute an example with which utilitarianism should be expected to deal.

However, critics of utilitarianism might respond, with some justice, that something very much like Williams's example could happen in wartime. Critics can also respond that the point of such examples is not always to create a realistic scenario but rather to bring out controversial implications of utilitarianism by isolating relevant factors and making them explicit, much as a controlled experiment does in science. In fairness to utilitarianism, let us note the objection to examples like this but use it nevertheless to illustrate some commonly held objections to the utilitarian theory.

Thus, it would seem that on any utilitarian analysis, even in the complex versions of Brandt and Braybrooke, Jim ought to kill one Indian so that nineteen others would be saved. A utilitarian of any stripe should find Jim's question rather easy to answer. However, those who are not utilitarians might find Jim's question very difficult to answer. What makes the question difficult for the nonutilitarians is that they believe something other than future consequences should be considered. Jim must consider not only the number of deaths that might result but the fact that if he chooses one way he is a killer, whereas if he chooses another way he is not. If Jim kills an innocent person, then Jim himself has killed. However, if Jim refuses to kill an innocent person then we cannot say that Jim has killed twenty other people who will die; perhaps we cannot even say that Jim caused the twenty Indians to be killed.

What we think Williams is driving at is the fact that one's position in a situation makes a difference. There is an integrity of a position or role that cannot be captured under the utilitarian umbrella. Jim does not have the same responsibility to the twenty Indians that Pedro would kill as Jim does to the one Indian he would kill. Of course, it may be that he nevertheless should kill one to save nineteen, but there are complications in that question that no utilitarian can understand.

The utilitarian's failure to consider the position or role one holds in the chain of consequences is symptomatic of a serious deficiency in the way utilitarians consider individuals. John Rawls, at one time an adherent of rule utilitarianism but now the adherent of perhaps the most important nonutilitarian theory of justice, one that we will consider later, charges the supposedly individualist theory of utilitarianism with ignoring the distinctions that exist among persons. Since utilitarianism has traditionally been viewed as an individualist theory par excellence, how is it possible that it ignores personalities? Rawls says that utilitarianism extends to society the principle of choice for one man:

> It is customary to think of utilitarianism as individualistic, and certainly there are good reasons for this. The utilitarians were strong defenders of liberty and freedom of thought and they held that the good of society is constituted by the advantages enjoyed by individuals. Yet utilitarianism is not individualistic, at least when arrived at by the more natural course of reflection, in that, by conflating all systems of desires, it applies to the society the principle of choice for one man. . . . There is no reason to suppose that the principles which should regulate an association of men is simply an extension of the principle of choice for one man.[19]

What Rawls seems to be saying is that under utilitarian theory each person strives to maximize his net happiness with due account given to the intensity of his desires. The satisfactions and frustrations of desires of the individuals in society are summed up, with the frustrations of some individuals canceling out the happiness of others. The policy that ought to be adopted is the one that maximizes net happiness. This answer looks at society as if it were an individual who has balanced the gains and losses in order to achieve the greatest balance of happiness. Note the contrast in point of view, however. When Jones's desire for a third martini is denied because Jones wishes to avoid a headache tomorrow, both the desire frustrated and the desire fulfilled are desires of the same individual. However, when policy X, which leads to the greatest happiness on balance, cancels out the wants of Smith in favor of the wants of Jones, the analogy with a single individual is no longer legitimate. The frustration of Smith is not like the frustration of Jones's desire for a third martini. In the case of Smith, the benefits and burdens do not fall on the same individual; rather the losses for some are balanced by gains for *others*.

Thus, even though rule utilitarians and some nonutilitarians might endorse the same rules, and even though some rule utilitarians might support individual rights, utilitarians and many of their critics look at the people governed by the rules in very different ways. The critics of utilitarianism do not treat people as means toward achieving maximum net satisfaction.

Moreover, even though rule utilitarianism is presented as an approach that reconciles utilitarianism with a concern for individual rights, rule utilitarianism might not in the last analysis constitute a distinct position of its own. Thus, David Lyons has argued that ultimately there is no real difference between rule and act utilitarianism.[20] Consider how Lyons reduces rule to act utilitarianism. His main point is that if a rule turns out to permit bad consequences in a given situation, utilitarianism would require that the rule be modified to allow for an exception. For example, the rule against lying should allow an exception in cases where lying is necessary to save another person's life. Other exceptions surely will be needed as well. However, as the rule is amended to allow more and more exceptions, it looks more and more like a rule of thumb. Thus, when doubts arise about whether good consequences will follow from applying the rule in a specific case, for all practical purposes we might as well proceed as act utilitarians. That is, for all practical purposes, there is no significant difference between act utilitarians who treat moral rules as rules of thumb and rule utilitarians who allow exceptions to be built into the rule whenever a situation arises where following the rule leads to bad consequences.

If Lyons is right, then the appeal to rule utilitarianism in order to avoid objections to act utilitarianism will not work. Of course, the rule utilitarian could avoid the objection by not allowing exceptions and making the rules inviolable. However, rule utilitarianism will then be committed to rigid, inflexible rules that cannot be violated even when making an exception would produce far greater good than blindly following the rule. Thus, rule utilitarians may be trapped between the erosion caused by an indefinite number of exceptions, which may make the position indistinguishable from act utilitarianism, and inflexible rule worship.

CONCLUSION

In general we have criticized utilitarianism for failing to give an adequate account of how to ensure protection of an individual's rights. The story of Jim's dilemma illustrates how utilitarians ignore the roles individuals play in the causal chain. One cannot say what a person ought to do by ignoring past obligations, commitments, and responsibilities. Neither can a state treat society as a superperson where canceling a desire of Smith to fulfill a desire of Jones is analogous to an individual's frustration of his one desire to fulfill another desire of his own. In addition, a state should not treat all desires of its citizens as equal. Moreover, it should not expect the less fortunate to make greater sacrifices for the more fortunate simply because total utility is thereby increased.

Utilitarians like Brandt and Braybrooke would respond that their more complex utilitarian formulas do take these complicating factors into account. They would argue that the more complex constructions of the utilitarian formula do not conflict with our widely cherished moral beliefs. Brandt would argue that his formula allows utilitarianism to take account of such antiutilitarian sentiments. For example, some people's belief that they ought to tell the truth may be based on nonutilitarian considerations, for example that it is commandment of God. However, such a position, even though it is not based directly on utilitarian considerations, may still be useful because it leads people to generally tell the truth, a practice that actually is beneficial for utilitarian reasons.

Perhaps, assuming that rule and act utilitarianism really are distinct positions, one might refine utilitarianism so that rules and practices justified on utilitarian grounds were identical with the rules and practices that would be justified on some other nonutilitarian ethical theory. In other words, utilitarianism and at least one of its main rivals would sanction the same acts as morally right and condemn the same acts as morally wrong. So it might appear that we have a case of the chicken and the egg problem. However, that would be misleading. Even if the utilitarians and their rivals agreed about what was right or wrong, they would continue to disagree on the reasons. For the utilitarian, the rules and practices that protect individual rights are justified because such rules lead to the greatest good for the greatest number. Should the world change and such utilitarian results no longer obtain, the rules and practices that protect individual rights would be surrendered. For the nonutilitarian, the fact that the rules no longer bring about utilitarian results need not be a reason for abandoning them. The question now becomes what perspective should one take toward rules that protect individual rights or that specify how happiness should be distributed.

We believe that the utilitarian perspective is inadequate, and in the next chapter we develop a competing theory that places ultimate value on the rights of the individual. The answers to the questions of political philosophy are then assessed in terms of how well the rights of individuals are supported. Even if a sophisticated utilitarianism such as Brandt's or Braybrooke's could give the same answers to these questions that we do, we would prefer our rights perspective to that of the utilitarian for two reasons.

First, the utilitarian support for rights rests on too shaky a foundation. As we noted, Braybrooke argued that there is an impressive empirical consideration that offers a strong defense, indefinitely continuing, for the inalienability of certain rights. "Mindful of the weakness of human nature and aware of the imperfections of provisions for legislation, people believe that they will be safer if certain rights are kept out of reach." We suggest that this kind of protection for fundamental rights is too insecure. Let people's attitudes about the frailty of human nature become less pessimistic and human rights will be in danger.

Second, the very complexity of the utilitarian attempt to find a place for human rights suggests that we might do better to let human rights serve as the focal point at the outset. However, the reader is urged to wait until completing chapter 3 before making a final decision on the question.

In concluding this chapter, let us return to at least two of our original questions concerning the state. Our first question asked under what conditions a state should actually have authority. A utilitarian would answer that the state should have authority to provide for the public good. Immediately one would then ask our second question: "What is the proper scope or extent of its authority?" To this question, a utilitarian would respond that the extent of the state's authority should be sufficient to enable it to provide for the public good as long as the cost of expanding state authority is taken into account. Let us now consider how an adherent of fundamental human rights would delineate the function of the state and the scope of its proper authority.

NOTES

1. Jeremy Bentham, *Principles of Morals and Legislation*, 1789, widely reprinted. (Quotations from reprint, Garden City, NY: Dolphin Books, 1961, 17.)

2. Bentham, *Principles of Morals and Legislation*, 38–39.

3. This point, using the schema of both our examples, is made by Nicholas Rescher in his *Distributive Justice* (New York: Bobbs-Merrill, 1966) in chapters 2 and 3. This problem could be avoided if the utilitarian simply used the greatest good as the criterion. There is some evidence that Bentham actually gave up the double criterion of the greatest good for the greatest number. See Bhikhu Parekh, ed., *Bentham's Political Thought* (London: Croom Helm, 1973), 309–10.

4. John Stuart Mill, *Utilitarianism* (1863. Reprint Indianapolis: Bobbs-Merrill, 1957), 12.

5. Mill, *Utilitarianism*, 12.

6. Richard B. Brandt, *Ethical Theory* (Englewood Cliffs, NJ: Prentice-Hall, 1959), 384.

7. Some philosophers argue that a rule utilitarian who successfully formulated the rules that pass the utilitarian test would justify the same actions as an act utilitarian who successfully measured all of the consequences of any individual act. This is because the rule utilitarian would have to add so many exceptions that the extended "rule" would simply be a summary of decisions about individual cases. The most influential book arguing for this equivalence is David Lyons's *Forms and Limits of Utilitarianism* (New York: Oxford University Press, 1965), which we will discuss briefly later in the text.

8. John Stuart Mill, *Considerations on Representative Government*, chapter 8, "Of the Extension of the Suffrage" [1865] (Albany, NY: Prometheus Books, 1991).

9. John C. Harsanyi, "Morality and the Theory of Rational Behavior," *Social Research* 44 (Winter 1977): 623–56.

10. Ronald Dworkin has discussed this problem under the heading of external and internal preferences in his *Taking Rights Seriously* (Cambridge, MA: Harvard University Press, 1977).

11. See John Rawls, *A Theory of Justice* (Cambridge, MA: Harvard University Press, 1971), 30–31, for a similar point.

12. Thus, a contemporary act utilitarian counterpart to Bentham is J. J. C. Smart. A rule utilitarian counterpart to Mill is Richard Brandt. See Smart's "An Outline of a System of Utilitarian Ethics," in *Utilitarianism: For and Against*, ed. J. J. C. Smart and Bernard Williams (Cambridge: Cambridge University Press, 1973), 3–74, and Richard B. Brandt, *A Theory of the Good and the Right* (Oxford University Press, 1979).

13. Richard B. Brandt, "Toward a Credible Form of Utilitarianism," in *Morality and the Language of Conduct*, ed. Hector-Neri Castaneda and George Nakhnikian (Detroit: Wayne State University Press, 1965), 109–10.

14. Brandt, *A Theory of the Good and the Right*, 290.

15. David Braybrooke, *Three Tests for Democracy: Personal Rights, Human Welfare, and Collective Preference* (New York: Random House, 1968), 39.

16. Braybrooke, *Three Tests for Democracy*, 42–43.

17. Bernard Williams, "A Critique of Utilitarianism," in *Utilitarianism: For and Against*, ed. J. J. C. Smart and Bernard Williams (New York: Cambridge University Press, 1973), 98–99.

18. See, for example, R. M. Hare, *Moral Thinking: Its Levels, Method, and Point* (New York: Oxford University Press, 1981), 131–52.

19. John Rawls, *A Theory of Justice*, 28–29.

20. David Lyons, *The Forms and Limits of Utilitarianism*.

QUESTIONS FOR FURTHER STUDY

1. Bentham's version of utilitarianism has been criticized because it seems to imply that it is better to be a satisfied pig than a dissatisfied Socrates. Explain why Bentham's utilitarianism may seem to have that implication. Do you agree with the criticism? Why or why not?

2. Hedonistic utilitarianism urges us to maximize pleasure. Should we maximize the total amount of pleasure in society or the average amount of pleasure per person? Does it really make any difference: for example, what are the implications for population policy?

3. Explain the objection that utilitarianism would justify punishment of the innocent in some circumstances. Does rule utilitarianism avoid that objection? Why or why not?

4. How have modern economists changed the classical utilitarianism of Bentham and Mill? Does their reformulation allow them to escape objections to the earlier versions? Is their version subject to new criticisms? If so, what are they?

5. How might utilitarians incorporate human rights into their theory? Evaluate their account.

6. What is the point of the story of Pedro, Jim, and the rebels? Do our moral intuitions regarding the story undermine utilitarianism? Why or why not?

7. Is Lyons right to argue that act and rule utilitarianism come to the same thing? Why or why not?

8. Rawls says that utilitarianism extends to society the principle of choice for one man. Explain why Rawls thinks this is a criticism of utilitarianism. Do you think the utilitarians have a good response? Explain your answer.

SUGGESTED READINGS

Bentham, Jeremy. *Principles of Morals and Legislation*, in *The Utilitarians*. Garden City, NY: Doubleday, 1961.

Brandt, Richard B. *A Theory of the Good and the Right*. New York: Oxford University Press, 1979.

Braybrooke, David. *Three Tests For Democracy: Personal Rights, Human Welfare, and Collective Preference*. New York: Random House, 1968.

Frey, R. G., ed. *Utility and Rights*. Minneapolis: University of Minnesota Press, 1984.

Gibbard, Alan. *Utilitarianism and Coordination*. New York: Garland Publishing, 1990.

Glover, Jonathan, ed. *Utilitarianism and Its Critics*. New York: Macmillan, 1990.

Hare, R. M. *Moral Thinking: Its Levels, Method, and Point*. New York: Oxford University Press, 1981.

Lyons, David. *Forms and Limits of Utilitarianism*. Oxford: Clarendon Press, 1965.

——. "Utilitarianism," in *The Encyclopedia of Ethics*, ed. Lawrence C. Becker and Charlotte B. Becker, second ed. New York: Routledge: 2001, 1737–44.

Mill, John Stuart. *Utilitarianism*. Indianapolis: Bobbs-Merrill, 1957.

Regan, Donald. *Utilitarianism and Cooperation*. Oxford: Clarendon, 1980.

Sen, Amartya, and Bernard Williams. *Utilitarianism and Beyond*. Cambridge: Cambridge University Press, 1982.

Sidgwick, Henry. *The Methods of Ethics*, seventh ed. Chicago: University of Chicago Press, 1962.

Smart, J. J .C., and Bernard Williams. *Utilitarianism: For and Against*. Cambridge and New York: Cambridge University Pres, 1973.

3

HUMAN RIGHTS: MEANING AND JUSTIFICATION

The twentieth century has seen some of the greatest evils in human history. During the Holocaust, millions upon millions of people were murdered as the Nazis attempted to carry out their goal of exterminating the Jewish people and eliminating other "undesirables" from their Reich. The racist policy of apartheid was a dominant system in South Africa until well into the second half of the twentieth century. More recently, "ethnic cleansing" has claimed a still unknown number of victims in the Balkans. Mass slaughter in Rwanda and ongoing massacres, rapes, and assaults in the Darfur region of Sudan have elicited widespread condemnation but little in the way of intervention to prevent what plausibly might be regarded as genocide.

Indeed, it sometimes seems that abuse of our fellow humans is almost everywhere. In its report of 1996, Amnesty International describes violations of basic rights virtually around the globe. "Arbitrary killings by government forces and armed opposition groups go unpunished and unchecked. Torture is rife. Prisoners of conscience are confined behind bars. Political prisoners face trials that are a travesty of justice—or are jailed with no trial at all."[1] The history of the United States, although in many ways showing remarkable progress toward respect for universal rights, includes a legacy of slavery, racial segregation, gross mistreatment of native peoples, and a continuing battle against racial discrimination and prejudice, as well as controversy over alleged torture of suspects in the war on terrorism and in Iraq.

Many of these gross violations are carried out by governments and other organized political groups. Individuals can be victimized because of their political views, or simply because they belong to a racial, ethnic, gender, or religious group that has been targeted by oppressors. Victims of terrorism may have nothing in common other than their humanity and may be guilty only of being in the wrong place at the wrong time. The doctrine of human rights is designed to provide certain fundamental protections for individuals against the state, against other political and social organizations, and against other individuals as well. Such rights create basic protections for the individual that morally may not be ignored, even to provide gains for a greater number of people.

Although, as we will see, human rights can be conceived of as devices that promote long-term utility, they may best be thought of as protections for individual persons that are of sufficient moral weight to shield us against being sacrificed for the greater good of the greater number. In our view, the principal function of the state is to protect the human rights of its citizens. Unfortunately, as indicated above, states have often been among the greatest abusers of human rights. However, the doctrine of human rights, properly implemented by the state, can provide a powerful protection for all of us against the kind of systematic abuses of persons that have been all too frequent throughout human history.

Our first task will be to clarify the notion of a human right. In particular, the concept of a right, and especially the concept of a human right, must be explained and examined.

ANALYSIS

Rights

Compare two universities, which will be referred to as university A and university B. In each, it is sometimes the case that a professor grades a student's paper unfairly. The reasons for this vary from case to case, and the incidence of unfairness is no greater at one institution than at the other. What does differ, however, are the methods and procedures for dealing with unfairness when it does arise.

In university A, if students believe their papers have been unfairly graded and if they wish to appeal, they must petition the professor who graded the paper for an appointment. According to the rules of the university, however, it is entirely up to the professor whether such petitions are granted. Even if the petition is accepted, the rules of the university leave it entirely up to the professor whose fairness is being questioned whether the paper will be reviewed and the grade changed. There is no higher court of appeal. Of course, many faculty members at this university are conscientious and kind men and women. Most would not dream of turning down a student's petition for an appointment. However, according to the rules of the university, whether a professor chooses to act conscientiously and kindly is solely up to that professor. Students have no claim on the faculty nor are they entitled to impartial review. If some professors choose to act properly and others do not, then, as far as the rules of the university are concerned, it is a matter between them and their own conscience. At university A, then, faculty consideration of student complaints is a gratuity that may or may not be dispensed at will.[2]

In university B, things are quite different. Student complaints of unfairness in grading must be dealt with through established procedures. All complaints not resolvable by informal discussion between the parties must be investigated by faculty who are previously uninvolved in the case. In university B, it is not up to the professor involved as to whether the grievance machinery is called into play. Rather, the student is *entitled* to impartial review upon request.

In university B, but not in university A, students have rights in the area in question. The example illustrates the difference between having and not having rights. The example also brings out the point that rights are entitlements. The students in university B are *entitled* to impartial review. Their claim to review is not dependent upon faculty good will or permission. Indeed, the domain of rights is to be contrasted with that of permissions, on the one hand, and benevolence, on the other.

The notion of an entitlement has justificatory import. If someone is entitled to something, his claim to it is justified, at least prima facie. The justification may be institutional, legal, or moral, depending upon the kind of right considered. Such a justification need not be conclusive. For one thing, rights may clash. My right to ten dollars from Jones and your right to ten dollars from Jones cannot both be honored if Jones has only ten dollars. Moreover, if Jones has only ten dollars, perhaps none of us is justified in claiming it in the first place, all things considered.[3]

If students in university B have a right to impartial review upon request, then they are entitled to such review. And if they are entitled to it, others—in this case, the faculty—are under at least a prima facie obligation to provide such a review. Rights imply obligations in the sense that if some person has a right to something, some other persons are under an obligation either to provide it or at least not to interfere with the rights bearer's pursuit of it.

While some philosophers believe that rights can be defined in terms of the obligations of others, we suggest that it is of crucial moral importance to distinguish obligations that arise from rights claims from obligations of what may be a different sort, particularly those that arise from noblesse oblige or "one's station and its duties." A useful example has been provided by Richard Wasserstrom. Wasserstrom points out that during the civil rights movement of the late 1950s and early 1960s, white southerners frequently asserted that they had great concern for the welfare of "their Negroes." According to Wasserstrom, "What this way of conceiving most denies to any Negro is the opportunity to assert claims as a matter of right. It denies him the standing to protest the way he is treated. If the white southerner fails to do his duty, that is simply a matter between him and his conscience."[4]

The white southerner of Wasserstrom's example views kind treatment of black people as a matter of personal benevolence. If indeed there are any obligations involved, as Wasserstrom's (perhaps confusing) use of the word "duty" may suggest, such obligations do not arise from the correlative rights but rather from something like a duty to act charitably. However, if we view persons as possessors of rights, we view them as agents, as makers of claims, as beings who are entitled to certain considerations whether or not others feel like going along. It is this aspect of the emphasis on rights that, as we will argue later, accounts for the important connection between human rights, on the one hand, and human dignity, autonomy, and respect for persons on the other.

An objection may be that to explicate rights in terms of entitlements is to offer a circular account. For what can it mean to say that someone is entitled to something other than that he or she has a right to it?

However, even if the analysis is circular, it is not necessarily unhelpful for our purposes. For our goal is not to offer a formal definition but rather to demonstrate the normative function of rights talk—namely, to demarcate an area of individual inviolability that may not be invaded on grounds of benevolence, social utility, the public interest, or charity.[5] In any case, it may well be that terms like "rights," "entitlements," and "obligations" are a family of conceptually related terms none of which is primitive or basic but all of which together help to distinguish the realm of rights from that of charity, benevolence, and the direct pursuit of utility.[6]

If moral rights were at issue, different kinds of moral theories could then provide different sorts of justifications for particular normative judgments about when X ought to have Y and why deprivations would normally be impermissible. Thus, rule utilitarians might see rights as institutional devices that forbid violation of the individual's claims in order to directly pursue utility precisely because such a prohibition would indirectly promote the most utility in the long run. Others might argue, as we will do later in this chapter, that certain fundamental moral entitlements must be protected if persons are to be respected as rational, autonomous agents.

For our purposes, then, rights are best construed as entitlements. Legal rights are entitlements that are supportable on legal grounds, while moral rights are entitlements that are supportable, perhaps in the ways suggested above, on moral grounds. What then are human rights? The idea of human rights evolved out of the older tradition of natural rights.

Natural Rights

The doctrine of natural rights evolved over a long period of time and was often the center of political and philosophical controversy. The roots of the doctrine go back at least as far as debates among the Sophists of ancient Greece over whether justice is conventional or objective and universal. Plato and Aristotle argued that the nature of justice could be discovered by reason and so was accessible to all rational persons. And the later Stoic philosophers emphasized a natural law, binding on all men, that takes precedence over the particular laws embodied in human political institutions. As natural laws were held by the Stoics to be independent of existing legal principles, they constituted an Archimedean point from which the legal order could be evaluated.

The concern for the rule of law as manifested in ancient Rome led to further emphasis on the Stoic ideal of a law of nature. In 534 AD, Emperor Justinian presided over the completion of the *Corpus Iuris Civilis*, a great codebook of Roman law.[7] This codification of the law of the Roman Empire was to have remarkable influence, for one of the great gifts of Rome to later civilizations was appreciation of the significance of the rule of law. Justinian's law books claimed universal validity and so reinforced the Stoic ideal of a law over and above the law of any particular community, applying equally to all. This conception of a "higher" law than that of one's community was acknowledged by many educated Romans during various stages of the Empire's development. Perhaps none expressed the idea as well as Cicero, who declared:

> There is indeed a law, right reason, which is in accordance with nature; existing in all, unchangeable, eternal. . . . It is not one thing at Rome, and another thing at Athens . . . but it is a law, eternal and immutable for all nations and for all time.[8]

This conception of natural law was developed by Scholastic philosophers during the Middle Ages. The account defended by Thomas Aquinas has been especially influential. It fitted the Stoic belief in a rational moral order, analogous to an (allegedly) rational natural order, into the framework of Judeo-Christian theology, which sometimes identified moral laws with commands of God or with conceptions of human flourishing built into our very nature by God. Thus, some Scholastic natural law theorists, following ideas of Aristotle, regarded us as social beings by nature, so natural law would tell us that the good for human beings consists at least in part in living in a well-ordered society. Since the natural laws were identified with outpourings of divine reason, they were open to discovery by other rational beings. Aquinas maintained that:

> [I]t is clear that the whole community of the universe is governed by divine reason. This rational guidance of created things on the part of God . . . we can call the Eternal Law. . . . But of all others, rational creatures are subject to the divine Providence in a special way . . . in that they control their own actions. . . . This participation in the Eternal Law by rational creatures is called the Natural Law.[9]

Aquinas emphasized that this natural law is a higher law than that of such man-made institutions as the state:

> And if a human law is at variance in any particular way with Natural Law, it is no longer legal but rather is a corruption of law.[10]

This conception of natural law, like that of the Stoics, provides an external, rational standard against which the laws and policies of particular states are to be measured. The Scholastic conception of natural law, however, was intimately tied to a theological foundation and tended to be embedded in a theistic political framework. Although natural laws were held to be discernible by reason, they were also held to be promulgated by divine will. The political order, in turn, was held to serve a function determined by that will—namely, the development of distinctively human nature within a given social framework.

However, in the seventeenth and eighteenth centuries, growing rationalism and growing individualism led to revision of the classical account of natural law and natural right. Such documents as the French *Declaration of the Rights of Man* and the American *Declaration of Independence* asserted the rights of humans qua humans against the state. The foundation of natural law and of the rights of the individual was placed in reason rather than in theology. The political order, in turn, was viewed as an instrument through which diverse and essentially egoistic individuals could pursue their private ends and not as an agency for socialization through which the citizen would become fully human. Natural rights were appealed to in defense of human liberty and autonomy against what came to be perceived as the potentially (and often actually) oppressive power of the state.

However, with the rise of utilitarianism in the nineteenth century, the natural rights approach no longer held a position of dominance in political theory. Utilitarians, with their forward-looking consequentialist ethical theory, regarded only the effects of action or policy as relevant to moral evaluation. Right and wrong were held to depend on consequences, not on allegedly pre-existing natural rights. Thus, Jeremy Bentham attempted to relegate the doctrine of natural rights to the graveyard of abandoned philosophies when he held that "Natural rights is simple nonsense: natural and imprescriptible rights, rhetorical nonsense—nonsense upon stilts."[11]

But, as we have seen, a basic problem for utilitarian ethics is how to avoid permitting the oppression of a minority so long as the result is the production of the greatest overall good. The horrors of the Nazi Holocaust and the struggle for the civil rights of black people in America seem to have motivated many to search for a normative political theory that asserts the inviolability of the individual. While utilitarianism, on any plausible interpretation, would condemn Nazi genocide, many reflective people have regarded the kind of protection utilitarianism provides for the individual as inadequate, resting at best on complex empirical calculations, and have tried to argue for the inviolability of persons on non-utilitarian grounds. Thus, the doctrine of natural rights has resurfaced, shorn of much of its metaphysical and theological baggage, in the form of a plea for human dignity and for the kind of treatment that makes at least a minimally decent human life possible. We will refer to the modern version of the doctrine as a doctrine of *human rights* to indicate that the theoretical framework in which such rights are embedded and justified is independent of theology and of older accounts of natural law. We will reserve the expression "natural rights" for older historical versions of the doctrine.

Of course, those who view morality as commands of God may continue to perceive human rights as constraints on human behavior promulgated by divine will. However, such a theological approach is unlikely to command wide assent in a diverse society such as the United States, where people hold divergent religious views or no religious views at all, let alone in the wider world community. Moreover, viewing human rights merely as commands of God raises the problem perhaps first stated by Socrates in Plato's dialogue *The Euthyphro*. Is X right because God commands X or does God command X because it is right? The major problem with the first formulation is that it seems to imply that God's commands are totally arbitrary, which raises the question whether they are truly good (what significance can it have to call a command morally good if there is no reason why that command rather than its opposite was issued?) and why such a command should be obeyed, other than through fear of punishment. On the other hand, if God commands us to respect human rights because it truly is the right thing to do then we, as philosophers, can use our reason to try to explain why respecting human rights is morally so important.

How then are we to conceive of human rights? Traditionally, natural rights and natural law have been thought of as independent of any given social or political order. Thus, they can serve as external standards for the evaluation of such institutional frameworks. This explains the point of calling a certain class of rights natural ones. "Natural" has many opposites, including "artificial," "social," "conventional," "abnormal." In the context of natural rights, "natural" is in contrast with "social" and "conventional."

We will follow this account in explicating human rights. Human rights are rights that do not arise from any particular organization of society or from any roles their bearers may play within social institutions. They are to be distinguished from the rights of parents against children, teachers against students, and clients against their lawyers. Instead, they are rights possessed on grounds other than the institutional role of the holders or the nature of the society to which they belong. They belong to human beings as such.[12] Conversely, human rights impose obligations on anyone, regardless of rank or position. Since such rights are not held in virtue of social status, everyone is obliged to respect them.

Human rights also are thought of as morally fundamental. That is, the justification of other rights claims ultimately involves appeal to them. They are the most basic of our moral rights. Thus, the right to pursue a hobby in one's spare time can be defended as deriving from a more basic natural right to liberty from interference by others.

Moreover, human rights are general rights, not special rights. Someone, for example, may have the right to limit your freedom because of some special arrangement to which you and he previously had agreed. Thus, if you promised Reed to carry his packages home, then he has the right to have you do your duty, even though you would rather do something else at the time. Such a right is a special right, one "which arises out of special transactions between individuals or out of some special relationship in which they stand to each other."[13] General rights, however, are rights that hold independent of the existence of such special arrangements. Human rights are general rights, then, in that their existence is not dependent upon special relationships or previous agreements that rights bearers may have entered into. Human rights are not only logically prior to social and political institutions but they also are logically prior to human agreements as well.

In addition, many writers, including the authors of the American *Declaration of Independence*, have held that such rights are inalienable. If this claim is taken to mean that it is always wrong to fail to honor a claim of human rights, we suggest it is mistaken. Since rights claims can clash, situations may arise in which we can honor the fundamental rights of some only at the expense of failing to honor the equally fundamental rights of others. Although this is lamentable, it hardly can be wrong if some such rights are not honored in this sort of context. No other alternative is available.

Perhaps more plausible interpretations of the claim that human rights are inalienable are available. Perhaps they are inalienable in the sense that they must always be counted fully from the moral point of view, unless waived by the rights bearer under special sorts of circumstances. Thus, if there is a human right to life, perhaps it cannot legitimately be disregarded unless the rights bearer himself decides that life is no longer worth living. Or perhaps human rights are inalienable in the sense that even the rights bearers themselves cannot waive their claims of natural right. Thus, if someone were to say, "I give up my right to life, so go ahead and kill me," this would not entitle anyone to kill the speaker. However, requests for beneficent euthanasia in order to avoid the suffering of a terminal illness may constitute counterexamples to this formulation. Many of us are inclined to accept a waiver of the right to life in such circumstances. Perhaps, most plausibly, human rights are inalienable in the sense that they cannot be waived except by the bearer and then only to protect another right of the same fundamental order. Thus, in the case of a request for beneficent euthanasia, we may view the patient as waiving the right to life in order to better implement the right to a minimal degree of well-being, which would be destroyed by purposeless suffering.

Someone has a human right to something, then, if and only if (a) he or she is morally entitled to it; (b) the entitlement is morally fundamental; (c) it does not arise from the bearer's social status, the prescriptions of a legal system, or from any institutional rules or practices; and (d) it is general in the sense discussed above. In addition, human rights may be inalienable in one of the several plausible senses mentioned. Condition (a) places human rights within the broad category of rights while the other conditions identify human rights as moral rights of a distinctive and fundamental kind.

THE STATE AS PROTECTOR OF HUMAN RIGHTS

As we have seen, utilitarian theorists regard the state as a maximizer of utility. But, as we have also seen, it is far from clear that utilitarianism provides sufficient protection for the individual or, if it does, whether it does so for the right reasons. That is, human rights may be thought of, not implausibly, as rule utilitarian devices for securing future utility, but this would call into question their fundamental character. They would be a means to a more important end rather than rock bottom protections for the inviolability of individual persons.

This leads to a nonutilitarian view of the state. From the point of view of the human rights tradition, it is the function of the state to protect and implement the human rights of its citizens.

Perhaps the most influential spokesman for this tradition in political philosophy was John Locke. Locke, like Hobbes, used the social contract as a device to show that if the state did not exist, we would need to invent it. However, unlike Hobbes, Locke did not view all political and social relations as power relations. For Locke, human behavior was morally constrained by claims of what he regarded as "natural" rights grounded in natural law. It was precisely the job of the state to secure such rights.

But just what rights do people have? It is something of an embarrassment to rights theory that its proponents have been unable to agree on just which natural or human rights people possess. For example, the American Declaration of Independence speaks of the rights to life, liberty, and the pursuit of happiness. The French Declaration of the Rights of Man speaks of the natural right to security. Many contemporary theorists defend rights to the material prerequisites of at least a minimal degree of well-being, for example, the right to a guaranteed annual income. The Universal Declaration of Human Rights of the United Nations even includes the right to vacations with pay on its list.

Part of this divergence doubtless can be attributed to the fact that not every list is presented as a complete list. In addition, many lists do not distinguish fundamental from derivative rights. Thus, the right to paid vacations listed in the Universal Declaration, to the extent that its inclusion can be defended at all, probably can be best understood as a derivative right necessary to implement the more fundamental right to the minimal prerequisites of well-being.

Although some disagreement among advocates of human rights can be explained away along such lines, deep differences remain. One such difference that is particularly fundamental concerns the shift in emphasis from negative rights to personal liberty—rights to be free of interference with one's person or property—to the positive rights to material prerequisites of well-being, which have been of concern to many contemporary defenders of human rights. Negative rights impose obligations on others to refrain from interfering with the rights bearer in the protected area. Positive rights, however, impose obligations to provide (or at least to support the sort of institutions that do provide) those goods and services necessary to secure at least a minimally decent level of human existence.

As many persons regard positive rights with grave suspicion, primarily because they impose extensive obligations to provide things to others, it will be worthwhile to examine both kinds of rights.[14] The political philosophy of the seventeenth-century theorist John Locke is a paradigmatic example of a position that places nearly exclusive emphasis on negative rights. We will examine Locke's system in order to see if such an emphasis is justified. After considering Locke's position, we will go on to compare it with the expanded conception of natural rights suggested by the Universal Declaration of the United Nations. Next, we will consider the views of the critics of the modern expanded notion of rights. We will then be in a better position to decide just which fundamental rights, if any, the state ought to secure.

John Locke and the Referee State

John Locke (1633–1704) was not only an important political thinker of the first order, indeed one of the founders of the liberal tradition, but he also made important contributions to epistemology and metaphysics. In particular, his *Essay Concerning Human Understanding* is one of the classic texts of the empiricist tradition, which bases knowledge on experience. The *Two Treatises of Government*, Locke's major work in political philosophy, is connected with the Revolution of 1688 in England, serving both as a stimulus to and justification of it. The *Treatises*, particularly the *Second Treatise*, have exerted an important influence on liberal thought up to our own day, particularly through the United States Constitution, which embodies many Lockean ideas.

Both Locke's empiricism and his political philosophy were bulwarks in the seventeenth-century struggle against the entrenched privileges of the monarchy and nobility. Each stresses the tests of experience and reason in an attempt to question dogmatism in both epistemology and politics.

Locke's method in the *Second Treatise* (like that of Hobbes, whom we discussed in chapter 1) is to postulate a state of nature within which no political sovereign exists. He then goes on to establish what sort of government the inhabitants of such a state could rationally establish. Locke may have thought there actually was such a state of nature. After all, as he points out, the different nation-states can be regarded as being in the state of nature with respect to one another. However, the actual existence of such a historical stage in human history is irrelevant to the force of his argument. Rather, as was the case with Hobbes, we can analytically reconstruct Locke's purpose as that of showing what problems would arise if there were no state and hence why it would be rational to create one. Locke, like Hobbes, argues that if there were no such thing as the state, it would be necessary to invent it.

The Lockean State of Nature

For Hobbes, the state of nature is one of war between each person and every other person. Life there is depicted as "solitary, poor, nasty, brutish and short." In contrast, Locke's state of nature "has a law to govern it which obliges everyone; and reason which is that law teaches all mankind who will but consult it that being all equal and independent, no one ought to harm another in his life, health, liberty or possessions."[15] Moral principles, what Cicero and the Stoics might call natural laws, apply to the Lockean state of nature.

This natural law stipulates that all persons are equal in possessing the human or what Locke would call "natural" rights to life, liberty, and property prior to the establishment of government. If we view Locke's state of nature as hypothetical rather than historical, this can be understood as claiming that the justification for natural or human rights is logically more fundamental than that of the state. These rights are negative in that they impose obligations on others to refrain from interfering in the protected areas. Each person is given a sphere of autonomy that others may not violate. However, even though others may not deprive anyone of life, liberty, or possessions, they need not in addition take positive steps to provide property, or maintain life, or supply the conditions under which liberty may be meaningfully exercised. It is one thing, for example, to say that we may not prevent you from seeing a particular movie. It is quite another to say we must provide you with the price of admission. The equality of the state of nature is of the former sort, consisting only of "that equal right that each has to his natural freedom without being subjected to the will or authority of any other man."[16]

What justification might Locke have offered for these claims about natural law and natural or human rights? Although he may have regarded them as commands of God, he also refers to them as dictates of reason. Locke may have thought belief in human rights was rational since the differences among humans are not sufficient to support discrimination against any one person or group with respect to such fundamental moral protections. That is, given important similarities among people in basic characteristics such as human vulnerability, reasoning abilities, and capacities for love and affection, protections for all against violence and tyranny is justified, since there is no non-arbitrary basis for anyone to control the lives and safety of others without consent. We will discuss this and other possible justifications for claims to human rights later in this chapter.

In any case, Locke goes on to argue that natural rights in the state of nature would include the right to private property that one has acquired justly. This is important for, as we shall see, one of the terms of the social contract that establishes the state is that the state is morally required to protect the private property of its citizens. The Lockean argument here is that the world is a storehouse created for the benefit of humans. Consequently, persons may appropriate the goods in the storehouse for their own use. The means of appropriation is labor: "for this labor being the unquestionable property of the laborer, no man but he can have a right to what that is at once joined to, at least when there is enough and as good left for others."[17]

Property arises from labor, according to Locke. But, we are told, labor yields property only when there is "enough and as good left for others." If we assume approximate equality of ability and need, this requirement seems to lead to a fairly egalitarian distribution of goods, where all those willing and able to work end up with about the same amount of possessions.

In fact, if any person were to take more than could be used, the surplus would spoil, thus depriving others of their due. This spoilage problem could be avoided, however, if an imperishable medium of exchange were to be introduced. Money is precisely such a thing. If a farmer, for example, "would give his nuts for a piece of metal, pleased with its color, or exchange his sheep for shells, or wool for a sparkling pebble or diamond, and keep these . . . he invaded not the right of others."[18] For, as we have seen, Locke limits the property owner, not in the amount of possessions that can be accumulated but rather to the accumulation of what will not spoil, so long as enough and as good is left for others. As long as one's possessions do not spoil and others have the liberty and opportunity to try to accumulate possessions of their own, no limit is set on the amount one might own. Consequently,

> It is plain that men have agreed to a disproportionate and unequal possession . . . having by tacit and voluntary consent found out a way how a man may fairly possess more than he himself can use the product of by receiving in exchange for the surplus gold and silver.[19]

Through the introduction of money, the state of nature becomes one of unequal distribution in which some persons amass huge amounts of property through talent, effort, exchanges on the marketplace, and plain good fortune. Locke could have used his restriction on accumulation of personal property in defense of an egalitarian distribution of wealth. Instead, he introduced inequality into the state of nature, thereby justifying inequality in civil society. Inequality results since people differ in talent, willingness to exert effort, business acumen in market transactions, and good fortune. Such difference produces inequality in possessions. Since, as we will see, people enter civil society at least in part to preserve their property, this inequality will carry over into the state itself.

For Locke, then, inequality in possessions is not necessarily injustice. An inequality might be unjust if, for example, it arises from one person stealing what another has legitimately acquired. But it is not unjust if it results from harder work, acuity in trade, or even good luck.

The right to property, like the other Lockean rights we have considered, is negative. No one is obliged to provide property for anyone else. Rather, the only obligations are those of noninterference. Inhabitants of the state of nature are obligated not to deprive each other of the fruits of their labor or of possessions secured through contractual arrangements for the exchange of such possessions.

What rational consideration might induce an inhabitant of such a state to contract with others to establish political society? Several reasons are cited by Locke, although he does not always clearly distinguish them. For one thing, there is no impartial judiciary to enforce the law of nature. Consequently, persons become judges in their own case. Moreover, after such "judges" hand down their decisions, there is no one to enforce them save the parties to the dispute themselves. This hardly makes either for fair and impartial decisionmaking or for peaceful acceptance of decisions by all parties concerned. Even worse, everyone cannot be counted upon to obey the natural law at all times or to respect the rights of others. Indeed, any dispute might end in conflict. Although the Lockean state of nature, unlike the Hobbesian one, is governed by a moral law, even well-intentioned people who wish to carry out that law might disagree on its application and enforcement. Locke's state of nature is at best unstable and in danger of reverting to one of conflict. Consequently, "to avoid the state of war—wherein there is no appeal but to heaven and wherein even the least difference is apt to end where there is no authority to decide between the contenders—is one great reason of men's putting themselves into society and quitting the state of nature."[20]

However, since "no rational creature can be supposed to change his condition for an intention to be the worse,"[21] people do not give up all of their rights to the state. The Lockean state is not the Hobbesian leviathan. Rather, the individual insofar as he is rational only surrenders his right to executive and judiciary power. And he does so only on the condition that the state secure his own natural rights to life, liberty, and property.[22] Moreover, since for Locke the state is simply the community formed by the contract, the policy of the state is to be determined by the community, or where unanimous agreement is unobtainable, by a majority vote of the members.[23] Of course, such a majority vote cannot override the basic terms of the social contract: namely, that the individual surrender his right to interpret and enforce the laws of nature and that the state protect his rights to life, liberty, and property within a framework of public law governing everyone equally. The state, then, is the protector of the natural rights of its citizens. For, in Locke's view, it is only to form such a state that it would be rational to leave the state of nature in the first place.

Locke, then, like Hobbes, uses a hypothetical social contract to justify a particular kind of state. The contract is hypothetical in that it is one we ourselves supposedly would have signed had we been in the state of nature, not one we actually did sign. Locke is justifying a certain sort of state, not by its utility which might benefit the majority at the expense of the minority but by showing that all of us would agree to it if we were rational and in the appropriate position in the state of nature. It is our hypothetical consent and not the calculus of social interest that justifies the Lockean state.

The state's function, then, is to protect our fundamental rights. These natural rights, as Locke thinks of them, are primarily negative rather than positive—that is, the rights obligate others not to provide essential goods and services but simply to refrain from interfering with each individual's attempt to provide such goods and services for himself. Similarly, the state is not conceived of as a provider of welfare but rather has the negative role of referee. Its job (aside from providing defense against external enemies) is to regulate economic competition by making sure that each competitor respects the rights of others. The Lockean state is an umpire or referee making sure that all citizens, in freely pursuing their own welfare, do not infringe on the similar free enterprise of others.

Critique of Locke's Theory

A principal objection to the Lockean account of the state is that it permits too unequal a distribution of economic wealth. Put more accurately, the criticism is that the degree of inequality allowed by Locke's theory is *unjust* or *unfair*. As we have seen, inequality is introduced into the state of nature through the medium of monetary means of exchange, and is perpetuated into society through the social contract. Indeed, significantly unequal distribution of wealth is characteristic of many Western countries and of most other developed societies throughout the world.

In the ideal Lockean state, inequality of wealth arises basically from open competition on the free market. But, in competition for property, children of the previous generation's winners will have far more chance for material success than those of the previous generation's losers. So, in any generation after the first, many competitors will accumulate material goods at least partially because of their advanced starting position rather than because of their own abilities. Although all will have the right to property, citizens will be unequal in their actual power to amass it. Indeed, the rules of the Lockean free market competition seem to allow a small group of successful entrepreneurs and their descendants to control an overwhelming amount of property indefinitely. Accordingly, critics of the Lockean minimal state argue that if defenders of an unregulated free market actually favor fair competition, they must supplement the rules of free market exchange with some form of income, property, or power redistribution. This amounts to allowing other rights over and above the negative right to liberty and consequently entails abandonment of the referee theory of the minimal state.

It might be objected that if people earn money, they are entitled to it.[24] Redistribution is unjust when it involves violation of rights, and persons surely have a right to that which they earned. We will discuss this entitlement theory at length in chapter 4, but perhaps the following will suffice for now. For people to be entitled to what they acquire in the free market, the initial conditions under which market transactions take place must be fair. But the initial bargaining position is not fair if some people, through no fault of their own, are so deprived of basic necessities and education that they cannot develop skills or compete with any real chance of success. Accordingly, the very idea of an entitlement presupposes at least a minimal welfare base that guarantees each competitor access to education, health care, and adequate diet and other necessities. Thus, the protest that redistributive measures fail to respect the entitlements of property owners is open to the objection that such entitlements can arise only when redistributive measures guarantee fair access to the competition for property in the first place.

The case that fairness requires more than minimal Lockean rights to liberty also can be based upon Locke's own model of the social contract. The usefulness of the contract model is that it can function as a test for fairness. If we ourselves would agree to a particular social contract under reasonable conditions of choice, the terms of the contract arguably are fair. Conversely, if the terms are such that it would be irrational for us to consent to them, they arguably are unfair. In order to test the fairness of Locke's minimal state, then, we can ask whether contract makers would agree to the social contract that creates it.

Locke assumes that the contract makers would build the economic inequality found in the state of nature into the structure of political society. But surely this assumption is questionable. Why would the have-nots in the state of nature enter such an inegalitarian society in the first place? Surely, as Locke himself acknowledges, they would only sign the contract if they realized some gain from doing so. The rule of law, as Locke would argue, is indeed a gain, but it is much more of a gain to those who have property that the law can protect than for those who are poor. It seems plausible, then, that rational contractors would only agree to enter the state if they were guaranteed at least a minimal level of goods and services which would enable them to function as citizens and to benefit from the protection of the law in the first place.

In addition to redistributive arguments based on the requirement of fair competition (arguments that in some interpretations of what fairness requires may have quite strong redistributive implications), we can also argue that the very factors that guarantee Lockean rights to liberty also count in favor of positive rights to necessities. After all, liberty surely is important because it allows us to determine the course of our own lives and to function autonomously. But arguably, medical care, education, food, and shelter also are necessary if we are to develop as autonomous agents with plans of life worth living by.

Thus, even if people are entitled to what they earn, it does not follow that such an entitlement is absolute. For persons may also have positive rights to sufficient goods and services to make at least a minimally decent human existence possible. If so, persons may not have an absolute right to everything they earn. Rather, they may be obligated to contribute to efforts designed to satisfy the basic needs of others. Proponents of the entitlement theory, then, cannot simply assume that the only fundamental rights are Lockean negative ones.[25]

Consequently, defenders of the minimal state, which protects only negative rights to liberty, are open to the charges that (1) the economic competition it referees is unfair; (2) the inequalities it sanctions are not likely to be acceptable to all rational individuals under reasonable conditions of choice; and (3) the exclusive emphasis on negative rights is arbitrary.

We conclude that Locke's general account of the principal function of the state is sound. That function should be to protect the natural or human rights of its citizens. However, as our discussion suggests, it does not follow that the state's exclusive concern should be with negative rights to liberty, as exercised in the free market. In addition, there is a case for what might be called positive rights, rights to the receipt of basic goods and services.

Positive Rights—The Universal Declaration of Human Rights and the Welfare State

The Universal Declaration of Human Rights was adopted and proclaimed by the General Assembly of the United Nations on December 10, 1948. An examination of this document reveals that many of the rights included go far beyond the negative ones protected by Locke's referee state. For example, consider the following articles:

> Article 22: Everyone, as a member of society . . . is entitled to realization . . . in accordance with the organization and resources of each State, of the economic, social, and cultural rights indispensable for his dignity and the free development of his personality.
>
> Article 25: Everyone has the right to a standard of living adequate for the health and well being of himself and his family, including food, clothing, housing and medical care and necessary social services. . . .
>
> Article 26: Everyone has the right to education. Education shall be free, at least in the elementary and fundamental stages.

Unlike Lockean rights, which obligate others not to interfere with personal liberty, the positive rights of the Universal Declaration require more. In addition, they obligate each of us to support or, where they do not exist, work for the creation of institutions that can provide the necessary goods and services. The state, which is presumably the fundamental political unit capable of guaranteeing such rights, becomes responsible for the welfare of its citizens as well as their liberty.

The Critique of Positive Rights

The concept of positive natural or human rights has been criticized on several grounds. We will consider some of the most important criticisms.

One principal objection to the kind of social and economic rights mentioned in Articles 22, 25, and 26 of the Universal Declaration is that they do not fulfill some of the conceptual requirements for counting as natural rights. The first requirement is that of practicality. As Maurice Cranston has pointed out:

> The traditional "political and civil" rights can . . . be readily secured by fairly simple legislation. Since those rights are for the most part rights against government interference with a man's activities, a large part of the legislation needed has to do no more than restrain the government's own executive arm. This is no longer the case when we turn to "the right to work," "the right to social security," and so forth. . . . For millions of people who live in those parts of Asia, Africa, and South America where industrialization has hardly begun, such claims are vain and idle.[26]

Moreover, it is held that natural or human rights must be rights that impose obligations on everyone. Yet such rights as the right to work or to free education seem to be, at best, rights against one's government and not rights against all humankind.[27] Since social and economic rights fail these tests of practicality and universality, they cannot be natural rights to begin with.

Yet another objection rests on still another important conceptual difference between the two kinds of rights—namely, a difference in the kind of obligation they impose on others. Negative rights, by definition, impose obligations to refrain from acting in proscribed ways. Positive rights impose obligations to act in a required manner. But, so the objection goes, no one is morally required to perform the kinds of acts enjoined. Such acts may be beneficent and altruistic and, as such, should be encouraged. However, they are not morally obligatory. Thus, it may be praiseworthy for a family to give half its annual income to those less affluent, but they are hardly blameworthy if they fail to do so. According to this objection, then, there are no positive natural rights. For if there were positive natural rights, people would be obligated not simply to refrain from harming others but to go out of their way to benefit others. And, it is held, there is no such obligation.

Sometimes positive rights are criticized on the grounds that their implementation is incompatible with the attainment of other important goods. Thus, it frequently is claimed that the implementation of positive rights would involve drastic and unjustified restrictions on liberty. In order to appropriate resources needed to honor claims to positive rights, the state would have to limit our right to do with our property what we choose. One cannot spend for oneself that portion of one's income that the government taxes in order to make Medicaid or welfare payments to others. Indeed, some critics have gone so far as to characterize the welfare state as a near slavemaster that in effect forces people to work in order to appropriate earnings for the support of others.[28]

To review, positive rights have been criticized on the grounds that (a) they are impractical since they cannot be readily secured by fairly simple legislation, (b) they do not impose universal obligations, (c) they impose positive obligations to act when there can be no such obligation, and (d) their implementation would require extensive violations of the right to liberty. Are these objections decisive?

A Response to the Critique

While critics are right to worry that with the addition of positive rights, the idea of natural or human rights may become too bloated, their wholesale dismissal of positive rights is open to question. Indeed, some contemporary philosophers have argued that the whole distinction between positive and negative rights is a confused one and that all rights have positive and negative elements. Thus, as Henry Shue argues, if the negative right to liberty is to be significant, citizens have a positive obligation to provide the resources to support the police and judiciary system.[29] Similarly, all rights may sometimes require us simply to refrain from harming others and at other times to provide positive aid. Before deciding whether the distinction between positive and negative rights makes sense, however, we need to assess points (a)–(d) summarized above.

Consider the practicality objection (claim a). According to this objection, positive rights, such as a right to a decent standard of living, are impossible to implement for less developed and less affluent countries, and so such states cannot be obligated to honor them. It surely is true that poor nations will have a harder time satisfying social and economic rights claims than will rich countries. In some cases, they may find it impossible. However, exactly the same situation can arise with respect to negative rights. In a technologically underdeveloped country, there may not exist the efficient means of communication and transportation, or the development of a legal system, so necessary to prevent acts of violence, or even the extermination of one group by another. Here, we should note that Article 22 specifies that each country is obligated to honor social and political rights *in accordance with its available resources*. In other words, each state (and individual too, for that matter) is obligated to do what it can in light of its individual situation.[30] This applies to both negative and positive rights alike. Both kinds of rights need support if they are to be enjoyed.

What about the requirement of universality (claim b), which states that natural rights impose obligations on everyone? It supposedly follows from this requirement that positive rights cannot be human rights. For, in this view, the bearers of positive rights have claims only against their own governments, not on everyone wherever they may be. For example, if you have a negative right to liberty, all people—even those on the other side of the world—are under an obligation to avoid illegitimate interference with your activities. There seem to be no conceptual difficulties here, for the obligation imposed does not call on anyone to perform any positive act but only calls on them to refrain from acting in certain proscribed ways. Suppose, however, you have the positive right to a free education. Surely, it is implausible to say that inhabitants of some faraway country have an obligation equal to that of your fellow citizens to provide you with the needed schools. Rather, it is up to your government to provide the needed institutions and so the scope of your positive right is limited.

However, we suggest that this objection to positive rights is overstated. The distinction it attempts to draw does not stand up under examination. True, it normally is the state's job to implement positive rights, but this is often true of negative rights as well. If you have a negative right to liberty, the primary obligation imposed is the negative one of noninterference. But, as in Lockean theory, it may be rational to delegate to the state the authority to enforce laws designed to protect liberty. Of course, it is one thing to say that the state ought to protect citizens from illegitimate interference with their activities and quite another to say the state ought to provide positive goods and opportunities. But, in either case, the conceptual point remains the same. The special responsibilities of the state do not replace those of private citizens. Rather, the good state is an instrument through which citizens can most efficiently discharge their obligations. Thus, in the case of both negative and positive rights, such obligations are not restricted to one's fellow citizens alone, although the responsibilities of citizens to their fellow compatriots often may be stronger and more specific than duties to foreigners.

Thus, while the state may be the primary instrument for discharging our positive obligations that arise from human rights, these obligations may not simply disappear at the nation's borders. The issues of ethics in international affairs are complex, however, and we will devote special attention to them in chapter 8. For now, note that some states sometimes may have obligations to protect the negative rights of citizens of other states (for example, from genocidal policies by their own government) and to protect their positive rights as well (for example, by providing food and other forms of humanitarian relief after a disaster, such as the aid provided to the people of South East Asia after the tsunami of 2005).

What about claim (c)—the claim that there can be no positive obligations? This claim seems to simply beg the very question at issue. To assume that we cannot be obligated to do something (rather than refrain from doing something) is to deny just what is being argued for. One cannot establish that there are no positive obligations as a conclusion by simply asserting that very same point as a premise.

Finally, would recognition of positive rights require extensive violations of the negative right to liberty, as claim (d) asserts? Is it ever justifiable to infringe on someone's liberty to implement a positive right? This issue will be discussed more fully in chapter 4, but some important points need to be considered here as well.

There certainly is a danger that positive rights can become so bloated that the individual becomes a mere resource for satisfying the claims of others. This is the worry of the libertarians, who fear that the welfare state will turn productive citizens into natural resources for helping the less fortunate. We agree that there is a genuine problem in specifying just where positive rights claims become so extensive as to violate the liberty of others but suggest the libertarian worry is not justifiable.

Thus, as Henry Shue points out, negative rights may also impose positive obligations that can threaten liberty.[31] How much can the state ask you to give up to support the police, who in turn protect others from coercion? Can't the state ask you to pay taxes to support the court and prison system, which may protect citizens from assault by criminals? Negative rights, when enforced and protected by the state, impose positive obligations just as positive rights do. The very same problem arises for each kind of right. Accordingly, Henry Shue's claim that the distinction between negative and positive rights is a confused one does have force. Perhaps we should abandon the distinction and conceive of all rights as imposing both positive and negative obligations, as our discussion above indicates.

Whether or not the positive-negative distinction should be dispensed with, we conclude that arguments (a)–(d) against positive rights fail. Our discussion does call the wholesale critique of positive rights into question. Thus, either there is as good a case for positive rights as for negative ones or, if Shue is correct, no rights are altogether positive or altogether negative. Rather, each right imposes both negative and positive obligations depending upon context. In either case, the Lockean's exclusive emphasis on the "negative" right to liberty has been misplaced. The case for the minimal state based on the assertion that the only human rights the state can legitimately protect are purely negative freedoms from interference by others is far from self-evident. This issue will be pursued further in our discussion of justice in the next chapter. However, our arguments so far strongly suggest that, to the contrary, claims to at least minimal levels of welfare warrant equal protection as well.

If these arguments have force, the real question is not whether we have positive as well as negative rights. Rather, the real question is what fundamental entitlements must be protected if our status as rational and autonomous agents is to be protected. Our discussion suggests then that if claims based on appeal to human rights are justified, these rights claims include entitlements to the basic conditions necessary for a minimal standard of living as well as entitlements to be free of coercion by others. This does not mean that such economic and social rights must be given constitutional status, as in the American Bill of Rights, for they may best be implemented through the democratic political process rather than through the courts.[32] Nevertheless, we conclude that some claims made on the basis of positive human rights are as justified as some claims made on the basis of negative ones.

But are any claims of human rights justified? Let us now turn to the issue of whether any claim to a human right can be justified, warranted, or adequately supported.

JUSTIFICATION

We can show that people have justified claims based on human rights by showing they have fundamental moral entitlements of the kind specified in the first section of this chapter: namely, entitlements that are not due to social, institutional, or legal status or rules but that are general and perhaps inalienable. In this lies the importance of analysis. If we do not have an adequate analysis, we cannot be clear about what conditions must be satisfied if a human rights claim is to be justified.

But how are we to show that claims that appeal to human rights are justified? That is, how can we show that the conditions specified in the first part of the chapter are satisfied? While a full treatment of the issue would require a long digression into ethical and metaethical theory, we believe that at least a plausible case for human rights can be developed here.

The Egalitarian Argument

When unequal treatment is regarded as unjust, it is often because it seems to ignore the basic similarity of all affected. Those who receive beneficial treatment do not seem to be significantly different from those who do not, and so the inequality is held to be arbitrary and unfair.

HUMAN RIGHTS: MEANING AND JUSTIFICATION

This type of egalitarian argument is often employed in defense of human rights. The point of the argument is that in view of the factual equalities or similarities between persons, it is arbitrary to distinguish between them with respect to such rights. Since human rights are entitlements to those goods and opportunities that make a distinctively human sort of life possible, all humans are sufficiently alike to qualify as possessors. As John Locke puts it:

> There being nothing more evident than that creatures of the same species and rank . . . born to all the same advantages of nature and the use of the same faculties should also be equal one amongst another without subordination and subjection.[33]

Locke can be read here as maintaining that since humans are basically similar (equal, in fact), it would be indefensible to regard some humans as having a greater claim than others to fundamental rights. People who are basically similar would be treated dissimilarly and hence the distinction would be arbitrary and unjustified.

Unfortunately, there are difficulties with this type of argument. First, even if all humans are so similar that if anyone has human rights then everybody does, how do we know anyone has such rights in the first place? Second, although it may be conceded that humans are alike (equal) or nearly alike in some respects, they are notoriously different (unequal) in others. Locke's argument is that given human similarity, any presumption of superiority would be groundless. It is simply arbitrary, and hence irrational, to treat equals unequally. But are humans *sufficiently* similar or alike? The egalitarian must show that it is the similarities and not the differences that are relevant to justifying claims of natural right. Persecution of minorities, discrimination against women, slavery, and genocide all have been defended by reference to allegedly relevant differences between victims and oppressors.

The egalitarian will reply that it is the similarities and not the differences that are relevant where possession of human rights is of concern. Common human qualities that often have been cited as the grounds of such rights include rationality, the capacity to feel pain and undergo suffering, the ability to form a rational plan of life, and the need for the affection and companionship of others. But even within these categories, people differ. How is the egalitarian to show that it is the differences that are actually irrelevant?

There are at least two problems, then, with the egalitarian argument. At best, it seems to show only that *if* anyone has natural rights, all relevantly similar beings have the same rights. Second, even if it can be shown that some persons have such rights, it still must be shown that all humans are relevantly similar to the rights bearer(s).

However, these problems are not immune to resolution. In what follows, we suggest lines of response that may be satisfactory. While no presently available defense of a fundamental moral outlook is philosophically uncontroversial, this applies as much to utilitarianism or other moral theories (as well as to moral skepticism and relativism) as to the human rights approach. In moral philosophy, the choice is probably not between strict knock-down, drag-out proof of one's moral position, on the one hand, or irrational whim on the other. We hope that by developing lines of argument that can be advanced by proponents of human rights, we can show that there are good theoretical reasons for accepting human rights as fundamental elements of our moral system.

Human Rights, Human Dignity, and Respect for Persons

Rights as Rule Utilitarian Devices

Human rights, as we have indicated, might be compatible with a utilitarian framework. That is, some utilitarians might argue for human rights on the grounds that a moral system that provided such protections would produce more utility in the long run than one that lacked them. Sophisticated rule utilitarians might even agree that human rights function as trumps that can override the direct appeal to utility in judging individual acts, because in the long run it produces more utility to block such direct appeal in fundamental areas than to allow it. For example, if we were to try to decide in each individual case whether it promotes utility to prohibit a citizen in a democracy from speaking freely, we often would decide wrongly because we might be influenced by personal bias, our own political views, and the emotions of the moment in a crisis. A human right to liberty could promote utility in the long run by prohibiting such interference and allowing society to enjoy the benefits of open debate on issues.

However, even if in spite of some of the criticisms of utilitarianism advanced in chapter 2, such a rule utilitarian case for human rights can be made good, it does not make human rights fundamental moral commodities. Rather, such rights are regarded as means to the production of greater utility and are contingent on their success in producing desirable consequences. Another approach to justifying human rights regards them as more fundamental, as protections for the fundamental dignity and respect due to all persons as human beings, as rational agents with goals and purposes of their own. It is this nonutilitarian approach we will explore below.

Rights as Fundamental Moral Commodities

Consider as best one can a society whose moral code does not include the concept of a claim of right. People in it may act benevolently most of the time and are not cruel or unfeeling. Indeed, they may be imagined as kinder and more sensitive than the inhabitants of our own planet. What such a culture would lack, however, is the notion of persons as makers of claims upon one another, as having basic entitlements that others would be obligated to respect. And if occasional improper treatment occurs, there is no cause to complain:

> The masters, judges and teachers don't have to do good things, after all, for anyone.
> . . . Their hoped for responses, after all, are gratuities, and there is no wrong in the

omission of what is merely gratuitous. Such is the response of persons who have no concept of rights.[34]

In a society without the concept of rights, we all would be in a position analogous to that of the students at university A or the southern blacks prior to the civil rights movement, as viewed through the framework described by Richard Wasserstrom in the example we discussed earlier. We would lack the conceptual apparatus for asserting that some treatment was owed to us as a matter of right. If we are mistreated, that is a matter between our oppressor and his own conscience.

Rights, we are suggesting, are fundamental moral commodities because they enable us to stand on our own two feet, "to look others in the eye, and to feel in some fundamental way the equal of anyone. To think of oneself as the holder of rights is not to be unduly but properly proud, to have that minimal self-respect that is necessary to be worthy of the love and esteem of others."[35] Conversely, to lack the concept of oneself as a rights bearer is to be bereft of a significant element of human dignity. Without such a concept, we could not view ourselves as beings entitled to be treated as not simply means but ends as well.

To respect persons as ends, to view them as having basic human dignity, seems to be inextricably bound up with viewing persons as possessors of rights—as beings who are owed a vital say in how they are to be treated, and whose interests are not to be overridden simply in order to make others better off. Consequently, to opt for a code of conduct in which rights are absent is to abandon the kind of respect for persons and human dignity at issue. This price, we submit, is simply too high. Thus, one important answer to the questions of why people should be regarded as having claims of fundamental rights at all is simply that a world in which no such claims were ever made or ever regarded as justifiable would be a world that was morally impoverished, and very significantly so.[36]

The Challenge of Elitism

What if members of some special group were to accept the considerations cited above, but maintain that only members of their allegedly elite or "superior" group possessed any rights at all? Others, perhaps blacks, perhaps Jews, perhaps women, perhaps the less intelligent, are held to be inferior or not fully human. In this elitist view, there may well be reasons for recognizing fundamental rights. But, the elitists hold, in view of allegedly significant differences among humans, no reason has been given for thinking such rights belong to all humans. Why, asks such a proponent of discrimination, are these rights *human* rights rather than rights belonging to some allegedly superior elite? Perhaps, as many Nazis might have claimed, they belong only to the "Master Race."

In evaluating this kind of elitist challenge to equality, one must first get clear exactly what the ground of the proposed discrimination is supposed to be. Often, proponents of an elitist morality will base their discrimination on alleged empirical differences between their own group and the supposed inferiors they victimize. For example, women have been held to be too emotional or too unaggresive to hold responsible positions. Slave owners in pre–Civil War America argued that blacks were too simple and childlike to handle freedom, while allegations about differences in the brain size of white ethnics from Eastern Europe were used to justify immigration restrictions against them earlier in this century.

The proper line of defense against such elitists is to challenge their allegedly factual story of the difference between them and their supposed inferiors. That blacks are less sensitive than whites, that Jews are conspiring to control economic and political power, that women are unfit for professional success, and other such elitist generalizations are blatant falsehoods that should have been laid to rest long ago. Moreover, elitism of this sort is often applied inconsistently. Thus, proponents of racial segregation in the pre-1954 south sometimes justified their view by appealing to unequal educational attainments of black and white pupils. Leaving aside the entirely plausible point that segregation itself, to say nothing of poverty and deprivation, was responsible for what differences there actually were, the most that such an argument justifies is segregation by educational attainment, not by race.

What if the elitist does not appeal to alleged factual differences between his group and those who are oppressed? What if the elitist instead simply asserts that his group, by virtue of its very nature, is superior? Men, by their very nature, should be dominant. The more intelligent should control the less intelligent. Whites (or blacks) just are the superior group. How can such elitist moralities be rationally discredited when they do not rest on empirical claims to begin with?

A particularly plausible response to such assertions is that they are arbitrary. They seem to be baseless assertions of purely personal preference rather than expressing a reasoned moral position. As Bernard Williams has pointed out, "The principle that men should be differently treated . . . merely on grounds of their color is not a special sort of moral principle but (if anything) a purely arbitrary assertion of will like that of some Caligulan ruler who decided to execute everyone whose name contained three 'R's'"[37]

Can't the elitist respond that if elitism with respect to rights is arbitrary, is the commitment to equal rights is arbitrary as well? Why should equality be in a privileged position? If "All persons are not moral equals" is arbitrary, why isn't "All persons are moral equals" arbitrary as well?

However, the egalitarian has a number of effective responses to this move. In particular, elitism of a fundamental kind may beg the question against its victims. Thus, it is important to note that within the elitist group itself, characteristics that all humans possess are accorded significant recognition. These include the capacity to experience pain and suffering, the desire to be treated with respect and dignity, the sense of oneself as a conscious entity persisting over time with distinctive wants, ideals, and purposes, as well as the ability to view the world from a distinctive, self-conscious point of view. Among themselves, white supremacists, for example, weigh these factors heavily. They do not inflict gratuitous pain on one another, destroy or enslave one another on whim alone, or regard each other's life plans as of no value whatsoever. Rather, they seem to hold that each member of the elite should be treated just as the egalitarian thinks all human beings should be treated.

In view of the basic similarities among all humans, discrimination at the fundamental level does seem arbitrary and irrational. It seems unintelligible that a mere difference in skin color could by itself negate the importance of the factors enumerated above—the factors whose importance is already acknowledged within the elitist community itself. Thus, it hardly seems unreasonable to require the elitist to spell out the connection between any proposed ground of discrimination and the worth of individual persons. Indeed, in view of the great plethora of elitist positions (for example, anti-Semitism, sexism, and various forms of racism) it seems far from arbitrary to once again place the burden of proof on the elitist. In practice, elitists themselves give testimony to the arbitrariness of their fundamental discriminatory principles since they themselves generally seek to justify their discrimination by appeal to principles intelligible to everyone. Thus, although neither claim can be justified, the claim that "Women should not hold positions in business or government because they are emotionally fitted for raising children" seems to be at least intelligible in ways that "Women should not hold positions in business or government because they are women" is not.

Not only is elitism of the kind in question arbitrary, it also is doubtful if elitist principles could withstand impartial scrutiny. Would reasonable impartial people find it justifiable to deny people the most fundamental of rights on such grounds as skin color, religion, gender, ethnicity, or sexual preference? We believe not. It seems far more plausible to think people hold such elitist views because they have not considered the matter impartially but only from their own perspective, usually that of the allegedly elite group itself. Of course, actual elitists, such as the Nazis or various contemporary racist groups, may refuse to view things impartially, but then they must pay the philosophical price. That is, they cannot claim that their position is justifiable in the sense that it has grounds that can appeal to impartial, unbiased observers. They have, in fact, opted out of the process of justification. While they may continue to hold their position, they have forfeited any basis for claiming that their view is defensible in the arena of public reason and debate.

Cultural Variability

Not all challenges to human rights come from elitist moralities such as those of the Nazi or white supremacist. Perhaps more frequent are those that come from people impressed by cultural diversity who see an ethics of human rights as a Western attempt to impose our own morality on cultures very different from our own. For example, who are Westerners to say that what we call the genital mutilation of women in some African cultures is a violation of human rights when it is acceptable to the indigenous people themselves?

While we recognize that "cultural imperialism" or the imposing of one culture's values on another by force can be seriously wrong in many contexts, we suggest that applying such a critique to human rights is seriously mistaken for at least three reasons. First, it is far from clear that human rights reflect only Western values. The Nobel Prize–winning economist and philosopher, Amartya Sen, gives several examples ranging from defenses of open discussion and rights to dissent in Buddhist councils arising shortly after the Buddha's death 2500 years ago to Nelson Mandela's description of how he learned about individual rights while growing up by observing fair and open procedures in Mqhekezweni.[38] Mandela describes these meetings in a way that might also be applied to the tradition of New England town meetings.

> Everyone who wanted to speak did so. It was democracy in its purest form. There may have been a hierarchy of importance among the speakers, but everyone was heard. Chief and subject, warrior and medicine man, shopkeeper and farmer, landowner and laborer.[39]

Second, the excuse of "our morality is different" is often used to suppress dissent within a culture rather than to protest the imposition of an alien morality. Thus, many women within the African societies that practice genital mutilation protest the practice and even flee to avoid it, just as many Islamic women and other progressives protest what they regard as a too narrow interpretation of Islam that denies women fundamental rights.[40] Rather than human rights being a Western imposition on other cultures, it extends protection to those groups in every culture that work for change in oppressive practices in their own societies.

Third, and perhaps most important, the argument for human rights as outlined above appeals to fundamental values whose force should be apparent to reasonable people everywhere. Thus, the capacity of human rights claims to survive criticism in open debate and attract adherents from every culture (remember the United Nations' Declaration of Human Rights) is a tribute to the force of the arguments in their favor. As Sen writes,

> What are taken to be perfectly "normal" and "sensible" in an insulated society may not be able to survive a broad-based and less limited examination once the parochial gut reactions are replaced by critical scrutiny. . . . The viability and universality of human rights are dependent on their ability to survive open critical scrutiny in public reasoning . . . but the impartiality that is needed cannot be confined within the borders of a nation.[41]

We hope that our argument that egregious denials of human rights can be criticized as either based on especially dubious and stereotypical empirical generalizations on one hand, or arbitrary and indefensible distinctions on the other, contributes to the ability of human rights to survive and flourish in a context of open critical scrutiny and discussion.

The belief in equal human rights for all people does not imply the absurdity, sometimes wrongly attributed to egalitarians by their critics, that all people should be treated identically in all respects. For example, only the best players ought to make the all-star team. However, it does suggest that attempts to exclude some humans from the basic fundamental rights that ought properly to belong to all of us should be condemned as among the most serious crimes against humanity.

SUMMARY

Our discussion suggests that human rights are justified as conditions that must be satisfied if humans are to live and develop as autonomous moral agents. They protect us from being reduced to mere means in the pursuit of the overall social good, or being victims of oppressive elitist moralities. While the claim that human rights are fundamental requires more examination than we can give it here, we hope to have made a plausible case for it. (Remember that human rights also might be viewed as rule utilitarian devices for securing the greatest good in the long run.) While it is doubtful whether claims about human rights (or any other fundamental basis for morality) can be strictly proved in any mathematical sense, a moral perspective based on rights does seem to capture our firmest intuitions about the foundations of our moral view. Those who demand strict proof for everything probably will not find it in ethics but probably will not find it in many other domains as well. It is important, therefore, not to apply a standard to ethics that is so high that it would be judged absurd in other contexts. So while we clearly have not *proved* that some human rights claims are justified, we hope we have advanced significant reasons for accepting such a conclusion, reasons that when fully developed and examined will even more forcefully indicate that all humans have fundamental rights that it would be terribly wrong to violate. Perhaps the ultimate justification of the human rights perspective, however, is its application in practice—a task to which we will turn in later chapters. Human rights in the actual world are sometimes implemented and, unfortunately, far too often violated by states. Accordingly, let us turn from questions of theory to issues of implementation, and the role of governments in that process.

In our view, human rights are those entitlements whose protection and implementation are needed to safeguard human dignity, autonomy, and respect. In claiming that the human rights approach is warranted, we are claiming that it would not be discredited by extended evaluation of its theoretical justification and of its implications for action, and that it would survive such an examination at least as well as any of its competitors. In particular, egregious denials of human rights would be found to rest on false or dubious generalizations, or to be arbitrary and indefensible within impartial critical inquiry.

What are the implications of the human rights perspective for political philosophy? Surely, those who believe that humans should be regarded as possessors of fundamental rights, whether such rights are regarded as natural ones or as rule utilitarian devices, would be sympathetic to the Lockean view of the state. According to Locke, the primary function of the state is to protect the fundamental rights of the individual. States can be ranked according to how well they fulfill their function. Moreover, the Lockean approach provides a framework for criticizing the excesses of the state. The state calls its own reason for being into question when it violates the fundamental rights of its citizens.

Unlike Locke, however, we argue for both positive and negative rights. Implementation of positive rights is just as much a prerequisite of promoting human dignity, autonomy, and self-respect as is implementation of negative ones. Accordingly, the proper response to a Lockean defender of exclusive emphasis on negative rights is that there seems to be no way of defending one kind of right without also defending the other. At the very least, perhaps the burden of proof has been shifted so that it is up to the defenders of purely negative rights to mount a defense of their position.

We conclude that the primary function of the state is to protect and where necessary implement the positive and negative human rights of its citizens. Although any attempt to list all human rights is likely to fail, surely any such list should include the rights to liberty and life, on the one hand, and to the material prerequisites of a minimally decent human life on the other. (The content of these rights will be discussed in the remaining chapters of this book.)

However, rights can clash. Perhaps my right to well-being can be secured only by failing to protect your right to liberty. Or in cases of scarcity, it may not be possible to honor everyone's claim of right. Such conflicts among competing rights claims constitute especially poignant moral dilemmas, for any resolution is imperfect from the moral point of view. Thus, even a satisfactory human rights position is only a necessary constituent of an acceptable framework for adjudication of moral disputes. Where conflicts between competing claims arise, appeal is frequently made to social justice. Parties to the conflict may request, for example, that the dispute between them be justly settled. Accordingly, if one function of the state is to protect and implement natural rights, it is also plausible to think that it is the state's responsibility to adjudicate the clash of rights justly. In fact, the need for fair, just, and impartial adjudication of competing rights claims forms the basis in Locke's argument for the transition from the state of nature to the state of government. In the next chapter, we will extend the human rights approach by examining issues that arise where just adjudication of competing claims is at issue. What is justice and how is to be understood?

NOTES

1. *Amnesty International Report 1996* (London: Amnesty International Publications, 1996), 1. Also available online at Amnesty International, www.amnesty.org/ailib/aireport/ar96/index.html.

2. Joel Feinberg, in "The Nature and Value of Rights," *The Journal of Value Inquiry* 4, no. 4 (1970): 243–57, provides an example of a world without rights. We rely heavily on Feinberg's treatment, particularly his claim that in a world without rights, good treatment would be regarded as a gratuity.

3. This has been pointed out by Joel Feinberg in "Wasserstrom on Human Rights," *Journal of Philosophy* 61 (1964): 642–43.

4. Richard Wasserstrom, "Rights, Human Rights and Racial Discrimination," *The Journal of Philosophy* 61 (1964): 640. Our discussion of the nature of human rights is in great debt to Wasserstrom's article, which was particularly noteworthy for applying the insights of analytic philosophy to important social issues at a time when philosophy was dominated by the view that substantive issues were not within the scope of legitimate philosophical analysis, which then was conceived of as primarily linguistic and conceptual.

5. Even if, as some philosophers claim, rights are definable in terms of obligations, it does not follow that rights talk and obligation talk have the same practical or pragmatic consequences. Rights talk emphasizes the status of persons as active makers of claims, as possessors of entitlements that should be honored rather than as passive recipients of the duties of others. Hence, there are practical reasons for adopting the vocabulary of rights even if rights are nothing but the reverse side of obligations. We do doubt, however, whether rights can be fully defined in terms of obligations. As the example of the attitude of Wasserstrom's "white southerner" illustrates, it seems possible that some obligations may not involve correlative rights. A related example concerns the possibility of obligations that arise from one's station and its duties. For example, the faculty of university A may have professorial obligations to hear student complaints fairly, but the students have no correlative right to such fair treatment.

6. Alternately, a full analysis of rights might go on to explicate "X is entitled to Y" roughly as "X ought to have Y and it would be impermissible to deprive X of Y in the absence of a compelling justification." But the problem of conceptual interrelationships still might remain as "it would be impermissible to deprive X of Y" might have to be explicated in terms of "X is entitled to Y" or "X has a right to Y." As suggested in the text, this apparent circularity need not be vicious but might just draw out the conceptual connections among a family of concepts that together help distinguish the realm of rights from other areas of moral concern.

7. See A. P. D'Entreves, *Natural Law: An Historical Survey* (New York: Harper & Row, 1965), 17ff. Our historical survey of the natural rights tradition relies heavily on D'Entreves's excellent study.

8. Cicero, *Republic*, translated by G. W. Featherstonhaugh (New York: G. & C. Cavill, 1829), 31.

9. Thomas Aquinas, *Summa Theologica*, 1ae, 2ae, quae 91, arts. 1 and 2.

10. Thomas Aquinas, *Summa Theologica*, 1ae, 2ae, quae 95, art. 2.

11. Jeremy Bentham, "Anarchical Fallacies," in *The Collected Papers of Jeremy Bentham 2*, ed. John Bowring (Edinburgh, 1843), reprinted in *Human Rights* (Belmont, CA: Wadsworth, 1970), edited by A. I. Meldan, 32.

12. This is not to deny that such rights also may belong to wider classes of beings, such as higher animals or intelligent extraterrestrials. It also is meant to leave open whether they belong to potential humans, such as fetuses. Those issues are not central to our main task and so are not discussed here.

13. H. L. A. Hart, "Are There Any Natural Rights?" *Philosophical Review* 64, no. 2 (1955): 183.

14. Thus, if I have a positive right to education, medical care, and a minimal standard of living, you and other citizens may have an obligation to pay taxes to support the schools, pay for medical care, and provide a decent minimal standard of living, perhaps through a welfare system.

15. John Locke, *Second Treatise of Government*, 1690, chap. 2, sect. 6. All quotations are from Thomas P. Peardon's edition of *The Second Treatise* (Indianapolis: Bobbs-Merrill, 1952).

16. Locke, *Second Treatise*, chap. 6, sect. 54.

17. Locke, *Second Treatise*, chap. 5, sect. 27. See also chap. 5, sect. 26.

18. Locke, *Second Treatise*, chap. 5, sect. 46.

19. Locke, *Second Treatise*, chap. 5, sect. 50.

20. Locke, *Second Treatise*, chap. 3, sect. 21.

21. Locke, *Second Treatise*, chap. 9, sect. 131.

22. Locke, *Second Treatise*, chap 2.

23. Locke, *Second Treatise*, chap. 8, sect. 95–99.

24. See Robert Nozick's *Anarchy, State and Utopia* (New York: Basic Books, 1974) for an important defense of such an entitlement theory.

25. We consider the entitlement theory, and the case for a relatively unregulated free market, more fully in chapter 4.

26. Maurice Cranston, "Human Rights, Real and Supposed," in *Political Theory and the Rights of Man*, ed. D. D. Raphael (Bloomington: Indiana University Press, 1967), 50.

27. Cranston, "Human Rights, Real and Supposed," 51.

28. See Nozick, *Anarchy, State and Utopia*, 172.

29. Henry Shue, *Basic Rights: Subsistence, Affluence and U.S. Foreign Policy* (Princeton, NJ: Princeton University Press, 1980), 37–40.

30. D. D. Raphael makes a similar point in his paper "Human Rights Old and New," in Raphael, *Political Theory and the Rights of Man*, 63–64.

31. Shue, *Basic Rights: Subsistence, Affluence and U.S. Foreign Policy*, 40.

32. For a fuller discussion of this point, see Brian Barry, *Justice as Impartiality* (New York: Oxford University Press, 1995), 93–99. The basic point is that legislatures may be better suited than courts to deal with the issues of economics and social policy needed to implement welfare rights.

33. Locke, *Second Treatise*, chap. 2, 4.

34. Feinberg, "The Nature and Value of Rights," 247. See also Wasserstrom, "Rights, Human Rights and Racial Discrimination."

35. Here we are indebted to Feinberg's similar argument in "The Nature and Value of Rights."

36. Feinberg, "The Nature and Value of Rights," 252.

37. Bernard Williams, "The Idea of Equality," in *Philosophy, Politics and Society*, second series, ed. Peter Laslett and W. G. Runciman (Oxford: Basil Blackwell, 1962), reprinted in *Justice and Equality*, ed. Hugo A. Bedau (Englewood Cliffs, NJ: Prentice-Hall, 1971), 119.

38. Amartya Sen, "Elements of a Theory of Human Rights," *Philosophy and Public Affairs* 32, no. 4 (2004): 352–53.

39. Nelson Mandela, *Long Walk to Freedom* (Boston: Little, Brown, and Co., 1994), 21, quoted by Sen in "Elements of a Theory of Human Rights," 353.

40. For discussion of genital mutilation and cultural relativism, see Martha Nussbaum's discussion in her *Sex and Social Justice* (New York: Oxford University Press, 1999), reprinted as "Judging Other Cultures: The Case of Genital Mutilation," in *Reason and Responsibility*, ed. Joel Feinberg and Russ Shafer-Landau, twelfth ed. (Belmont, CA: Wadsworth, 2005), 622–31.

41. Sen, "Elements of a Theory of Human Rights," 355–56. See also Xiaorong Li, "'Asian Values' and the Universality of Human Rights," *Report from The Institute for Philosophy and Public Policy* 16, no. 2 (1996): 18–23.

QUESTIONS FOR FURTHER STUDY

1. What distinguishes human rights from other kinds of rights? Can a right be a moral right without being a human right? Justify your view.

2. How would Locke argue that an unequal distribution of resources is not necessarily a violation of fundamental rights and is not necessarily unjust? Is his position defensible? Why or why not?

3. Explain the distinction between negative and positive rights. State and evaluate a criticism of the view that positive rights are as morally fundamental as negative ones.

4. If one views a hypothetical social contract as setting down the terms under which reasonable people would agree to live in civil society, do you think the terms of such a contract should protect negative rights? Should the terms also protect positive rights? Justify your view.

5. What is the egalitarian argument for human rights? What is the rule utilitarian argument for human rights? What is the relation of impartial critical discourse to the justification of human rights claims? Explain your view by assessing the strengths and weaknesses of each approach.

6. Do you believe claims that people have fundamental human rights are justified? If not, what reason do you have, if any, for condemning such moral horrors as Nazi genocide and slavery, as well as contemporary evils ranging from "ethnic cleansing" to crimes such as murder and rape? Does the fact that some Nazis might not believe their position is wrong show that their views are as justifiable as those of their critics? Is moral skepticism about the justifiability of any moral claims the most justifiable position? Can it itself be justified? How?

SUGGESTED READINGS

Books

Becker, Lawrence. *Property Rights: Philosophic Foundations*. Boston: Routledge and Kegan Paul, 1977.

CHAPTER 3

Dworkin, Ronald. *Taking Rights Seriously*. Cambridge, MA: Harvard University Press, 1977.

Gewirth, Alan. *Human Rights*. Chicago: The University of Chicago Press, 1982.

Leiser, Burton, and Tom Campbell, eds. *Human Rights in Philosophy and Politics*. Abington, UK: Ashgate, 2001.

Locke, John. *Second Treatise of Government*. 1690 (widely available in a variety of editions).

Nickel, James W. *Making Sense of Human Rights*. Boston: Blackwell, 2006 (revised ed.).

Nussbaum, Martha. *Sex and Social Justice*. New York: Oxford University Press, 1999.

Raphael, D. D., ed. *Political Theory and the Rights of Man*. Bloomington: Indiana University Press, 1967.

Shue, Henry. *Basic Rights: Subsistence, Affluence and U.S. Foreign Policy*. Princeton, NJ: Princeton University Press, 1980.

Thomson, Judith Jarvis. *The Realm of Rights*. Cambridge, MA: Harvard University Press, 1990.

Wilson, John. *Equality*. New York: Harcourt Brace Jovanovich, 1966.

Articles

Berlin, Isaiah. "Equality." *Proceedings of the Aristotelian Society*, vol. 56 (1955–1956).

Ethics 92, no. 1 (October 1981). The entire issue is devoted to the topic of rights.

Feinberg, Joel. "The Nature and Value of Rights." *The Journal of Value Inquiry* 4, no. 4 (1970): 243–57.

Gewirth, Alan. "Are All Rights Positive?" *Philosophy and Public Affairs* 30, no. 2 (2001): 321–33.

Li, Xiaorong. "'Asian Values' and the Universality of Human Rights." *Report from the Institute for Philosophy and Public Policy* 16, no. 2 (1996): 18–23.

Nickel, James W. "Human Rights," in *Encyclopedia of Ethics*, ed. Lawrence C. Becker and Charlotte B. Becker, vol. 1. New York: Garland, 1992.

Sen Amartya. "Elements of a Theory of Human Rights." *Philosophy and Public Affairs* 32, no. 4 (2004): 315–56.

The Monist 52, no. 4 (1968). The entire issue is devoted to human rights.

Wasserstrom, Richard. "Rights, Human Rights and Racial Discrimination." *The Journal of Philosophy* 61 (1964): 628–41.

● 4

JUSTICE

When conflicting rights claims are pressed under conditions of relative scarcity, under which all claims cannot easily be met, problems of justice typically arise. Consider for example the problem of distribution of organs for transplant discussed in chapter 1. More patients require organs than there are organs available. Since there are not enough organs available some of those patients who need them will die. How are the available organs to be allocated? What is the just distribution?

If plenty of organs were available, the issue of a just distribution would not arise. In that situation, everyone who needed one could receive one and no problem would exist. But in the absence of this ideal world, competition for the available organs does exist, and the resulting conflicting claims must be resolved. But how should this be done?

In the case of organ transplants, should organs be distributed by lottery? A lottery would at least count all applicants equally. But is equal treatment necessarily just treatment? People often differ in merit. Perhaps organ transplants should go first to the most meritorious. After all, some people need organ transplants because they disregarded their physician's orders. Why should those patients be treated as equals with those patients who followed their physician's orders? Is a patient's need relevant? Suppose one patient is the sole supporter of several children while another is only responsible for herself. Indeed, what if the patient who disregarded his physician's orders is responsible for the support of four children, while the person who followed her physician's orders is only responsible for herself? How are need and merit to be traded off against one another? Perhaps the strongest argument for the lottery procedure is the difficulty of assessing the weight to be assigned to other factors that seem significant.

Similar problems arise with more general discussions of justice. Is it just to distribute wealth, honor, or positions on the basis of merit? After all, who is to say what merit is or who has more of it than another? Even if we could identify the meritorious, what of those with great need but little merit? Are they to be left to

CHAPTER 4

starve in the streets? On the other hand, are all inequalities in wealth arbitrary? Don't those who work harder than others or perform better deserve more of a reward? How are all these different values to be weighed on the scales of justice?

In this chapter we will consider three main theories on the nature of justice, beginning with the theory developed by John Rawls (1921–2002). Rawls's theory has been criticized from opposite sides by libertarians and egalitarians or socialists. We then explain and critique Robert Nozick's (1938–2002) libertarian theory and Karl Marx's (1818–1883) socialist theory. We conclude with our own comments on how justice fits in with our theory of rights. Later we will extend the analysis to contemporary issues of justice.

JOHN RAWLS'S THEORY OF JUSTICE

Many philosophers would contend that John Rawls's book *A Theory of Justice* is the most important work on the topic of justice in the twentieth century. He received both his undergraduate and doctoral degrees from Princeton University. Between receiving these degrees, he served his country in the United States Army during World War II. Before joining the Harvard faculty, Rawls held positions at Cornell and M.I.T. In 1979 Rawls was appointed Conant University Professor. *A Theory of Justice* received the kind of widespread attention and acclaim seldom accorded to works of academic philosophy. Rawls served as president of the American Philosophical Association and the American Association of Political and Legal Philosophy. He was a member of the American Academy of Arts and Sciences, and in 1999 he received the National Humanities Medal from the National Endowment for the Humanities. As we will see, he continued to work on and develop his ideas about justice until his death in 2002.

The Argument of *A Theory of Justice*

In *A Theory of Justice*, Rawls argues that the primary task of social and political institutions is the preservation and enhancement of social justice, which he understands to include both principles of individual liberty and principles of well-being or welfare. Rawls tries to develop a procedure that would yield principles of justice. These principles of justice would then serve as guides in the construction and evaluation of social and political institutions.

In Rawls's view, questions of justice arise when a society evaluates the institutions and practices under which it lives with an eye toward balancing the legitimate competing interests and conflicting claims that are recognized as legitimate by the members of that society. If we adopt the language of rights, we can say that Rawls sees the problems of justice arising when legitimate rights claims come into conflict.

84

Rawls does not view the citizens of a state as naive moralists searching for a utopian ideal. Rather, these citizens are sufficiently self-interested to wish to pursue their own individual interests or those of their families and loved ones. Given inevitably competing interests and conflicts, Rawls's task is to attempt to provide a procedure that will enable the members of the society to adopt principles for resolving conflicts and for putting in place just practices and institutions. In other words, his question is this: By what procedure can persons primarily concerned with their own interests and the interests of those close to them, such as family members, adopt principles of just institutions and practices?

Rawls's answer is to appeal to a contract process constrained by certain assumptions. Rawls's contract is not an actual contract made in history but rather a thought experiment or hypothetical state called the original position. Assumptions governing contracting in the original position include that (1) human cooperation is both possible and necessary, (2) the contractors adhere to the principle of rational choice, (3) all contractors desire certain primary goods that can be broadly characterized as rights and liberties, opportunities and powers, income and wealth—in other words, general goods that it is reasonable to think are necessary to the attainment of any other individual goods persons may desire, (4) the contract process is constrained by a minimal morality, which stipulates that principles adopted by the contractors be general, universal in application, public, and the final court of appeal for ordering the conflicting claims of moral persons, and (5) the parties to the contract are capable of a sense of justice and will adhere to the principles adopted.[1]

The force of these five conditions is to put moral limits on the kind of contract that can be produced. With these five conditions acting as constraints, Rawls's strategy is to ask us to conduct a thought experiment. What principles of justice would we come up with if we were placed behind a veil of ignorance with all other rational agents and instructed to devise a set of principles for organizing society so that justice in the society would be achieved? The key to understanding how the principles of justice are to be selected is the veil of ignorance, or the ignorance principle. The ignorance principle states that the contract makers are to act as if they did not know their place in society. Such ignorance guarantees impartiality and prevents us from arguing on selfish rather than general grounds. The veil of ignorance would exclude knowledge of one's class position or social status (including the probability of occupying any position or having any specific degree of status), one's fortune in the distribution of natural assets and abilities, one's intelligence, one's physical strength, the nature of one's society, and one's individual conception of the good and other values. Operating in this way, none of the contract makers would have any special interests to defend, nor would they have any reasons to form alliances to adopt principles that work to the disadvantage of a minority of other contract makers.

In effect, as Rawls applies it, the requirement of ignorance tells us to act as if our enemy were to assign our place in society. For example, suppose the issue were the distribution of income. Since the veil of ignorance prevents you from knowing how wealthy you are or will be, and it prevents you from knowing your occupation and talents, what strategy would it be rational for you to adopt? Surely, Rawls argues, you would want to protect the position of the least well-off. Similar thought experiments would assure that there would be no racist principles for the organization of social institutions. After all, you cannot be sure that you would not be a member of the race that would be discriminated against. Since the contract makers are rational egoists operating from behind a veil of ignorance, they would adopt the general principle of seeking to minimize their losses. Since they are ignorant of the probability of any specific outcome and know that some outcomes, such as being a member of a despised minority, are unacceptable, they would guard against the worst possible outcomes by making the people in the worst-off position as well-off as possible.

We can now see how unanimous agreement on the principles of justice is possible. Since everyone agrees that it is rational to reduce one's losses and since no one knows what position he or she holds in society, the following two principles would be adopted unanimously: (1) Each person is to have an equal right to the most extensive total system of equal basic liberties compatible with a similar system of liberty for all. (2) Social and economic inequalities are to be arranged so that they are both (a) to the greatest benefit of the least advantaged, and (b) attached to offices and positions that are open to all under conditions of fair equality of opportunity.[2]

These principles, which are the result of the contract, are just because the procedure that produced them is just. Indeed, it is the just procedure that makes the principles just. Rawls's hypothetical contract is an example of pure procedural justice. These are the principles that persons operating under the constraints of Rawls's original position behind the veil of ignorance would choose as the requirements of justice. Since they did not know particular facts about themselves, they have no specific interests to protect. Rather, the concern is with those goods Rawls calls primary goods—namely, general goods that are reasonably thought to be necessary to the attainment of any other individual goods persons may desire.

One of the most important of these primary goods is liberty, which is protected by the first principle. Since no one will know his or her place in society, it is in everyone's interest to adopt the first principle, which provides a system of equal liberty for all. Otherwise, one might turn out to be at the mercy of more powerful individuals or groups.

What are the constituent liberties that make up the system of liberty? Rawls answers this question by providing a list of basic liberties. The list includes political liberty (the right to vote and to be eligible for public office) together with freedom of speech and assembly; liberty of conscience and freedom of thought; freedom of the person along with the right to hold (personal) property; and freedom from arbitrary arrest and seizure as defined by the concept of the rule of law.[3]

The second principle is concerned with the primary goods of opportunities and power, income and wealth. Rawls's method is to consider his principle in contrast with several competing ones and then ask which principles would be selected by self-interested persons constrained by the veil of ignorance. Rawls first considers the principle of natural liberty. In the system of natural liberty, positions are open to those able and willing to strive for them. As for the distribution of wealth in the system of natural liberty, it is determined by the principle of efficiency. In terms of his theory, Rawls defines the position as follows:

> Thus we can say that an arrangement of rights and duties in the basic structure is efficient if and only if it is impossible to change the rules, to redefine the scheme of rights and duties so as to raise the expectations of any representative man (at least one) without at the same time lowering the expectations of some (at least one) other representative man.[4]

Rawls argues that this principle of efficiency within a system of natural liberty would be rejected, however. If after the initial distribution, someone had vastly more wealth than others, nothing could be done to correct the situation that would not run afoul of the efficiency principle. Moreover, the distribution of wealth at any given time has been strongly influenced by the cumulative effect of the natural and social contingencies of past distributions. Accident, past injustice, and good fortune play an important role in determining who is wealthy at any given time. Since the veil of ignorance prevents us from knowing our own fortune and since, according to Rawls, it is rational to seek to minimize our losses, the principle of efficiency would not be accepted in the contract. Rational contractors would seek to avoid the risk of turning out to be on the bottom in the efficient society.

Rawls has more positive reactions to the principle of equal opportunity. This principle asserts that people with the same ability, talents, and expenditures of effort should have roughly the same prospects for success in given fields of endeavor. One's family background, race, religion, sex, or social background should not act as an impediment to success. To assure equality of opportunity, society should impose heavy inheritance taxes, offer a broad public education, and pass antidiscrimination legislation. To the extent that such social measures are successful, the distribution of goods and services will depend on ability, talent, and effort. This principle is implicitly supported by broad segments of the American public.

However, in Rawls's view, the principle of equal opportunity is still not sufficient as an adequate principle of justice. Rawls argues that the distribution of talent, ability, and capacity for effort is just as arbitrary from the moral point of view as the distribution of sex, family wealth, and social class. A person has no greater right to more wealth because he is smarter than because he is of a certain religion.

In part, Rawls seems to be claiming that behind the veil of ignorance it would be no more rational to gamble on being smart, talented, or dedicated than on being a member of a dominant group in other areas, so we would reason conservatively and try to protect ourselves against bad outcomes. However, he also seems to appeal to our considered ideas about fairness. Distribution is fair, in Rawls's view, only if assets are treated as collective social goods. After all, none of us deserves to have been born into favorable circumstances or with personal traits such as a disposition to work hard. These are gifts distributed at birth as if by a natural lottery and are not earned by us as individuals. Moreover, the distribution of goods and services is a cooperative effort on the part of all. Given the cooperative effort and the morally arbitrary distribution of natural assets and favorable family circumstances, the fairest principle is the one that accepts inequalities only if the inequalities work to the advantage of the least well-off.

> It seems to be one of the fixed points of our considered judgments that no one deserves his place in the distribution of native endowments, any more than one deserves one's initial starting place in society. The assertion that a man deserves the superior character that enables him to make the effort to cultivate his abilities is equally problematic: for his character depends in large part upon fortunate family and social circumstances for which he can claim no credit. The notion of desert seems not to apply to these cases. Thus the more advantaged representative man cannot say that he deserves and therefore has a right to a scheme of cooperation in which he is permitted to acquire benefits in ways that do not contribute to the welfare of others. There is no basis for his making this claim. From the standpoint of common sense, then the difference principle appears to be acceptable both to the more advantaged and to the less advantaged individual.[5]

What the quoted passage shows, Rawls would maintain, is that his principles of justice conform to our own considered judgments about justice, those judgments in which we place the most confidence. Perhaps what ultimately justifies the Rawlsian contract procedure is its ability to explain, support, and provide grounds for reconsideration of our intuitive sentiments about social justice.

When fully spelled out, then, the Rawlsian argument is that the two principles of justice are justified because they and they alone would emerge from a fair procedure of rational choice. The procedure itself is warranted because of its coherence with our most firmly held judgments about justice and fairness. Finally, Rawls maintains that a society in which the political, social, and economic institutions were constructed in conformity with the principles of justice would be a highly stable one. The citizens of such a society would recognize that the society is basically just and thus would desire to act as the principles of justice require. These citizens would also be inclined to support society's basic institutions. In this way, such a society would be well-ordered and stable.

Assessment of Rawls's Theory

Naturally there was and continues to be considerable criticism and assessment of a project of this magnitude. Critical reaction to *A Theory of Justice* came from both those on the political right and the political left. Libertarians and others who supported capitalist economic institutions thought that Rawls's theory sacrificed liberty for greater equality. Those on the left thought that Rawls conceded too much to the self-interested side of human nature and thus overemphasized the inequalities from the necessity of providing incentives to the more talented. Moreover, even if such incentives were required, that did not make them just. To see the strength of these critical reactions, we consider the theories of the libertarian Robert Nozick and the socialist theory of Karl Marx. Marx developed his theory more than a hundred years before Rawls developed his. Nonetheless, Marx's theory captures many of the significant concerns of those who would challenge Rawls from the political left. We will consider the merits of these criticisms below.

Some readers consider Rawls's contract procedure to be too abstract and maintain that it is impossible psychologically to actually go beyond the veil of ignorance. While we have some sympathy for this sort of reaction, we suggest it may be overdrawn. The veil is not an actual device, as in a science fiction story, but is a way of expressing a relatively strong requirement of impartiality. It can be understood as a ground rule for actual discussions of justice. The rule tells us to reject a proposed principle of justice if it is unreasonable to think that people would hold it unless they occupied a social position where application of the principle provided some special benefit to them. That is, the veil asks us to use our imagination to test whether a proposed principle of justice seems attractive because it helps us or whether we genuinely think it can be the basis of cooperation between equal persons under conditions of freedom of choice. Having said that, Rawls seems to have de-emphasized more abstract elements of the contractual argument in his later work and has developed other lines of argument, as indicated below and more fully assessed in chapter 7 (where we also assess various criticisms of the notion of impartiality).

Criticism of Rawls's project was not limited to criticisms of his principles of distributive justice or his contract procedure. Rawls was also criticized because his account could not apply to all political societies but only to liberal democracies. Rawls accepted this criticism and wrote a second book, *Political Liberalism*, which further developed his ideas on justice and stability for a liberal democracy. Since we will be using a central idea from that book—the notion of an overlapping consensus—from here on, let us explain that notion before commenting on the criticisms of *A Theory of Justice*.

An overlapping consensus exists where there is agreement on certain principles for carrying on a debate and for making decisions in the political realm. True to his procedural inclinations, Rawls believes that people with competing conceptions of the good can nonetheless accept certain common political ground rules.

For example, religious fundamentalists and atheists can both agree to respect equal human rights—the fundamentalists because they believe all humans are equal before God and the atheists because they believe human rights can be justified by philosophical and ethical arguments, perhaps those we considered in chapter 3. In that way we have an overlapping consensus on these ground rules based on moral commitments rather than an unstable agreement of convenience. To achieve this consensus on ground rules, there must be some kind of limit on conceptions of the good that can be tolerated. For example, those who have no wish to get along with others and who actively seek to eliminate those with different religious beliefs would not be given credence.

The notion of an overlapping consensus as well as other ideas in *Political Liberalism* have also come under critical scrutiny. These criticisms of Rawls's later work will be discussed in chapter 7. In this chapter, we will consider alternatives to the views advanced by Rawls in *A Theory of Justice* and offer suggestions of our own about how to adjudicate conflicts among different approaches to justice. Since Rawls's theory is so influential and complex and has been developed in a number of stages, it will be discussed in a number of places throughout the book and should be viewed as a major statement, probably the most important, of liberal democratic principles of justice.

ROBERT NOZICK'S ENTITLEMENT THEORY

Robert Nozick (1938–2002), like Rawls, was a professor of philosophy at Harvard. In his book *Anarchy, State, and Utopia* (1974), Nozick developed an alternate theory of justice based on the primacy of our natural right to liberty. Nozick's theory has become a highly influential version of libertarianism, a political philosophy that emphasizes individual freedom and severely restricts the role of government in order to protect individual choice. Since Nozick's position has much in common with those who regard free competitive capitalist markets as the basis for an account of justice, it should be emphasized that Nozick supports free markets on grounds of the freedom of economic exchange and personal liberty they involve rather than by appeal to their economic efficiency.

Entitlement Theory

In *Anarchy, State, and Utopia* Robert Nozick developed an alternative theory of justice based on the primacy of our natural right to liberty. For a number of theoretical reasons that will be explained below, Nozick believed that Rawls's theory would require large and unacceptable violations of our right to liberty.

To make his point, Nozick used as an example the former basketball great Wilt Chamberlain (1936–1999). Chamberlain was a dynamic, high-scoring player who attracted large crowds whenever his team was in town. In one game he scored

100 points. Nozick then provided a thought experiment of his own. Suppose that people were willing to pay $1 of their ticket price to Chamberlain himself for the privilege of seeing him play. If one million people were so willing, Chamberlain would have an extra million dollars. Certainly Chamberlain was not responsible for his height and vast athletic ability. And if Rawls were right, Chamberlain would not even be responsible for his extraordinary work ethic. Unless one could establish that Chamberlain would only play if he received the extra million dollars, a Rawlsian would tax away that extra million. But that would be contrary to the free choice of the million people who were more than happy to provide Chamberlain with the extra million dollars. And to make matters worse, if a million people paid him a total of a million dollars next year, it would have to be taxed away again. A commitment to Rawls's theory of justice would require constant interference with the free choices of individuals.

What went wrong with the Rawlsian project? To see what Nozick regards as a fundamental flaw in Rawls's approach, we need to unpack his distinction between historical principles of justice and non-historical principles of justice. Nozick calls these non-historical principles end-state principles and believes that they are inadequate as principles of justice. Rawls's two principles are end-state principles.

With respect to the distribution of wealth, a defender of historical principles would argue that in assessing the justice of a distribution of income, it is not enough to simply look at the distributions. We must also look at how the goods were produced and how the distribution came about. As Nozick put it, "historical justice holds that past circumstances or actions of people can create differential entitlements or differential deserts to things."[6]

Another distinction Nozick makes is between patterned and non-patterned principles of justice. A patterned principle selects some characteristic or set of characteristics that specifies how the distribution is to be achieved. Any formula that fills in the blank "to each according to _____" is a patterned principle. Rawls's two principles of justice are patterned principles.

Nozick finds any patterned principle objectionable because the attempt to have the distribution be in accordance with the pattern is an infringement of liberty. This is the theoretical point of the Wilt Chamberlain example. With respect to Rawls's second principle, we would need to tax people in order to remove any inequalities that do not work out to the advantage of the least well-off representative man. But Nozick believes that is unfair. What is the difference, Nozick asks, between forcing someone to work five hours for the benefit of the needy and involuntarily taxing someone five hours' worth of work? Nozick claims that there is no difference. He maintains that taxation of earnings from labor is equivalent or virtually equivalent to forced labor. Thus the attempt to achieve patterned distributions results in an infringement of one's right to liberty.

As an alternative to patterned theories, Nozick develops a non-patterned theory that he calls the theory of entitlements. In Nozick's view, a distribution is just if people have what they are entitled to. To determine what people are entitled to, we must discuss the original acquisition of holdings, the transfer of holdings, and the rectification of holdings. Nozick's theory of acquisition is a variant of the theory of property rights developed by the philosopher John Locke, whose views we discussed in chapter 3. For Nozick, any person has a right to any owned thing so long as ownership by that person does not worsen the situation of others. Suppose I farm a plot of land that is neither used nor owned by anyone else. I cultivate the land, plant the seeds, and weed and water the garden plot. Surely I am entitled to the fruits of the harvest. What Nozick attempts to do is to accommodate all types of legitimate ownership to the case of the garden plot. We are entitled to what we have worked for or freely received by transfer from others.

The scarcity of goods and resources complicates Nozick's account. After all, whenever someone owns something, he usually diminishes the opportunity for someone else to own it. There are not enough resources for a swimming pool and three cars for all. It is the recognition of this problem that accounts for Nozick's addition of the phrase "does not worsen the situation of others."

However, this phrase needs considerable interpretation. For Nozick, someone's situation is not worsened just because his opportunities become more limited. At times Nozick speaks as if someone's situation would be worsened if he fell below a certain baseline.[7] It is tempting to think that the phrase "baseline situation" means something like "minimum standard of living" or "welfare floor." If this were the case, fairly extensive violations would be allowed to keep people from falling below the baseline. For example, taxes for the purpose of providing a safety net would interfere with people's liberty to spend their income as they wished.

However, the examples that Nozick chooses for discussion and other, more extensive comments that he makes indicate that his view of how one's ownership of something makes another worse off is far narrower. Nozick seems to indicate that we should compare the situation of a person as it would be with a system of property rights and as it would be without a system of property rights. If Jones acquires something, Smith is not made worse off unless Smith's situation deteriorates to the point where he is worse off than he would be in a system without property rights. Thus Jones could not own the only waterhole in the desert. However, Jones could own the only effective drug against a new pandemic if he himself discovered and developed it because in this case his property rights have not made others worse off than they would have been in the state of nature.

The end result of Nozick's discussion of how one person can be harmed by another's acquisition of property is that nearly everyone is entitled to everything he acquires so long as coercion or fraud is not involved. The theory is rounded out by the contention that what one has justly acquired, one is entitled to transfer to others. Once can see why Nozick would adopt the slogan "from each as they choose, to each as they are chosen." A person is entitled to something if he acquired it without worsening the situation of others or if he received it as a transfer from one who had acquired it without worsening the situation of others.

Assessment of Nozick's Theory

Nozick presents several solid objections to Rawls's theory. At a minimum, his point that those who produce goods and services have special claims of entitlement or ownership (claims allegedly unacknowledged by theories that focus only on distribution) deserves full consideration. However, his own libertarian theory of entitlement is not without problems of its own. The major criticism of Nozick is that he gives too much weight to the right to liberty and not nearly enough weight to the right to well-being. After all, why should we build a theory of justice in terms of liberty alone? A consequence of Nozick's position is that it would be unjust for even a wealthy state to tax individuals in order to provide better food, clothing, or housing for the poor. In Nozick's view we are entitled (have a right) to our legitimate acquisitions, but the poor have no right to a minimum standard of living. In chapter 3, we examined defenses of human rights. If rights claims are justified on the basis of our recognition of the dignity and self-respect of every individual, then the right to a minimum standard of living is as firmly justified as our right to liberty. Nozick not only ignores our right to well-being but utterly annihilates it, as it comes into conflict with one's right to liberty. Such an extreme point of view needs considerable defense, which unfortunately Nozick does not supply.

The extreme flavor of Nozick's theory is clearly seen in his discussion of how A's ownership of X can worsen the condition of B. How does Nozick justify his suggestion about how people's condition can be worsened? In his view, people's condition is worsened only if they are worse off than they would be in a system without property rights. It is most remarkable that Nozick provides no defense at all for this interpretation of worsening. Surely it needs a defense because it implies that workers laid off by a company that downsizes are not really made worse off since they would be even poorer in a system without property rights. Since Nozick's interpretation is so counterintuitive, surely it calls for some justification.

Our criticism of Nozick would be less severe if we could interpret more broadly how people's condition could be worsened. We might say that someone's condition is worsened when it falls below a certain baseline (welfare floor). In this way, our liberty as expressed through property rights would not be rejected but would be checked or limited in the face of extreme need. This interpretation would be inconsistent with most of what Nozick says, however.

In addition, as he himself seems to concede, Nozick does not offer a full-fledged theory of acquisition, or indeed, of what it means to own anything. With respect to the former there is no discussion of what counts as fraudulent acquisition. Stealing is clearly illegitimate since it violates one's right to liberty. Is emotional or subliminal advertising legitimate? Can an advertiser or salesperson prey upon the ignorance of the poor? Must products be proven safe or should society adopt the philosophy of "let the buyer beware"? With respect to the concept of ownership, when does someone own something? Can property owners forbid jet planes to fly over their homes? Do minerals at the bottom of the ocean or on Mars belong to the person who gets there first? If so, can an explorer own all of Mars by arriving five minutes before a second explorer? What account can be given of public goods or collective ownership?

Nozick's account of justice is severely limited in scope. By failing to place some constraints on the means of acquisition and by failing to define how someone can be said to own something, Nozick ignores many of the important issues. In addition, Nozick must deal with Rawls's contention that much of what we acquire is the result of moral luck and may be wholly or partially undeserved. A Rawlsian can point out with respect to the Wilt Chamberlain example that Wilt was able to achieve his success in great part because of his height, which resulted in part from a fortunate genetic endowment. Since Wilt was not personally responsible for all of his assets, on what basis can it be said that he deserves that extra million dollars that people are willing to pay? On what basis can he be said to deserve *all* of it?

While we suspect that this Rawlsian point is not decisive and is sometimes overdrawn—we ourselves criticize it below—we also think Nozick and the libertarians need to pay more attention to the result of moral luck in the market and its implications for deserts and entitlements. Do we want an individual's fate to be largely determined by the luck of the draw in either genetic endowment or the distribution of the most favorable environments for growth?

Nozick's theory also has difficulties with fairness. Suppose, for example, that a first generation of colonists establishes a settlement in a new land. They operate according to a capitalist market where economic goods are concerned. As a result, some do far better than others economically since their goods and services are more highly valued than those of the other colonists. What happens, however, to the children of the first generations? Some, through no fault of their own, are born into poverty, while others, with better luck, are born into affluent homes. Some have lost their parents to accidents or ill health. Others become ill and cannot work themselves. Is it *fair* that such individuals must depend on the charity of others?

Nozick might reply that, whether the situation is fair or not, to appropriate the products of the work of other people against their will in order to help the disadvantaged violates the human right to liberty of the property owners. However, our arguments in chapter 3 suggest that, on the contrary, the disadvantaged have a human right to a minimum standard of living, as well as a right to liberty. To deny such a right and opt for Nozick's unmitigated entitlement theory is to fall prey to the Rawlsian objection that an individual's fate should not be the result of accidents of birth or factors for which the person is not responsible.

Perhaps we should examine a theory that focuses on well-being rather than on liberty. Marxism presents us with such a theory.

MARXIST THEORIES OF JUSTICE

With the collapse of the Soviet Union in 1989–1990 and the spread of one form or another of capitalism throughout the industrial world and even in the developing world, it is easy to be dismissive of the thinking of Karl Marx (1818–1883) and later theorists who have reflected on justice in the Marxist tradition. However, that would be a mistake, because Marx identified a number of important issues, particularly with respect to economic justice, that remain important today. However, today these issues are not often identified with Marx and Marxism, but nonetheless Marx and his followers were the ones who articulated them.

Before beginning our explanation of Marx, a few caveats are in order. First, Marx often spoke as if his theory of capitalist exploitation and the transition from capitalist to socialist to communist society is scientific. Thus, some have argued, not implausibly, that Marx is less a moralist than a social scientist.[8] However, since this chapter is dealing with justice, we will treat and evaluate Marx's theory as if it were a theory of *justice*. Secondly, Marx's critique of capitalist exploitation rests on something called the labor theory of value. Economists no longer adopt the labor theory of value, and to explain Marx in terms of it would be unduly complicated for modern readers. Therefore we will put Marx's basic point in more contemporary language. In doing so we will nonetheless attempt to be faithful to Marx's argument.

The starting point for Marx's theory is with class struggle in capitalist markets. Marx believed that in the employer-employee relationship, the owners of the means of production (the capitalists) had the advantage. (Marx referred to the workers as the proletariat and to the capitalists, among others, as the bourgeoisie.) To oversimplify a bit, a manufactured product is the result of inputs from labor, capital, management, and machines. This product is then sold in the marketplace. How should the money received from the product be divided among the factors of production? Marx argued that the workers never receive their fair share because the capitalists could keep wages low and extract some of the workers' share of their actual contribution to production for themselves. The capitalists could do this because there was a large number of people who wanted work (a reserve army of the unemployed) and because the capitalists were always using technology to improve machines so that the machines could take the place of laborers. Indeed Marx thought that the capitalists could keep wages at or near subsistence.

> The greater division of labor enables one worker to do the work of five, ten or twenty; it therefore multiplies competition among the workers fivefold, tenfold, and twentyfold. The workers do not only compete by one selling oneself cheaper than another; they compete by one doing the work of five, ten, twenty, and the division of labor, introduced

by capital, and continually increased compels the workers to compete among themselves in this way:

Further as the division of labor increases, labor is simplified. The special skill of the worker becomes worthless. He becomes transformed into a simple, monotonous productive force that does not have to use intense bodily or intellectual faculties. His labor becomes labor that anyone can perform. Hence competitors crowd in upon him on all sides. . . . The more simple and easily learned the labor is, the lower the cost of production needed to master it, the lower do wages sink, for like the price of every other commodity, they are determined by the cost of production.

Therefore, as labor becomes more unsatisfying, more repulsive, competition increases and wages decrease. . . .

Machinery brings about the same results on a much greater scale, by replacing skilled workers by unskilled, men by women, adults by children. It brings about the same results, where it is newly introduced, by throwing the hand workers on to the street in masses.[9]

Marx was wrong about the tendency of wages to remain at subsistence in a capitalist economy. However, he was right to focus on how the returns from the productive effort, both sales and profits, are to be divided among the factors of production. Contemporary debates about executive compensation and the percentage of productivity increases that go to workers as opposed to managers or shareholders have Marxian origins. Productivity increased markedly during the 1990s as the benefits of information technology flowed to business. There is an increasing consensus that a disproportionate share of the gains from increased productivity have gone to managers rather than employees. Thus the ratio between the salary of a CEO and the lowest-paid person in a manufacturing enterprise has gone from 50/1 to 400/1 at one point in the early 2000s.

Those who defend this increase in executive compensation point out that good managers are in short supply and that huge compensation packages are necessary to attract good managers. If this argument is true, then a Rawlsian would be required to support the current distribution if it worked to the benefit of the least well-off. That is why socialists and those of a more egalitarian persuasion were critical of Rawls. Rawls conceded too much to motivation by incentives. The greedier a talented person is, the more he can withhold his services and thus get an income that would pass the Rawlsian difference principle test. If these services really are necessary for the business enterprise to succeed (which is highly debatable), it seems that rich rewards for those with managerial talent are also necessary. Marx, and many who do not call themselves Marxist, think this is unfair (although Marx himself avoided such ethical language, given his materialist and scientific orientation). Since the individual worker is powerless to effect change in the system and to acquire his share of the productivity gains, the worker is being exploited.

But exploitation is not the only question of justice that a Marxist raises about capitalist economic systems. Marx also believed that the worker is alienated in a number of senses. First, with wages so low, workers needed to work long hours in order to achieve a subsistence existence. Thus the worker sacrificed family time, time as an active citizen participating in civil society, and even church time in order to work. Since these activities are arguably necessary for self-realization, and since the opportunity to exercise one's capacities and abilities and to achieve a wide range of one's goals, is necessary for self-respect, a Marxian could argue that a capitalist economic system denies a person's self-respect. (Rawls, too, regards self-respect as an especially significant primary good.) In all these ways, workers become alienated from all other aspects of their lives.

The worker is also alienated from the product that he helps produce. In precapitalist societies, a worker made the whole product. In industrialized society, people on the assembly line have only one function to perform. They might never even see the final product that they helped produce. Another way of expressing the resulting alienation is to say that such work is not meaningful. Think of Adam Smith's pin factory, which reduced the making of a pin to eighteen individual operations. As a result of this specialization, many more pins were produced. However, no individual worker ever made a pin. Marx put it this way:

> Owing to the extensive use of machinery and the division of labor, the work of the proletarians has lost all individual character, and consequently all charm for the workman. He becomes an appendage of the machine, and it is only the most simple, most monotonous, most easily acquired knack that is required of him.[10]

Even the father of capitalism, the great eighteenth-century economist and moral philosopher Adam Smith, recognized the deadening effects of such a division of labor and anticipated some of Marx's criticism:

> The man whose whole life is spent in performing a few simple operations, of which the effects are, perhaps always the same, has no occasion to exert his understanding, or to exercise his invention in finding out expedients for removing difficulties which never occur. He naturally loses, therefore, the habit of such exertion, and generally becomes as stupid and ignorant as it is possible for a human being to become. The torpor of his mind renders him, not only incapable of relishing or bearing a part in any rational conversation but of conceiving any generous, noble, or tender sentiment, and consequently of forming any just judgment concerning many of the ordinary duties of private life. Of the great and extensive interests of his country he is altogether incapable of judging.[11]

On this point as well, Marx is relevant to contemporary issues. Contemporary critics of capitalist society point out that one wage earner is not sufficient for achieving a salary that can pay for the goods and services an average family wants or needs. The two-earner household is now the norm. As a result, serious questions about the care of children and the time available for civic and religious activities have arisen. The dilemma is posed as one of balancing work and the rest of life rather than involving Marx's term of alienation, but the issues raised are similar.

In addition, fewer and fewer workers consider their work to be meaningful or fulfilling. You see this in our language, in the phrase "TGIF" (Thank God It's Friday) and in references to Blue Monday and Wednesday as hump day (halfway to Friday). An economic system that requires the neglect of family, that often precludes participation in the political process, and in which so few people find work to be meaningful and joyful can be called an unjust system.

Although we find that Marx's theory gives too little weight to individual rights, including rights to choose ways of life that a Marxist might reject, such as a choice to prefer repetitive work and a higher standard of living over more interesting work and less disposable income, some of Marx's criticisms do raise legitimate questions about the values of our own society. For example, Marx's concern that the demands of a largely free market economy may unduly pressure many of us into working longer and longer hours at the expense of other important aspects of our lives surely has force. Similarly, the question raised by his work of whether increasingly larger concentrations of economic power in the hands of a few may undermine the freedom as well as the welfare of the many is especially significant in view of growing inequalities of wealth in the United States. How such issues are best resolved remains debatable, but Marxist thought at its best contributes to a critique of current society by bringing them to the forefront of our thought.

Finally, although Marx may not have seen himself as engaging in moral criticism rather than social analysis, Marxism as a philosophy is associated with two principles of distributive justice. In socialist economies, Marx wanted the worker to receive the fair value of his work. As we saw above, much of Marx's analysis of capitalism was to show how the worker was prevented from receiving this fair value. After the transition from socialism to communism, perhaps the final stage in Marx's "scientific" theory of socioeconomic evolution, Marx endorsed the distributive principle "from each according to his ability, to each according to his need." Although Marx applied the formula to communist societies, the formula itself is attributed to the French socialist Louis Blanc. It was one of the elements of the German socialists' Gotha Program of 1875. Although Marx was critical of that program,[12] this principle of distributive justice was accepted as the governing distributive principle in the final stages of communism by both Marx and Lenin. If the economic institutions of society were organized around this principle, people would contribute to economic production based on their skills. However, their pay would not be based, or simply based, on supply and demand in a competitive market. What people received in economic goods and services would be based on what they need rather than on how much their productive power could bring them in the marketplace.

Our criticism of Marx is the mirror opposite of the criticisms we made of the work of Robert Nozick. Whereas Nozick sacrificed the human right to well-being to give priority to the right to liberty, Marxist theory sacrifices the human right to liberty to give priority to need. (Recall that Marx does not have a place for rights in his theory.) Similarly, even if Rawls conceded too much to the necessity of unequal distributions, Marxian theory is unrealistic and utopian in that it does not make any concession to the necessity of incentives that result in unequal distribution. Why would workers produce enough to satisfy needs, for example, without incentives? A possible reply is that workers in the final stages of communism would find work to be its own reward, just as an athlete may practice hard for love of the game, but this may presuppose a level of economic development so far advanced from our own that issues of justice become irrelevant.[13] Justice may not be needed in utopia. In any case, many of Marx's predictions and recommendations seem naive or outlandish today. There has been no revolution of the proletariat against the bourgeoisie. Few, if any, serious thinkers would recommend the abolition of private property and the abolition of the family as Marx and Engels did in *The Communist Manifesto*. On the other hand, few economies today are purely capitalistic, and the liberal democracies of Europe have at times combined economies that are in some respects socialistic (not communist or Marxist) with respect for fundamental human rights, reflecting to some degree arguably positive influences of Marxist thought.

JUSTICE WITHIN THE CONTEXT OF NATURAL RIGHT

While the theories of justice that we have considered conflict on many points, some principles emerge as especially reasonable. In particular, Rawls's insistence that fundamental aspects of justice are procedural seems salient and is a key element of our own suggestions about justice. Our suggestions work at two levels.

Our starting point is egalitarian in the sense that we believe all human beings are entitled to basic human rights, the two primary human rights being the right to liberty and the right to a minimum standard of well-being. However, how rights claims are to be honored and how disputes between rights claims are resolved depend on specific situations. The implementation of rights claims constitutes the lower level. We use the word "lower" because the decisions made at this level implement the rights claims to which we are entitled at the higher level. For example, the dispensing of anti-typhoid vaccine to those and only to those exposed to typhoid is a working out in specific situations of the human right to well-being. Medicine should go to the sick and not to everyone, food to the hungry and not to everyone and so on. Indeed, with respect to the right to well-being, need is usually the most relevant factor. However, recognizing need is relevant because it enables us to implement a human right, not because (as in some versions of Marxist thought) a basic principle of justice is "to each according to need." On our view a necessary condition for justice is that it must represent an attempt to implement a human right.

Although we believe that Rawls is correct in providing a procedural theory of justice by adopting the original position and the veil of ignorance, we do not accept Rawls's second principle of justice, the difference principle, because we believe he does not give an adequate place to individual desert. We believe the problem originates in Rawls's view that our talents, capacities, and even our character are the arbitrary results of a natural environmental/genetic lottery and so are social assets. Isn't this view vulnerable to the charge of being disrespectful to persons, the very charge that Rawls made against utilitarianism? For example, why should Rawlsians value protection of individual choice so much if what we choose depends on such "accidents" as our tastes, inclinations, and skills? Isn't this letting the natural lottery affect outcomes just as much as rewarding talents and abilities? Why shouldn't our kidneys be viewed as social assets, since the luck of the draw determines who has and who lacks healthy kidneys? What is left of the individual once skills, capacities, and character are stripped away? Perhaps Rawls is just as guilty as the utilitarian of not taking seriously the differences between persons. At least on the intuitive level, it often seems just, as in competitive athletics, to let outcomes be determined by individual skills, effort, and ambition, so long as such practices do not undermine the rights of others, positive and negative alike. Perhaps that is all Rawls meant to say, as some of his later writings suggest, but his remarks quoted above (from the 1971 edition of *A Theory of Justice*) about the natural lottery and the rejection of merit and desert as a basic element of justice suggest a reluctance to give due weight to individual responsibility that seems open to moral question.[14]

Our own view is that it is the task of the state to provide justice by adjudicating conflicting rights claims fairly. We agree with Rawls that fairness is a fundamental aspect of justice and that what is required is a fair procedure. However, rather than the hypothetical original position constrained by the veil of ignorance, we opt for actual democratic decisionmaking, although democratic decisionmaking subject to certain moral constraints. We shall discuss the specific nature of those constraints in the next two chapters, but the first and foremost constraint is that democratic decisionmaking should be consistent with human rights. In other words, democracies need to balance human rights and make tradeoffs among them. However, they are not morally permitted to ignore human rights. Our view of justice might be characterized as the liberal theory of justice since it is based on implementing and adjudicating conflicts among individual human rights in part through application of fair democratic procedures constrained by individual rights.

As a starting point, here is a brief outline of our liberal theory of justice:

1. Problems of justice arise as individuals attempt to implement their rights.
2. The function of the state is to provide a mechanism for adjudicating the conflicts of individual rights claims and for implementing the claims.
3. Suitably constrained, a form of democracy is the appropriate procedure for providing justice.
4. Our individual rights framework provides some limitations on the kinds of questions that can be submitted to the democratic mechanism.
5. Other moral principles place additional constraints on the democratic mechanism, but these supplementary principles can be discovered only by analyzing particular problems in particular historical circumstances.

Our approach views the individual person as the bearer of fundamental rights. This emphasis on the individual is a crucial value we share with Nozick and Rawls, and other major thinkers in the liberal tradition, including earlier philosophers such as John Locke. But this emphasis on the individual and democratic decisionmaking has come in for strong criticism. Among the critics are those identified as communitarians and radical feminists. Indeed some feminists, such as Iris Young, have charged that liberal approaches have been too concerned with issues of distribution of resources and not enough with the elimination of oppression, while communitarians and some feminists as well have rejected liberalism because of what they regard as excessive individualism. In the next two chapters, we will more closely examine the notions of individual liberty and democracy in order to flesh out the fundamental values of liberal democratic thought. Then, in chapter 7, we will consider these critiques and indicate how a political liberal might respond.

NOTES

1. John Rawls, *A Theory of Justice* (Cambridge, MA: Harvard University Press, 1971), 126–42.

2. Rawls, *A Theory of Justice*. Rawls provides more complicated formulations throughout his book.

3. Rawls, *A Theory of Justice*, 61.

4. Rawls, *A Theory of Justice*, 70.

5. Rawls, *A Theory of Justice*, 104.

6. Robert Nozick, *Anarchy, State, and Utopia* (New York: Basic Books, 1974), 155.

7. For example, Nozick uses the idea of a baseline when talking of transferring property from one person to another. "This excludes his transferring it into an agglomeration that does violate the Lockean proviso and excludes his using it in a way . . . so as to violate the proviso by making the situation of others worse than their baseline situation." *Anarchy, State, and Utopia*, 180.

8. A strong proponent of this view is Robert C. Tucker. See his "Marx and Distributive Justice," in *Justice* (Nomos 6), ed. Carl Friedrich and John Chapman (New York: Atherton Press, 1963), 306–25.

9. Karl Marx, "Wage Labour and Capital," in *The Marx-Engels Reader*, ed. Robert C. Tucker, second ed. (New York: W. W. Norton, 1978), 214–15.

10. Karl Marx and Friedrich Engels, *The Communist Manifesto* (New York: Appleton Century Crofts Inc., 1955), 16.

11. Adam Smith, *The Wealth of Nations* [1776], ed. Edwin Cannan (Chicago: University of Chicago Press, 1976), Part II, 303. For those using other editions, see Book V, chapter 1, article 2d, "Of the Expense of the Institutions for the Education of Youth."

12. This critique was made in a letter to the leaders of the Eisenach faction of the German Social Democratic movement. The letter was written in early May of 1875.

13. For discussion, see Edward Nell and Onora O'Neill, "Justice Under Socialism," *Dissent* 18 (1972): 483–91.

14. Rawls's later work suggests a different interpretation that gives more weight to questions of individual entitlement and desert without regarding them as morally fundamental. For example, see his *Justice as Fairness: A Restatement*, ed. Erin Kelly (Cambridge, MA: Harvard University Press, 2001), 72–74.

QUESTIONS FOR FURTHER STUDY

1. What function or purpose are the original position and veil of ignorance intended to serve within Rawls's theory? Do they serve that purpose? Explain.
2. State and explain Rawls's two principles of justice. Assess a major criticism of each.
3. In what respect is Rawls's theory procedural? Explain.
4. What are Nozick's chief criticisms of Rawls?
5. What is a patterned principle of justice? What is the Wilt Chamberlain example designed to show about patterned principles of justice?
6. Describe Nozick's entitlement theory of justice. What do you think are major criticisms of the theory? Are they successful?
7. Critics claim that Nozick's theory allows a few to accumulate too much. Yet Nozick says that no one should "worsen the situation of others." Does this requirement or proviso answer the worry about excessive accumulation by the few? Why or why not?
8. What is Marx's central criticism of capitalism? Evaluate this criticism.
9. Evaluate Marx's claim that the worker in capitalistic societies is alienated. What does Marx mean by this claim?
10. Is Marx's formula of "from each according to his ability, to each according to his need" a defensible principle of distributive justice? Why or why not?
11. What relationship between justice and human rights is postulated in this chapter?

SUGGESTED READINGS

Books

Ackerman, Bruce A. *Social Justice in the Liberal State.* New Haven, CT: Yale University Press, 1980.

Barry, Brian. *Justice as Impartiality.* New York: Oxford University Press, 1995.

Daniels, Norman, ed. *Reading Rawls: Critical Studies of "A Theory of Justice."* New York: Basic Books, 1975.

Miller, David. *Principles of Social Justice.* Cambridge, MA: Harvard University Press, 1999.

Narveson, Jan. *Respecting Persons in Theory and Practice.* Lanham, MD: Rowman & Littlefield, 2002.

Nozick, Robert. *Anarchy, State and Utopia.* New York: Basic Books, 1974.

Pogge, Thomas. *Reading Rawls*. Ithaca, NY: Cornell University Press, 1989.

Rawls, John. *A Theory of Justice*. Cambridge, MA: Harvard University Press, 1971.

——. *Political Liberalism*. New York: Columbia University Press, 1993.

——. *The Law of Peoples*. Cambridge, MA: Harvard University Press, 1999.

Sher, George. *Desert*. Princeton, NJ: Princeton University Press, 1987.

Articles

Miller, Richard W. "Marx's Legacy," in *The Blackwell Guide to Social and Political Philosophy*, ed. Robert L. Simon. Malden, MA: Blackwell Publishers (2002), 131–53.

Nell, Edward, and Onora O'Neill. "Justice Under Socialism." *Dissent* 18 (1972): 483–91.

Okin, Susan Moller. "Poverty, Well-Being, and Gender: What Counts, Who's Heard?" *Philosophy and Public Affairs* 33, no. 2 (2003): 280–316.

Wellman, Christopher Heath. "Justice," in *The Blackwell Guide to Social and Political Philosophy*, ed. Robert L. Simon. (2002), 60–84.

Wood, Allen W. "The Marxian Critique of Justice." *Philosophy and Public Affairs* 1 (1972): 244–82.

5

LIBERTY

Although virtually everyone claims to be a friend of liberty in the abstract, many turn out to be only fair-weather friends in the concrete. Although most Americans willingly pledge allegiance to their flag and to the liberty and justice for which it stands, all too frequently the very values the flag supposedly symbolizes are lost sight of in the heat of controversy. This is especially true of liberty. Liberty enables people to act in ways others cannot control. People are left free to act in ways that some might find repulsive, immoral, and subversive. Those affronted may react by trying to limit liberty itself.

Thus, fundamentalist religious groups have tried, with some success, to eliminate those textbooks that they believe undermine their own religious and political values from the public schools. Similarly, guardians of the public's virtue have tried and continue to try, again with some success, to remove controversial books from library shelves. Throughout our history, those who have dissented from official policy often have been faced with economic and even physical retaliation. Without freedom, we would live in a totalitarian state, but often those who exercise freedom in controversial ways face many risks, even in those countries where political liberty is most valued and protected.

Other problems concerning liberty arise, even if those involving its infringement are ignored. Thus, even the staunchest friends of liberty disagree over its scope and limits. Your liberty to swing your arm may end where your neighbor's nose begins. But should you be free to take high risks even if the only reason for doing so is to show off to friends? Should attempts at suicide be prevented or should people be free to end their own lives if they wish? Are there limits to free speech? If so, what are they? If not, does it follow that racist speech is protected by law? Can colleges or universities promulgate and enforce speech codes prohibiting what has come to be called "hate speech" directed against various minority groups? If colleges can prohibit "hate speech," can religious or political groups prohibit speech, for example certain kinds of rap music, that they consider anti-Christian, anti-family, or anti-female? Can behavior be prohibited simply because it is offensive to others? If so, how offensive must it be? On the other hand, if the offensiveness of behavior is not a good reason for prohibiting it, does it follow that even behavior that deeply disgusts virtually all who witness it must be allowed? Finally, in an age of terrorism, how are possible conflicts between our freedoms and our security to be reconciled?

Our concern in this chapter is to delineate the scope of a fundamental human right, the right to individual liberty, and also to indicate how the right to liberty can act as a needed constraint on the democratic process. Consideration of the scope and limits of individual liberty will also enable us to demarcate the proper limits of the state's authority over the individual. It is to such questions concerning liberty that we now turn.

THE CONCEPT OF POLITICAL LIBERTY

Our concern is with political liberty. Thus, some disputes over liberty of other kinds need not concern us. For example, there has been dispute over whether humans have free will or whether the laws of nature are restrictions on human liberty. Are our personalities, and hence our choices, determined by our environment and our genetic heritage? Do humans have free will? Fortunately for us, no stand need be taken on these issues here since our concern is purely with political liberty. Political liberty seems to be associated with the presence or absence of constraints imposed directly or indirectly by persons or associations of persons. Thus, an earthquake that destroys roads and bridges may make it impossible for inhabitants of an area to leave, but it is not their *political* liberty that is restricted.

There is some temptation to identify liberty with the ability to satisfy one's wants and desires. Suppose that Jones is locked in a room but wants nothing more than to remain there. Is Jones free? After all, Jones can do exactly what he wants to do. If Jones is free, then are the subjects of a ruthless dictatorship, where criticism of the despot is not permitted, also free so long as they actually support the government and do not want to criticize the dictator?

One difficulty with the view that one is free if one does as one wants is that wants can be coercively imposed. John Stuart Mill, in his essay "On the Subjection of Women," suggests that even if women act as they want, they are not free if what they want to do is itself the result of coercion:

> All causes, social and natural, combine to make it unlikely that women should be collectively rebellious to the power of men. . . . Men do not want solely the obedience of women, they want their sentiments. . . . They have therefore put everything in practice to enslave their minds. . . . When we put together three things—first, the natural attraction between opposite sexes; secondly, the wife's entire dependence on the husband, every privilege or pleasure . . . depending entirely on his will; and lastly, that the principal object of human pursuit . . . and all objects of social ambition, can in

general be sought or obtained by her only through him, it would be a miracle if the object of being attractive to men had not become the polar star of feminine education and formation of character. . . . Can it be doubted that any of the other yokes which mankind have succeeded in breaking, would have subsisted till now if the same means had existed, and had been so sedulously used, to bow their minds to it?[1]

If Mill is correct in claiming that the wants of many women have been formed coercively, then surely such women are not free even if they are doing what they want to do. One might as well say that we can liberate prisoners simply by getting them to want to remain in prison.[2] On the other hand, we must be careful of dismissing others as "brainwashed" or "socialized" just because we reject their views. Thus, the tendency of some feminists to dismiss the criticism of women who hold more traditional values as merely the result of social indoctrination too often functions as a device for avoiding the need to deal with objections and to take opponents seriously as persons. Nevertheless, it surely is too simple to say people are free simply because they can do what they want, since it is at least possible that what they want itself is the result of coercion and oppression.

Joel Feinberg has pointed out another unacceptable consequence of the view that one is free if what one does as what one wants to do. Feinberg asks us to consider

the case in which Doe can do one thousand things including what he most wants to do, whereas Roe can do only the thing he most wants to do. On the (freedom as the ability to do as one wants) model, Doe and Roe do not differ at all in respect to freedom.[3]

Surely such a consequence is unacceptable. But since any account of freedom that has such an unacceptable consequence is itself unacceptable, the account that identifies freedom with doing what one wants must be rejected. Accordingly, liberty ought not to be confused with being able to do as one wants. The willing slaves of a dictator may be happy but they are not free!

But what is liberty? Some valuable suggestions are found in Sir Isaiah Berlin's important paper "Two Concepts of Liberty."

Berlin's "Two Concepts of Liberty"

In his influential essay "Two Concepts of Liberty," British philosopher and prominent intellectual Isaiah Berlin (1909–1997) attempted to distinguish negative from positive liberty. The first, negative liberty, is involved in the answer to the question "What is the area within which the subject . . . is or should be left to do or be what he is able to do or be, without interference by other persons?" The second, positive liberty, is involved in the answer to the question "What, or who, is the source of control or interference that can determine someone to do, or be, this rather than that?"[4] Negative liberty concerns the absence of external constraints imposed by others. Positive liberty concerns self-mastery, or control over one's own fate. Let us examine negative and positive liberty more closely.

Negative Liberty

According to Berlin, one lacks negative liberty "only if you are prevented from attaining a goal by human beings."[5] Negative freedom is the absence of coercion. Coercion "implies the deliberate interference of other human beings."[6] Such interference prevents action that the agent otherwise could have performed.

Must constraints be *deliberately* imposed for negative liberty to be violated? It seems mistaken to require that constraint be intentional for negative liberty to be violated. If Bradley accidentally locks Adler in his room, Adler is as unable to leave as he would be if Bradley's behavior were deliberate. Similarly, if through a series of accidents, people are locked between floors in a stalled elevator in a high rise, they are not free to leave. Lack of intention may well mitigate personal responsibility for any harm people in the elevator may suffer. Nevertheless, these examples indicate that freedom can be restricted unintentionally. We conclude, therefore, that constraints on negative liberty need not be deliberately imposed.

Negative liberty is the absence of constraint imposed by others. Such liberty is embodied in the notion of civil liberties, which are barriers against interference by the state. Lockean natural rights, as we have seen, were concerned primarily with negative liberty. What then is positive liberty?

Positive Liberty

Berlin tells us that the "Positive sense of the word 'liberty' derives from the wish on the part of the individual to be his own master. I wish my life and decisions to depend on myself, not on external forces . . ."[7] Positive freedom, according to this account, is self-mastery. One might be subject to no constraints imposed by others yet lack positive freedom. For example, if one is neurotically indecisive, then even if no one else prevents one from attending a movie, one may not be free to go because of inability to make up one's mind. Likewise, compulsive desires, overwhelming depression, and perhaps even ignorance can restrict positive liberty.

Berlin believed that the concept of positive liberty is dangerous. Demagogues might claim that just as the neurotic is in the grip of irrational desires that prevent free choice, so too might the citizenry need to be forced to be free of their "irrational" desires for democracy. Once demagogues take this position, they may ignore the actual desires of the citizenry in order to "bully, oppress, torture [the citizens] in the name . . . of their 'real' selves."[8] Berlin is quite right to point out the fallacy here: namely, that of equating what we might want if we were not what we are with what we do want, and then assuming that if we are forced to promote the former, we are being liberated. This fallacy may lie behind the claim of some totalitarians that the citizens of a dictatorship have true freedom in spite of their protests to the contrary. It may also lie behind the claim of some allegedly progressive political movements that discount criticism on the ground that their opponents have been so corrupted by the existing system that they are incapable of critically examining it.

Berlin's essay is a warning against the appeal to positive liberty, with all the abuses to which such appeal may lead. The idea of "forcing people to be free" in the name of their deeper selves certainly can lead to terrible abuses of human rights. However, the fault may lie more in the misuse of positive liberty than in the logic of the concept. Surely, there is nothing absurd in the claim that mental illness, exhaustion, or even lack of knowledge constrain one's decisionmaking ability and obstruct autonomous deliberation. The danger lies either in the misapplication of the claim, as when radical social critics mistakenly dismiss the arguments of opponents by claiming they have been brainwashed by the system and have lost the power to critically examine it, or in the additional step that the opponents must be coerced in order to be freed. This additional step is the one that we should be especially wary of taking, although sometimes, as in the treatment of the psychotic, we may be warranted in taking it. Be that as it may, the fault seems not to lie in the claim that there are constraints on self-mastery but rather with the further claim that the victim should be forced to be free.[9]

Accordingly, we should first of all be very careful not to dismiss the critical arguments of opponents on the grounds that they lack positive freedom, for this not only deprives them of their standing as moral agents but also insulates our own view from criticisms they might make, which often will deserve consideration. In fact, such a device can be used as a political weapon to avoid criticism in the first place. Second, even in the perhaps infrequent cases when political opponents do lack positive liberty, it does not follow that they should be forced to be free. Berlin is right to warn us of the dangers of this road to tyranny. Rather, we need to consider noncoercive measures to raise critical awareness, such as increased exposure to education and to the argument of others. Perhaps there are occasions when people need to be forced to be free, as when a drug addict is made to go "cold turkey," but we need to keep in mind the abuses that might follow from such a conclusion when it is wrongly drawn. Refusing to consider others as responsible moral agents and reducing them to the status of slaves of their passions or of the social system to which they belong can be a way of depriving them of human dignity and human rights.

Nevertheless, the concept of positive liberty, while easy to misapply, is not inherently defective. There can and have been cases where human freedom has been severely restricted not by clear-cut external barriers to liberty, such as chains and iron bars, but by molding the victim's wants and desires to produce "happy slaves" who accept their plight regardless of its lack of justification or the damage it does to their self-respect and self-interest.

Finally, note that while Berlin's comments suggest a rather sharp distinction between positive and negative liberty, perhaps the distinction is not sharp or clear-cut. More to the point, perhaps all liberty claims, when fully unpacked, have both positive and negative components. For example, to fully specify my liberty to speak, we must fill in not only the lack of negative constraints on when and where I may exercise my liberty but also the positive acts my liberty protects. Does it protect only my liberty to discourse politely in limited forums? Does it include my freedom to offend others with my words or the liberty to burn my country's flag? Is it truly liberty if such acts arise from irrational desires, neuroses, or conditioning of which I am unaware? Surely a degree of self-mastery or autonomy is required for our acts to be ours rather than the result of outside influence, nonrational or irrational inner states, or coercion. A full account of a liberty claim, on this view, must include an account of both its positive and negative elements. "Whenever the freedom of some agent or agents is in question, it is always freedom from some constraint or restriction on, interference with or barrier to doing, not doing, becoming or not becoming something."[10] This conception of liberty often is called "triadic," since it implies that all liberty claims have three elements: an agent who is free or not free to act, a range of negative restrictions on action, and a range of positive acts, opportunities, or powers that are protected.

Constraints on Liberty and the Value of Liberty

Much controversy arises over what counts as a constraint on liberty, either as a negative restriction on action or as a barrier to autonomous decisionmaking. Should we view poverty, ignorance, lack of opportunity, and lack of health as constraints on liberty? If so, we might justify the liberal welfare state (as well as attempts to implement the Rawlsian difference principle discussed in chapter 4) as a means for implementing the right to liberty by freeing us from constraints imposed by poverty, ignorance, disease, and lack of genuine opportunities to improve our condition. Other theorists argue, however, that liberty ought to be distinguished from the conditions under which liberty is significant or valuable. Suppose, for example, that Smith will not be admitted to college because he does not realize that certain college preparatory courses must be taken in secondary school. In the first view, Smith may be considered to lack the freedom to attend college. His ignorance is a constraint on his freedom. In the second view, he is perfectly free to go. No one is stopping him from taking the appropriate courses. Unfortunately, because of his ignorance, his freedom is not of much value. But he is free, nevertheless. Similarly, someone in poverty is in this view perfectly free to buy a million-dollar home as there are no legal or explicit political constraints prohibiting him from doing so; it is just that his liberty is of no value to him since he lacks the resources to exercise it. Proponents of the second interpretation, particularly the kinds of libertarians we discussed in chapter 4, often criticize the activities of the welfare state as actually limiting liberty through excessive regulation. In this view, the welfare state spends so much time trying to improve the value of liberty that liberty itself gets lost in the shuffle.

This dispute seems largely verbal, however. While our sympathies lie with exponents of the broader interpretation in part because they correctly point out that such conditions as ignorance and poverty often result from human action, the truth of their point does not depend on the language used to describe it. If we consider poverty a constraint on liberty, then, all else being equal, if we want to extend liberty, we will want to eliminate poverty. But equally, if we believe that poverty diminishes the value or significance of liberty, then, if we value liberty, we will still want to eliminate poverty all else being equal, since liberty that lacks value seems of little use to anyone.

Thus, someone who distinguishes between liberty and the conditions of liberty need not be a defender of a laissez-faire free-market economy. Similarly, one can adopt the broad interpretation of liberty while defending laissez-faire. One would simply maintain that liberty from centralized government regulation is more important than liberty from poverty, ignorance, or lack of opportunity. Accordingly, whether one adopts the broad or narrow interpretation, the *verbal issue* of what is a constraint on liberty and what is a condition of liberty having value should be distinguished from the *substantive issue* of what conditions must be altered if liberty is to be extended (made more valuable).[11]

The following conclusions emerge from this discussion of the *concept* of political liberty.

1. Liberty claims are often elliptical and need to be filled in as indicated by the triadic schema.
2. Liberty should not be confused with other values, such as want satisfaction, with which it can conflict.
3. Restrictions on liberty need not be deliberately imposed.
4. Conditions such as poverty and ignorance can restrict liberty or (depending upon one's choice of vocabulary) significantly lower its value.

With these points in mind, some of the political and social issues concerning the scope and limits of individual liberty will now be considered.

LIBERTY: ITS SCOPE AND ITS LIMITS

Liberty is considered to be of great value because of its intimate connection with human dignity and self-respect, autonomy and individuality, free inquiry, and a host of other values. To be always at another's beck and call, to be always dependent on someone else's permission for action, to always be under constraints that severely limit one's ability to act (or even to choose to act) is incompatible with the development of self-respect and the retention of human dignity and autonomy. It also precludes the kind of growth and exploration that inquiry requires. Moreover, lack of freedom arguably is itself an intrinsic evil even apart from its connections with other related values since a life under restraints imposed by others arguably is one that all rational people will avoid all else being equal.[12]

However, one person's liberty can conflict with another's. Moreover, other values can conflict with liberty. One individual's liberty can conflict with another's welfare. Individual liberty may be threatened by the state when it attempts to improve our security by spying on suspected criminals. It is not surprising, then, that those in the liberal democratic tradition have been concerned with demarcating the proper scope or range of individual liberty. The problem is that of deciding just when it is justifiable for individuals, groups, and institutions to impose barriers on choice or action. For example, should someone be free to watch pornographic movies at home? At a movie theater? In a kindergarten classroom? Should free speech be extended to those who support racist and totalitarian ideologies? Does freedom include the freedom to advocate the elimination of freedom? Virtually all parties to the discussion agree both that some degree of liberty is desirable and that liberty is not without limits. As a prominent Supreme Court justice once noted, your freedom to swing your arm stops where my nose begins. But where should the line between permissible and impermissible exercises of liberty be drawn in more complex cases?

What is wanted is a criterion for distinguishing those areas in which restraint on others is permissible from those in which such restraint is illegitimate. John Stuart Mill proposed what is perhaps the most influential criterion of demarcation in his eloquent defense of individual freedom, *On Liberty* (1859*)*. In *On Liberty*, Mill declares that:

> the sole end for which mankind are warranted individually or collectively in interfering with the liberty of action of any of their number is self-protection. That the only purpose for which power can be rightfully exercised over any member of a civilized community, against his will is to prevent harm to others. His own good, either physical or mental, is not a sufficient warrant.[13]

This passage has long been cited in defense of civil liberties and individual freedom. Each person, it asserts, is to be granted a sphere of inviolability in which to do as he or she wishes. Paternalistic coercion for the good of the agent is ruled out. Interference with one person is justifiable only when necessary to protect others from harm. Self-regarding actions—those that affect only the agent—may not be interfered with. Other regarding actions, those that may lead to harm to others, are fair game for regulation in the interests of public safety.

Sometimes, the significance of a proposal becomes clearer if we understand what it is attempting to rule out. In asserting what has come to be called the *harm principle*, Mill is ruling out paternalistic interference with the liberty of persons—that is, limiting their freedom for their own good. Thus, if the harm principle is in effect, physicians cannot treat a patient without the consent of the patient even if they believe the patient might die if left untreated. So long as patients are competent and informed, interference with their liberty without their informed consent, even to preserve their lives, is unjustified according to the harm principle.

The harm principle prohibits more than paternalistic interference. It also forbids interference with behavior that is merely offensive to others, or with behavior that others believe is immoral but which is not harmful to third parties. Thus, even if the majority of the population finds homosexual relations offensive or even immoral, the harm principle forbids any prohibition of this kind of sexual conduct on the grounds of its offensiveness or alleged immorality alone.

If Mill is correct in suggesting that the only permissible ground for interference with liberty is prevention of harm to others, it becomes crucial to understand what counts as harm. How are we to understand "harm"? If we do not know what is to count as harm to others, we cannot apply the harm principle to begin with.

Perhaps physically hurting or causing someone pain is the criterion of harming. However, one can hurt or cause someone pain without harming them, so this proposal fails. For example, a dentist may hurt someone when filling a cavity, but the dentist is helping and not harming the patient. Likewise, someone may be harmed without being physically hurt or being caused to experience a painful sensation, for example, by having valuable possessions stolen.

Harm seems to be a broader notion than that of physical hurt or pain. We will assume here that interests delimit harm. To harm X is to damage X's interests.[14] Since it normally is not in one's interest to be physically hurt or caused to experience pain, physically hurting or causing pain normally are ways of harming. But they are not the only ways. Insulting, excluding, discriminating against, and degrading are other ways of harming that need not involve physical hurt or pain. While the concept of an interest is far from clear, an interest at least seems to be something necessary for carrying out our actual or potential desires, or for securing our good. Understood in this way, the harm principle states that interference with anyone's action is justifiable only when necessary to prevent damage to the interests of others.

But is the distinction Mill attempts to draw between self- and other-regarding actions viable? Aren't all acts really other-regarding? Even the reading of a book in the privacy of one's own home can change one's character in a way that is ultimately detrimental to others. Thus, Mill's contemporary James Fitzjames Stephen, maintained that:

> the attempt to distinguish between self-regarding acts and acts which regard others is like an attempt to distinguish between acts which happen in time and acts which happen in space. Every act happens at some time and in some place, and in like manner every act that we do either does or may affect both ourselves and others.[15]

Mill is not without reply to this objection. He acknowledges, for example, that acts performed in the privacy of one's home might constitute a bad example for others who learned of them. The problem this raises for Mill's position is that the distinction between self- and other-regarding actions seems to collapse if even acts performed in private contexts can affect others. Mill rejoins, however, that if the example is truly a bad one, others, seeing the harm brought about to the agent, will not follow it.[16] This particular reply, however, seems weak since it rests on the questionable empirical claim that people do not follow bad examples.

Perhaps a better rejoinder available to Mill is that the original private act does not cause harm directly. Rather, harm is caused by other people—namely, those who have chosen to follow the bad example of the original agent. Thus, suppose X is influenced by Y's habit of getting drunk in private and gets drunk and then drives. It is X's public behavior, driving while intoxicated, that may be criminalized and punished, not Y's private drinking habits.

On this view, for an act to be other-regarding, it must cause harm directly rather than merely influence another free agent to choose to do wrong. In a similar fashion, Mill denies that long-range, indirect consequences of an action render it other-regarding. He distinguishes harmful consequences of neglect of a duty from remote long-range consequences of ordinary human actions. If we were to interfere with the latter, no sphere of liberty would exist at all. Hence, "No person ought to be punished simply for being drunk: but a soldier or policeman should be punished for being drunk on duty."[17] It is only the immediate, direct risk of harmful consequences, not merely an indirect effect or influence, that renders an act other-regarding.

Whether the distinction between self- and other-regarding acts can be defended along such lines is controversial. However, even if these replies are satisfactory, the harm principle still faces many serious objections of other kinds. For example, some apparently harmless acts seem subject to criminalization: for example, someone enters your home without permission (trespass), takes a nap on your bed, but steals nothing and does no physical harm to anyone.[18]

Whether or not the harm principle can be defended against this and related objections, and whether alternate principles such as those formulated in terms of individual control over one's choices and use of one's faculties (personal sovereignty) are more satisfactory, continue to be discussed by philosophers and legal theorists. (A principle of sovereignty would characterize the sphere of liberty more in terms of an individual's entitlement to control his or her choices and use of personal capacities than in terms of preventing harm to others, but might also face the problem of determining the limits of each individual's liberty.)[19]

Rather than come to any final conclusion about the justifiability of the harm principle, which still dominates philosophical discussions of issues of liberty, we will consider attempts to override liberty of the person in three areas, namely, those concerning offensive acts and the enforcement of morality, paternalistic interference, and interference with freedom of thought and discussion. Although much of our discussion will be framed in terms of the harm principle, it can also be read as considering the limits of our freedom to make our own decisions and use our faculties, such as reason, independent of the control of others. Thus, the considerations we advance can be understood and examined even if one has doubts about the validity of the harm principle itself.

Offensive Acts and the Enforcement of Morality

Offensive Acts

The moral significance of the distinction between self- and other-regarding actions has been attacked by appeal to the idea of an offensive act. The claim here is that offensive acts may be prohibited simply because they are offensive to others. If this claim is true, Mill's harm principle must be modified since it only allows interference with harmful acts, not offensive ones.

However, there are difficulties with the view that offensive acts may be prohibited just because they are offensive. How many people must be offended? How offensive must the act be?

It would seem that on this view, almost any act might be subject to prohibition since almost any act might offend someone. For example, should we prohibit a philosophy professor from discussing criticisms of the classical proofs for God's existence because some believers might be offended? Should we prohibit homosexual relationships because some people are offended by them? Should we prohibit certain forms of music or art because those styles offend some people? The principle of prohibiting acts just because they are offensive is too broad, since almost any act might be offensive to some groups or individuals. Such an approach also is objectionable because it prohibits some conduct, such as free discussion in philosophy class, that ought to be allowed.

Sometimes, of course, offensive acts also are harmful. For example, degrading epithets directed at a minority group on a college campus may not only be offensive to many people but may harm those targeted by making them feel unwelcome or threatened, thereby decreasing their capacity to work effectively. We will discuss the case of hate speech more fully later in this chapter, but we acknowledge that where offensive action is also harmful in ways that violate the harm principle, regulation of such behavior may be permissible. However, it remains unclear that offensive actions may be regulated on grounds of their offensiveness alone.

But while there is danger in allowing regulation of offensive acts simply on grounds of their offensiveness, is it plausible to say offensiveness *never* is a ground for regulation? People may be deeply offended at witnessing what they regard as immoral or obscene acts and behavior. A deeply religious person may be significantly pained by seeing or hearing about what he regards as a sacrilegious speech, work of art, or play. Virtually anyone in contemporary Western societies would be disgusted by public defecation. In at least some such cases, the offense given can not only be upsetting but can induce rage, affect health, and perhaps even alter the course of a person's life, for example, as when someone makes it her or his life work to stamp out pornography. Does acceptance of Mill's harm principle imply that we must be prepared to be constantly offended in the name of liberty?

Perhaps individual liberty can be reconciled with the desire to be safe from constant offense. A first step at reconciliation would involve distinguishing easily avoidable from unavoidable offensive acts. If the act or behavior that is regarded as offensive can be avoided with a minimum of effort, it is not unreasonable to expect those who object to make the minimal effort required. Surely, liberty is of great enough value to outweigh the minimal effort required to avoid offense. Thus, having sexual relations on the subway may be legally prohibited. Sex between the proverbial consenting adults in private should be beyond the scope of the law. Again, nudity in a posted area that may be easily avoided by those likely to be offended surely is far easier to justify than allowing nudity on major public city streets.

How exactly is the boundary between avoidable actions and unavoidable ones to be drawn? Just how easy must an act be to avoid for it to be classified as avoidable and exactly how hard must an act be to avoid for it to be classified as unavoidable? It is doubtful if any precise formula can be constructed that then can be applied to cases in a mechanical fashion. In practice, the boundary should be established by democratically enacted statutes, as applied by the judiciary. However, there are limits on how far democracy may go here. These limits are set by the value of liberty itself. In view of the importance of individual liberty, the burden of proof is on those who would limit it to show at least: (a) that the allegedly offensive behavior cannot be easily avoided; (b) that it is not feasible to provide a restricted area where the behavior in question need not be witnessed by the general public; (c) that the behavior is widely regarded as deeply offensive in the community as a whole; and (d) that the allegedly offensive behavior is not the expression of an ideology or ideal that ought to be protected under the heading of free speech or does not involve legitimate artistic expression. We also should remember that since any act may offend someone, we cannot prohibit all offensive behavior without surrendering liberty entirely.

In practice, the courts often have appealed to the standard of what the community in general finds offensive, obscene, or revolting. The trick, which may not yet have been performed satisfactorily, is to characterize the relevant community properly. Presumably, one should not define the community so narrowly that the showing of the very same movie is allowed in one and prohibited in the other of two neighboring suburbs. Yet one might not want to define the community so broadly that what is permissible on 42nd Street in New York City must also be permissible in an Amish community.

The guidelines sketched above should be interpreted as placing a heavy burden of proof on those who would restrict liberty in order to minimize offense. Protecting liberty normally is more important than protecting people from being offended. This is a moral judgment concerning the importance of liberty that we hope is warranted in view of the arguments for human rights in chapter 3, and as developed in later sections of this chapter.

The Enforcement of Morality

In 1957, in Great Britain, the Wolfenden Report concluded that homosexual behavior between consenting adults in private should not be subject to criminal sanction. In the spirit of Mill's harm principle, the report argued that the law should not favor particular patterns of behavior or ways of life unless necessary to protect others. The Wolfenden Report reflects the view of those liberals who follow Mill in maintaining that the widespread belief that a practice is immoral, or that it is offensive to many, even if true, is not itself a reason for imposing criminal penalties. In this view, crime and sin are not coextensive categories. Prohibition and punishment, on the view as developed by Mill and defended by many liberals, may be used to prevent harm to others but not simply to enforce prevailing moral standards alone.

This liberal view was attacked in Mill's time by James Fitzjames Stephen and also was criticized sharply at the time of the Wolfenden Report by the distinguished British jurist Lord Patrick Devlin. Let us consider Devlin's case for the enforcement of morality, for it raises important issues of contemporary concern. For example, does society have a right to prohibit gay people from marrying each other because the majority believes that gay marriages are immoral?

Devlin on Enforcing Morality

The foundation of Lord Devlin's position lies in the claim that society has a right to protect its own existence. He then maintains that a common public morality is one necessary condition of a society's survival. But certain acts, even though they may not harm other individuals in Mill's direct sense, undermine the public morality. Accordingly, society has the right to regulate such acts in self-defense. "Society may use the law to preserve morality in the same way as it uses it to safeguard anything else that is essential to its existence."[20]

Devlin does not maintain that every act widely believed to be immoral should be legally prohibited. In fact, he favors maximal tolerance consistent with the security of society. The position Lord Devlin takes, then, is that "without shared ideas on politics, morals and ethics no society can exist."[21] This central core of the public morality, which is essential to society's very existence, can and should be protected by the criminal sanction. In this way, Devlin's position has some resemblance to that of the communitarians whose views we discussed earlier since he is defending the right of community to preserve essential elements of its way of life through its legal system.

Hart's and Dworkin's Counterattack

There is a serious problem for Devlin, however, which critics have not hesitated to exploit. The problem is this: How are those elements of the public morality essential for society's survival to be distinguished from those elements unessential for society's survival?

Devlin responds that the proper test is the reaction of the "reasonable man." The reasonable man or woman should not be confused with the rational one:

> He is not expected to reason about anything, and his judgment may be largely a matter of feeling. . . . For my purpose, I should like to call him the man in the jury box, for the moral judgment of society must be something about which, any twelve men or women drawn at random might after discussion be expected to be unanimous.[22]

It is this feature of Devlin's position that has drawn fire from such liberal legal theorists and prominent contributors to recent legal philosophy and jurisprudence as H. L. A. Hart and Ronald Dworkin. Hart and Dworkin argue that Devlin is confused about the nature of morality. Hart maintains that if all that Devlin means by "morality" is widely shared feelings of indignation, intolerance, and disgust, there is no justification for giving such prejudices the status of law. Rather, Hart asserts that "the legislator should ask whether the general morality is based on ignorance, superstition, or misunderstanding . . . and whether the misery to many parties, the blackmail and the other evil consequences, especially for sexual offenses, are well understood."[23] In a similar vein, Ronald Dworkin maintains that Devlin has not distinguished moral convictions from personal prejudices. At the very least, moral convictions must be based on reasons rather than emotion, must be arrived at autonomously, and must pass minimal standards of evidence and argumentation. The trouble with Devlin's position, Dworkin tells us, "is not his idea that the community's morality counts, but his idea of what counts as the community's morality."[24]

In other words, Hart and Dworkin fear that society's worst prejudices and most irrational phobias may be supported under Devlin's banner of the enforcement of a public morality. On the other hand, does it follow that simply because Devlin's position can be abused that it is never justifiable to legally prohibit acts simply on grounds of their immorality?

Reflections on the Debate

In our view, the criticisms of Devlin by Hart and Dworkin have considerable force. Devlin, for example, seems committed to prohibiting interracial handholding if a randomly selected jury in a segregated racist society would find such behavior intolerable. Surely, Devlin's critics are right in contending that the "reasonable man" is not the proper source of wisdom on the nature of the public morality. But then, Devlin is left without means of distinguishing essential from unessential elements of the public morality. He relied on the "reasonable man" to make the distinction but that reliance is unwarranted.

However, Devlin and his critics do seem to agree on one point—namely, that *if* essential aspects of the public morality could be identified, they may be protected by the law. But surely there are enormous problems about identifying the essential aspects. Social scientists might tell us what people believe are essential but this would not show if such beliefs are correct. Who is to be the final arbiter? Do we want physicians making the decision? Philosophers? CEOs of major corporations? Labor leaders? No answer of this kind seems convincing. Perhaps we ought to appeal to the democratic process, the decision of the majority of all the people. But doesn't this bring us right back to Devlin's "reasonable man" standard, one that has already been rejected as inadequate?

One suggestion, one we ourselves made in an earlier edition of this book, is that the whole issue can be avoided. Devlin and his critics each make an assumption

that can be rejected, namely, the assumption that a society is entitled to protect itself from any kind of assault on the essential elements of common public morality through use of the criminal sanction. Perhaps society has no such right. That is, it is always an open moral question whether any society *ought* to survive, where "survival" is understood merely in terms of "survival of an essential public morality." Perhaps the shared morality ought to be changed, even if this means bringing a new society into existence. According to this suggestion, Devlin, and perhaps even Hart and Dworkin, do not clearly distinguish between legitimate and illegitimate methods for bringing about change. Respect for others forbids forcing change down their throats. Society surely has the right to protect its members against coercion. On the other hand, as Joel Feinberg points out:

> a citizen works legitimately to change public moral beliefs when he openly and forthrightly expresses his own dissent, when he attempts to argue, persuade and offer reasons and when he lives according to his own convictions with persuasive quiet and dignity, neither harming others nor offering counterpersuasive offense to tender sensibilities.[25]

Thus, if one is really committed to the legitimacy of change through the democratic process, one must be prepared for public debate and decision on what the public morality ought to be. (We discuss issues of democracy in the next chapter.)

While we still think this point has considerable merit, we point out that it does not settle the issue of whether it is ever permissible to prohibit action solely on grounds of its alleged immorality. It is one thing to say that the nature of public morality should be debatable. It is quite another to say that no element of the public morality ever can be legally protected. Even liberal academics probably would want to enforce the moral standards necessary for preservation of academic communities, such as respect for evidence and scholarship and censure of plagiarism, while acknowledging that those standards can be criticized and discussed within the academic community. But, some social conservatives may argue, if the academic community has the right to enforce its academic ethic in the name of preserving academic communities, why doesn't the broader community have the same right to preserve its most sacred standards as well? Thus, social conservatives may argue, a prohibition of gay marriages can be debatable and legally enforceable at the same time. If this rejoinder has force, Devlin's views may not be so easy to dismiss as liberal critics, ourselves included, have thought.

However, we also need to make sure the force of the Hart-Dworkin critique has been properly appreciated. Their point may well be not simply that it is hard to distinguish the enforcement of morality from the enforcement of personal or community prejudice. Rather, it may be that if some factor like harm to others or infringement of individual autonomy is not involved, the appeal to morality is in principle nothing more than an appeal to prejudice. What distinguishes a moral argument from mere personal preference is that moral argument appeals to reasons that can be impartially appreciated and approved. But then such reasons must be provided. Devlin's response is that the continued survival of the community is such a reason, but there must be a moral case that the community is worth preserving. Does the continued survival of a community that is founded on racism and bigotry automatically merit preservation? Ultimately, it seems that the kind of reasons that must be provided involve such factors as human welfare, preservation of rights, and protection from harm and not simply enforcement of morality itself.

Thus, briefly consider the debate over whether gay marriages ought to be permitted by law. Gay rights advocates often defend the claim that such marriages ought to be legal on grounds of equality and antidiscrimination. Why should gays have fewer rights than anyone else simply because of sexual preference? Isn't the right to marry a human right? Are opponents simply homophobic?

If opponents simply were to argue that gay marriage should be prohibited because it is immoral, without giving any further reason for their view ("Why is it immoral?" "It just is!"), it would appear as if they were trying to enshrine their personal prejudices into law. However, opponents may have other arguments they can present for public debate. For example, they might argue that marriage is a special institution with some specific functions (namely, to promote monogamous relationships most suitable for the rearing of children) and deny that homosexual couples could successfully fit into this paradigm.

Proponents of gay marriage might rejoin that couples who intend to remain childless are allowed to marry and that gay couples are permitted to adopt children, so the conservative argument is specious. Conservatives may reply that their point is not that every marriage must produce children but that special preference may be granted to a practice, heterosexual marriage, the main and usual point of which is to raise a family. Proponents might reasonably counter that gay partners may have just as much of a desire to raise a family, and do it just as well as straight couples.

What is relevant about this debate for our discussion of liberty is that each side should appeal to factors such as the welfare of children and consistency in applying the law that are topics for public debate and assessment rather than appealing to intuitive and perhaps groundless and prejudicial feelings of Devlin's "reasonable man."

Religious Belief and Community Morality

What of those citizens whose objection to some social practices, such as gay marriage, is based neither on pure emotion that amounts to prejudice or on reasoned argument reached through impartial consideration? Rather, these citizens may base their belief on their religious views, including their reading of holy texts or scriptures.

Is it proper to support laws, including criminal sanctions, for what might be regarded as a sin according to a particular religious perspective? Is there an obligation or duty of citizens who have strong religious views to argue using only reasoning that their fellow citizens can accept, or can they simply assert their religious views? These issues are especially vexing in pluralistic societies where the religious views of citizens differ, and may even conflict on many points, and where many have no religious views at all. In fact, in his later work (which we discuss more fully in chapter 7), John Rawls has argued that perhaps the major problem for liberal democratic societies concerns the following question: "How is it possible that there may exist over time a stable and just society of free and equal citizens profoundly divided by reasonable though incompatible religious, philosophical and moral doctrines?"[26] The violence between Sunni and Shiite Muslims in Iraq and struggles between Catholics and Protestants in Northern Ireland give dire warning of what can ensue if Rawls's question cannot be answered.

Some philosophers in the liberal tradition have argued that controversial religious, moral, and philosophical beliefs that cannot be debated within the confines of reasoned critical inquiry, perhaps because they are based on alleged revelations available only to true believers, should be bracketed in public discourse. As Rawls puts it, we must distinguish "between a public basis of justification generally acceptable to citizens . . . and the many nonpublic bases of justification belonging to the many comprehensive doctrines and acceptable only to those who affirm them."[27]

Why should believers subject themselves to the restraint suggested by Rawls and refrain from voicing their religious values in public debate unless they can provide a basis for them in the kind of reasonable public discourse open to all? Such a restraint may prevent them from voicing the deepest aspects of their conscience and perhaps load the dice in public discussion against their point of view.

In response, two sorts of replies can be given. First, it would be unreasonable to expect fellow citizens, especially those whose deepest religious values conflict with those of the first group, to simply surrender their own religious convictions in the face of a rival view of revelation of scripture. A second related consideration is that those with whom we disagree on fundamental moral issues are also free agents and deserve our respect as such. In terms of the moral framework developed in this book, they have a human right not to have deep moral values or religious convictions imposed on them from the outside. Surely it is unreasonable and unjust for you to expect me to abandon my religious convictions on a moral issue simply because you assert that is want God wants, even though my religion teaches the opposite. Rawls himself, as we discuss in chapter 7, believes it is possible to build what he calls an overlapping consensus on political values, such as respect for our fellow citizens as free and equal beings, even if we cannot agree on some fundamental philosophical issues.

Is bracketing of those beliefs that cannot be defended in reasoned public discourse (using ordinary tools of empirical inquiry, logic, and elements of moral reasoning such as impartiality that are open to all) morally required? Do those who refuse to bracket behave immorally?

An effective argument can be made that failure to bracket those of our opinions that cannot be defined within public reason is *not* immoral. One line of argument, advanced by Christopher Eberle, suggests that we must distinguish between the duty of a citizen to try to find reasoning that is accessible to reasonable people within critical discourse and the duty to refrain from political activity on behalf of one's religiously based views if the attempt to use reasonable discourse fails.[28] In other words, citizens should try out of respect for the freedom and equality of others to find common bases of argument to employ in debate with their fellow citizens. However, they need not refrain from acting on their own commitments should it prove impossible to find such common grounds of reasoned inquiry (or even if reasoned inquiry finds against their views which ultimately are based on alleged divine revelations).

We agree with Eberle that it is not immoral for people to continue to assert their religious views in cases where the appeal to reasoned inquiry breaks down. However, we point out that it surely is unreasonable to expect others to give up their own deep convictions simply on the basis of a claim to revelation or an interpretation of holy texts that they themselves reject. Hence, if liberal democracy, and the human rights on which it is grounded, especially freedom of conscience, are to survive, public discourse and appeal to kinds of argumentation theoretically open to all should have a fundamental place in the political order that simple appeal to religious revelation, no matter how firmly believed, does not.

Summary

We have been discussing whether the alleged immorality of a belief or action is sufficient grounds for legally prohibiting it. While we are not prepared to rule out entirely the immorality of an act or kind of act as a ground for prohibiting it, especially where a community tries to protect what it *reasonably* regards as its core values (and these values actually are morally defensible), we conclude that a heavy burden of proof rests on proponents of such prohibition to show that their conception of immorality is not merely personal prejudice or preference. Moreover, if the core values of a community cannot be defended through public debate in democratic forums, it is not clear that the community's code should be preserved rather than changed. Accordingly, unless this heavy burden of proof is met, the immorality of an act or kind of act is not by itself a reason for prohibiting it through the legal system. However, it may be that in some cases, the burden of proof can be met. Thus, we view the harm principle (or the alternate approach based on a principle of respect for individual sovereignty over belief, choice, and use of one's faculties) as providing the framework for discussion about the grounds for limiting liberty, a framework that may be abandoned only for the weightiest of reasons, but not as an absolute principle that must be adhered to without exception no matter what.

Paternalistic Interference

Paternalistic interference is interference for the benefit of the agent whose liberty is infringed upon. Its aim is the good of the person coerced, or at least the prevention of harm to that person, not the prevention of harm to others. According to both the harm principle and the idea of individual control or sovereignty over one's choices and faculties, paternalistic interference is unjustified, at least where competent adults are involved. But is such a view acceptable?

Examples of allegedly paternalistic interference range from suicide prevention and involuntary confinement of mentally ill but not dangerous patients to passage of statutes requiring motorcycle riders to wear helmets and automobile occupants to wear seat belts, to refusing to serve ice cream to dinner guests who suffer from high cholesterol in spite of their expressed desires to the contrary. To be sure, such interference need not always be paternalistic. Accident victims may have to be cared for at the public expense, for example, so the statutes requiring helmets and seat belts can be viewed as protecting the public from undue medical costs. For the moment, however, let us consider whether such statutes, and other similar kinds of interference, are justifiable when they are paternalistic in character. Perhaps this issue can best be explored by considering in detail a kind of intervention that is often regarded as both paternalistic and justified, namely, intervention to prevent suicide.

Paternalism and Interference with Suicide

Suicides are not always or even usually self-regarding. Loved ones, dependents, and associates of the victim frequently are liable to harm. Accordingly, in a number of cases, intervention may be justified on other-regarding grounds. However, even here, it is doubtful if extensive, lengthy interference with freedom is justifiable on other-regarding grounds alone. The loss of liberty may outweigh the benefits received. (In any case, a person who is suicidal over extended periods of time is unlikely to be helpful to family, friends, and associates.) So, while remembering that suicide prevention often can be justified on other-regarding grounds, it is also well to remember the costs of ruling that a person's life is really not his or her own but is under the control of others. The case that is of interest here, however, is that of suicide that does not harm others. Is purely paternalistic interference with a potential suicide justifiable?

Most of us will be moved in two apparently conflicting ways on the issue of the legitimacy of suicide prevention. On the one hand, at least in cases where either there are no dependents or dependents are unlikely to be seriously harmed, we are inclined to say that a person's life is that person's own business. At least in cases where suicide is unlikely to involve harm to others, interference seems to imply that the agent in question is really like a child, unable or unwilling to make responsible decisions. On the other hand, it seems to show a callous disregard for the value of human life to merely stand by and do nothing. Is there any way to reconcile these two opposing views?

One strategy of reconciliation is to restrict the applicability of the harm principle so that it allows at least some kinds of suicide prevention. Mill himself suggests one such approach when he declares that:

> It is, perhaps, hardly necessary to say that this doctrine is meant to apply only to human beings in the maturity of their faculties. . . . Liberty, as a principle, has no application to

any state of things anterior to the time when mankind have become capable of being improved by free and equal discussion.[29]

This passage suggests a position according to which intervention with another's action in order to prevent suicide is justifiable where there is reason to believe the agent in question has not made a rational, responsible decision.

How might one fail to make such a decision? For one thing, a person might be in the grip of an abnormal, highly emotional mental state, for example, anxiety or depression. While in such a state, suicide might seem a desirable alternative. However, if the person were to return to normal, suicide no longer would seem acceptable. Surely it is justifiable to intervene in such cases to make sure that a person's decision to commit suicide is one that has been given sufficient consideration and examination. To allow a fleeting desire or an unusual emotional state to bring about such an irrevocable decision is to ignore the agent's own rational plan of life that might be adhered to given further opportunity for reflection. As one proponent of intervention has declared of the proverbial businessman on the ledge of a tall building, "He is on the ledge rather than in his office because he wants to jump. But he is on the ledge rather than in the air because he wants to live."[30] Moreover, the potential suicide might not just be in the grip of a fleeting depression or an abnormal mood. Such a person may be highly neurotic, mentally ill, or under the grip of a recurring compulsive desire. In such cases, it may be doubted whether the person involved has decided to commit suicide at all. Suicide becomes more like something that happens to one rather than something one does and so the act of attempting suicide is not the kind of behavior the harm principle (or the idea of individual sovereignty over our choices and faculties) was intended to protect.

Care must be exercised, however, in avoiding two kinds of mistakes. First, it should not be concluded that simply because a person is a potential suicide, that person necessarily fails to be rational or responsible. This would be to rule out the possibility of a rational, responsible suicide by definition. Such a move is trivial for it can alter only what we call the facts, not the facts themselves. We would simply have to invent a new word to refer to rational, responsible agents who take or attempt to take their own lives. The danger here is that of mistaking linguistic legislation for fact and on the basis of such a confusion, interfering with the freedom of autonomous agents. Second, one must be wary of too extensive interference in the lives of potential suicides. Thus, it seems incompatible to say both that a patient's mental state is fleeting or abnormal and that the patient must be confined for long periods of time. Intervention of some preliminary sort may be justified in all cases of potential suicide as a fail-safe device, designed to allow the agent to think through his or her situation or to provide counseling. But the assumption that an agent is not rational or responsible can be overridden in particular cases. Indeed, when the person in question is suffering from a painful terminal disease, failure to allow suicide may not only unreasonably infringe on liberty but may be just plain cruel as well.

On the other hand, as recent discussions of the permissibility of euthanasia have brought out, by making suicide, including physician-assisted suicide, too easy an alternative to obtain, pressure may be brought on seriously ill patients who would not otherwise do so to ask for euthanasia.[31] Their decision, in such a case, may be coerced rather than voluntary. (It should be noted, however, that we already allow patients to refuse lifesaving treatment even though this may create pressure on some patients to reject treatment in order to reduce health care costs for others.)

The burden of the discussion so far is that individuals who are competent and autonomous ultimately have the moral right to control their own lives, so long as the rights of others are respected. But can't this reasoning be carried too far? For example, does it imply that a person should be allowed to contract into slavery? Suppose, for example, some individuals would be willing to become slaves in return for financial benefits for their families. It might seem as if such an act should be permitted under some circumstances. Interference might be justified to ensure that the agent is rational and autonomous. But once such a conclusion is established, and the subject freely contracts into perpetual slavery, there would seem to be no grounds for interference.

While some extreme libertarians might be willing to allow even slavery contracts, we suggest that the reasoning justifying such contracts fails. Moreover, the reasoning suggesting that suicide sometimes may be permissible and the reasoning suggesting that slavery contracts ought to be permitted are not really parallel after all. The decision to commit suicide, especially when motivated by a desire to escape the ravages and indignities of a painful terminal illness, can itself be an expression of autonomy and dignity. Suicide may be contemplated because illness or some other evil would rob the subject of autonomy and dignity. Without these, the subject believes, life is not worth living. To contract into slavery, however, is to choose a life without autonomy or dignity. While suicide can be committed out of respect for such values, the decision to become a slave represents their abandonment. Hence, we suggest that the harm principle and respect for sovereignty of the individual are overridden in cases where the agent would choose such extreme degradation that the very values of human dignity and respect for persons are irrevocably abandoned.

We also point out that it is highly unlikely a person would voluntarily enter into slavery. Rather, slavery contracts are most likely to be signed by poor people anxious to protect their families from the ravages of poverty at almost any cost to themselves. It is at best extremely doubtful that such contracts in such circumstances could be entered into freely rather than under duress. (It is also possible, however, that suicide might seem attractive because of external pressures, such as the desire on the part of terminally ill patients to spare their family the costs of medical care, and for this reason it is important that strong procedural safeguards are in place to prevent subtle forms of coercion.)

Extension to Other Cases

This discussion of suicide prevention suggests that the following are acceptable principles of paternalistic interference.

1. One may paternalistically interfere with another in order to ensure that that person's behavior is autonomous.
2. One may paternalistically interfere with the behavior of nonresponsible persons, for example, children or the severely depressed and disturbed.
3. One may paternalistically interfere with the behavior of others in order to prevent acts which (a) irrevocably commit the agents to situations or ways of life which are seriously harmful to them, and (b) which commit such agents to abandonment of the very values of rationality and autonomy that justify the concern for liberty in the first place.

These principles constitute guidelines that indicate the sort of considerations relevant to justification of paternalistic interference. Each, we suggest, is compatible with the harm principle and individual autonomy and sovereignty. The first principle allows interference to ensure that the agent's behavior is truly free and autonomous. The second principle makes clear that paternalism is permissible when the individuals being interfered with are not competent to decide for themselves. The third principle maintains that paternalism may be justified to prevent competent agents from irrevocably abandoning the very values of rationality and autonomy that support both the harm principle and individual freedom to decide for ourselves how our own life is to be lived.

How might these principles apply in practice? We can give only some brief suggestions here that indicate how the principles might apply to more complex cases. Mountain climbing, for example, although risky for the participants, could not be interfered with justifiably. Normally, mountain climbers are autonomous rational agents. Although the decision to climb may turn out to be harmful, in the sense of clause (a) of the third principle, it surely does not represent an abandonment of autonomy and rationality or self-respect. The decision to participate in an activity like mountain climbing that, although dangerous and requiring great skill, gives participants a sense of achievement and exposes them to the beauty and majesty of our world not only is an intelligible decision but often may be an admirable one as well.

On the other hand, a more plausible, if not fully satisfactory, case can be made for legislation that requires that seat belts be worn in motor vehicles. The failure to wear such belts is more often a matter of lack of proper habits than conscious choice. The third principle, however, does seem to sanction interference with activities that will lead to drug addiction. Heroin addicts, for example, certainly seem to run afoul of both 3a and 3b.

In *On Liberty*, Mill maintained that

> the human faculties of perception, judgment, discrimination, feeling, mental activity and even moral preference are exercised only in making a choice. . . . The mental and the moral, like the muscular powers, are improved only by being used. . . . He who lets the world, or his own portion of it, choose his plan of life for him, has no need of any other faculty than the ape like one of imitation.[32]

Those who find a society of apelike mimics abhorrent have good reason to be skeptical of paternalistic intervention. However, such skepticism admits of justified exceptions where paternalism is designed to protect the autonomy of the agent in the long run.[33]

FREEDOM OF THOUGHT AND DISCUSSION

The second chapter of *On Liberty* is entitled "Of the Liberty of Thought and Discussion." It is perhaps the most eloquent and moving defense of virtually absolute freedom of thought and discussion available. In this chapter, Mill claims that interference with thought or discussion in itself is almost never warranted. "If all mankind minus one were of one opinion, mankind would be no more justified in silencing that one person than he, if he had the power, would be justified in silencing mankind."[34]

Mill's Defense of Freedom of Thought and Discussion

How might the harm principle apply to freedom of thought and its natural extension, freedom of speech? Exactly how Mill himself thought the harm principle would apply in this area is unclear. Perhaps he believed that virtually no harm to others could arise from freedom of thought and discussion. Such a view seems implausible, however. After all, speech can have effects. Thus, a radical tract can lead to a violent revolution, or the lyrics of a popular song can make a life devoted to drugs and violence seem attractive to vulnerable young people. Surely, in some such cases, the effects of speech are clearly harmful. Although it is possible to argue that such effects are indirect and hence outside the scope of the harm principle because the harm is mediated by the choice of autonomous agents, as when a person *decides* to take heroin after listening to a song glorifying drug use, another more plausible reading of Mill is possible.

Remember that Mill is a utilitarian. As a utilitarian, Mill needs to establish the usefulness of freedom of thought and discussion apart from any appeal to abstract rights or justice. If he were to reason as an act utilitarian, he might be able to argue that allowing freedom generally or normally is more useful that prohibiting it. However, as critics have rightly pointed out, this would not lead to any strong principle of liberty in this area but at best only to a presumption in its favor. As James Fitz-james Stephen pointed out in Mill's own time,

> the question whether liberty is a good or bad thing appears as irrational as the question whether fire is a good or bad thing. It is both good and bad according to time, place and circumstances. . . . We must confine ourselves to such remarks as experience suggests about the advantages and disadvantages of compulsion and liberty in particular cases.[35]

Stephen's point is that utilitarians cannot have a general principle supporting freedom of thought and expression but must look on each particular occasion at whether allowing such freedom produces better consequences than suppressing it. But such a contextual approach hardly amounts to a robust defense of liberty, since whether or not liberty is protected depends on contingent circumstances. Our Bill of Rights would hardly provide fundamental protections if each right were amended so that we could exercise it only when it was useful for the rest of society to allow us to do so.

However, Mill plausibly may be regarded as a *rule utilitarian*. If Mill can show that the rule or practice of allowing freedom of thought and discussion has utility, and that judging in each individual case whether to allow such freedom has disutility, he will have made a strong case for the general principle that freedom of thought and discussion should be inviolate. Moreover, such a defense might have great value for those who are not utilitarians but who, like ourselves, argue from a human rights perspective. This is because if Mill is a rule utilitarian, he construes utility rather broadly and in fact ends up appealing to some of the same factors that support a defense of fundamental individual rights. Thus, if we approach the issues of liberty of thought and discussion from the perspective of human rights and concern for the entitlement of individuals to control their own decisions and faculties (individual sovereignty), we might end up with conclusions similar to those of the thoughtful rule utilitarian. Let us examine this approach further.

Perhaps Mill's strongest and most famous argument along such lines is that freedom of thought and discussion are valuable because of their intimate connection with rationality. To be rational is at least in part to use procedures that enable us to detect our errors and arrive at more warranted belief. Mill held that open critical discourse involving freedom of thought and expression is the principal procedure that allows us to attain such a goal:

> the particular evil of silencing the expression of an opinion is that it is robbing the human race, posterity as well as the existing generation—those who dissent from the opinion still more than those who hold it. If the opinion is right, they are deprived of the opportunity of exchanging error for truth: if wrong, they lose what is almost as great a benefit, the clearer perception and livelier impression of truth produced by its collision with error.[36]

Without freedom of discussion, and the open exchange and criticism such discussion involves, we are deprived of the chance of having our errors corrected and condemned to hold the views we do hold as prejudices without rational foundation. This is precisely why it is important to present our views in rational debate before intellectually diverse critics. Just as a sports team proves its mettle by defeating worthy opponents, a belief or claim is tested by exposure to the objections of worthy critics. Free discussion is the mechanism for detecting and correcting error, and for providing support and understanding for those views that emerge from critical inquiry unscathed. Institutions and practices that permit and encourage free inquiry and discussion provide the framework within which our views can be supported or refuted. "Complete liberty of contradicting and disproving our opinion is the very condition which justifies us in assuming its truth for purposes of action."[37] On the other hand, if an opinion is protected from criticism by the suppression of dissent, its adherents have no basis for claiming it to be justified, for they have not submitted it to rigorous testing.

Mill's first premise of his defense of freedom of thought and discussion is that such freedom is necessary for the correction of error and appreciation of truth. As a utilitarian, Mill also must establish a second premise, namely, that correction of error and appreciation of truth are useful in some utilitarian sense of that term. Presumably, Mill would argue that the process of inquiry would allow society to avoid serious error by exposing mistaken reasoning or dubious assumptions. Hence, it is more likely that a free society will choose optimal policies than it is that an unfree society will make such choices. Moreover, Mill also argues forcefully that freedom of thought and discussion leads to a diversity of points of view, which in turn produces inventiveness and independence among the citizenry. New ideas produced by an inventive and independent people lead to social, technological, scientific, and intellectual progress, which in turn benefits the society as a whole.

Assessment of Mill's Argument

While we are sympathetic to Mill's approach as developed above, we question whether rule utilitarianism alone provides the strongest defense for liberty of thought and expression. First, as we saw earlier in our discussion of utilitarianism in chapter 2, there is the danger of rule utilitarianism collapsing into act utilitarianism due to the weight of thousands of exceptions. That is, should exceptions to the rule permitting liberty of thought and discussion be allowed on utilitarian grounds alone? This issue has been at the center of public debate since 9/11 and the War on Terrorism as Americans have debated how to balance the competing roles of liberty, privacy, and government surveillance in the interests of national security and public safety. Moreover, does utility itself provide a firm enough foundation for freedom of thought and discussion? Are we really sure that a free society will always be happier in a utilitarian sense than an unfree one? Those who believe freedom is a human right might want to place it on a more secure foundation.

However, it is important to remember that Mill is not always best read as if he supported traditional utilitarian theories. In fact, we suggest that one of Mill's best arguments is not in the mainstream utilitarian tradition at all. Rather, although he often equivocates, Mill suggests that the development of critical, autonomous individuals, not simply pleasure in a hedonistic sense, is the intrinsic good to be produced. For Mill, "The worth of a state in the long run is the worth of the individuals composing it."[38] Social institutions are to be judged according to the kind of individuals they develop. Thus, even if freedom does not always produce the most favorable attainable ratio of happiness to unhappiness, free discussion does promote the creation of critical, autonomous individuals. Such people are developed, Mill believed, through participation in free and open critical discussion and inquiry. Since the goal is development of an atmosphere where such individuals can grow and flourish, Mill held that an absolute prohibition on interference was justified.

Whether Mill ever unequivocally adopted such a position is unclear, although he surely was attracted by it. In any case, we suggest that a stronger defense of liberty of thought and discussion can be made along such lines rather than through appeal to quantitative considerations of utility.

A very important line of argument for a human right to liberty, which also can be understood independent of utility, can be developed with help from Mill's suggestion that critical inquiry is the medium through which our opinions are justified. According to this line of argument, the right to individual liberty is best justified by showing it to be a precondition for the promotion and protection of personal autonomy. Whether or not liberty best promotes the overall general happiness, without it individuals cannot determine the course of their own lives. Freedom of thought and discussion are particularly important aspects of human liberty. The exchange of ideas it protects provides the framework within which we can make informed and intelligent choices, influence the views of others by appealing to their own rational capacities, and function as autonomous and sovereign moral agents within a community of equals.

Finally, as Mill argued, a framework of rights that guarantees liberty of thought and discussion provides the very background within which claims can be examined and criticized. Without such a framework, it is doubtful if our views can be properly examined since they might well be insulated from serious challenge. To use the analogy we developed earlier, they would be like teams that always avoided competition with opponents that might provide a challenge. Just as such a team could not claim to be excellent, untested and unchallenged opinions have no reasonable claim to be justified. Liberty, then, constitutes the framework within which other claims can be rationally evaluated. It is a fundamental element of any acceptable political order, for without it we are in no position to critically examine the major choices before us or to rationally examine the moral foundations of the political order itself.

This implies that the best remedy for bad, misleading, erroneous, and oversimplified speech is more speech. Debate, discussion, and inquiry provide the context in which flaws in our own position or those of others can be detected and pointed out. By restricting speech, such flaws might never be detected and our system of belief never improved.

But even if freedom of thought and discussion is of fundamental value, it does not mean that such liberty can never be limited by other considerations. Liberty is not license. To better understand both the importance and the possible limits of liberty of thought and discussion, we will briefly consider a particularly controversial issue involving individual liberty: the recent attempts by some colleges and universities to prohibit what has come to be called hate speech through the passage of campus speech codes.

LIBERTY AND THE RESTRICTION OF HATE SPEECH

Unfortunately, recent years have seen a series of deplorable expressions of hate speech against racial, religious, and ethnic minorities, as well as women and gay people, on many of the nation's campuses. While we will not attempt to provide a precise definition here and doubt whether necessary and sufficient conditions can be provided, by "hate speech," we mean roughly the verbal or written expression of visceral hatred against distinct social groups, such as African Americans or Jews, employing epithets and slurs in a hostile, intolerant manner. For example, in January 1987 at the University of Michigan "unknown persons distributed a flier declaring 'open season' on blacks . . . referred to as 'saucerlips, porch monkeys, and gigabits.'"[39] Soon afterward, a student disc jockey allowed racist jokes to be broadcast on an on-campus radio station and a Ku Klux Klan uniform was displayed at a demonstration protesting the earlier events. Similar episodes directed against various social groups, denigrating their race, religion, gender, or sexual orientation, have taken place at far too many academic institutions throughout the country.

In an attempt to prevent some incidents and to protect members of the target groups from them some academic institutions promulgated speech codes designed to prohibit and punish hate speech on campus. Such codes restrict freedom of speech but do so to protect people from denigration based on their group membership. Does hate speech fall outside the realm of protected speech, or are speech codes an unjustified limitation on freedom of expression?

Speech Codes and Hate Speech

In order to focus our discussion, we will examine the code that was adopted by the University of Michigan in response to the incidents described above and which was challenged in the courts by an instructor at the university.

The code adopted by Michigan applied specifically to educational and academic areas such as "classroom buildings, libraries, research laboratories, recreation and study centers" and probably to university housing, although various public parts of the campus were exempted, as were publications sponsored by the university, such as the campus newspaper. In areas covered by the policy, persons were subject to disciplinary action for:

Any behavior, verbal or physical, that stigmatizes or victimizes an individual on the basis of race, ethnicity, religion, sex, sexual orientation, creed, national origin, ancestry, age, marital status, handicap, or Vietnam veteran status and that

a. Involves an express or implied threat to an individual's academic efforts, employment, participation in University sponsored extracurricular activities or personal safety: or
b. Has the purpose or reasonably foreseeable effect of interfering with an individual's academic efforts, employment, participation in University sponsored extracurricular activities or personal safety: or
c. Creates an intimidating, hostile, or demeaning environment for educational pursuits, employment, or participation in University sponsored extracurricular activities.

To help explain the code to members of the campus community, Michigan published an interpretative guide that contained the following examples of prohibited behavior.

- A flyer containing racist threats distributed in a residence hall.
- Racist graffiti written on the door of an Asian student's study carrel.
- A male student makes remarks in class like "Women just aren't as good in this field as men," thus creating a hostile learning atmosphere for female classmates.
- Students in a residence hall have a floor party and invite everyone on their floor except one person because they think she might be a lesbian.
- A black student is confronted and racially insulted by two white students in a cafeteria.[40]

Evaluation of the Michigan Code

How might colleges and universities who develop such speech codes justify their action? The first and perhaps most important consideration is protecting the victims from harm. While many people may maintain that "Sticks and stones will break my bones but names will never harm me," in fact the opposite seems true where hate speech is concerned. Racial epithets, for example, can cause great psychological stress to those they are directed at and make them fearful for their lives as well. This can affect their ability to work and function effectively as full members of the college community. "The symbols and language of hate speech call up historical memories of violent persecution and may encourage fears of current violence. Moreover, hate speech can cause a variety of other harms, from feelings of isolation, to a loss of self-confidence, to physical problems associated with serious psychological disturbance."[41]

In addition to harming students, hate speech can also wrong them by denying them equal opportunity to benefit from the academic institution they attend simply because of their race, religion, sexual orientation, ethnicity or some other educationally irrelevant factor. In other words, the targets of hate speech are being discriminated against. Moreover, the kind of discrimination in question is especially invidious since hate speech in effect states or implies that its targets are not fully persons and are not equal members of our moral community. In effect, hate speech, like racism, excludes its victims from the human race and from full and equal membership in the moral community. Surely, proponents of speech codes will argue, academic institutions have not only the right but also the duty to protect their students from being harmed and from being dehumanized. Therefore, they conclude, the imposition of speech codes like that implemented at Michigan is justified.

Is that conclusion warranted? Consider the case of *Doe vs. Michigan*, in which a graduate student at Michigan who wished to remain anonymous and who hence is known as "John Doe" successfully challenged the university's speech code in court. Doe's specialty was the study of the biological basis of individual differences in personality traits and mental abilities.

> Doe said that certain controversial theories positing biologically based differences between the sexes and races might be perceived as "sexist" and "racist" by some students and he feared that discussion of such theories might be sanctionable. . . . He asserted that his right to freely and openly discuss these theories was impermissibly chilled . . . [42]

In fact, as the courts pointed out, Doe had a basis for his fears since, as we have seen, the guide to the code published by the university specifically cited remarks made in class such as "Women just aren't as good in this field as men" as in violation of the code.

At this point, those disposed to favor the code might deny that Doe has the right to question the abilities of major social groups in class. After all, doesn't that create a hostile classroom environment in which members of those groups may have trouble learning precisely because their confidence in their own abilities has been undermined?

But then what other issues and questions also would be out of bounds? Could a critic of affirmative action say that it lowers the standards of those admitted to the school since that also might insult or undermine the confidence of beneficiaries of affirmative action policies? Could a philosophy professor maintain that adherence to a religion was an irrational superstition since such talk might create an intimidating or unfriendly atmosphere for religious fundamentalists? Could a psychiatrist argue that homosexuality was a disease?[43]

Proponents of the code might rejoin that their intent was not to create a politically correct atmosphere in which controversial issues could not be discussed but to prohibit slurs and insults directed against groups. However, it is not clear that the Michigan code draws a clear line between controversial political discourse and purely emotive slurs and epithets. In fact, the code prohibits verbal behavior that creates an "intimidating, hostile, or demeaning environment for educational pursuits." Unfortunately, words such as "intimidating," "hostile," or "demeaning" are just too vague to provide a reasonably clear boundary between controversial and possibly offensive intellectual discourse, which must be permitted if we are to have genuine intellectual disputes on important topics, and pure cases of hate speech that proponents of the code would assert fall outside the boundary of intellectual discussion.

A major problem with the Michigan speech code, then, is that it is both too vague and too broad. It is too vague because it is not clear how words such as "hostile" and "intimidating" are to be applied and too broad since it appears to rule out controversial (and possibly highly offensive) comments on issues that are under intellectual discussion.

Would the code be more defensible if it could somehow be amended to apply only to clear ethnic slurs, insults, and epithets? Even then, problems remain. We have already seen that there are problems with the view that speech or behavior should be prohibited simply because it is (or is believed by the majority to be) morally wrong or offensive. Yet speech codes, such as those of the University of Michigan, appear to prohibit racist, homophobic, anti-Semitic, and sexist speech simply because such speech is immoral or offensive.

Surely racist, homophobic, anti-Semitic, and sexist speech is wrong. Why shouldn't it be prohibited, then, on grounds of its wrongness? As we have seen, however, there are at least three major problems with enforcing morality in this way. First, where do we stop? Suppose the majority thinks homosexual behavior is morally wrong. Can it prohibit and punish such behavior? One problem with enforcing morality is that of whose morality is to be enforced. Second, can we clearly separate genuine moral positions from purely emotional reactions without appealing to some additional factor such as harm to others, unfairness, or violation of rights? As Hart and Dworkin argued against Devlin, without such a check, the criterion of enforcement of morality can too easily degenerate into enforcement of the prejudices of the majority. Third, as Mill argued, if we do not subject our views to challenge, we are in no position to assert they are justified. Consider Doe's point that men and women may not have equal capacities to engage in all areas of inquiry. How can we be justified in rejecting such a view without even examining it?

In addition, while there is an intuitive distinction between ethnic slurs and epithets on one hand and intellectual discourse on the other, it is not always easy to say where one ends and the other begins. Valuable debate is not always fully civil or polite. While we agree that civil debate is most likely to be productive, sometimes individuals believe they can get their point across only by being shocking or outrageous. It seems dangerous to us to cede to officials of major organizations, whether they are speaking for the state or the university, the power to draw lines here, since it will often be their own conduct that is at the center of the dispute. (We concede, however, that some lines do need to be drawn. Debate in the classroom normally should be civil and respectful of dissent, and disruptive verbal behavior in class or at a lecture may be prohibited and sometimes may warrant punishment.)

In addition, it is important to note that the Michigan speech code is not viewpoint-neutral. For example, it does not prohibit the use of epithets by feminists against traditionalists or by radicals against flag-waving patriots. Is dismissing someone's arguments by calling them "homophobic," or a "heartless Republican," or a "pro-life dogmatist brainwashed by the Church," or a "religious fanatic," or a "godless atheist who will burn in Hell," using epithets or slurs? Is dismissing the viewpoints of rural southern citizens by contemptuously referring to them as the "Bubba vote" or as "rednecks" allowable? Should the university favor one set of political positions and disfavor opposing views by prohibiting one set of alleged slurs while allowing others? As Judge Avern Cohen maintained in his opinion in *Doe*, "What the university could not do . . . was establish an antidiscrimination policy which had the effect of prohibiting certain speech because it disagreed with the ideas or messages sought to be conveyed."[44] The *Doe* opinion then goes on to quote with approval an important passage from the United States Supreme Court's decision in an earlier case protecting free speech.

> If there is any star fixed in our constitutional constellation, it is that no official, high or petty, can prescribe what shall be orthodox in politics, nationalism, religion, or other matters of opinion.[45]

The problem with speech codes such as the one examined in the Doe case is that they are overbroad, vague, and arguably partisan rather than content-neutral. While we agree that the harms caused by hate speech are real and serious, we do not believe for these reasons that codes such as the one at Michigan are justifiable forms of response.

Speech Acts, Narrow Speech Codes, and Civil Rights

While the Michigan code may be defective in the ways cited, perhaps we have not done justice to the case for some sort of regulation of hate speech. Thus, while we have emphasized the value of liberty, what about equality? As we have seen, hate speech results in some members of the academic community being treated as moral inferiors, as not full human beings. Aren't the targets of such speech entitled to some protection?

Moreover, considerations of free speech may not be all on one side. If members of less powerful groups are harassed by hate speech, they may feel threatened. As a result of such intimidation, they may be less likely to participate in the public life of the institution or even to attend. Hence, their contributions to open discussion are lost and we have a less diverse set of participants in debate than would otherwise be the case. In other words, by not limiting hate speech, we reduce the value and effectiveness of free and open inquiry far more than a narrowly tailored speech code would do. Indeed, this may be a reason for rejecting the requirement of content-neutrality; it unfairly assumes a level playing field when some groups on campus are more vulnerable than others.

Such considerations have led some writers to develop a parallel between hate speech and harassment. While the parallel is far from exact—for example, harassment usually is a pattern of behavior but hate speech may occur only once—it is worth considering further since regulating harassment is far less controversial than regulating the content of speech and expression. The main thrust of such an approach is that it would not be the content of the speech that is regulated but rather the act of directing certain "speech acts" at specifically targeted individuals.

Such an approach has been developed by Andrew Altman, a philosopher and law professor, who emphasizes the connection between his argument and the speech act theory developed earlier in the twentieth century by J. L. Austin at Oxford. Austin's main point was that by saying certain things in certain contexts, we also were performing certain acts. For example, by saying "I do" during a wedding ceremony, the bride and groom marry. By saying "I promise" in the appropriate circumstances, one promises.

Altman starts off with a statement by the writer Mari Matsuda, who claims that "racist speech is particularly harmful because it is a mechanism of subordination."[46] Altman suggests that such a comment is best understood as maintaining not merely that racist speech causes harm but that such speech *is* an act of subordination just as saying "I promise" in the right circumstances is promising. According to Altman, hate speech wrongs its targets by subordinating them and depriving them thereby of their equal standing as persons. However, as we have seen, just because such speech acts wrong others doesn't mean they can be regulated. Regulation of a narrow sort may be justified, Altman maintains, because of its connection with antidiscrimination and antiharassment legislation:

> The wrongs of subordination based on such characteristics as race, gender, and sexual preference are not just any old wrongs. . . . Historically, they are among the principal wrongs that have prevented—and continue to prevent—Western liberal democracies from living up to their ideals and principles.[47]

Altman's point is that just as the state can enforce civil rights and antidiscrimination legislation, universities may be permitted to regulate acts of subordination, which are, as well, a form of discrimination.

The harassment or subordination approach has implications quite different from speech codes such as the Michigan speech policy that are very broad in scope. Discrimination, harassment, and subordination injure specific individuals. For this reason, some proponents of the harassment approach, such as Altman, favor narrowly drawn codes that prohibit specific acts of subordination directed against specifiable individuals. The expression of ideas, however repugnant, is not punishable, but the subordination or harassment of identifiable individuals through hate speech is punishable.

The speech policy adopted by Stanford University in the 1990s is one that reflects Altman's approach. As drafted by law professor Thomas Grey, the Stanford policy provides that "'protected free expression ends and prohibited discriminatory harassment begins' at the point where expression of opinion becomes 'personal vilification' of a student on the basis of one of the characteristics stated in the policy."[48] More specifically, to fall under the policy, speech or other expression constituted harassment by personal vilification if it

a) is intended to insult or stigmatize an individual or a small number of individuals on the basis of their sex, race, color, handicap, religion, sexual orientation, or national and ethnic origin; and

b) is addressed directly to the individual or individuals whom it insults or stigmatizes; and

c) makes use of insulting or "fighting" words or nonverbal symbols.[49]

Insulting or fighting words and symbols are those "'which by their very utterance inflict injury or tend to incite an immediate breach of the peace,' and which are commonly understood to convey direct and visceral hatred or contempt for human beings on the basis" of the designated characteristics cited earlier.[50]

Assessing the Civil Rights Approach

The advantage of the approach suggested by Altman and expressed in the Stanford code is that it does not prohibit expression simply on the grounds that the majority does not like what is said, or even that the ideas expressed are grossly repugnant or immoral. As we have seen, to limit expression on such grounds is highly problematic. Rather, the approach we are considering limits expression of a narrowly circumscribed sort to protect the civil rights of the victims. Is this approach defensible?

Some critics might object to the very feature of the Stanford code that makes it attractive to Altman and Grey: namely, its narrowness. Thus, the 1987 racial incident at Michigan described earlier in which a flier was distributed declaring among other things "open season on blacks" might not be covered by the Stanford code since the element of personal vilification and face-to-face insults seems missing. Certainly, more general statements such as the posting of an anti-Semitic flier or the use of epithets directed generally against homosexuals or people of color also would not be covered for similar reasons. However, any speech policy that does cover such events, such as the Michigan speech code, is likely to be vague, overbroad, and non-neutral, so we do not favor rejecting the emphasis of the civil rights approach on such grounds.

There are two other criticisms of even narrowly drawn speech codes, based on the civil rights model, that we think must be given significant weight. First, considerable leeway is given to those whose job it is to enforce the speech policy to interpret such expressions as "insult," "stigmatize," and "insulting or fighting words."

While unfortunately there are many clear cases of the use of hate-laden epithets, nevertheless ceding to authorities the discretion to decide where the boundaries of permitted discourse end and violation of the rights of others begins is all too likely to have a chilling effect on speech in other areas. For example, suppose that during an argument on gay rights, some students use offensive language to express their personal view that gays are promiscuous and lack any kind of sexual morality. Just when do comments such as these constitute harassment or subordination rather than crudely expressed claims that need to be examined and questioned through free debate?

This point while important may not be decisive, however, since other policies, such as those prohibiting sexual harassment or campus disruptions, have similar areas of vagueness. However, while not decisive, the point suggests a second worry. Normally, policies such as those prohibiting sexual harassment or disruption of legitimate campus activities are not partisan. Democrats and Republicans receive the same protection from harassment, and both liberal and conservative rallies are protected against illegitimate interference. Students with conflicting political perspectives may debate each other freely in class. However, speech codes like the Stanford code are not content-neutral in the same way. For example, the Stanford code does not include speech that insults on the basis of class, so yelling at students that they are "rednecks" or "white trash" presumably would not be punishable.[51] Thus, the Stanford code does not apply evenly to all use of degrading and insulting forms of personal vilification.

This degree of partisanship may be defensible, as Thomas Grey has suggested, on the grounds that there are asymmetries of power among groups in our society. Thus, as Grey notes, "there are *no* epithets in this society at this time that are 'commonly understood' to convey hatred and contempt for whites *as such*."[52] People of color, gays, and other groups may be in a vulnerable and isolated position on many predominantly white campuses, or at least face special problems of adjustment that create educational inequities. It is this imbalance that the apparent "partisanship" of the Stanford code is designed to address.

Nevertheless, there surely is a case that our colleges and universities should not adopt policies that may punish one group of students for personal vilification using one set of epithets but not punish others for personal vilification using a second set of epithets, which also deeply wound the victims. Even if one agrees, as we do, that racial incidents directed against, say, African Americans reflect a unique history of oppression in America, and that some racial epithets have no antiwhite counterpart, it does not follow that educational institutions, let alone the state, should adopt a partisan speech code. Not only is lack of evenhandedness likely to breed resentment and make cooperative social union difficult to achieve, it elevates a particular set of moral and political perspectives to the level of official status, thereby insulating them to a significant degree from debate and challenge. As we have seen, such protection goes too far since it chills discussion and thereby undermines the very framework of debate under which such a position can be justified in the first place. Moreover, if the neutrality of a framework for discussion was replaced with overt partisanship, it is not necessarily the case that views regarded as progressive would dominate. Once it is permitted to institutionalize an orthodoxy, there is no guarantee that the orthodoxy one favors will actually win.

Moreover, and perhaps most important, in evaluating the case for policies restricting speech and expression, we need to keep in mind that the best remedy for bad speech almost always will be good speech rather than repression. Let us consider this point further.

Good Speech as a Remedy for Bad

Sometimes policies have unintended consequences that are more significant than the intended ones. In particular, while the imposition of speech policies may be intended to protect members of designated groups from harassment and subordination, they may have broader unintended consequences. For example, individuals may become fearful of expressing controversial views that may offend members of protected groups because they may fear (perhaps wrongly) that the code will be extended in a partisan way to silence their position. They also may fear the reaction of their peers who may regard them as "virtual" racists, homophobes, or anti-Semites. As a result, a whole range of debate over significant issues may be eliminated without anyone actually meaning to do so.

Perhaps even worse, truly objectionable views may simply be pushed underground. If such a view is expressed openly, it can be debated and refuted, but if it is circulated underground, it is more likely to survive until it explodes dangerously into the light of day. Generally, our best protection against hateful views is to debate them and expose their flaws, but speech codes unintentionally may make such debate virtually impossible.

Finally, members of protected groups may view speech codes as overly paternalistic, implying they are less able then others to defend themselves in open discourse. African Americans, Jews, gay students, and others may much prefer to stand up for their rights in free debate rather than be protected by the institution.

For these reasons, we conclude that even narrowly drawn speech codes are at best the last resort in the liberal democratic state. However, while we categorically reject the imposition of broad speech codes, such as the one at Michigan, we do acknowledge that narrow codes based on protection of civil rights are more difficult to evaluate and that their imposition may be justified in special circumstances. While we are troubled by the power they cede to officials and by their lack of neutrality, they avoid many of the difficulties of the broader approaches and may in some special contexts actually improve the climate for debate by protecting those who might otherwise be intimidated into silence.

However, while individuals are entitled to protection from harassment and subordination, such protection normally should be tied to freedom from threatening conduct and not be defined in terms of the content of the expression employed. In fact, we can distinguish two separate goals speech codes might have: (1) protection of individuals from harassment and from what Altman calls subordination; and (2) the prohibition of certain kinds of slurs and epithets. Problems arise when the two goals are blurred together because it may not be possible to define just the language that is to be forbidden in a politically neutral way. While it may not always be desirable or even possible to be neutral, neutrality is an important virtue in many contexts, particularly in colleges and universities, which must provide acceptable forums for broad and vigorous debate.[53] The problem with distinguishing between politically unacceptable and politically acceptable slurs and epithets is that the political perspectives of some groups are placed in a privileged position by institutions. (In fact, the Stanford code was rejected by state courts in California in 1995 on grounds of lack of content neutrality.) This is all too likely to limit the degree to which people will challenge the dominant perspective since they feel it is already officially entrenched, and that criticism of it may lead to punishment. It is also important to remember that once neutrality of a framework for discussion is replaced with partisanship, it may be the views we oppose or find oppressive that become officially entrenched.

Thus, while a *total* rejection of narrowly drawn speech codes is not justified, we suggest that proponents of their implementation in a given context face a burden of proof that we believe will be met only on very rare occasions. (For example, a campus climate may be so intimidating and hostile that open debate becomes at least temporarily impossible to carry on.) This does not mean hate speech against African Americans, gays, and other targeted groups should be tolerated but rather that in many contexts the best response is speech itself—for example, widespread condemnation of the acts of hate speech and broad-based expressions of support for the targeted groups. For example, a widely supported rally endorsing the equal rights of all members of the campus community might be part of an appropriate response to the hate incidents at Michigan. Remember, however, that some highly controversial comments might not consist of epithets and slurs but might have intellectual content, such as claims about alleged sex differences in mathematical abilities. These can be explored in the appropriate academic forums.

Political orthodoxies, however, must be avoided, even if they are our own orthodoxies, for we all lose when the very conditions of free and open debate which themselves make justification possible are limited and eroded.

THE PRIORITY OF LIBERTY: FREEDOM, WELFARE, AND SECURITY

The Conflict of Rights

The right to liberty is one among several fundamental rights that the good state ought to protect and implement. However, these rights can conflict. In such cases, where some rights claims must remain unfulfilled in order that others can be implemented, the choice is to be made by suitably constrained democratic procedures, as outlined in chapter 6 where we examine issues raised by democracy.

Influenced by John Rawls's work, philosophers have been paying increasing attention to what has been called the priority of liberty. Within the liberal tradition, liberty has always been assigned an especially fundamental place. Thus, we have already seen that in Locke's political philosophy, basic rights were rights to liberty from interference by others. Nozick's contemporary libertarianism seems to recognize only the right to negative liberty. Even many of those whose work defends nonmarket principles of distribution, such as Rawls, either give priority to liberty or argue that economic equality contributes to greater liberty.

In our view, when the right to liberty conflicts with rights to material prerequisites of a minimally decent human life, a choice must be made as to which gets priority. We see no grounds for saying liberty must always receive priority in all circumstances and all times and places, although we maintain, as did Rawls, that liberty is particularly fundamental once a minimally decent level of economic well-being has been achieved. However, we point out that since poverty, ignorance, and ill health can constitute barriers to liberty, or at least conditions that rob liberty of its value, there is no *necessary* conflict between liberty and economic redistribution. Liberty and equality can conflict, but they need not necessarily do so, and making people better off economically may also help enhance the degree of liberty (or the value of liberty) that they enjoy.

However, as we just suggested, our position does provide grounds for assigning a special priority to considerations of liberty. That is, it seems wrong, from a human rights perspective, to trade away the right to liberty for wealth or community and harmony, once one has already obtained material prerequisites of a minimally decent human existence. This is not a psychological assertion about what *causes* what. Rather, it is a *moral* claim to the effect that autonomy and the freedom to carry out one's choices are more *significant* constituents of a meaningful human life than is great affluence. Moreover, liberty provides the framework within which democratic debate can take place and within which we test our ideas by exposing them to critical review.

But aren't we just expressing our own personal preferences for a liberal society? Are other preferences, such as enforcement of a religious code by the state, entitled to equal weight? Are such preferences rationally binding on everyone?

In response, we would point to two considerations, both of which arise from points made by John Stuart Mill. First, the exercise of liberty is a major, perhaps the major, element in living a life of human dignity—of living as a moral person. Thus, would anyone really say that a society of affluent slaves who, while wallowing in luxury, were always at their master's call, led lives in which the values of human dignity and respect for persons were exemplified? Similarly, people would not be exercising autonomy if they lived in a rigid community in which traditions were viewed as beyond question or change.

Second, as Mill argued, liberties are essential for rational inquiry. Liberty is required to safeguard access to information, to protect critical discussion, and to allow for the formulation and communication of new points of view. How can citizens in a democracy assess foreign policy, for example, if it actually is determined by covert intelligence operations that are not exposed to public scrutiny or evaluation?

Similar considerations apply to limiting liberty in order to enhance the wealth of society. Once the material prerequisites of a minimally decent human life have been secured for everyone, loss of additional wealth is less likely to hinder inquiry than loss of liberty. Accordingly, as affluence increases, there seem to be good reasons for weighing liberty more and more heavily relative to competing values. Liberty is needed for full critical examination of how best to use our wealth and to justify our conclusions about the fair distribution of social assets. Liberty may be overridden on occasion, and perhaps properly so, but our argument seems sufficient to shift a heavy burden of proof to those who would constrain liberty in particular cases.

An additional consideration in favor of the priority of liberty is Rawlsian, arising particularly from Rawls's later work. The point, already alluded to in our discussion of the appeal to religious values in democratic debate, is that in democratic and pluralistic societies, people will reasonably disagree on all sorts of fundamental religious and metaphysical ideas, such as the existence of God, the interpretation of religious-ethical imperatives, and the morality of some apparently harmless acts. Accordingly, it is important for the state to remain neutral in many such areas in order to respect the freedom of conscience of its citizens. A highly partisan state, for example, one that imposed the views of one religion against the conflicting view of others, would violate the conscience of some on grounds that cannot be reasonably justified to them. Liberty is required to protect our ability to choose our way of life for ourselves and not have one imposed on us for what must seem to us to be arbitrary and unsupported grounds.

Fundamental liberties are central both to the idea of respect for persons as free, autonomous agents and to the democratic process, since that process cannot proceed unless the fundamental freedoms of citizens to inquire, discuss, investigate, and argue are preserved. Core or basic liberties will normally be promulgated as provisions of a constitution, exempted from the normal majoritarian voting process, and interpreted and limited, if necessary, by the courts. Other aspects of liberty—more controversial and less central—may sometimes be open to democratic review. However, as liberty is a right, core areas of freedom covered by the right are not subject to the direct democratic process or to limits imposed simply by the pursuit of affluence, utility, or communal harmony.

Liberty and Security

Since the attacks on the World Trade Center and Pentagon on 9/11, another potential conflict between liberty and other values has come into sharp focus. Liberty can clash not only with paternalism, with limits on offensive behavior, and with attempts to prohibit allegedly immoral action. It also can conflict with our own security and safety.

Following the attacks, President George W. Bush and prominent members of his administration have argued that traditional liberties enjoyed by Americans and rights accorded to enemy combatants captured in war need to be modified or limited, sometimes quite substantially, as in the case of foreign fighters and others suspected of involvement with terrorism. The Bush administration has argued at various times since 9/11 that enemy combatants may be imprisoned for indefinite periods of time without being charged or having recourse to due process, has kept secret prisons in Europe, and has argued forcefully that the Geneva Convention protecting prisoners of war from inhumane treatment may not apply to those opposing America in the War on Terror. Those suspected of being terrorists or having relevant information may have been farmed out to foreign countries where torture is practiced, and President Bush himself, at times against opposition even from members of his own party and within the military, has argued for wide latitude for government agencies in employing highly debatable techniques, regarded as torture by many, for interrogating prisoners.[54]

Since we discuss the principles of just war in chapter 9, we will focus on the issue of covert surveillance of Americans in this section. This is especially appropriate since it bears directly on the topic of this chapter—liberty itself. However, whether or not policies of the Bush administration are legal or moral, we note that it is controversial whether they actually make Americans safer. The abuses of prisoners at Abu Ghraib prison in Iraq may well been a tipping point in influencing many Iraqis to either lose faith in America's good intentions or actively oppose the American occupation. Similarly, critics of the Bush administration argue that American limitations of due process and employment of abusive techniques of interrogation have blurred the moral lines between the United States and those it opposes and in fact have provided material used by Islamic terrorist groups to create grievances and better recruit angry young Islamic men to their cause.

On the domestic front in the battle against terrorism, many Americans have been concerned about once-secret domestic wiretapping programs, some reported by the *New York Times* in December 2005 and acknowledged by the Bush administration, allowing government intelligence agencies to eavesdrop on conversations between American citizens and foreign nationals without a warrant. These programs are defended on the grounds that they allow the government to obtain information about terrorists and their plans that may prevent attacks and save American lives. How are such claims to be evaluated and how are we to reconcile liberty and security when under the threat of terrorism?

These issues raised concern over the power of the president and the executive branch of government to go beyond the sorts of surveillance authorized by the Foreign Intelligence Surveillance Act (FISA), federal legislation that allows covert surveillance, including monitoring of private telephone conversations, subject to approval of special FISA courts. These courts have granted warrants in almost every case in which they have been requested by intelligence-gathering agencies. Furthermore, FISA allows covert surveillance for up to seventy-two hours without a warrant just in case intelligence agencies must act quickly to get needed information, so a warrant need not be obtained before surveillance operations begin.

The important point for our purposes is that FISA represents a balancing of liberty and security arrived at through the democratic process. It preserves the idea of checks and balances among branches of government so that no one branch can accumulate and abuse power without knowledge or review by the others. Indeed, American history reveals too many instances of such abuse. (Examples include the involvement of President Nixon in the Watergate burglary of offices of the opposition party and J. Edgar Hoover's and the FBI's covert surveillance of such civil rights leaders as Martin Luther King Jr. and others they deemed to be political opponents during the 1950s and 1960s.)

However, it can be argued that in order to protect us from terrorism, intelligence agencies should not be constrained by the need to get a warrant or have each operation be subject to review by the courts. Moreover, the executive can claim that it cannot defend this view by providing specifics, for that would require it to reveal state secrets, such as methods of surveillance, and results of specific operations, that might endanger operatives or sources.

Are these points determinative? The legal issues are complex and involve questions about whether the president has special indeterminate powers in wartime, and how such a view is to be balanced with our Constitution. For example, the Fourth Amendment in the Bill of Rights states:

> The right of the people to be secure in their persons, houses, papers and effects, against unreasonable searches and seizures, shall not be violated, and no Warrants shall issue, but upon probable cause, supported by Oath or affirmation, and particularly describing the place to be searched, and the persons or things to be seized.

On the other hand, presidents and the executive branch of government traditionally have been given some leeway during wartime and rights of Americans have been circumscribed, sometimes in ways we deeply regret, such as the internment of Japanese-Americans during World War II. At the time of this writing, the FISA program has been upheld and the case for covert surveillance without warrants has been rejected by a U.S. District Court (with an appeal by the government likely to be heard by the U.S. Supreme Court).[55]

Is the moral case for surveillance without judicial review (without warrants) decisive? We suggest not. Let us begin by making several relatively narrow points concerning whether such surveillance in the context of the FISA controversy would improve the security of Americans. First, it is unclear whether FISA does significantly restrict surveillance operations since it allows covert operations for seventy-two hours without a warrant. Moreover, if the executive branch believes it needs even more leeway, it can make its case to Congress that FISA should be amended. To go further, in case of imminent danger, courts have always allowed some leeway when law enforcement is in "hot pursuit" of criminal agents. Finally, if intelligence agents believe a substantial threat is so immediate that they must violate the law, they can do so, then later report their actions and stand in judgment of the courts. Indeed, FISA might be amended to allow a legal defense for intelligence agents based upon the reasonable presumption that danger was immediate and court review unfeasible. All these considerations indicate that judicial review does not threaten our security or undermine the need for traditional checks and balances that protect our liberty.

> If we do remain receptive to the need to compromise civil liberty, we must insist that those who talk the balancing-talk step up to the plate with some actual predictions about effectiveness. We should not give up our liberties, or anyone else's liberties, for the sake of purely symbolic gains in the war against terrorism.[56]

Thus, the needs of security need to be balanced and checked by a concern for the very values that make our way of life morally defensible. If we abandon or unduly restrict our fundamental rights in the name of security, it becomes less and less clear why our political system is worthy of defense or worth dying for. More pragmatically, if our own citizens, as well as much of the world, regard the lines between America and tyranny as becoming fuzzier and fuzzier, our policies will secure less and less support not only from our own people, who are already becoming increasingly cynical about their own government, but also from the international community, whose support is vital if terrorist operations are to be disrupted before they can be launched.

We agree that liberty is not an absolute but must sometimes be weighed against other values, including national security.[57] However, we emphasize that this balancing must be done within the democratic process, that no branch of government should be above the check and review of others, and that rights should at most be compromised at their periphery and core elements preserved (except perhaps in case of the most dire emergencies). While reasonable people may disagree over whether FISA has drawn lines at the proper place, whatever lines are drawn should be in accord with the principles just stated. As former Supreme Court Justice Earl Warren once wrote:

> Implicit in the term "national defense" is the notion of defending those values and ideals which set this Nation apart. . . . It would indeed be ironic if, in the name of national defense, we would sanction the subversion of . . . those liberties . . . which make the defense of the nation worthwhile.[58]

Concluding Comments

We see no reason, then, to abandon a modified form of the priority of liberty. Each person is to be viewed as possessing a right to liberty. This right protects freedom of thought and action, and can be overridden only when it conflicts with equally fundamental rights. Even in cases of such conflict, liberty can only be limited by especially weighty considerations and (except in the direst emergencies) at its periphery rather than its core. That is, limitations on liberty should be as minimal as possible to accommodate core considerations of conflicting rights; liberty should not be limited in order to only minimally secure conflicting rights and entitlements.[59]

The right to liberty, as so understood, significantly limits the scope of the state's authority. States may override the right to liberty only in order to protect and implement other rights *and* when such a policy has been arrived at by a just adjudication procedure suitably constrained, such as legitimate proceedings through a court system as defined by a democratic constitution. The right to liberty cannot be overridden on paternalistic grounds, to enforce the moral beliefs or personal tastes of the majority, or to suppress unpopular, merely offensive, or allegedly dangerous ideas. In some cases, such as speech codes designed to protect the civil rights of vulnerable minorities, it will be controversial whether limitations are justifiable. Even when some limitations on liberty are warranted, as perhaps when needed for purposes of national security in time of war, limitations need to be peripheral (barring extreme emergency) and above all adjudicated within the democratic process to ensure the separation of powers and minimize chances of abuse.

In any case, the existence of controversial cases does not undermine fundamental principles; in fact, the cases often arise precisely because fundamental principles sometimes clash. Thus, while controversy will rightly arise over difficult cases, such as the promulgation of speech codes as a weapon against hate speech and covert intelligence gathering in an age of terrorism, we suggest that the ground rules of freedom and respect for persons are morally fundamental. If we too easily compromise perhaps the most fundamental of rights in the democratic state, the right to liberty, we risk undermining the very values that make liberal democracy worth defending in the first place.

NOTES

1. John Stuart Mill, *The Subjection of Women* (1869, reprinted London and New York: Longmans, Green and Co., 1911), 42–43.

2. This point is made by William A. Parent, "Some Recent Work on the Concept of Liberty," *American Philosophical Quarterly* 2, no. 3 (1974): 151.

3. Joel Feinberg, *Social Philosophy* (Englewood Cliffs, NJ: Prentice-Hall, 1973), 7.

4. Isaiah Berlin, "Two Concepts of Liberty," in Berlin's *Four Essays on Liberty* (New York: Oxford University Press, 1969), 121–22.

5. Berlin, "Two Concepts of Liberty," 122.

6. Berlin, "Two Concepts of Liberty," 122.

7. Berlin, "Two Concepts of Liberty," 131.

8. Berlin, "Two Concepts of Liberty," 133.

9. For fuller consideration of this point, see C. B. Macpherson's discussion in *Democratic Theory: Essays In Retrieval* (New York: Oxford University Press, 1973), chap. 5.

10. Gerald C. MacCallum Jr., "Negative and Positive Freedom," *Philosophical Review* 76, no. 3 (1967): 314. MacCallum's discussion of liberty as a triadic relationship between X (an agent), Y (negative constraints on the agent's acts), and Z (a range of positive acts or goals the agent is free to attempt or pursue) has been especially influential.

11. This is not to deny that the choice of conceptual frameworks may have important consequences. Given the favorable connotations of "liberty," it is probably easier to muster political support for elimination of what are termed constraints on liberty than for efforts to increase the value of liberty one is already believed to possess. On the other hand, in some contexts, the blurring of the distinction between liberty and conditions under which liberty is of value may result in concern for negative rights being unduly subordinated to concern for implementation of positive ones. Hence, the intelligent choice of conceptual schemes requires thorough investigation and evaluation of the consequences of adoption in particular contexts.

12. This point is argued for at length by Bernard Gert in his *Morality: Its Nature and Justification* (New York: Oxford University Press, 1998). Following the general line of Gert's discussion, we include the *ceteris paribus* clause since some rational people may be willing to trade off liberty to prevent even greater evils (including loss of liberty) for themselves or their loved ones.

13. John Stuart Mill, *On Liberty*, 1859. Passages quoted are from Currin V. Shield, ed. (Indianapolis: Bobbs-Merrill Library of Liberal Arts edition, 1956), 13. All subsequent quotations from *On Liberty* are from this edition.

14. The connection between harm and interests has been argued for by a number of philosophers. See, for example, Brian Barry, *Political Argument* (New York: Humanities Press, 1965), 176f., and Joel Feinberg, *Harm to Others: The Moral Limits of the Criminal Law* (New York: Oxford University Press, 1984), esp. chap. 2.

15. James Fitzjames Stephen, *Liberty, Equality, Fraternity* (London: Smith, Elder & Co., second ed., 1874), x.

16. Mill, *On Liberty*, 101.

17. Mill, *On Liberty*, 99–100.

18. Perhaps a proponent of the harm principle might reply that the laws against trespass are designed to prevent the general harm resulting from the practice of invasion of another's property without permission and do not suppose that harm takes place in every individual case (rule utilitarianism). This example is proposed by and discussed in depth by Arthur Ripstein in his paper "Beyond the Harm Principle," *Philosophy and Public Affairs* 34, no. 3 (2006): 215–45. In this paper, Ripstein defends what he calls the sovereignty principle as an alternative to the harm principle.

19. See Thomas Scanlon, "A Theory of Freedom of Expression," *Philosophy and Public Affairs* 1, no. 2 (1972). A principle of sovereignty, presented explicitly as an alternative to the harm principle, is defended by Arthur Ripstein in "Beyond the Harm Principle."

20. Lord Patrick Devlin, "Morals and the Criminal Law," from Devlin's *The Enforcement of Morals* (New York: Oxford University Press, 1965), reprinted in *Morality and the Law*, ed. Richard A. Wasserstrom (Belmont, CA: Wadsworth, 1971), 34.

21. Devlin, "Morals and the Criminal Law," 33. For his discussion of the range of tolerance and its limits, see 39–41.

22. Devlin, "Morals and the Criminal Law," 38.

23. H. L. A. Hart, "Immorality and Treason," *Listener* 30 (July 1959), reprinted in Wasserstrom, *Morality and the Law*, 54. For a fuller discussion of Hart's views on the scope and limits of the criminal law, see his *Law, Liberty and Morality* (New York: Random House, 1966).

24. Ronald Dworkin, "Lord Devlin and the Enforcement of Morals," *Yale Law Journal* 75, as reprinted in Wasserstrom, *Morality and the Law*, 69.

25. Feinberg, *Social Philosophy*, 39.

26. John Rawls, *Political Liberalism* (New York: Columbia University Press, 1993), xviii.

27. Rawls, *Political Liberalism*, xix.

28. Here we rely on a distinction suggested by Christopher Eberle, although we may not have captured his exact point. See Christopher J. Eberle, "Religion and Liberal Democracy," in *The Blackwell Guide to Social and Political Philosophy*, ed. Robert L. Simon (New York: Blackwell, 2002), 300-301.

29. Mill, *On Liberty*, 13-14.

30. We have been unable to identify the source of this remark but first heard it on a tape of a debate on suicide prevention between Dr. Thomas Szasz and an unidentified opponent. The opponent was the source of the remark.

31. For a thoughtful discussion of the dangers of legalizing physician-assisted suicide, see Leon R. Kass and Nelson Lund, "Courting Death: Assisted Suicide, Doctors, and the Law," *Commentary* 102, no. 6 (December 1996): 17-30.

32. Mill, *On Liberty*, 71.

33. Another related approach of interest has been proposed by Gerald Dworkin who has argued that paternalistic interference is justified if rational, autonomous persons would consent to it in the given circumstances. The limits of paternalism are set by what might be thought of as an ideal or hypothetical contract. See Dworkin's "Paternalism," in Wasserstrom, *Morality and the Law*, 107-26.

34. Mill, *On Liberty*, 21. Most liberals would agree that speech may be interfered with in certain special cases such as to prevent a "clear and present" danger from arising. But care must be taken not to construe "clear and present" so broadly that legitimate protest is silenced. In any case, the goal here is to prevent a dangerous action, not to interfere with communication as such.

35. James Fitzjames Stephen, *Liberty, Equality, Fraternity*, 49.

36. Mill, *On Liberty*, 21.

37. Mill, *On Liberty*, 24.

38. Mill, *On Liberty*, 141.

39. *Doe v. University of Michigan*, 721 F. Suppl 852 (E. D. Mich, 1989). Excerpts from this important opinion on speech act codes have been widely reprinted, for example in John Arthur and Amy Shapiro, *Campus Wars: Multiculturalism and the Politics of Difference* (Boulder: Westview, 1995), 114-21, and John Arthur and William H. Shaw, eds., *Readings in the Philosophy of Law* (Englewood Cliffs, NJ: Prentice-Hall, 1993), 537-44.

40. This summary relies on the treatment of the University of Michigan policy found in *Doe v. Michigan*, 721 S. Supp 852 (E. D. Mich, 1989).

41. Andrew Altman, "Liberalism and Campus Hate Speech," *Ethics* 103 (January 1993), reprinted in *Campus Wars: Muticulturalism and the Politics of Difference*, ed. John Arthur and Amy Shapiro, 124.

42. *Doe vs. Michigan*, 721 S. Supp 852 (E. D. Mich, 1989) as reprinted in Arthur and Shaw, 539.

43. In fact, according to the court in *Doe*, at least one student was disciplined or threatened with discipline "because he stated in the context of a social work research class that he believed that homosexuality was a disease that could be psychologically treated." *Doe vs. Michigan*, as reprinted in Arthur and Shaw, 540.

44. *Doe vs. Michigan*, as reprinted in Arthur and Shaw, 541.

45. *West Virginia State Board of Education v. Barnette*, 319 U.S. 624 (1943), as quoted in *Doe vs. Michigan*, as reprinted in Arthur and Shaw, 541.

46. Mari Matsuda, "Legal Storytelling: Public Response to Racist Speech: Considering the Victim's Story," *Michigan Law Review* 97 (1989): 2329–434, esp. 2352.

47. Altman, "Liberalism and Campus Hate Speech," 128.

48. Thomas Grey, "Civil Rights Versus Civil Liberties: The Case of Discriminatory Verbal Harassment," *Social Philosophy and Policy* (1991), reprinted in Joel Feinberg and Hyman Gross, *Philosophy of Law*, fifth edition (Belmont, CA: Wadsworth, 1995), 299.

49. Grey, "Civil Rights Versus Civil Liberties," 305.

50. Grey, "Civil Rights Versus Civil Liberties," 307.

51. This point is discussed by Grey, 301.

52. Grey develops this argument more fully in the course of his paper.

53. For discussion of the role of neutrality in colleges and universities, see Robert L. Simon, *Neutrality and the Academic Ethic* (Lanham, MD: Rowman & Littlefield, 1994).

54. Thus it is alleged that the CIA used "waterboarding," or the technique of strapping a prisoner face-up and pouring water into his nose to cause the sensation of drowning, during the interrogation of Khalid Sheikh Mohammed, the suspected director of the 9/11 attacks. President Bush has maintained that this interrogation yielded vital information about the plans of terrorists. To our knowledge the use of waterboarding in this investigation has never been confirmed by the Bush administration and, again to our knowledge, is an allegation rather than a substantiated fact.

55. *ACLU et al. v. National Security Agency, Central Security Service, and Lt. General Keith B. Alexander*, U.S. District Court, Eastern District of Michigan, Case No. 06-CV-10204, presided over by the Hon. Anna Diggs Taylor in 2006. The plaintiffs were lawyers, scholars, and journalists who claimed that covert surveillance chilled the carrying on of their legitimate duties. For example, sources of information may not reveal information to journalists.

56. Jeremy Waldron, "Security and Liberty: The Image of Balance," *Journal of Political Philosophy* 11, no. 2 (2003): 210.

57. For a cautionary discussion about balancing liberty against other values, see Waldron, "Security and Liberty: The Image of Balance."

58. *U.S. v. Robel*, 289 U.S. 258 (1967): 264.

59. Assuming, as we stated earlier, that other rights, particularly rights to a minimally decent standard of living, are already secured to a significant degree.

QUESTIONS FOR FURTHER STUDY

1. What are some of the problems with the claim that liberty is being able to do what you want?

2. Explain Berlin's distinction between positive and negative liberty. Do you think the distinction is helpful? Why does Berlin think positive liberty is or can be dangerous? Is he right? Justify your view.

3. Explain the harm principle as defended by John Stuart Mill. What is its purpose?

4. Do you believe that it is ever defensible to prohibit an action just because it offends others? Which, if any, of the following do you think should be prohibited simply because of the offense it might cause: advocacy of socialism, advocacy of atheism, advocacy of racial supremacy, exhibiting art that might offend believers of a particular religion, use of lyrics in a song that glorify violence against women, use of lyrics in a song that glorify violence against the police?

5. Explain Mill's argument defending freedom of speech and expression. Do you think his argument justifies protecting any or all of the following: speech advocating legalization of marriage between people of the same sex, speech advocating the view that homosexuality is an illness (or a sin against God), burning the American flag, flying a Confederate flag on a college campus?

6. Do you think your college or university ought to have a code prohibiting hate speech? How might such a code be formulated? Defend your view by replying to a major objection to it.

7. Is liberal neutrality (the view that the state should be neutral with respect to theories of the good life) biased against religious believers in that it actually imposes a liberal theory of the good (namely: the ideal that society should be composed of free and autonomous individuals who engage in free debate) but rules out the state imposing Christian values or Islamic law?

SUGGESTED READINGS

Books

Berger, Fred R., ed. *Freedom of Expression*. Belmont, CA: Wadsworth, 1980.

Berlin, Isaiah. *Four Essays on Liberty*. New York: Oxford University Press, 1969. See particularly the essay "Two Concepts of Liberty."

Feinberg, Joel. *Harm to Others: The Moral Limits of the Criminal Law*. New York: Oxford University Press, 1984.

——. *Offense to Others*. New York: Oxford University Press, 1985.

——. *Harm to Self*. New York: Oxford University Press, 1986.

——. *Harmless Wrongdoing*. New York: Oxford University Press, 1988.

Gary, Tim. *Freedom*. London: Macmillan, 1991.

Hart, H. L. A. *Law, Liberty and Morality*. New York: Random House, 1966.

Mill, John Stuart. *On Liberty*. 1859. (Widely available in a variety of editions.)

Nielsen, Kai. *Equality and Liberty*. Totowa, NJ: Rowman and Allenheld, 1985.

Wasserstrom, Richard, ed. *Morality and the Law*. Belmont, CA: Wadsworth, 1971.

Wertheimer, Alan. *Coercion*. Princeton, NJ: Princeton University Press, 1987.

Articles

Altman, Andrew. "Liberalism and Campus Hate Speech." *Ethics* 103 (January 1993): 302–17.

Daniels, Norman. "Equal Liberty and the Unequal Worth of Liberty," in *Reading Rawls: Critical Studies of "A Theory of Justice,"* ed. Norman Daniels. New York: Basic Books, 1975, 253–81.

Eberle, Christopher J. "Religion and Liberal Democracy," in *The Blackwell Guide to Social and Political Philosophy*, ed. Robert L. Simon. New York: Blackwell, 2002, 292–18.

Grey, Thomas. "Civil Rights Versus Civil Liberties: The Case of Discriminatory Verbal Harassment." *Social Philosophy and Policy* (1991); reprinted in Joel Feinberg and Hyman Gross, *Philosophy of Law*, fifth ed. Belmont, CA: Wadsworth, 1995.

Jacobson, David. "Mill on Liberty, Speech, and the Free Society." *Philosophy and Public Affairs* 29, no. 2 (2000): 276–309.

MacCallum, Gerald C., Jr. "Negative and Positive Freedom." *The Philosophical Review* 76, no. 3 (1967): 312–34.

Matsuda, Mari. "Legal Storytelling: Public Response to Racist Speech: Considering the Victim's Story." *Michigan Law Review* 87 (1989): 2339–34.

Ripstein, Arthur. "Beyond the Harm Principle." *Philosophy and Public Affairs* 34, no. 3 (2006): 215–45.

Scanlon, Thomas. "A Theory of Freedom of Expression." *Philosophy and Public Affairs* 1, no. 2 (1972): 287–300.

Steiner, Hillel. "Liberty," in *The Encyclopedia of Ethics*, ed. Lawrence C. Becker and Charlotte C. Becker, second ed. New York: Routledge, 2001, 978–81.

Waldron, Jeremy. "Security and Liberty: The Image of Balance." *Journal of Political Philosophy* 11, no. 2 (2003): 191–210.

Wertheimer, Alan. "Liberty, Coercion, and the Limits of the State," in *The Blackwell Guide to Social and Political Philosophy*, ed. Robert L. Simon. New York: Blackwell, 2002, 38–59.

6

DEMOCRACY

"Democracy" is an honorific term in the sense that normally to call people democrats is to praise them, and to call people undemocratic is normally to suggest that their political morality is questionable. The honorific connotations of "democracy" have become so powerful that even totalitarian states have taken to calling themselves "true" or "people's" democracies.

But if the meaning of "democracy" is stretched so wide that virtually any government counts as one, the word is trivialized. In calling a state democratic, we would not be ruling out any particular way it deals with its citizens. So if any examination of the purported justifications of democracy is to prove fruitful, it is important to be clear about what is and what is not to count as a democracy.

Such clarity is especially important because of the prominent place given democracy in the writings of such political theorists as Locke, Madison, Rousseau, and Rawls. Moreover, we have argued that states or governments are to be evaluated according to the degree to which they satisfy two fundamental criteria. First, they must protect and, where appropriate, implement the natural or human rights of their citizens. Second, they must institute just procedures for the adjudication of conflicting claims of right. We maintain that democracy, as suitably constrained by individual rights, ought to be the principal procedure for adjudication.

Some political thinkers consider democracy valuable in and of itself; that is, democracy is intrinsically valuable. For example, although his considered view of democracy may be broader, some of George W. Bush's remarks about how voting in such Middle Eastern areas as the Palestinian territories, Iraq, and Egypt constitutes an advance for democracy suggest that we should identify democracy with voting and promote voting for its own sake. However, events in the Middle East cast doubt on this view. A "democracy" that does not recognize the rights of its own citizens, that does not tolerate those who hold different religious beliefs, and does not recognize the integrity of other democratic states is not valuable in and of itself. Thus we insist that the "goodness" of democracy has to do with its ability to protect and promote the rights of its citizens and to fairly adjudicate conflicts of rights that emerge in the society.

To say that democracy achieves its value in fulfilling its purpose rather than that it is intrinsically valuable itself is not to diminish the importance of democracy or its moral standing. The protection and implementation of human rights is intrinsically valuable as in resolving rights conflicts among citizens of a state. We believe that when the value of democracy is clearly understood, some of the mistakes in public policy that occur when democracy is taken as the be all and end all are avoided.

THE DEFINITION OF DEMOCRACY

Any account that purports to provide necessary and sufficient conditions for democracy is likely to be controversial. To avoid such a lengthy controversy, we attempt to provide not an exhaustive list of defining conditions, but rather an admittedly incomplete list of paradigmatic features of a democracy. A paradigmatic feature of democracy is an attribute so characteristic that (1) one would point to it in teaching a child the meaning of the word "democracy," and (2) to the extent that any government fails fully to exemplify the feature, then to that extent it becomes less clear that the government in question is a democracy. An analogy will illustrate the point. A paradigmatic feature of baseball is that it is played by two teams of nine players each. However, if we were to witness a sandlot game in which each team had eight players we would still call it baseball. Presumably if there were only two on a side, we would be reluctant to call what was going on baseball. Perhaps we would say that the players were only practicing. Similarly, a government may still be a democracy even if it does not fully exemplify a paradigmatic feature of democracy. However, any government that fails to a significant extent to exemplify one or more features is at best a defective form of democracy and at worst no democracy at all. As with the baseball example, borderline cases are possible.

Three characteristics that seem to be paradigmatic features of democracy are (1) holding regular elections whose results can alter policy and the people who make it, (2) the existence of virtually universal suffrage, and (3) providing civil liberties, including in the election process itself. Let us examine each of these characteristics in turn.

The first excludes from the category of democracy those states whose rulers claim to follow the will of the people but never allow that will to be expressed in genuine periodic elections. In particular, genuine elections must be a contest between different points of view such that the election results can alter policy and the people who make it. One-party "elections" are not genuine in this sense.

The second condition, virtual universal suffrage, rules out a state where a significant number of persons are denied the franchise for morally unacceptable reasons. Thus a state in which women are denied the vote is not a democracy. Morally acceptable cases of exclusion include disenfranchisement of young children, the psychotic, and the severely retarded. Exclusion of criminals might well constitute an arguable borderline case. In view of the arguments in chapter 3, factors such as race, religion, sex, or ethnic or social background cannot justify exclusion.

The third requirement—provision of democratically required civil liberties—distinguishes the democratic state from the majoritarian state. Majoritarianism is the view that all political issues ought to be settled by a majority vote or by those elected officials who have received majority support.[1] Historically, however, democracy has been thought of as containing built-in safeguards for individual rights. The U.S. Constitution's Bill of Rights is an example. Such checks are justified as safeguards against a dictatorship of the majority, a group that can be as tyrannical as any individual despot. At the very least a democracy must protect those procedural rights, such as the right to vote and the right to free speech, without which elections become a mockery.

It is the violation of these procedural rights that makes such features of many proclaimed democracies as excessive government secrecy or harassment of dissenters so reprehensible. By depriving the citizenry of information needed for intelligent voting or by intimidating or harassing those who dissent from official policies, such abuses undermine the democratic process itself. And, as we will see, where the democratic process is significantly undermined, the obligation to abide by the dictates of so-called democratic decisions becomes weaker. Exactly where the point of vanishing obligation is to be located is controversial. Surely, however, the officials of a democratic government have a special obligation not to undermine the very process they have sworn to uphold.

Each of the attributes—regular genuine elections, universal suffrage, and protection of individuals' rights—is a paradigmatic feature of democracy in the sense already explicated. The dispute over whether or not a given state is a democracy is not merely verbal. As will be argued later, the extent to which a state is democratic determines the extent to which we ought to support it, and perhaps even whether we are under any special political obligation to respect its authority. Let us now consider what, if anything, might justify allegiance to a democracy.

THE JUSTIFICATION OF DEMOCRACY

Utilitarian Arguments

Utilitarian arguments for democracy are those that argue from the good consequences promoted by democracy to the desirability of democracy as a form of government. The utilitarian is concerned with the consequences promoted by the working of an institution and not with those of any one action. The utilitarian is evaluating the system of democracy rather than any individual act performed within the system and so is employing a form of rule rather than act utilitarianism. The utilitarian arguments we will consider below are individualistic because, as in the arguments of Bentham and Mill, the good consequences to which they appeal are individual goods for individual persons. In the next section, we will consider the arguments of collectivists or holists, who appeal to a group under the terms of "the general good."

Here, as elsewhere in this book, it is understood that the utilitarian cannot appeal to considerations of justice or natural rights as last resorts in political argument. Rather the utilitarian must base natural rights and justice on their utility.

One kind of utilitarian defense of democracy appeals to the material benefits enjoyed by citizens of the Western democracies. It is true that currently most, or at least a great many, of the citizens of such states enjoy a higher standard of living than do most citizens of most other countries. So, in political argument, the democratic form of government is sometimes defended by appeal to the material benefits that accrue to those who live under it. A form of this argument appears in the work of the Nobel Prize–winning economist Amartya Sen, who points out that there has never been a famine in a country with a democratic form of government.[2]

However, this argument is far from decisive. It is unclear, for one thing, whether the standard of living in a democracy is a result of its being democratic, of its plentiful natural resources, of its capitalist economic system, or of a host of other possible explanatory factors. Several countries rich in oil are not democracies, and China, which has one of the fastest growing economies in the world, is not a democracy either. Thus a cause-and-effect relationship between democracy and having a high standard of living is difficult to establish.

More important, proponents of such an argument, by their own logic, would be forced to admit that if a totalitarian country did come to enjoy a higher standard of living than a democracy, there would be reason for preferring the former to the latter. But surely a ruthless totalitarian government does not become morally acceptable just by making its citizens, or a majority of its citizens, richer. In fact, as subsequent arguments will show, there are good moral reasons for preferring a democracy to other forms of government, even at a significant cost in material wealth.

A second utilitarian argument maintains that democracy by distributing power among the people is most likely to avoid the abuses of power that result from its concentration in too few hands. If any group of leaders does misuse its power, in a democracy there are regular procedures that the people may use to separate such leaders from their power.

This is indeed a strong argument for democracy and there are historical instances where this has occurred. Many are in the United States, where the Congress has curtailed an overreach by the president or where the Supreme Court has declared an act of Congress unconstitutional. The Supreme Court, in 2006, ruled against the Bush administration for its setting up of special military tribunals for accused terrorists at Guantanamo Bay, in part because these tribunals were in violation of international law and in part because they had not been constituted in consultation with Congress.

We should point out, however, that the argument that democracy provides a check on the abuse of power is two-edged. The totalitarian can reply that the very success of democracy in curbing abuse of power, or at least acting as a check to abuse, may also be its Achilles' heel. When quick and effective use of power is needed, democracy may not be able to supply it. Thus the good consequences of curbing an abuse of power can be offset by the bad consequences of a democracy's failure to be able to take strong, decisive action when it is needed.

We believe that the misuse of power is generally more to be feared than failure to use it. However, that is not our main point. Rather our point is that the conflict between these two points of view cannot be fully resolved within a utilitarian framework. Both sides are appealing to consequences. The issues between them are the empirical ones of whether misuse of power is worse than failure to use it in various contexts, or whether one is more likely to occur than the other. In a later section of this chapter we will argue that power ought to be distributed among the people not simply to maximize want satisfaction and minimize want frustration but because the people have a right to such a distribution. Thus we will maintain that democracy is best justified from the point of view of equality, justice, and rights rather than that of utility and efficiency. This is not to deny the legitimacy of certain utilitarian arguments for democracy, but to suggest that they are far from the whole story.

In that vein, John Stuart Mill has provided perhaps the most effective utilitarian defense of democracy. In his *Considerations on Representative Government*, Mill argued that participation in the democratic process developed the intellectual and moral capacities of citizens, while under other forms of government, the citizens, or more accurately, the subjects, remained passive and inert.[3] In a democracy, according to Mill, people are encouraged to understand issues, develop and express points of view, and implement desires through political involvement. In a despotism, however, citizens are passive receptors for the will of the governing elite. Therefore, Mill maintains, those who value individual development are committed to valuing the form of government that best fosters individual development and that form of government is a democracy. Employing this argument, Mill broadens the conception of utility from the idea of individual happiness and personal pleasure to include development of important human capacities and talents as well.

While we are very sympathetic to Mill's approach here, some qualifications must be made. First, precisely because Mill transforms what counts as utility, it is not clear that Mill's position is genuinely utilitarian. In emphasizing the development of each individual's intellectual and moral capacities, and in deemphasizing such quantitative factors as production of pleasure, Mill has moved a great distance from classical utilitarianism.[4] Instead, Mill seems to have shifted to a self-realizationist or "perfectionist" perspective where the goal is to promote the rational development of persons, to achieve a perfected or improved idea of human development.

One problem with such a view is that of determining how any one ideal of human nature or development can be shown to be better than any other. Another is that even if one conception of the human good can be shown to be most defensible, why should it be made the basis of public policy in a pluralist society in which many citizens hold opposing conceptions of the good? Many liberal democrats advocate state neutrality toward conceptions of the good. This issue will be discussed in detail in chapter 7.

Nonetheless, Mill's argument does have features that are similar to our position. Mill's self-realizationist philosophy is grounded on an imperative to be rational. One can interpret Mill as arguing that one can never be justified in abandoning rational discourse. Since justification requires the giving of reasons, the claim that one is justified in abandoning reasoned discourse is incoherent. It amounts to claiming that one has reasons for not having reasons. This is similar to our own position regarding the imperative of rationality. Our own arguments for human rights rest on this rational imperative. This rational imperative can be rejected only by those willing to lead the unexamined and therefore unjustifiable life. Thus, it is plausible to think that Mill's ideal of developing human rational capacities and talents is not just another conception of the good but rather is a prerequisite for even considering the questions of political and social policy, including evaluation of conceptions of the good in the first place.

Mill's argument is that participation in the democratic process promotes rational development. However, there have been a number of disturbing developments that cause one to doubt Mill's factual claim. George Washington warned of the dangers of partisanship in his farewell address, yet bitter partisan rivalries have been the norm in American politics. Talk show hosts, particularly on the right, have been especially shrill. Redistricting has created safe districts for both parties. As a result, the far left and the far right have gained influence at the expense of the middle, which has inflamed partisan passions even more. Television provides an excellent opportunity for attack ads. Internet blogs, while sometimes valuable, also allow everyone a voice no matter how outrageous, allowing insult and invective to overwhelm reasoned discourse. Many have argued that there has been a decline in civil discourse in the United States and that the increased partisanship and lack of reasoned debate present a danger for democracy. Mill's arguments represent a noble theoretical ideal, but the empirical reality regarding reasoned discourse in actual democracies is quite distant from the ideal.

To sum up this discussion, some of the utilitarian arguments for democracy have considerable merit. In some if not all cases, democratic checks on power function effectively. A democracy may have some effect on developing the rational capacities of its citizens. It certainly does a better job of that than any theocracy.

Even if these utilitarian arguments are correct, they are not sufficient in making the case for democracy. By the very logic of utilitarianism, if a totalitarian state were to produce the greatest good, that state would be rated best. If the utilitarian were to reply, following Mill, that dictatorships do not contribute to the rational development of citizens and so cannot produce the greatest good, then critics would claim with some force that a new nonutilitarian value, rational development, has been introduced into the argument. This is an important argument, but there is nothing distinctively utilitarian about it. Thus at best, classical utilitarian defenses of democracy provide an important but only a contingent defense of democracy. Where other political systems provide good results, those systems pass the utilitarian test as well. We agree with the utilitarian's assertion of the importance of the individual and it is central to the egalitarian defense of democracy, as we shall see as the discussion proceeds.

Nonindividualistic Defenses

One of the standard criticisms of individualistic defenses of political institutions is that they ignore the role that the group plays in individual life. We will consider some of these critiques of individualistic liberal theories such as Rawls's and our own view in chapter 7. Here we consider two nonindividualistic defenses of democracy: the pluralist defense and the defense of the classical political theorist Jean-Jacques Rousseau.

Pluralism

Pluralism can be conceived of both as a descriptive account of democracy advanced by analytical social scientists and as a normative justification of democracy. A pluralist normative justification of democracy is best exemplified by *Federalist Paper 10* by James Madison. Madison accepted the basic Hobbesian account of human nature, that persons are basically selfish and take any opportunity to dominate their fellows. In order to prevent dominant individuals or groups from controlling the political process, Madison thought it was necessary to distribute power widely. Democracy was the form of government that best accomplishes this end.

Madison's approach is called pluralism because he advocated multiple centers of power. He believed wide distribution of power, rather than constitutional checks and balances, was the best protection against tyranny. It is the pluralistic society that prevents despotism. Democracy, by allowing for the give-and-take of bargaining between competing centers of power, promotes pluralism.

So far, Madisonian pluralism resembles the utilitarian argument for the wide distribution of power that was considered earlier. Madison is perhaps the finest articulator of that argument. What is of interest here is the union of this pluralistic approach with an emphasis on the role and value of group life in a democracy.

What the major modern pluralist theorists add to the Madisonian account is an emphasis both on the importance of interaction between groups and on extra-constitutional checks on the accumulation of power. The two additions are related in that it is the competition and compromise between groups that constitute the extra-constitutional checks on government, such as the decision of a legislator from Maine to support a program for Alabama on the understanding that the representatives from Alabama will support a project that benefits the citizens of Maine.

When pluralists look at democracy, they do not see isolated individual utility maximizers. Rather they see individuals as members of groups, coming out of traditions, embedded in a social structure. By raising the ethnic and religious group to the center of attention, the pluralist theorists have provided the framework within which a theory of democracy based on group interaction can be constructed.

In the pluralist view, the democratic process is a set of ground rules within which different groups can pursue their particular interests. Ground rules are necessary, for without them we would revert to a Hobbesian state of nature, a war of every group against every other group. Within the ground rules, the plurality of groups provides a check on the power of any one element in society. What we have is a shifting majority made up of many minorities temporarily voting alike in the pursuit of their share of the pie.

> Constitutional rules are mainly significant because they help to determine what particular groups are to be given advantages or handicaps in the political struggle. . . . Thus the making of governmental decisions is not a majestic march of great majorities united upon certain matters of basic policy. It is a steady appeasement of relatively small groups.[5]

It is this competitive extra-constitutional balance of power among groups that protects us from despotism.

Such a view has several advantages. In particular, it incorporates the importance of tradition, identification with a group, and social structure in the life of individuals. A significant loyalty of many individuals is to the group with which they identify. Moreover, pluralism incorporates this emphasis on the value of group life, on community rather than possessive individualism, into a traditional defense of democracy as a check upon tyranny. However, regardless of its merits as a descriptive theory about how democracy works, pluralism has serious weaknesses as a normative theory about how democracy ought to work.

In particular critics have emphasized that, regardless of the intentions of pluralists, pluralism has unacceptably conservative implications. "The very passivity of government as 'referee' suggests that the 'game' is likely to be dominated by the oldest and strongest players."[6]

The pluralists themselves are not unaware of this difficulty. Robert Dahl, one of the leading pluralists, acknowledges, for example, that "if a group is inactive, whether by free choice, violence, intimidation, or law, the normal American system does not necessarily provide it with a checkpoint anywhere in the system."[7] While the system often has expanded to include previously unrepresented groups, it need not do so, nor need it provide opportunities for new groups to be heard or recognized. Accordingly, a major disadvantage of a normative defense of democracy based on pluralism is that pluralism contains no built-in protections for emerging or less powerful groups. Democracy should encompass more than simple power relationships, whether it is relationships between individuals or between groups that are at issue.

A second difficulty with pluralism arises from the competitive picture it paints of the democratic process. With each group struggling to attain its own interest, there is no incentive for any group to defend the public interest. Each party to the political struggle can hope that the common good will be taken care of by others and concentrate its energy on securing its own private benefit, but what reason do we have to think that that hope will be realized? Forty years ago Robert Paul Wolff noted:

> America is growing uglier, more dangerous and less pleasant to live in, as its citizens grow richer. The reason is that natural beauty, public order and the cultivation of the arts, are not the special interest of any identifiable social group . . . To deal with such problems, there must be some way of constituting society as a genuine group with a group person and a conception of the common good.[8]

This quotation is true today as well. We note that this is the very problem that Rawls tried to deal with in *A Theory of Justice*, and especially in *Political Liberalism*, with his idea of a just framework and an overlapping consensus to which all groups are committed. According to Rawls's thought, all groups would commit to respecting persons as free and equal individuals in a democratic society. However, Rawls's vision is a moral one, not simply a framework of competition among groups each simply pursuing its own interests.

We recognize that the pluralists, as political scientists, have presented an interesting hypothesis about how democracy actually works, one that surely warrants extensive consideration. However, pluralism is at best incomplete as a theory of how democracy ought to work. It is true that the importance of groups is often ignored by the individualist and it is also true that many individuals place a high, perhaps even the highest, value on the group. But even if we accept that the group is the proper unit of analysis here, pluralism contains no account of the fair or just apportionment of power among groups. Moreover, it seems to replace the individualist picture of society as composed of isolated, competing individuals with the hardly more edifying picture of society as composed of isolated, competing groups. In each case, the common values that are essential to all are left out of this picture. It is precisely these problems that the political philosopher Rousseau hoped to avoid.

Rousseau, Democracy, and the General Will

Perhaps the difficulties noted above arise because the assumption on which they are based—that democracy involves conflict between different interest groups—is itself faulty. An alternative account of democracy can be based on the views of the

French political philosopher Jean-Jacques Rousseau (1712–1778). In his book *The Social Contract*, Rousseau formulates the problem of justifying the state's claim to authority over the individual as follows: The problem is to determine if there is "a form or association which will defend and protect with the whole common force the person and property of each associate and by which each person while uniting himself with all, shall obey only himself and remain as free as before."⁹ Rousseau is asking the question we considered in chapter 1: How can the individual retain autonomy while acknowledging political authority?

Rousseau's solution is in the social contract tradition that we have already encountered in the work of Locke, Hobbes, and, in contemporary form, Rawls. But while Hobbes's contractors give up all their power to a sovereign to enhance security and Locke's contractors give up some rights to better protect others, Rousseau's associates give up all their rights to enhance their personal autonomy. They do this by ceding their rights to the association or community. Since each is an equal member, none is disadvantaged more than any other. Each is to have the same voice in group decisionmaking.

Rousseau is making the important point that equality is a fair compromise between parties contracting to create a collective decision procedure. If no party has any threat advantage over any other and if principles are not arbitrarily tailored to favor any particular group, then equality in the sense of one person, one vote seems to be the favored result. (Rousseau seems to have anticipated the kind of contractual argument employed by Rawls. Rawls himself acknowledged a great debt to Rousseau.)

But how does Rousseau deal with the problems facing pluralism? The answer lies in Rousseau's conception of the political community. For Rousseau, the community is not simply an aggregate of individuals to be swayed by majority vote, as in Locke's thought, nor is it a disunited collection of competing groups. On the contrary, the parties to the contract could not retain their autonomy, Rousseau argues, if they were to accept the Lockean idea of majority rule. Majority rule involves abandoning autonomy since one suspends one's individual judgment when it is not in accord with the majority view.

Rousseau's contractees, unlike Locke's, surrender all their rights to the community only because it is the function of the community to pursue the common good. Hence, each individual remains "as free as before" since, unlike in the case of majority rule, no individual's or group's good is to be subordinated to any other's. The community, guided by its general will, is to pursue the general or common good, which is as much any one citizen's good as any other's.

Rousseau, like Hobbes, Locke, and Rawls, should not be read as offering a historical account of the social contract. Rather Rousseau is exploring the rational basis of the state by asking under what conditions reasonable persons could accept the political order. His answer is that it is rational to acknowledge the authority of the state only if the state is a political community, not merely an aggregation. In the latter, each individual or group selfishly pursues its own interests, leading to the kinds of problems facing pluralism. A community is not simply an aggregation of egoists. Rather it is a group with a common goal: securing the common good for its members.

But how is the common good to be discerned? Rousseau believed that the *general will* of the community could discern the common good. The general will is to be distinguished from particular wills, even when the particular wills of all citizens agree. "There is often a difference between the will of all and the general will; the general will studies the common interest while the will of all studies private interest and is indeed no more than the sum of individual desires."[10] Individuals express their particular will when they vote their own personal preferences and desires. The general will is expressed only when citizens assume an impersonal standpoint and vote to secure the common good. One votes the general will when one abandons one's own selfish perspective and attempts to see things from a point of view common to oneself and others.

It is the merit of Rousseau's approach that he focuses our attention on the common good and the public interest, namely on what unites a collection into a community rather than an aggregation of competing individuals or interest groups. Many fear that in the contemporary United States we have lost the sense of the common values that make us a political community, and that we have become simply an aggregation of competing individual wills. In Rousseau's state, no individual or group can dominate another for the only interests the state can legitimately pursue are the interests of all. Rousseau's political philosophy serves as a counterweight to competitive individuals and pluralism alike; as a counterweight to a world where some affluent egoists or groups live in private splendor while such public goods as parks, clean air and water, and a beautiful and healthy environment vanish. But while Rousseau's emphasis on the common good is valuable, his approach is open to serious criticism on a number of points.

Evaluation of Rousseau's Position

Rousseau's argument can be stated as follows:

1. A political association has authority only if it preserves the autonomy of the associates, that is, keeps them "as free as before."
2. It preserves the autonomy of any given associate only if it does not subordinate the pursuit of his or her interests to the pursuit of those of others, for he or she could not rationally consent to such a system.
3. Such subordination can be avoided only if the association is restricted to pursuing only the common interests of the associates.
4. Therefore a political association has authority only if it restricts itself to pursuit of the common interests of its members.

163

5. The general will and only the general will discerns the common interest.
6. Therefore a political association has authority only if it allows for expression of the general will, that is, for democratic voting in which each votes from the point of view of all.

How is this argument to be evaluated? One problem is presented by premise 5. Is it really true that if voters try to discern what is in the common interest, they will succeed in doing so? On the contrary, it can be argued that there is little reason to think that the majority will usually perceive the common good, or wherein the common good lies, let alone that it will always do so. Indeed, critics contend that Rousseau's apparent assumption that the general will is (virtually) infallible is actually dangerous to civil liberties. Rousseau has argued that those who oppose the general will must be "forced to be free."[11] Since only the general will expresses the common good, and since each rational citizen has consented to pursue the common good, each rational citizen has consented to obey the general will. Hence, in forcing the citizen to abide by its dictates, we really are carrying out the dictates of the citizen's rational self and so are not coercing him after all.

As critics have pointed out (see the first section of chapter 5), this argument confuses satisfaction of rational wants with freedom. Coercion in people's interest, even coercion designed to get them what they would want under certain conditions, is still coercion. "Forcing people to be free" is forcing them, not liberating them, as Berlin emphasized in his discussion of positive liberty in chapter 5.

Rousseau assumes that the general will is infallible, or at least is likely to be correctly expressed on any given occasion. Hence, there is no need to protect individual rights; such rights are not needed as checks against a mistaken majority since the majority cannot be wrong. But since this assumption of the infallibility of the majority surely is mistaken, individual rights need to be protected against the tyranny of the majority. Indeed, if the considerations presented in favor of natural rights have force, claims of natural rights ought to be honored even if the majority is infallible. If a physician knows that informing a patient of a diagnosis of cancer will severely depress that patient, it does not follow that the patient ought not to be told. The patient's right to control his or her own life may be paramount. Indeed, if the individual has a natural right to liberty, such paternalistic interference may be in violation of it.

If individual rights are honored, then a sphere of individual, private entitlement is protected. Within that sphere, individuals may follow their own possibly selfish judgments. It seems that we can eliminate such pursuit of private ends only by ignoring claims of individual right as well. Accordingly, Rousseau's view of the state is open to the criticism that pursuit of the common good is allowed unduly to dominate the pursuit of individual interest.

This is not to deny the importance of the common good or the public interest. However, the common good or the public interest does not automatically take precedence over all other values in all contexts. Surely a healthy environment is in

the public interest if anything at all is. But suppose that we could prevent a 1 percent increase in cancer caused by pollution only by suspending the rights of those
who have caused the pollution from even having a say or vote on the matter,
on the grounds that they would only express their individual, selfish interests.
Whether the gain is worth the loss is at least controversial. Rousseau's emphasis on
the common good remedies a serious deficiency in pluralist theory but perhaps at
the price of going too far in the opposite direction. In accepting premise 3, that the
state avoids subordination of some citizens to others only by pursuing the common
good, Rousseau opens himself to the objection that the common good should not
always take precedence over the pursuit of private satisfactions. Rousseau thinks
he has eliminated subordination but actually he simply subordinates private interests to those that everyone has in common. By insisting that the general will
represents the real will of each individual, he overlooks the private wants of the
actual individual. Conflicting interests seem to be a central feature of political life.
Rousseau obscures this conflict and so provides no practical mechanism for dealing with it.

A second problem with Rousseau's argument arises in connection with premise
2. This premise states that any citizen's autonomy is preserved only if the political
association never subordinates the individual's interests to those of others. However, while a majoritarian democracy often pursues some people's interests at the
expense of others, it may well be in everyone's rational interest to consent to a decision procedure that allows just that to happen. Rousseau may not have given adequate weight to the distinction between (a) adoption of a decision procedure being in everyone's interest and (b) the actual decisions resulting from its application
being in everyone's interest. Where (a) holds, it may be rational to consent to the
procedure in spite of the fact that its application may not always work to everyone's benefit. Imagine, for example, two children who constantly quarrel over who
is to make the first move in a board game. Rather than constantly fight, it may be
rational for them to agree to a rule determining who goes first. Perhaps the rule is
"Each participant shall roll a die and the one with the highest number on the face
of the die shall move first. In case of ties, the procedure is to be repeated until a
winner emerges." On any given occasion, one child will lose if the rule is followed.
Nevertheless, it may be rational for them both to adopt the rule and avoid inter-
minable quarrels.

Accordingly premise 2's identification of an autonomous decision as one that
never leads to the subordination of interests confuses the rationale for consenting
to a decision procedure with that for evaluating the outcome of individual decisions. As in the case of the children, it may be rational to allow for some subordination of interests in the application of a procedure when it is significantly in
everyone's interest to adopt such a procedure. (See chapter 1 for a discussion of
this point.)

In spite of these criticisms, Rousseau has called our attention to the importance of
common interests and the value of community. Moreover, Rousseau leaves democrats

with some perplexing questions. If each group is to pursue its own interests, as pluralism suggests, how are permanent minorities—groups that can always be outvoted by the others—to be protected? And how are egoistic individuals or groups to protect public interests as well as private ones? Rousseau may have unduly subordinated the private to the public, but critics, with some force, have pointed out that our society tends to the opposite. How is a proper or appropriate balance to be achieved? Even if the criticisms of Rousseau's approach are decisive, the problems he set out to solve still remain.

PROBLEMS WITH REPRESENTATION: MINORITIES IN A DEMOCRACY

One of the defining characteristics of a democracy is the existence of nearly universal suffrage. However, there is wide disagreement among democrats regarding what universal suffrage entails and how it is to be implemented. In a direct democracy all citizens would vote on all the issues that come before the body politic. The New England town meetings of the seventeenth and eighteenth centuries represented this ideal. However, in the large industrial democracies of the twenty-first century, citizens cannot vote on every issue. Direct democracy is just not practical. (It might be noted that a few thinkers have argued that the existence of computer technology would make direct democracy feasible, but few support either its feasibility or its adequacy.)

The practical alternative to direct democracy is representative democracy where citizens choose people to represent them in the various institutions that govern them. Thus, periodic elections are another defining characteristic of democracies. However, almost any representative scheme can be criticized as being undemocratic.

Again as a practical matter, a democracy is divided into voting districts. In the United States where the Constitution limits the number of seats in the House of Representatives and requires a census at ten-year intervals, districts need to be realigned. The political parties have sought to gerrymander districts both to provide "safe" districts and to give advantage to the party in power. This tactic was taken to a new height when the Texas legislature undertook a redistricting in the middle of the ten-year cycle. At that time, the Texas legislature was under the control of the Republican party, and the result of the redistricting was to create an additional five "safe" seats in the U.S. House of Representatives for the Republican party. In 2006 the Supreme Court in a divided opinion upheld the Texas plan.

The creation of "safe" seats for one party or another raises a number of disturbing questions. Political scientists believe that these "safe" seats help explain the approximately 90-percent reelection rate of incumbents that we see currently in the United States. In addition these political scientists believe that these "safe" districts encourage the electorate to choose people at the extreme ends of the political spectrum. The extremes attract intense participants who vote in the primaries where turnout is often low. Once candidates at the political extremes are successful in the primaries, their election is virtually certain. At the national level, this leads to an increase in partisanship.

Another perverse feature of "safe" districts also deserves our attention here. Democrats that reside in safe Republican districts are permanent minorities in those districts just as Republicans in safe Democratic districts are permanent minorities in those districts.

Where voting takes place on racial, ethnic, or religious lines, persons who are in the minority in those districts become permanent minorities. During the civil rights movement, some argued that some districts should be redrawn so that they would be safe African-American districts. Otherwise, the argument went, African Americans would not be represented in Congress. In the New York primary in 2006, a white office-seeker in a safe Democratic-majority African-American district was criticized because with the large number of African-American candidates running, it was possible that the white office-seeker would win, and thus an African-American seat would be lost. Did those who were concerned about the possible loss of African American representation in the House of Representatives have a valid point?

Given the fact that historically African Americans have had difficulty in having their interests represented, it might seem that the answer to the question is "yes." But there are countervailing considerations. Perhaps districts that become safe for African-American representation may actually dilute the voting power of African-Americans rather than enhance it. By concentrating African Americans in districts where they constitute a majority, elected whites from other districts may feel less of a need to respond to the concerns of African Americans than they would if there were a substantial number of African Americans in their own districts. "Let the African-American officials look after African Americans. My job is to look after my own constituents," such officials might respond. Our point is that when structural revisions make a minority a majority in a local area, the group's minority status may well reemerge in the larger system.

Deliberative Democracy

These concerns about adequacy of representation have led to the development of a variation of democratic theory known as deliberative democracy. Among the leading exponents of deliberative democracy are Seyla Benhabib, Joshua Cohen, John Dryzek, James Fishkin, Amy Gutmann, Dennis Thompson, and Melissa Williams. Benhabib's characterization of deliberative democracy is representative:

> According to the deliberative model of democracy, it is a necessary condition for attaining legitimacy and rationality with regard to the collective decisionmaking processes in a polity, that the institutions of this polity are so arranged that what is considered in the common interest of all results from processes of collective deliberation conducted rationally and fairly among free and equal individuals.[12]

The concern of the deliberative democrats is that the underrepresented groups in a democracy have their interests fairly represented. These democratic theorists realize that the needs of the poor, for example, are often ignored. Hurricane Katrina, the storm that devastated New Orleans in August of 2005, provided a tragic reminder of this issue. Many believe that the government's response to Katrina, particularly in New Orleans, would have been quicker and more efficient if affluent whites rather than often poverty-stricken African Americans were primarily affected. We accept the point that the poor and other minorities are too frequently underrepresented or even ignored in a liberal democracy and that this is wrong. The question is: How can this unfortunate situation be corrected? We believe that a fundamental focus on protecting human rights is a better way of addressing this problem than the focus on deliberation, as we argue in chapter 7, although deliberation and reasoned discourse should play a crucial role in the democratic process.

For now, it should be pointed out first that deliberative democracy is hardly a cure-all for the problem of underrepresentation. As we will see in chapter 7, deliberative democracy in some of its forms gives prominence to those who are good at public speaking and at using the political process to achieve their ends. In other words, there is a danger that those unskilled at deliberation will constitute a permanent minority of their own in a deliberative democracy.

Second, does every opinion deserve to be heard and considered? The deliberative democrats seem to support an egalitarianism of opinion here, but should the voice of a racist count equally with the voice of a Native American seeking to protect tribal fishing rights? Should the voice of a religious fundamentalist count equally with the voice of a scientist in deciding whether creationism or intelligent design theory should be required in the science curriculum of the public schools? These are difficult questions that liberal theorists at least try to answer with their notions of impartiality and rights.

Third, the considerations raised above lead us to see that the deliberative democrats have no way to protect oppressed minorities once they get to the bargaining table. Some deliberative democrats seem to believe that if the homeless had significant access to democratic forums of opinion and were able to tell their stories to the public at large, the majority would devote more resources to them. Perhaps, but isn't it equally possible that the majority might feel contempt for the homeless once their story is told? Unscientific observation seems to indicate that the public is moved by tales of misfortune, but that is not always so.

When we reflect on the justification of democracy, we can formulate at least a partial response to these difficulties. On the human rights view, democracy imposes moral limits on the majority. As all citizens of a democracy are counted as moral equals, on this justificatory approach no citizen's rights should be overridden on the basis of mere power. Democratic government is not simply a matter of power but, as the exponents of deliberative democracy have emphasized, presupposes a model of critical rational dialogue among the citizens so that positions

taken by some can be justified to others. While it is true that in actual democracies sometimes the majority imposes its will on the minority, ideally the majority
should have a justification for its position that it believes the minority should at
least find intelligible. While the minority should not be expected to agree that the
majority is always right, the minority should at least be able to understand the reasons for the majority vote and be able to challenge them in open discussion. In this
way different sides have a fair chance to influence each other's supporters, and
each side can grasp what considerations will move its opponents. Of course, the
whole process is conducted within a broader constitutional framework that protects the fundamental rights of all.

Although democracy can degenerate into the kind of interest-group egoism that
critics describe, such egoism contradicts the very point of having a democracy.
Equals should not be treated as a mere means for the fulfillment of others' wishes.
The very point of having democratic procedures is to acknowledge the moral
equality of others. Thus it is morally self-defeating to use those same procedures
to violate or ignore the rights of others. Consider the homeless issue again. In most
cases, the fundamental issue is not that the homeless do not have sufficient voice,
although that is true. Rather, the issue is that many homeless persons are being denied their human right to a minimum standard of well-being. That is wrong even
if a democratic majority approves of it.

Of course, anyone is likely to be in a minority in democratic decisionmaking on
some occasions. Our concern is with groups whose interests have been ignored again
and again. Any democrat should be prepared to lose on occasion, but no one should
be a loser virtually all the time on a wide variety of issues. Hence to the extent that
a given democracy allows for the existence of permanent minorities, the reasons for
those minorities to abide by the democratic process are seriously weakened.

Multiculturalism and Democracy

The United States has long been considered the melting pot, as people from all
over the world have come to settle here. The notion of the melting pot is that there
is core set of values that all citizens of the United States should adopt, whatever
their ethnicity or religious preference.

For many, the image of the melting pot raises issues about the idea of assimilation. The United States does not differ in this respect from the European democracies although the degree of assimilation expected varies from country to country. France expects a great deal of assimilation, the Netherlands less assimilation.

Currently one of the most contentious issues in pluralistic democracies is how
much assimilation, if any, it is morally appropriate to require. One of the advantages of a core set of values is that it gives a unity among the diversity and provides
for stability within a society. But what are these core values? We would begin with
the acceptance and support of human rights, specifically the rights to liberty and a
minimum level of well-being. After all, we have argued that the primary function

of a democracy is the protection of human rights and the fair adjudication of rights conflicts. Obviously another core value is support of democracy itself. A democracy cannot function if its citizens do not believe in democracy and in democratic institutions. An implication of this acceptance of democratic values is that one will obey the laws democratically enacted, and if one feels that a law violates one's conscience then one would engage in peaceful civil disobedience to try to convince one's fellow citizens to change the law. Valuing the human right to liberty requires valuing free expression, freedom to worship as one sees fit, and, as a corollary, religious tolerance and indeed the toleration of opposing points of view generally. Toleration of other points of view in return requires eschewing violence to settle political disputes.

The critics of assimilation charge that the demand for assimilation is little more than a cover for maintaining a set of European or Western values. Molefi Kete Asante holds this point of view when he argues that "The idea of 'mainstream America' is nothing more than an additional myth meant to maintain European hegemony. . . .There is no common American culture as is claimed by defenders of the status quo. There is a hegemonic culture . . . pushed as if it were a common culture."[13]

To what extent are critics like Asante correct about assimilation? Much depends on what is being charged and how "assimilation" is understood. Often the charge focuses on groups that have been discriminated against in democratic societies or who have borne a disproportionate share of the burdens of political life. Women and the poor in all democratic societies and African Americans as well as Native Americans in the United States serve as examples. The critics charge that the culture and/or values of these groups has not received the respect and recognition that are deserved. What assimilation has meant is that Native Americans have been forced to abandon many of their traditional tribal ways and to adopt the culture of their white conquerors. Many feminists argue that women, until the advent of the feminist movement, were assimilated into what many now perceive as a male-dominated, subservient institution of marriage. In other words, what critics like Asante are contending is that assimilation perpetuates injustice against minorities.

Even if certain minorities have been treated unjustly, that does not speak against the concept of assimilation as we understand it. Assimilation need not refer to the absorption or elimination of a minority culture (strong assimilation), but assimilation in a liberal democratic state does require an acceptance of a common core of values supportive of human rights and democratic processes (moderate assimilation). Within that set of core values, individual cultures may flourish. Indeed, since freedom of expression and freedom of religion are two of those core values, we would expect a multicultural flourishing, and indeed, we argue that in the United States and European democracies we have such a flourishing and a greater sensitivity to the cultural traditions of others.

Some critics of assimilation might simply be arguing on behalf of moral relativism. Moral relativism is the claim that what is really right or wrong in a culture is what the culture believes is right or wrong. There are many arguments against moral relativism. We simply point out that if moral relativism were correct, then conflict resolution and cooperation among cultures on issues of culture and values could not take place on the basis of rational persuasion.

Another way of making this point is to contend that to the extent that the common core of values disappears and democracies become a collection of multiethnic and multireligious groups with no common bonds, then the possibility for dialogue among groups becomes difficult if not impossible. If members of different groups have no common standards of argumentation, logic, and moral justification that hold across group lines, dialogue itself becomes a conceptual impossibility. The price that marginalized groups pay for this kind of relativism can be quite high. If there are no common standards, why should members of other groups pay any attention to the critiques that the oppressed make of the existing system, since it is acknowledged that there are no common standards by which such critiques can be evaluated? "Perhaps your argument is good by your standards," a member of the dominant society might reply, "but not by ours." To the extent that the critique of assimilation rejects common principles of argumentation and justification that apply across group lines, it undermines the case for a social critique of existing institutions that has appeal to groups all across the social spectrum.

Moreover, if there is no notion of assimilation, how can a democratic society persist? An extreme emphasis on differences among groups can destroy the moral and social presuppositions necessary for a democracy to work.

This issue is not simply one of intellectual speculation. In the United States some Christians have sought to impose their own religious values on public institutions, such as demanding the teaching of Creationism and Intelligent Design in biology curricula in the public schools, and have called for boycotts of what they regard as threatening books and movies, such as *The Da Vinci Code*. European democracies have received large numbers of Muslim immigrants from different parts of the Muslim world. Segments of these growing Muslim communities have resisted assimilation in the strong sense in which it requires diluting their own culture and religious customs. In some cases, as when France attempted to prohibit Muslim schoolgirls from wearing distinctive religiously significant apparel to school, reaction by Europeans has been heavy-handed and open to serious moral question. (Under a French law passed in 2004, widely believed to be aimed at the wearing of headscarves by Muslim women and girls, students are prohibited from wearing overtly religious symbols, including not only Muslim headdress but also Jewish skullcaps, Sikh turbans, and large Christian crosses.) Muslim immigrants also have faced and continue to face unjustifiable discrimination in some European countries and sometimes in America.

Nevertheless, it is disturbing that some segments of the Muslim community in Europe, and certainly in predominantly Muslim lands throughout the globe, seem to reject assimilation in the weaker and more moderate sense of adherence to the freedoms of liberal democracy, including the freedom to criticize Islam. Reaction to cartoons that appeared in Danish newspapers that may well have been seen by many Muslims as not only extremely insulting but also blasphemous led to sometimes violent protests. To the justified horror of Europeans, a Dutch filmmaker, Theo van Gogh, who had produced a movie criticizing Islam's treatment of women, was assassinated in Holland in 2004 by a young Muslim man.

We sympathize with those religious communities, including such groups as the Amish, who resist strong assimilation and who do not wish to dilute their distinctive cultural and religious practices. Moreover, all of us, within the bounds of reasoned discourse, should avoid disrespect for the deepest religious views of others. However, we do not think resistance to and violation of the core values of liberal democracy by religious groups, especially lack of respect for the fundamental rights of others, can be justified. Although there may be some limits to free speech, criticism of another culture or religion must be permitted in a liberal democracy that supports and defends human rights. The use of violence or threats of violence to silence those with whom we disagree is impermissible, as we hope the bulk of religious believers of all faiths would agree. Finally, since liberal democracies are not theocracies, no one religion can claim exemption from criticism or special protection from the kind of vigorous debate that is essential to the workings of liberal democracy. Of course in a liberal democracy religious believers also are free to criticize and protest against those expressions of opinion they find insulting to their own religious perspectives.[14]

Another way of making our point is to say that we are recommending a moderate assimilation along the lines of promoting a Rawlsian overlapping consensus, mentioned in chapter 4 and discussed further in chapter 7. Citizens in a democracy need to understand the ethical and practical considerations underlying the democratic system, the different sorts of cases that can be made for liberal democracies, the great works that have shaped the democratic tradition, and of course the arguments of the critics of the liberal democracies and possible responses to them. This is turn implies that citizens need to be trained in critical thinking and analysis, so that they can make intelligent and informed political decisions. In other words, liberal arts education is a prime prerequisite for the success of democracy. Moderate assimilation, then, does not require abandonment of distinctive religious or cultural practices insofar as they are compatible with the rights of others, but moderate assimilation does presuppose the acceptance (or at least the willingness to abide by) the core principles and values of the liberal democratic state.

Moreover, we should not forget why a democratic form of government is justified in the first place. Democratic governments support and implement individual human rights. They also resolve conflicts among rights that occur as citizens in a democracy live their lives. If democracies are to achieve their purpose, then the citizens must accept some kind of human rights framework as part of the overlapping consensus.

DEMOCRACY AND THE COMMON GOOD

In addition to problems in representation and issues raised by multiculturalism, democrats also face the problem of reconciling the pursuit of individual and group interests with concern for the common good and the public interest. The concern is that people will vote for their own interests or those of their group and the public interest will be ignored.

There is no easy solution to the problem of how to interest rational individuals in sacrificing for the common good. If the public good in question is a common good, a good for all, it is always rational to contribute less than one's share in the hope that others will pick up the extra. Since everyone reasons in the same way, public goods receive inadequate support—hence the paradox of public squalor amidst private affluence. Where private goods are concerned, people will bid what they think the product is worth, for the highest bidder wins and everyone else loses. But where public goods are concerned it is rational to try to be a freeloader, which is exactly why labor unions favor closed rather than open shops.

On the other hand, if persons always functioned only as Hobbesian rational egoists, the political order would be impossible. Political institutions are themselves public goods. More dramatically, if persons were incapable of valuing anything but their own good, human life as we know it might well be impossible. Relationships such as love and friendship, as well as traits such as intellectual honesty, require the taking of an impersonal point of view rather than a narrow egoistic one. Perhaps understanding the foundations of the democratic process itself can provide moral motivation for concern with the public interest. And, as Rawls has argued, since the moral society is likely to win the loyalty of fair-minded citizens, and indeed promote fair-mindedness, it is likely to be the stable society as well.

In addition to the importance of fairness as a motivator, we can sometimes use rationality to overcome our short-term rational self-interest. This occurs when it is realized that it is sometimes rational for people to impose sanctions collectively on themselves in order to achieve their long-term collective interests. Contributions to social security are compulsory for most working people. They are compulsory because the data shows that we do not save enough for our retirement. A new law requires that employees in companies that offer 401k retirement plans are to be automatically signed up by management unless the employee explicitly opts out. Similarly, since all of us are hurt by significant injury to the environment, to the educational system, or to facilities for cultural and aesthetic expression, perhaps we can agree upon incentives that make it rational for us to help protect such public goods. Public interest lobbies, institutional devices such as the ombudsman, and the judicious use of tax benefits provide some of the required incentives. The trick is to design institutions that automatically perform functions that we might not carry out if left to our own devices. It is rational to support such institutions.

Although such moral and institutional incentives do not ensure the protection of the public interest, this approach is surely less unsatisfactory than Rousseau's method of forcing us to be free. People need not always function as rational egoists, and even when they do, it may be possible for them to voluntarily channel their egoism in a constructive direction. Providing institutional incentives strong enough to protect the public interest and weak enough to leave room for individual liberty remains a serious problem facing democratic theorists. This issue has become more acute, as many social commentators in the United States believe that American society has become increasingly egoistic and that American citizens are less inclined to sacrifice for the public good.

THE OBLIGATION TO SUPPORT A DEMOCRATIC STATE

In chapter 1, we asked under what conditions a state had political authority. As an aid to answering such a question, we suggested that the proper function or purpose of the state should first be identified. Our investigation so far indicates that the proper function of the state is (1) to protect and, where appropriate, implement the natural or human rights of its citizens; and (2) to provide for the just adjudication of competing claims (including claims of right) among citizens. The second criterion is a procedural requirement. In our view, procedures for adjudicating conflicting claims may fail to honor a claim of right only in order to protect or implement other claims of right. The argument of this chapter is that democracy is a paradigmatic procedure for conflict adjudication.

If a state satisfies the criteria listed above, it is doing what the political order is supposed to do. Consequently there are good reasons for supporting it. However, it does not follow that it has authority over us and that we are obligated to obey its edicts. Similarly there may be good reasons for following a low-cholesterol diet, but we may not be under any obligation to do so. What can be said on behalf of an obligation to support a democratic state?

The Theory of the Social Contract

The theory of the social contract, particularly as developed by the social contract theorists Hobbes, Locke, and Rousseau, contains an account of political obligation. In the contract view, obligations arise from special acts of commitment by agents. Thus, X becomes obligated to pay Y five dollars by promising to do so. Likewise, citizens acquire political obligations by contracting to acknowledge the state's authority. Political authority arises from the consent of the governed, and consent is expressed through the social contract.

However, well-known difficulties face the contract approach. If the act of signing the contract is viewed as a historical one, when did it occur? And since the current generation never signed the contract from where does its obligation, if any, arise? These questions appear unanswerable if the social contract theory is interpreted literally.

Locke attempted to modify the literal historical interpretation by relying on the notion of "tacit consent."

> Every man that has any possessions or enjoyment of any part of the dominions of any government does thereby give his tacit consent and is far forth obliged to the laws of that government during such enjoyment, as anyone under it; whether . . . his possessions be of land . . . or a lodging only for a week, or whether it be barely traveling freely on the highway.[15]

But surely this is unsatisfactory. If even use of public highways is construed as tacit consent, it is far from clear what would not count as withholding consent. By Locke's criterion, even revolutionaries plotting to overthrow a government have tacitly consented to obey it merely by their use of public roads. This Lockean account of tacit consent is too broad.

However, narrower criteria of tacit consent may not be any more satisfactory. Suppose it is maintained that voting is a necessary and sufficient condition of tacitly consenting. But this criterion seems to be too narrow. Voting can hardly be a necessary condition of consenting, for we would want to say that many of those who fail to vote nevertheless tacitly consent to obey the government. If a person who would have voted fails to do so because of illness on election day, it is surely plausible to think that such a person nevertheless consents to political authority. (Indeed, if we take this condition seriously, it follows that since only about half the electorate votes in United States elections, only about half are under the moral authority of the government.) Moreover, it is doubtful that voting is a sufficient condition of consent. It is at least controversial whether those who vote simply out of habit or because a boss-dominated political machine tells them to are consenting to the political order. Perhaps some criterion of tacit consent can be formulated that is neither too broad nor too narrow. At this point, however, other approaches seem more promising.

Suppose we consider hypothetical versions of the social contract approach. At first glance, it would seem that such an approach is unhelpful. Even if there were an ideal contract that all rational persons would sign under appropriate conditions, such as behind the Rawlsian veil of ignorance, these conditions are only hypothetical. How can persons be obligated by a contract that they would have actually signed but never did?

This question seems difficult to answer if we appeal to contract theory alone. Perhaps a contractualist could argue that if persons admit that they would have signed a contract under fair conditions of choice, they are acknowledging something like the conclusion that the contract is fair. Then, if there is an obligation to be fair, they would seem to be obliged to honor their hypothetical agreement, not because they actually agreed (they didn't), but because the hypothetical agreement is in fact fair. However, this argument is not purely contractual but appeals to an additional principle that philosophers have called the principle of fairness. Let us consider this principle further.

Fairness and Obligation

John Rawls has stated the principle of fairness as follows: "This principle holds that a person is under an obligation to do his part as specified by the rules of an institution whenever he has voluntarily accepted the benefits of the scheme or has taken advantage of the opportunities it offers to advance his interests, provided that this institution is just or fair."[16] The intuitive idea here is that if persons voluntarily accept the benefits of a cooperative arrangement, they have indicated to others their intention of playing a role in upholding the arrangement. Without this indication they could not accrue the benefits, for others would not cooperate without the assurance that everyone will bear their share of any burdens involved. Hence, it is illegitimate, a form of cheating, for anyone to act as a free rider without some special justification.

According to Rawls, the institution must be fair or just if obligations are to arise from participation in it. "It is generally agreed that extorted promises are void *ab initio* [from the beginning, eds.]. But similarly, unjust social arrangements are themselves a kind of extortion, even violence, and consent to them does not bind."[17] Rawls's theory of obligation has two parts. First, just or fair institutions are to be identified by appeal to an ideal hypothetical contract or, as in Rawls's later writing, by an overlapping consensus of the kind discussed in chapter 4. Second, we become obligated to follow the rules of any particular institution by voluntarily taking advantage of the benefits or opportunities it offers. It is in this second stage that the principle of fairness applies.

Unfortunately the principle of fairness is itself not sufficient. What is missing here is any kind of requirement of consent beyond accepting the benefits of the institutions. But surely one additional requirement is that the benefits must be voluntarily accepted. Nevertheless, even if we read the principle of fairness as requiring voluntary or consensual acceptance of the benefits of the practice, we still need to spell out what counts as consent. Is consent actual, explicit, tacit, hypothetical, or what? We seem to be back to where we were when we discussed "tacit consent." Perhaps an acceptable theory of consent in this area might be developed, but it also proves fruitful, we suggest, to follow another line of thought developed by Rawls.

Obligation and Rights

Suppose we could distinguish between institutions that we have a duty to support and those that we need to support only if we so desire. Consent would not be required where institutions of the first sort are concerned. Rather, we would have a moral obligation to support or enhance (and where they do not exist, to help create) institutions of the required sort. Then, once we actually reap the advantages provided by such institutions, we are politically obliged, by application of the principle of fairness, to carry our share of the burdens the institutions impose. In other words, participation in the institutions would be obligatory, and hence consent would not be required.

Rawls adopts just such a strategy by appealing to our natural duties, that is, duties that hold independently of any voluntary act of commitment to a particular institution or person. Thus, we have a natural duty not to be cruel. For example, if one were to be discovered abusing animals or children for fun, one could not excuse oneself by declaring, "I have never consented to the institution of avoiding cruelty." So, according to Rawls, we have a natural duty to support just institutions. Rawls holds that we have this duty because such a conclusion would be accepted by rational persons deliberating behind the veil of ignorance in the original position.[18]

Given the lack of agreement over just which principles would be accepted behind the veil of ignorance, let alone whether the contract approach is warranted, it would be helpful if conclusions similar to Rawls's could be derived from a human rights framework. We believe that they can. Human rights impose obligations on others. These obligations require us not only to refrain from interfering with others but also to do our share in supporting institutions that provide social and material prerequisites of an at least minimally decent human existence. Now it is the function of the state to protect and implement claims of human rights. Since we are obligated to respect such claims, and since the just state is the most efficient means of implementing them, we are obligated to support the just state.

On both the Rawlsian and the human rights view, we have a natural duty to support the just state. Once we are part of such an institution, we have a special duty, based on the principle of fairness, to carry out our share of the burdens, for example, by obeying the laws that such institutions impose. Natural duties bind us to support a legitimate political order. The principle of fairness creates the political obligation to acknowledge the authority of some particular political framework.

However, the problem of consent cannot be fully avoided. Citizens are not slaves. While they have an obligation to support the just state, which just state they support is up to them. That is, while citizens have an obligation to support the just state, which particular state they have an obligation to support depends upon which one they actually participate in. Furthermore, citizens normally have the right to leave one state and join another if they so wish.

Moreover, although obligations to the just state are genuine, they need not be absolute. Remember that by a just state we mean one that respects fundamental rights and has a just procedure for adjudicating conflicts among rights. However, a procedurally just political decisionmaking procedure may yield unjust decisions. While the requirement of respect for rights mitigates the degree to which injustice can exist, some injustices might be quite significant. In such cases, decent persons may find themselves with conflicting obligations. There is no a priori reason to believe that the obligations to follow the dictates of political authority will always take precedence. However, if the arguments of this section have force, there is a prima facie obligation to obey. If political obligation does not imply blind subservience, neither is it a myth. Rather it arises ultimately from our obligation to respect others as rights bearers equal to ourselves.

177

AN OVERVIEW

This completes our overview of a liberal theory of the state. In our view the state is justified when it protects, enhances, and implements the human rights of its citizens and when it provides for the just adjudication of conflicts among rights that inevitably arise. Central concepts here include the right to a minimum standard of well-being, the right to liberty, and the right to justice. The state that seems best able to accomplish these tasks, we have argued, is a liberal democratic state, although we admit that democracies are not perfect in this regard. Our view stands in contrast to a utilitarian justification for the liberal democratic state. Finally the liberal democratic state is usually entitled to the obedience of its citizens.

In the next chapter we consider and try to answer criticisms that have been leveled against the liberal democratic state. Finally, in the last two chapters we expand our analysis to the international arena, where we consider what the citizens of one country owe to the citizens of other, less prosperous countries. We also consider what morality requires in times of war and terrorist threats. We now turn to critics of liberal political theory.

NOTES

1. See Brian Barry, *Political Argument* (New York: Humanities Press, 1967), 58–66, for a discussion of majoritarianism.

2. Amartya Sen, *Development As Freedom* (New York: Anchor Books, 2000), 16, 51–53, 155–57.

3. John Stuart Mill, *Considerations on Representative Government* (1861) in *The Philosophy of John Stuart Mill*, ed. Marshall Cohen (New York: Modern Library, 1961), esp. 401–6.

4. See our discussion of Mill's utilitarianism in chapter 2.

5. Robert Dahl, *A Preface to Democratic Theory* (Chicago: University of Chicago Press, 1956), 137, 146.

6. Eugene Lewis, *The Urban Political System* (Hinsdale, IL: Dryden Press, 1968), 147.

7. Dahl, *A Preface to Democratic Theory*, 138.

8. Robert Paul Wolff, *The Poverty of Liberalism* (Boston: Beacon Press, 1968), 159.

9. Jean-Jacques Rousseau, *The Social Contract* (1762), trans. Maurice Cranston (Baltimore: Penguin Books, 1968), bk. 1, chap. 6, 60. Citations are to this edition.

10. Rousseau, *The Social Contract*, bk. 2, chap. 3, 72.

11. Rousseau, *The Social Contract*, bk. 2, chap. 7, 64.

12. Seyla Benhabib, "Toward a Deliberative Model of Democracy," in *Democracy and Difference*, ed. Seyla Benhabib (Princeton: Princeton University Press, 1996), 69.

13. Molefi Kete Asante, "Multiculturalism: An Exchange," in *Debating PC: The Controversy over Political Correctness on College Campuses*, ed. Paul Berman (New York: Dell, 1992), 305, 308. Originally published in *American Scholar* (Spring 1991).

14. For a sensitive discussion of the difficulties of reconciling some interpretations of Islam with the precepts of liberal democracy, see Andrew F. March, "Liberal Citizenship and the Search for an Overlapping Consensus: The Case of Muslim Minorities," *Philosophy and Public Affairs* 14, no. 4 (2006): 373–421.

15. John Locke, *Second Treatise of Government* (1690, reprinted, ed. Thomas R. Peardon, Indianapolis, IN: Bobbs-Merrill, 1952), chap. 8, sec. 119.

16. John Rawls, *A Theory of Justice* (Cambridge: Harvard University Press, 1970), 342–43.

17. Rawls, *A Theory of Justice*, 343.

18. Rawls, *A Theory of Justice*, 333ff.

QUESTIONS FOR FURTHER STUDY

1. What does it mean to say that democracy is instrumentally, not intrinsically, valuable?

2. Explain the utilitarian case for democracy. What are its strengths and weaknesses? Explain Mill's defense of democracy based on self-realization. In what way does it differ from classical utilitarianism?

3. What constitutes the pluralist defense of democracy and what objections can be made to the pluralist defense? How can pluralists best reply to these criticisms? Would this reply be successful? Defend your view.

4. How does Rousseau's justification for democracy differ from that of the utilitarians and that of the pluralists? What criticisms would Rousseau have of each? Are his criticisms valid? Defend your answer.

5. What does Rousseau mean by the "general will"? Can decisions made from the perspective of the general will guarantee that the common good is achieved? Why or why not?

6. What are the chief strengths and weaknesses of Rousseau's democratic theory?

7. What are some of the problems in a representative democracy in assuring that everyone really has some say in the decisionmaking process? Can an adherence to deliberative democracy resolve these problems? Why or why not? Would the existence of a fundamental right to participate in deliberative democracy avoid criticisms of the deliberative approach?

8. What is the argument for democracy based on equality of fundamental rights? How would a proponent of that argument reply to the objection that not everyone is equally capable of participating in the political process? Is that reply successful? Justify your view.

9. What amount of assimilation can a liberal democracy require of all its citizens? Explain your answer.

10. Are the citizens of a liberal democracy obligated to obey the state? Defend your answer.

SUGGESTED READINGS

Books

Braybrooke, David. *Three Tests for Democracy: Personal Rights, Human Welfare, Collective Preferences.* New York: Random House, 1968.

Galston, William A. *The Practice of Liberal Pluralism.* Cambridge: Cambridge University Press, 2005.

Gutmann, Amy, and Dennis Thompson. *Democracy and Disagreement.* Cambridge: Harvard University Press, 1981.

Gutmann, Amy, and Dennis Thompson, eds. *Why Deliberative Democracy.* Princeton, NJ: Princeton University Press, 2004.

Levine, Andrew. *Liberal Democracy: A Critique of Its Theory.* New York: Columbia University Press, 1981.

Locke, John. *Second Treatise of Government,* 1690 (widely available in a variety of editions).

Mill, John Stuart. *Considerations on Representative Government,* 1861 (widely available in a variety of editions).

Nelson, William. *On Justifying Democracy.* Boston: Routledge & Kegan Paul, 1980.

Parekh, Bhikhu. *Rethinking Multiculturalism,* second ed. New York: Palgrave Macmillan, 2006.

Pennock, Roland, and John C. Chapman, eds. *Liberal Democracy,* Nomos 25. New York: New York University Press, 1983.

Rawls, John. *A Theory of Justice.* Cambridge, MA: Harvard University Press, 1971, chaps. 4 and 6.

Rousseau, Jean-Jacques. *The Social Contract,* 1762 (widely available in a variety of editions).

Taylor, Charles. *Multiculturalism: Examining the Politics of Recognition.* Princeton, NJ: Princeton University Press, 1994.

Articles

Benhabib, Seyla. "Deliberative Rationality and Models of Democratic Legitimacy." *Constellations* 1 (1994): 26–52.

Buchanan, Allen. "Political Legitimacy and Democracy." *Ethics* 112 (2002): 689–719.

Copp, David. "The Idea of a Legitimate State." *Philosophy and Public Affairs* 28, no. 1 (1999): 3–45.

Dahl, Robert A. "Procedural Democracy," in *Philosophy, Politics and Society,* fifth series, ed. Peter Laslett and James Fishkin. New Haven: Yale University Press, 1979.

Estlund, David. "The Democracy-Contractualism Analogy." *Philosophy and Public Affairs* 31, no. 4 (2003): 387–412.

Fishkin, James. "Deliberative Democracy," in *The Blackwell Guide to Social and Political Philosophy,* ed. Robert L. Simon. Boston: Blackwell, 2002, 221–38.

Freeman, Samuel. "Deliberative Democracy: A Sympathetic Comment." *Philosophy and Public Affairs* 29, no. 4 (2000): 371–418.

Goodin, Robert E. "Democratic Deliberation Within." *Philosophy and Public Affairs* 29, no. 1 (2000): 81–109.

March Andrew F. "Liberal Citizenship and the Search for an Overlapping Consensus: The Case of Muslim Minorities." *Philosophy and Public Affairs* 14, no. 4 (2006): 373–421.

Monist 55, no. 1 (1971). The entire issue is devoted to the topic "Foundations of Democracy."

Spinner-Halev, Jeff. "Feminism, Multiculturalism, Oppression, and the State." *Ethics* 112 (2001): 84–113.

Swaine, Lucas A. "How Ought Liberal Democracies to Treat Theocratic Communities?" *Ethics* 111 (2001): 302–43.

Wellman, Christopher Heath. "Toward a Liberal Theory of Political Obligation." *Ethics* 111 (2001): 735–59.

7

LIBERAL POLITICAL THEORY AND ITS CRITICS

The liberal theory of the state and the principles of liberal democracy and social justice are not only targets of criticism from Western philosophers and political theorists, who often seek to advance what they think are more progressive views, but are also rejected by countries that are undemocratic and that embrace various forms of dictatorships, one-party rule, or theocracy. Among political theorists in the Western tradition, much criticism of liberal political theory has come from a group of thinkers who are commonly referred to as communitarians, although there is no established orthodox communitarian doctrine and many of those who are characterized as communitarians have not adopted the title. Social scientist Amitai Etzioni has embraced the term, and Robert Bellah and his colleagues are sympathetic to it. However, when political philosophers refer to communitarian writings, they most frequently refer to the writings of such contemporary political philosophers as Michael Sandel, Alastair MacIntyre, Charles Taylor, and Michael Walzer.

Other critics come from the feminist tradition, and, as with the communitarians, there is not unanimous agreement on the details of the feminist critique, nor would all feminist political theorists reject liberalism. Among the feminists we will consider are Susan Moller Okin, Carol Gilligan, and Iris Marion Young. Both the communitarians and the feminists were critical of John Rawls's *A Theory of Justice*. Let us look at the criticisms of Rawls and how he dealt with them and developed a more comprehensive liberal political theory as a result. In other words, in response to his critics, Rawls's *Political Liberalism* encompassed much more than a theory of justice.

CRITICISM OF RAWLS'S THEORY AND HIS RESPONSE

Criticism of Rawls's Theory

The criticism of Rawls that has had the most impact is the claim that his theory is biased in favor of liberal, individualistic Western values and so cannot succeed as a universal theory of justice for all. In part, this criticism is directed to Rawls's theory of the good. In the original position as described in chapter 4, Rawls rules out any knowledge of what each of us considers to be the good life. Rather, our knowledge of our desires is limited to what Rawls calls primary goods. Primary goods include rights and liberties, powers and opportunities, and wealth and income, which every rational person should want since these goods are necessary for achieving any other goods. By limiting our knowledge of the good in this way, Rawls can argue that no one would choose a society where the pursuit of any one nonprimary good prevailed at the expense of all the others. For example, no one would choose a society where religious persecution was practiced since behind the veil of ignorance one does not know if one is in the majority religion or not. But critics point out, isn't this stipulation biased against individuals who hold alternative theories of justice in which one value (such as the predominance of a religion) or a limited set of values is given preeminence? Rawls's refusal to rank particular perceptions of the good implies a very marked tolerance for individual inclination. Another way of putting this point is to say that Rawls has not shown that being neutral with respect to various theories of the good is itself a neutral decision. Thus, according to the critics, Rawls's theory reflects a built-in liberal, individualistic assumption that is undefended in the theory.

Rawls has at least a partial answer here. Rawls's theory of the good is a "thin" theory that is represented by his list of primary goods. Primary goods are those that all rational persons can be presumed to want regardless of the more comprehensive "thick" theories of the good they might hold, since the primary goods are the means to achieving a wide variety of conceptions of the good life. Thus whether one is religious or not, it is rational to want the liberty to live according to the beliefs one holds.

Suppose a religious fundamentalist argues that he finds toleration of other religions to be blasphemous. Behind the veil of ignorance, one would not know whether one would reject or endorse religious toleration. Rawls would think that in such circumstances the rational choice is to choose toleration in case it turned out that one had minority religious beliefs or even no religious beliefs at all. But why is that the rational choice? Couldn't one argue that if one were a religious believer who did not practice toleration, then the choice for toleration would have been a bad choice? What this shows, the critics argue, is that Rawls's theory is not universal but only applies to liberal democracies.[1]

Rawls's Political Liberalism

Over a period of twenty years Rawls reflected on criticisms like these, and he published a response in his book *Political Liberalism*. In this book Rawls agrees with his critics that his theory applies only to liberal democratic societies.[2] Toleration and stability are central themes of *Political Liberalism*. In it, Rawls holds fast to his belief that modern liberal democracies are characterized by intense competition among different, often conflicting theories of the good. How can people who hold these competing conceptions get along? As Rawls says in the introduction, "The problem of political liberalism is: How is it possible that there may exist over time a stable and just society of free and equal citizens profoundly divided by reasonable though incompatible religious, philosophical, and moral doctrines?"[3] This is a profound question for the United States at this time.

To answer this question Rawls distinguishes between a *modus vivendi* and an *overlapping consensus*. A modus vivendi occurs when people agree to grudgingly accept one another rather than fight. A tense stalemate is better than the Hobbesian war of all against all. A modus vivendi exists in many parts of the world today—in the Balkans, for example. However, a modus vivendi is inherently unstable since it will tend to break down once one side has sufficient power to impose its will on the others with impunity.

Rawls contrasts a modus vivendi with an overlapping consensus. In an overlapping consensus, there is genuine agreement on certain principles for carrying on a debate and for making decisions in the political realm. True to his procedural inclinations, Rawls believes that people with competing conceptions of the good can nonetheless accept certain common political ground rules. In that way we have an overlapping consensus on these ground rules rather than an unstable agreement of convenience. For example, religious evangelicals might support freedom of religion on the grounds of their view that God values only freely chosen belief. Atheists also might support freedom of religion for a variety of philosophical reasons—for example, that they accept Mill's defense of free thought and personal autonomy (as explained in chapter 5).

To achieve this consensus on ground rules, there must be some kind of limit on conceptions of the good that can be tolerated. Those who have no wish to get along with others and who actively seek to eliminate adherents of competing ideas of the good (for example, those with different religious beliefs) wish to impose their will on other citizens. Imposition of a conception of the good through coercion is not just. Rawls believes that such people do not have reasonable conceptions of the good.

To develop this concept of a reasonable account of the good, Rawls provides a normative characterization of citizenship in a democratic society. Citizens in a democratic society are committed to the use of evidence and to procedural rules for settling debates rather than to forms not available to other citizens or confirmable by public tests (for example, divine revelation). In addition, citizens should respect the reasonable conceptions of the good that other citizens might have, even when these conceptions are inconsistent with their own comprehensive view of the good. Citizens in a just democracy are appropriately tolerant of the reasonable positions of others.

Rawls is careful to insist that the reasonable is not simply reducible to the rational. From the normative point of view, citizens in a democracy are free and equal in the sense that they all have the capacity to have a sense of justice and a conception of the good. By "free" Rawls means having the moral autonomy to form one's own conception of the good, to regard oneself as a self-authenticating center of valid claims, and to view oneself as capable of taking responsibility for one's choice of aims. What the concept of the "reasonable" adds to the concept of the "rational" is a commitment to engage in the competition of competing goal realization on terms that others could be assumed to accept. Thus citizens would try to achieve their goals in ways that would be perceived as reasonable by others. Conceptions of the good that reject the normative account of citizenship as involving equality and freedom, or that involve achieving goals in ways that others could not accept, are unreasonable.

Rawls's account of the reasonable imposes additional requirements on the citizens in a just democracy. Citizens must be willing to let political values have priority over other values in public life. Political values are those that govern the basic structure of social life and are constituted largely by the principles that Rawls developed in *A Theory of Justice*: equal political liberty, fair equality of opportunity, economic reciprocity presumably implemented through the difference principle, and the social basis of mutual respect among citizens. To these principles, Rawls adds the value of public reason as explained above. Rawls believes that any person with a reasonable conception of the good will accept these political values and their priority.

But why should these political values and principles be given priority? Because only in this way is an overlapping consensus possible. And it is the overlapping consensus that makes a liberal democracy and social justice possible. One might characterize Rawls's theory as a theory of reasonable pluralism.

Rawls's analysis at this point may seem unduly abstract. What he is trying to do is to solve the problem of how people with very different conceptions of how life should be led, perhaps based on different religious, cultural, or ethnic traditions, can all get along in one society under a common set of guidelines that all can reasonably accept. Rawls provides the following example to illustrate the importance of reasonable pluralism:

> Now in holding these convictions, we clearly imply some relation between political and nonpolitical values. If it is said that outside the church there is no salvation, and therefore a constitutional regime cannot be accepted unless it is unavoidable, we must make some reply.... We say that such a doctrine is unreasonable; it proposes to use the public's political power—a power in which citizens have an equal share—to enforce a view bearing on constitutional essentials about which citizens as reasonable persons are bound to differ uncompromisingly. When there is a plurality of reasonable doctrines, it is unreasonable, or worse, to want to use the sanctions of state power to correct, or to punish, those who might disagree with us.[4]

Those who want to impose their conceptions of the good on those who do not share it are being unreasonable. In other words, Rawls comes close to saying that comprehensive conceptions of the good that are not committed to the basic political values of justice and the regulation of public debate are not reasonable.[5]

To a large extent, citizens in the United States have accepted something like Rawls's reasonable pluralism. Thus when authorities in Afghanistan threatened to execute a citizen who had converted to Christianity from the Muslim faith, there were cries of outrage. To prevent a citizen from changing his or her religion on pain of death is a violation of liberal justice. Such examples show how difficult it would be for a theocracy to be compatible with liberal democracy.

Rawls, then, made a number of concessions to the critics of *A Theory of Justice*. For example, he conceded that people might have major commitments to communities and groups organized around conceptions of the good, but he insisted that liberal democratic principles of justice are needed that allow for pluralism of reasonable conceptions of the good. However, some communitarians and feminists remained quite skeptical of a number of points in Rawls's theory.

THE COMMUNITARIAN CRITIQUE OF LIBERALISM

The Communitarian Critique of the Liberal Self

Michael Sandel's book-length critique of Rawls, *Liberalism and the Limits of Justice*, established the theme for the communitarian criticisms of a liberal theory of the state. One of its criticisms of rights theories and of political liberalism is that these ideas misunderstand the nature of the individual. The liberal notion of the individual is too abstract. It is a kind of X that stands outside experience and decides what it will become. Some, including Sandel, criticize this account of the self by arguing that the content of the self, the *what* that the self chooses to be, is provided by society, and that liberal political theory ignores this fact. The isolated X independent of social influences and totally free to choose among them is simply a myth.

However, liberals have a reasonable response to this version of the critique. Of course the choices that are presented to the self are by and large provided by society. Nevertheless, people do change their religion or give up religion altogether; some people even emigrate to foreign countries. The fact that relatively few people do these things is immaterial to the liberal position. That people can do these things and should have the right to do so is what matters. Thus, what the self decides to become need not be determined by society, although liberals acknowledge that the range of our choices comes from society. (However, individual creativity can extend the range of available choices, as in the introduction of new approaches in the arts, new techniques in sport, or new technologies or treatments in health care.)

Sandel's formulation of the argument cuts much deeper, though. Sandel admits that Rawls allows a greater place for community than do laissez-faire economic liberals like Nozick. These laissez-faire liberals are instrumentalists with respect to the individual's relation to the state. An instrumentalist views the community as a means to one's ends. It is a resource upon which one draws, but it has no intrinsic value. Rawls explicitly rejects the instrumentalist view and adopts instead what Sandel refers to as the sentimentalist view. Rawls argues that in a just society citizens are moved by a sense of community because they have shared final ends and a sense of cooperation. But Sandel thinks Rawls's account is still too individualistic because the starting point of the self is the individual. Sandel says that individuals are defined by their community. An individual is the individual she is because of the relationships she finds herself in.

> A theory of the community whose province extended to the subject as well as the object of motivation would be individualistic in neither the conventional sense nor in Rawls'. It . . . would describe not just a feeling but a mode of self-understanding partly constitutive of the agent's identity. On this strong view, to say that the members of a society are bound by a sense of community is not simply to say that a great many of them profess communitarian sentiments and pursue communitarian aims, but rather that they conceive their identity . . . as defined to some extent by the community of which they are a part. For them community describes not just what they have as fellow citizens, but also what they are, not a relationship they choose . . . but an attachment they discover, not merely an attribute but a constituent of their identity.[6]

Charles Taylor, another theorist sympathetic to many communitarian themes, has developed his own criticism of the liberal self. He has characterized the liberal self as monological. Here is what Taylor means by that strange term. According to a monological view of the self, the essential characteristics of an authentic self cannot be socially derived; rather they are internally generated and determined. Taylor contrasts this monological view of the self with what he calls the dialogical view. The dialogical view argues that a self becomes what it is in dialogue (broadly defined) with other human beings. Our identity is not self-determined but rather is determined in interaction with others. Taylor also notes as a matter of psychological fact that we cannot get the full enjoyment of some experiences unless we experience them with others. It is more fun to share. As Taylor says, "We define our identity always in dialogue with, sometimes in struggle against, the things our significant others want to see in us. . . . If some of the things I value most are accessible to me only in relation to the person I love, then she becomes part of my identity."[7]

We should note here that Taylor is making a stronger claim than merely asserting that the self we choose to be must select characteristics from an existing society. One cannot choose to be an airplane pilot in a world where there are no airplanes. Of course, the individualist liberal would concede this. Rather, Taylor is saying that the self who the individualist argues can choose is itself socially determined. There is no pure chooser. To the extent that a self chooses to be what it is, its status as a chooser is derived at least in part from its interaction with significant others. There is an important sense in which the self as chooser is already, at least in part, socially determined.

Michael Walzer also thinks Rawls and other liberals underestimate the importance of community and the social nature of the self. Yet he takes the critique of the liberal self further to develop a second but related point, namely that one's social relationships and circumstances play a crucial role in the development of the conception of justice as it applies in particular circumstances.

Walzer maintains that you cannot get principles of justice for real people in historical circumstances by asking what would rational persons who knew nothing of their culture or other social relationships choose as principles of justice. Rather, people ask what is just, given our culture at this particular time. Walzer puts it this way:

> The greatest problem is with the particularism of history, culture and membership. Even if they are committed to impartiality, the question most likely to arise in the minds of the membership of a political community is not, What would rational individuals choose under universalizing conditions of such and such a sort? But rather, What would individuals choose who are situated as we are, who share a culture and are determined to go on sharing it?[8]

What would these people choose? First, they would recognize that goods are socially determined. Rawls thought that there was a list of goods that all rational people would want because they are those necessary for securing any other goods at all (that is, primary goods). Walzer, on the other hand, argues that what counts as a good depends on the culture one is in. All goods are valued because they are shared with another group—in the widest sense, with a culture. Men and women take on the identities they do because of the way they relate to social goods.

Walzer then develops a normative theory for the distribution of social goods. He argues that there are many kinds of goods—money, free time, education, kinship, and love, to name but a few. It is important for justice that no one good dominate another good. For example, not all goods should be reduced to money, and the economic sphere should not invade every other sphere of our lives. Justice also requires that no one should be unequal across all goods in the sense of having dominant shares of a wide variety of different kinds of benefits. It is unjust that a person be rich, have great political power, be successful in love, have many fulfilling talents and abilities, and have lots of free time. These are the types of principles that are appropriate for dealing with the particularity of historical time and culture. Walzer also admits that three principles—free exchange, desert, and need—are relevant to issues of distributive justice, but that no one of them should dominate the other for all goods. Thus, it is not the case that all goods should be distributed according to the principle of need or the principle of desert.

The Communitarian Critique of Liberal Neutrality

A second communitarian objection to liberal political theory is that the liberal state is not neutral among conceptions of the good, and as a matter of logic it could not be. Some religious views have as their essential characteristic a commitment to a conception of the good that rejects and refuses to tolerate certain competing conceptions of the good. One historical example is provided by the Spanish Inquisition, which occurred primarily at the end of the fifteenth century and throughout the sixteenth century. During the Inquisition Jews were forced to convert to Catholicism or be killed or forced to emigrate. Protestants were also persecuted. Stuart Hampshire describes the outlook of the Inquisitors, who at the point of a sword demand adherence to what they regard as the true religion.

> Your belief in forcible conversion as a duty follows from your conception of the good, and even when you want to be tolerant, you think you ought not to be because you infer that it would be unjust—both to the faithful who would be scandalized, and to the infidel who would go to Hell. You are ready to argue against liberals in support of your conception of the good and of the consequent substantial conception of justice.[9]

To appreciate this objection, one need not look to history. The position characterized by Hampshire is exactly that taken by Islamists in many parts of the world. The communitarian is arguing that the liberal cannot assert priority of the procedural account of justice over the communitarian's substantive account. Hampshire, in effect, is suggesting that Rawls's procedural notion of justice is itself a substantive position. Liberals claim that they are defending neutral procedures but in reality they are themselves employing a disguised conception of the good.

Moreover, with respect to important moral issues, substantive matters of the good should be debated. As we have seen, Rawls is willing to suspend debate on nonpolitical matters of the good in order to attain an overlapping consensus on how politics should be conducted. Sandel disagrees with Rawls on this matter. Sandel points out that the setting aside (bracketing) of substantive moral issues was a major issue in the Lincoln-Douglas debates, which took place just before the Civil War. Douglas argued that since there was substantive disagreement about slavery, it should be set aside (bracketed) and not made a matter of political debate. Lincoln argued the contrary position. Thus, as Sandel sees it, the liberals are aligned with Douglas and the communitarians with Lincoln.

However, as Sandel himself realizes, this criticism is not truly effective against liberals because liberals reply that slavery should not be bracketed, since it is a violation of the requirement of equal respect for persons that constrains political debate. Slavery is inconsistent with the thin theories of liberal procedural justice. For example, slavery could not be accepted in Rawls's account. Rawls's theory is not entirely neutral because it rules out positions, such as slavery, that cannot coexist with the fundamental values of liberal democracy.

However, if the discussion is shifted to abortion, Sandel is on firmer ground. Many liberals argue that the issue of abortion should be bracketed and left to individual choice since its resolution depends on the solution of complex moral and metaphysical issues, such as the status of the fetus, which cannot be resolved by public reason. But surely this is to favor those who think that the fetus is not a person over those who think it is.

> Opponents of abortion resist the translation from moral to political terms because they know that more of their view will be lost in translation; the neutrality offered by minimalist liberalism is likely to be less hospitable to their religious convictions than to those of their opponents. For defenders of abortion, little comparable is at stake; there is little difference between believing that abortion is permissible and agreeing that, as a political matter, women should be free to decide the moral question for themselves. The moral price of political agreement is much higher if abortion is wrong than if it is permissible.[10]

Although liberals like John Rawls and Ronald Dworkin do have a limited theory of the good, communitarians argue against them and other liberals that the procedural notion designed to separate the political from the civil and to provide an overlapping consensus is too thin. Communitarians argue that a viable democracy needs a commonly recognized definition of the good life.

What definition of the good life do communitarians propose? In *Democracy's Discontent*, Sandel has argued for a republican (and here we refer to civil republicanism, not the policies of the contemporary Republican party) conception of the state rather than the liberal one. Civic republicanism emphasizes the life of participation in political institutions as part of the human good. Sandel argues that the participation by the citizen in the affairs of the state is part of the comprehensive theory of the good that a state should strive to achieve. Liberalism, he argues, has no place for such a general obligation: if citizens want to participate actively in the state, they of course have the right to do so, but there is no obligation. Moreover, on the republican conception, part of the activity of participation in civic affairs involves engaging in debates about the common good. Sandel puts it this way:

> To share in self-rule therefore requires that citizens possess, or come to acquire, certain qualities of character or civic virtue. But this means that republican politics cannot be neutral toward the values and ends its citizens espouse. The republican conception of freedom, unlike the liberal conception, requires a formative politics, a politics that cultivates in citizens the qualities of character self-government requires.[11]

Sandel would take exception to our construal of the state as the protector of individuals' fundamental rights. We see the state as a protector of the right to liberty, a right that can be overridden only by another human right. Sandel argues that the right to liberty emerges from democracy and is in some sense dependent on it. For Sandel's version of civic republicanism, a citizen is free as a participant in a free political community that determines its own fate. Freedom, in this view, entails participation in civic affairs and decisionmaking, or participation in ruling, rather than simply abstract freedom of choice. Sandel points out that there is a strong and a weak interpretation of the claim that freedom is participation in civic affairs. For Aristotle, participation in civic affairs is a necessary condition for freedom. On this more demanding Aristotelian interpretation, a person who does not take an active part in the polis is not really free. The weaker interpretation of this claim is that participation is instrumental to the exercise of liberty. Participation in the polis and public service help preserve liberty and thus strengthen it.

For civic republicans like Sandel, the liberal theory of freedom is too weak to sustain itself. People might use their freedom to get high on drugs or watch soap operas all day. At the very least, freedom is of value only when combined with correlative responsibilities to participate in the political life of the state and develop the civic virtues necessary to the good functioning of democracy.

A Liberal Response to Communitarianism

However, as liberal political theorists we have our own concerns about the republican conception of freedom. Our main concern is that the republican theory of freedom leaves fundamental human rights unprotected. Sandel seems close to admitting that in a democracy where all citizens actively engage in the political process, the state may adopt a notion of the public good that is shared by the majority. On certain issues, such as how much to spend on national defense and how much on welfare, we have no quarrel with this conception so long as the amount spent for defense in peacetime does not deprive a family of the right to a minimum standard of living. Yet we think there is a danger in Sandel's view that an active republican democracy could pass legislation that would in fact deprive a minority of basic human rights, such as the right to a minimum standard of living.

In addition, even if political participation is an important part of freedom, either intrinsically or instrumentally, does the state have a right to coerce us to be free, or to force us to cultivate the civic virtues? We think Sandel would have to answer that question in the affirmative. We find the dangers of state coercion and oppression to be greater than the dangers that citizens in a democratic state might neglect civic participation to an extent that threatens democracy itself. While we are alarmed at the cynicism that the American public has toward politics, we do not believe that mandatory participation in the political process is the answer.

While communitarians argue that liberals ignore the impacts of the liberal account of liberty on political and economic arrangements, liberals like us point out that in embracing substantive conceptions of good citizenship as enforceable by the state, communitarians reject the liberal idea of neutrality toward conceptions of the good life. We liberals do not want the Christian right or any other group with a controversial conception of the good forcing their view of the good life on every American.

Another aspect of the communitarian critique of liberal politics is the communitarian claim that the liberal overemphasizes the individual at the expense of the culture or group. Liberals focus on individual rights, but don't cultures have rights? In particular, doesn't a culture have a right to survive? The force of this question is seen when we consider the contentious issue of immigration and the assimilation of immigrants into American society. The communitarian Paul Taylor defends the notion of the right of a minority culture to survive. Indeed, from Taylor's perspective, the survival of such a culture is a public good, and a public good so important that it permits the violation of the right to equal treatment in certain cases. The example Taylor considers is the concern of French separatists in Quebec, Canada, who are afraid that their French culture will be assimilated into an English Canada and disappear. As a result, the Quebec provincial government has passed a number of laws that might seem to violate liberal norms of equal treatment. French-speaking people and immigrants are not allowed to go to English-speaking schools, the operative language in businesses employing more than fifty people must be French, and all commercial signs must be in French. Taylor defends these laws on the basis of the public good of cultural survival. On this issue the state cannot be neutral with respect to two competing theories of the good. As Taylor says:

> Political society is not neutral between those who value remaining true to the culture of our ancestors and those who might want to cut loose in the name of some individual goal of self-development. . . . It is not just a matter of having the French language available for those who might choose it . . . it also involves making sure that there is a community of people in the future that will want to avail itself of the opportunity to use the French language.[12]

This quotation from Taylor points to a potential difference between liberals and communitarians. For most liberals, it is individuals rather than cultures that have moral standing. In the language of this book, cultures do not have rights—even the right of survival.[13]

A few liberals have parted company with the tradition on this point. For example, Will Kymlicka has tried to integrate a concern with cultural survival into the liberal position.[14] Kymlicka has argued that persons, as individuals, have a right to have their culture protected. If Kymlicka's argument is successful, then he might accept Taylor's defense of the Quebec government's restrictions on traditional liberal rights, but on liberal rather than communitarian grounds.

In his later work *Multicultural Citizenship*, Kymlicka has provided a list of group-differentiated rights for ethnic groups and national minorities that would help guarantee cultural survival. In that work Kymlicka argues that the recognition of such group rights is consistent with the integration of such groups into a liberal society. We have doubts as to whether he has succeeded here, but a full consideration and rebuttal of his views cannot be undertaken here, so we shall limit our discussion to Kymlicka's defense of a right to cultural survival.

Kymlicka's attempt to establish a right to cultural survival is an interesting one. His position is consistent with the traditional emphasis on individuals as the locus of moral rights. However, the issue of cultural survival is fraught with difficulties when countries grapple with it as a matter of public policy. Nowhere is this clearer than in Europe as it struggles with a large number of Muslim immigrants who demand that they practice their religion as they see fit, even when from a liberal's point of view their practices violate the basic human rights of women. Although minority cultures need not fully assimilate in the strong sense identified in chapter 6, the arguments for human rights and other fundamental liberal values, such as liberty, imply that all cultures within a liberal democracy should accept the core values, including a commitment to honoring human rights. Perhaps France goes too far when it insists that Muslim women not wear their traditional garments in public schools. Perhaps those Americans who insist that everyone speak English also go too far. However, an insistence that other religions or cultures accept (or at least do not violate) human rights, religious toleration, and freedom of speech is not only morally acceptable, but we believe it is morally obligatory. In this view, the policy recently adopted by the Netherlands after the assassination of the Dutch filmmaker van Gogh, whose work criticized the treatment of women in some Muslim communities, of making sure immigrants, including Muslims, understand the traditional Dutch commitment to a free and open society where criticism of religious and traditional values, is quite acceptable (although exactly how this policy is best implemented might well be debatable).

Of course, liberals do see great value in cultural diversity. Seeing issues from different perspectives contributes to the individual growth of all. On the other hand, there can be dangers in an overemphasis on groups and cultural rights. Too much emphasis on groups can lead to pressures of conformity within the group, which can undercut the rights of an individual. Moreover, a heavy emphasis on group differences conjoined with an emphasis on loyalty to the group could create competition among groups that would tear society apart, undermining liberal democratic protection for all. Perhaps the greatest danger comes from those groups that would force an undemocratic theocracy on all those who do not accept their position.

FEMINIST CRITIQUES OF LIBERALISM

Feminist Themes

Although there are similarities between the feminists and the communitarians, there are important differences as well. Both are critical of the liberals' attempt to be impartial and neutral. Both wish to situate the subject or individual person in historical space and time. But most feminists tend to reject the notion that a state should seek a unified conception of the public good. These feminists fear that if such a conception were adopted, the opinions of certain groups, especially women, would be marginalized. In expressing this fear, the feminists have something in common with the liberal political theorists they criticize. Many feminists would agree with Amy Gutmann, who said of the communitarians:

> The communitarian[s] . . . want us to live in Salem but not to believe in witches. Or human rights. Perhaps the Moral Majority would cease to be a threat were the United States a communitarian society; benevolence and fraternity might take the place of justice. Almost anything is possible, but it does not make moral sense to leave liberal politics behind on the strength of such speculation.[15]

The guiding philosophy of feminist ethics is that the marginalization and oppression of women are wrongs that ought to be corrected. That conviction is shared by all feminists. However, feminists differ on what is needed to correct the wrongs that are committed against women and sometimes even over the nature of those wrongs themselves. Feminism is a diverse movement, and feminist theorists differ significantly among themselves over the extent and nature of oppression of women and over the proper remedies.

Liberal feminists have argued that women have been treated unequally from men and that justice requires that this unequal treatment cease and that genuine equal opportunity prevail. Liberal feminists do not reject liberal theory but want a fair and full application of it while other feminists find liberal theory incomplete or inadequate and strive to go beyond it. To make the transition from unequal to equal treatment, many liberal feminists maintain that the need for affirmative action and preferential hiring continues. Liberal feminists believe that men and women are not fundamentally different, and that both should have the same opportunity to become doctors or nurses, to serve in the armed forces, or to be physicists. To achieve that kind of opportunity, inequality in family life has to be addressed. So long as women bear unequally the responsibilities of family life, then equality in the workplace cannot be achieved. Liberal feminists would admit that there has been much discussion of this issue and that men may even do the dishes more. However, they would cite statistics to show that the bulk of household and family responsibilities still falls on the shoulders of women. In this respect there is not a significant difference between the beginning of the twenty-first century and the last quarter of the twentieth.

Susan Moller Okin (1946–2004) was the first major feminist to challenge the Rawlsian position on justice. In her book *Justice, Gender, and Family*, she argued that Rawls, throughout his work, had ignored the family and that as a result of ignoring what she regarded as the great inequalities of the division of labor between men and women in sustaining the family, Rawls had perpetuated this injustice in his own theory. Okin believed that liberal projects like Rawls's could be corrected to take care of these inadequacies. To the extent that the claims of inequality in liberal practice are true, we agree. We are as one with the liberal feminists in believing that inequalities resulting from family and household responsibilities should be addressed, although we note that there is room for debate over just which differences are unfair or inequitable.

Other feminists have parted ways from Okin and her liberal feminist colleagues. They reject liberal feminism because they challenge the assumption that there are no morally significant differences between men and women. These feminists have argued that there are important psychological as well as physiological differences between men and women and that these differences are morally significant. As a long-running popular book puts it, surely overstating the point, "Men are from Mars; women are from Venus." Lawrence Kohlberg (1927–1987), a psychologist of moral development, at one time interpreted data from his studies as suggesting that the most advanced stages of moral development emphasized impartial evaluation of the sort found in utilitarianism but especially Kantianism and the views of justice, such as that of Rawls, that developed in part from Kantianism. However, his former colleague Carol Gilligan argued in her influential book *In A Different Voice* (1981) that women tend to reason differently from the impartial perspective rather more often than men and that this alternative perspective, that of caring, is often ignored by Kohlberg and many traditional male liberal political philosophers.[16]

According to this approach men, including male liberal theorists, tend to argue abstractly, emphasizing impartiality, rights, and justice. Women, following this theory, tend to value the importance of relationships in the moral life, and the primary virtue for sustaining relationships is caring. Kohlberg, being male, undervalued caring, so women scored lower on the moral development tests, which allegedly are biased in favor of impartiality. In any case, some feminists emphasize giving equal respect and significance to the special ways that women contribute to our society or correcting the special problems women face, sometimes as a result of sexism (for example, an alleged lack of attention by medical researchers to women's medical needs).

In line with Gilligan's work, other feminists theorists, such as Nel Noddings, have attempted to build a full-blown ethical theory of caring. Central to Noddings's notion of caring is "apprehending the reality of the other." This can be done only by apprehending the other person in all her particularity, not by thinking of individuals as abstractions. Thus a math teacher who appreciates the situation of a child who fears math reflects caring. You can't simply treat all math students alike. Some fear math and some do not.

Feminists have reacted in different ways to the notion that there is a distinctively feminist theory of caring. Some have argued that any fully developed ethical theory must contain both an ethics of caring and an ethics of rights and fairness. Such a well-developed ethical theory would be neither distinctively feminine nor distinctively masculine. Thus ethical theory would in fact become gender neutral. Jean Grimshaw is a good spokesperson for that point of view:

The idea that women "reason differently" from men about moral issues should be questioned. Insofar as there are differences between men and women, it is better to see these as differences in ethical concern and priorities, rather than as differences in mode or style of reasoning. The idea that women "reason differently" rests on problematic oppositions between such concepts as "abstract" and "concrete" or on the notion that a morality of "principles" can be sharply opposed to one in which judgment is contextual.[17]

Our own view shares much in common with Grimshaw. Liberal political theorists and ethical theorists in the tradition of Kant have argued that liberal theory can take into account individual differences, and that caring need not be inconsistent with impartiality. Impartiality does not require that you always treat your mother the same as you would treat a stranger. This discussion, which is now several decades old, cannot be repeated here. Perhaps it is sufficient to note that liberals do recognize that one student fears math and one doesn't, and that that difference is morally significant in how the two students should be treated. Indeed, one should be more caring with respect to the one who fears math. In so doing, one need not have acted contrary to liberal theory. Indeed, impartiality does not require insensitivity to differences. Impartiality simply requires not being biased in favor of a difference due to self-interest.

Some feminists go much further. They argue that traditional liberal theories of rights and fairness that emphasize impartiality are fundamentally mistaken. These traditional liberal theories need more than supplementation. They need to be replaced. Feminists who think this way have tried to develop alternative feminist theories that include more than an ethics of care. Since we are defending a theory of ethics based on individual rights and democratic processes, it is important that we carefully consider and respond to this version of the feminist critique of traditional theories like ours.

The communitarians have criticized the notion that the state can be neutral with respect to competing theories of the good. Some feminists have also challenged the neutrality of liberalism at a deeper level. Specifically, they have argued that the notion of impartiality that is at the center of so much of ethical theory is itself biased—moreover, biased in a way that undercuts the plausibility of the ethical theory on which it is based. Thus, Iris Marion Young (1949–2006) began an important section of her book *Justice and the Politics of Difference* by saying, "A growing body of feminist inspired moral theory has challenged the paradigm of moral reasoning as defined by discourse of justice and rights."[18]

Young, who mounts a radical challenge to some key liberal values, has been among the most philosophically influential and important critics of liberal ethical theory. She charges that liberal theorists' use of impartiality is seriously flawed for three reasons. First, traditional theory is overly abstract. It denies the particularity of situations, treating all according to the same moral rules. Second, it seeks to eliminate feeling from discussions of politics and justice. Third, it reduces the plurality of reasons to one single or monolithic point of view.

Young's first point about abstraction has been developed by Jean Grimshaw. Grimshaw has argued that the charge of too great abstraction can be made in two distinct ways.[19] First, abstraction does away with the concrete particularities of each situation. In order to make comparisons, to apply a rule, what is unique about the forms to be compared is discounted. However, what is discounted is often what is most important, from the ethical point of view. Thus a morality based on rules and principles misses much that is essential. Second, a person can make a decision from a distance and thus not be able to imagine the consequences of that action. To be distanced in that way is to be abstracted from the situation. Bomber pilots are trained to abstracted themselves from their bombing missions in just that way. Because they are unable to see the direct results of the bombing, they are able to disconnect themselves from the harm their actions cause. Foot soldiers who confront the enemy face-to-face are unable to abstract themselves in this way.

Young's second charge is that this excessive abstraction leads liberals to value detached reasoning too much and to ignore the role of feeling and emotion in moral life. Moral claims become like moves in a chess game and lose all life and power.

Third, Young maintains that the liberal emphasis on the impartial point of view blurs the complexity of many moral situations and the very different factors that might apply to them. For example, an injunction simply to be impartial seems of little help when we must weigh a variety of competing factors in deciding whether more of our own personal resources ought to be spent saving for our children's education or helping our neighbors, the victims of a nearby tragedy such as a flood, get back on their feet.

A LIBERAL RESPONSE TO FEMINIST CONCERNS

Are these charges of excessive abstraction and emotional detachment justified? As we indicated earlier, liberal theorists have tried to find a place for particularity and for emotions like caring. However, liberal theorists are more than happy to plead guilty to the charge that rationality and impartiality are central concepts in a theory of ethics and in the political philosophy of the just state.

To see why this is the case, we need to see why liberal theorists emphasize rationality and impartiality. First and foremost, liberal theorists are trying to eliminate bias from ethical reasoning and the determination of the principles of justice. The point of Rawls's veil of ignorance in the original position is to eliminate knowledge of our particular selves so that we can eliminate bias. Rawls and most other liberal thinkers assume that if particularity enters in, people will try to invoke principles of justice that benefit themselves. Rich people will propose principles that benefit rich people, members of particular racial, ethnic, or religious groups might well propose principles that benefit their groups more than others, and so forth. By abstracting away these particulars we are less inclined to be biased in the selection of principles. Surely there is a lot of folk wisdom as well as social scientific work that supports liberal theorists here.

Moreover, an excessive concern with particularity can increase social strife and undermine democratic institutions. Those in any religion who would establish a theocracy are clear that they will make laws that favor those who hold their religious views. In more extreme cases they will try and sometimes succeed in imposing their religious views on others. Think of the Taliban, who are highly skilled in focusing on particularity. Liberals focus on what is common. Particularists focus on their group and thus have a tendency to emphasize difference and to see those who are different as the enemy. At this point in history the dangers of focusing on the particular should be all too obvious.

Similar considerations account for the devaluing of the emotions. Liberal theorists seek principles that are acceptable to all. Getting universal or near universal agreement on basic principles is extremely difficult since people initially tend to disagree over many basic principles. What is required in such circumstances is rational argument. Each citizen tries to persuade others as to the merit of the principles each proposes. Emotion is ill suited to accomplish this. When people's emotions get in the way, positions tend to harden and be less amenable to change. Consider the conflict between Israel and the Palestinians that dates from 1948. The emotional intensity in that dispute remains about as high as it was in the beginning; so does the distance to peaceful resolution.

And when emotional appeals do succeed in getting people to change their minds, the change of mind seems not to be totally legitimate. People should accept moral principles or principles creating the just state on the basis of reason rather than emotion. Rational persuasion functions as a deliberative ideal of objectivity.

Young and those who support her point of view would respond to this defense of rationality and impartiality by arguing that eliminating emotion and particularity does not eliminate bias. She claims that the liberal's emphasis on rational discourse and the elimination of particularity is ideological in the sense that "belief in it helps reproduce relations of domination or oppression by justifying them or by obscuring more emancipatory social relations."[20] How does it do this? The first move is to point out the facts of oppression in liberal societies with special emphasis on the oppression of women and of blacks in the United States. But of course the liberal has a ready response to that claim. Such oppression in liberal states, if and where it exists, should be eliminated. There is nothing wrong with liberal philosophy; rather any oppression in liberal societies is to be explained by the failure of democratic states to act in accord with liberal theory. The liberal position is that where discrimination and oppression can be shown to exist, the liberal is committed to removing them.

However, Young thinks that this response misses the point. Young's real challenge is to the role that the liberal gives to the state. For the liberal the state acts as a referee that is granted the authority to oversee and rule in matters of conflict. On our view, for example, the chief task of the liberal state is to settle conflicts regarding rights claims of citizens. In our discussion of democracy, we have argued that the liberal democratic state is most justified in acting in this role. Of course, working out the mechanics of democratic institutions so that they operate fairly is, we acknowledge, a challenge.

Young herself is certainly a supporter of democracy as the justified form that a state should take. Moreover, she thinks that deliberative democracy (see chapter 6 for an explanation of deliberative democracy) is a step in the right direction toward what she calls "communicative democracy," which she prefers. Young believes that deliberative democracy shares with liberalism in general a bias toward the rational. In deliberative democracy, those with the gift of speaking well have an advantage over those that do not. Young believes that differences in the ability to speak are culturally related; that is, speaking skills are less valued in some cultures than in others. For example, deliberation privileges male over female ways of speaking.[21] Those without such a gift are devalued and marginalized.

Thus, Young maintains, justice requires that equality of participation be broadened from equality to deliberate to equality to communicate where, in addition to standard discourse, greeting, narrative, and rhetoric are given standing as legitimate means of communication. We are familiar with the many forms of greeting, such as "Hello" and "How are you?" Young thinks that forms of speech like these encourage the willingness for discussion and thus play an important role in communicative democracy. So do narratives that provide personal accounts of the needs and values of the speaker: for example, a member of the Lakota tribe explains why the Black Hills of South Dakota have such meaning.

Liberals can accept Young's notion that greeting and narrative deserve standing in an expanded notion of citizen discourse. We do as well although we note that rhetoric that aims to persuade through nonrational devices, such as unreasonable appeals to emotion, should be viewed with suspicion. Moreover, narratives themselves are open to different interpretations and distortions and must be analyzed rationally to avoid the very same kind of bias that Young finds in liberal appeals to impartiality and neutrality. In other words, rationality and impartiality are needed to critically assess the use of such devices as narrative in discourse and discussion.

Remember also that in both deliberative and communicative democracy decisions have to be made. Once everyone who is affected and wishes to have a say has had it, what then? Must the resulting decision on a law or policy be unanimous, or is a majority vote good enough, or should some people or groups of people have a veto power? Neither deliberative democrats nor communicative democrats are as clear as one would like here and we have struggled with such issues ourselves in our chapter on democracy.

What of the central claim of both feminists and deliberative democrats that there should be a commitment to equal voice? Is that egalitarian commitment really justifiable? Should the voices of the ignorant and the prejudiced be given equal weight to the voices of the informed and the reasonable? There are difficult questions that liberal theorists at least try to answer with their accounts of impartiality and rights. Everyone's rights are protected subject to neutral constraints such as prohibition of threats, but what some people say may be judged far more worthy than what others say. Young's communicative democracy has no way of dealing with this problem. Should racists simply be silenced and barred from communicating if the majority doesn't like what they say? But if one group can be silenced, why not others, perhaps simply because their views are not in political favor with the majority? Aren't rights needed to protect access into the very kind of discussion Young endorses? Indeed, she seems to have little room for impartiality and for notions of rational deliberation such as Rawls's notion of public reason.

Even a deliberative democrat like Benhabib has argued that Young's own account requires a commitment to impartiality. Benhabib says, "Without some such standard Young could not differentiate a genuine transformation of partial and situated perspectives from mere agreements of convenience or apparent unanimity reached under conditions of duress."[22] Young herself at times seems to accept the force of this criticism, because she sees the necessity for some commonly accepted standards (unity) even in communicative democracy. At one point Young says, "The members of the polity . . . must agree on procedural rules of fair discussion and decisionmaking. These three conditions—significant interdependence, formally equal respect, and agreed-on procedures—are all the unity necessary for communicative democracy."[23]

Thus, there need to be some, even if thin, impartial rules if we are to have either deliberative or communicative democracy. Liberal concerns with impartiality cannot be entirely dismissed. It is especially important to realize that impartiality has its home in ordinary discourse and everyday practice. We distinguish partial from impartial basketball referees, partial from impartial jurors, and scholars who consistently are unfair to alternative positions from those who make a fair case for views that oppose their own. Impartial judgments in these areas do not involve taking an allegedly impossibly abstract view from nowhere but involve making judgments based on appropriate standards rather than on our personal preferences about outcomes. Thus, a basketball referee is impartial if he makes calls based upon a reasonable interpretation of the rules but is partial if he makes calls against one team because of a personal dislike for the coach. Impartiality, then, need not involve a view from nowhere, only a willingness to strive for supporting reasons that have force apart from our own interests in the matter.

Implicit in much of the work of Young is a concern that Native Americans, African Americans, and women have been marginalized in modern liberal democratic societies and that impartiality is in some way the cause of the marginalization. Even if the marginalization claim is partially true, we doubt that the liberal emphasis on impartiality leads to viewing all problems from one perspective, that of the dominant. Impartiality properly applied requires each of us to consider the viewpoint of others and to give no special weight to our own. Moreover, impartiality need not lead to simplistic and highly abstract rules. Liberal impartiality, as

Brian Barry has argued, is a second-order notion requiring that the major rules governing the political order be reasonable for all to accept, but it does not require that the rules themselves be simple or few in number.[24] On our view, especially complex political issues sometimes may need to be resolved by suitably constrained democratic procedures that allow for the play of a variety of perspectives in mutual dialogue.

So where does that leave us? We think that the feminists are right to point out the failures of liberal theory in the real world. Despite the claims of impartiality, great injustice still exists in the world, and it is statistically correct to say that injustice falls disproportionately on certain groups. However, liberals need not be convinced that this failure results from any errors of logic in the rights-based theory of the democratic state. Where violations of human rights or justice occur, liberals should remain committed to corrective action. Feminist theories have sensitized much of our society to potential blind spots, but they have not shown that rights-based theories of the democratic state are fundamentally flawed. Indeed, if Benhabib is right, and we think she is, feminism itself needs a rights-based ethical theory.[25]

Many "postliberal" thinkers tend to condemn or reject liberal attempts to ground political argument on impartial, neutral, or relatively objective grounds because they believe that such notions presuppose a "god's-eye view" or a neutral perspective of impartiality and objectivity that humans cannot attain. Of course, we agree that the language of neutrality, impartiality, and objectivity can be misused as a cover for self-seeking, especially (but not only) by those in power. And of course we realize that political claims regarding the attributes of the just state are not scientific claims.

However, there is widespread agreement that the function of the state is to preserve order, limit conflict, and assist its citizens as they seek fulfillment in their lives and that the state should do so justly. We believe that the liberal democratic state is best able to achieve those goals.

In the absence of a liberal state, here is what worries us. Unless there are acceptable points of view from which reason can proceed, impartial ground rules acceptable to all parties, it is hard to see how people on any side of a dispute can persuade those who disagree with them. What worries liberals is that if there are no preconditions on discussion and no human rights that are specifiable in advance, then there is the danger that individuals will be unjustly treated. The rights theorist believes that some things should be off the table, such as racism, if justice is to prevail. And a democracy should be constrained by rights. Otherwise a religious fundamentalist majority could elect to become a theocracy that would run roughshod over individual rights. The early twenty-first century provides vivid pictures of what happens in a fundamentalist theocracy, like that of the Taliban.

Accordingly, although liberal theory is far from perfect, and forceful objections have been brought against many of its key assumptions, such objections, we have argued, are far from decisive. The liberal democratic state, we have argued, provides protections for the individual that can be abandoned only at our great peril.

NOTES

1. Some Rawlsians might reply, however, that in a situation where one didn't know the odds of any given outcome, as in the original position, it is rational to avoid the worst outcome—namely, that of having religious beliefs one rejects forced on one at the point of the sword. Critics might rejoin that whether that is or is not the worst outcome depends on the degree to which one refuses to tolerate the allegedly blasphemous religious views of others. Whether or not there is a neutral account of what is the worst outcome (and whether a Rawlsian account must be neutral) continues to be a debatable issue in political philosophy.

2. Not all commentators agree that this is an improvement. Thus Brian Barry argues that Rawls's theory is strongest in the form published in *A Theory of Justice*. See Barry, *Justice as Impartiality* (New York: Oxford University Press, 1995), xi–xii.

3. John Rawls, *Political Liberalism* (New York: Columbia University Press, 1993), xviii.

4. Rawls, *Political Liberalism*, 138.

5. This idea is developed by Michael Sandel in his review of *Political Liberalism* in *Harvard Law Review* 107 (1994): 1777–82.

6. Michael J. Sandel, *Liberalism and the Limits of Justice* (New York: Cambridge University Press, 1982), 150.

7. Charles Taylor, "The Politics of Recognition," in *Multiculturalism*, ed. Amy Gutmann (Princeton, NJ: Princeton University Press, 1994), 33–34.

8. Michael Walzer, *Spheres of Justice* (New York: Basic Books, 1983), 5.

9. Stuart Hampshire, *Innocence and Experience* (Cambridge, MA: Harvard University Press, 1989), 154.

10. Michael Sandel, *Democracy's Discontent* (Cambridge, MA: Harvard University Press, 1996), 20–21.

11. Sandel, *Liberalism and the Limits of Justice*, 5–6.

12. Charles Taylor, *Political Arguments* (Cambridge, MA: Harvard University Press, 1995), 246.

13. We do not mean to rule out altogether the possibility of nonreducible group rights or responsibilities. But a culture seems to be too poorly defined to constitute the sort of entity that can have collective rights. In any case, not all cultures seem to have justified claims to survival. Does the culture of the Taliban have a right to survival? For a thoughtful discussion of collective responsibility, see Larry May, *Sharing Responsibility* (Chicago: Chicago University Press, 1992).

14. Will Kymlicka, *Liberalism, Community and Culture* (Oxford: Clarendon Press, 1989).

15. Amy Gutmann, "Communitarian Critics of Liberalism," *Philosophy and Public Affairs* 14, no. 3 (1985): 319.

16. Carol Gilligan, *In a Different Voice* (Cambridge, MA: Harvard University Press, 1982).

17. Jean Grimshaw, *Philosophy and Feminist Thinking* (Minneapolis: University of Minnesota Press, 1986), 224.

18. Iris Marion Young, *Justice and the Politics of Difference* (Princeton, NJ: Princeton University Press, 1990), 96.

19. Grimshaw, *Philosophy and Feminist Thinking*, 204–15.

20. Young, *Politics of Difference*, 112.

21. For a complete account of Young's argument here, see her "Communication and the Other: Beyond Deliberative Democracy," in *Democracy and Difference*, ed. Seyla Benhabib, (Princeton, NJ: Princeton University Press, 1996), 120–35.

22. Seyla Benhabib, "Toward a Deliberative Model of Democratic Legitimacy," in *Democracy and Difference*, 82.

23. Young, "Communication and the Other," 126.

24. Brian Barry, *Justice as Impartiality* (New York: Oxford University Press, 1995), esp. chap. 9.

25. Benhabib, "Toward a Deliberative Model of Democratic Legitimacy," 78.

QUESTIONS FOR FURTHER STUDY

1. Explain the charge that Rawls's theory of justice is not neutral. To what extent do you think that criticism of Rawls is justified? Explain your answer.

2. Describe the changes Rawls made in his theory as expounded in *Political Liberalism* as compared with the earlier *A Theory of Justice*. What problem in a liberal democracy is Rawls trying to resolve? Does his notion of "an overlapping consensus" succeed in resolving the problem? Why or why not?

3. What does Rawls mean by a "reasonable pluralism"?

4. On what basis do communitarians criticize Rawls as having an inadequate sense of community? Do you think that criticism is justified? Why or why not?

5. Communitarians also criticize Rawls's theory of the self. What is that criticism? Is it justified? Explain.

6. What is the basis of the communitarian critique of liberal neutrality? Do you agree with the critique? Why or why not?

7. Should there be a right to cultural survival? Why or why not?

8. Feminists have criticisms of both the communitarians and the liberal democrats. What are those criticisms? Are they justified? Defend your view.

9. Why would some feminists be opposed to the philosophies of such feminist thinkers as Carol Gilligan and Nel Noddings? Which feminist perspective do you think is more nearly correct? Explain.

10. Is liberal political theory guilty of excessive abstraction and emotional detachment? Explain in detail.

11. What do you think is a major strength of the theory of deliberative democracy? What do you think is a major criticism of it? Is the criticism successful? Defend your view.

12. Can deliberative democracy resolve the practical problems surrounding representation? Why or why not?

SUGGESTED READINGS

Books

Barry, Brian. *Justice as Impartiality*. New York: Oxford University Press, 1995.

Galston, William A. *The Practice of Liberal Pluralism*. New York: Cambridge University Press, 2005.

Gutmann, Amy. *Identity in Democracy*. Princeton, NJ: Princeton University Press, 2004.
—. *Multiculturalism*. Princeton, NJ: Princeton University Press, 1994.
Kymlicka, Will. *Multicultural Citizenship: A Theory of Minority Rights*. New York: Oxford University Press, 1995.
—. *Liberalism, Community and Culture*. Oxford: Clarendon Press, 1989.
Okin, Susan Moller. *Justice, Gender and the Family*. New York: Basic Books, 1989.
Sandel, Michael. *Liberalism and the Limits of Justice*. New York: Cambridge University Press, 1982.
—. *Democracy's Discontent*. Cambridge, MA: Harvard University Press, 1996.
Taylor, Charles. *Philosophical Arguments*. Cambridge, MA: Harvard University Press, 1995.
Walzer, Michael. *Spheres of Justice*. New York: Basic Books, 1983.
Young, Iris Marion. *Justice and the Politics of Difference*. Princeton, NJ: Princeton University Press, 1990.

Articles

Buchanan, Allen. "Political Liberalism and Social Epistemology." *Philosophy and Public Affairs* 32 (Spring 2004): 95–30.
Gutmann, Amy. "Communitarian Critics of Liberalism." *Philosophy and Public Affairs* 14, no. 3 (1985): 308–22.
Patten, Alan. "Liberal Neutrality and Language Policy." *Philosophy and Public Affairs* 31, no. 3 (2003): 356–86.
Simon, Robert L. "From Ethnocentrism to Realism: Can Discourse Ethics Bridge the Gap?" *Journal of the Philosophy of Sport* 30, no. 2 (2004): 122–41.
Taylor, Charles. "The Politics of Recognition," in *Multiculturalism*, ed. Amy Gutmann. Princeton, NJ: Princeton University Press, 1994, 25–73.
Williams, Melissa S. "Justice Toward Groups." *Political Theory* 23 (February 1995): 67–91.

8

ETHICS AND
INTERNATIONAL AFFAIRS

Do our moral obligations stop at the water's edge? Do individual citizens in the affluent nations have moral obligations to the less affluent and often severely disadvantaged millions of the Third World? Can one nation wrong another? What is the proper role of human rights in foreign policy? Should states aim only at enhancing their national interest or should their pursuit of national interest be constrained by moral norms? Can war ever be morally justifiable and, if so, under what conditions?

These and related questions raise the issue of whether at least some moral principles might apply across national boundaries. But what are these principles and upon whom are they binding? For example, are states sometimes morally required to sacrifice their national interest in order to meet the demands of morality?

In this chapter, we will explore questions concerning the role of morality in international affairs. Does morality even have any significant role in the international arena? The political realists answer that it does not. Let us begin by considering their views.

THE CHALLENGE OF REALISM

Political realism is a view about the limits of morality in international affairs. Although it has distinguished contemporary adherents, it was also defended in other eras and was perhaps first described by the ancient Greek historian Thucydides.

In his *History of the Peloponnesian Wars*, Thucydides describes the "Melian dialogue" between the generals of imperial Athens and the leaders of Melos, an isolated island colony of Sparta. The Athenians demanded fealty of Melos but the independent Melians refused to submit. In Thucydides' account of the negotiations between the two sides, the Athenian generals put morality to one side. According to the generals, the reality of the situation is, "They that have . . . power exact as much as they can, and the weak yield to such conditions as they can get."[1] The

Melians refused to surrender until required to do so by force of arms. Thucydides tells us that then "the Athenians . . . slew all the men of military age, made slaves of the women and children and inhabited the place with a colony."[2]

The Athenians, at least on Thucydides' account, are being "realists" in the sense of putting the interest of their city-state ahead of any moral considerations. Can such a dismissal of morality in international affairs possibly be justified?

Two Arguments for Realism

For analytical purposes, it will be useful to distinguish descriptive from normative political realism. The former is a descriptive doctrine about how nations do act while the latter is a normative doctrine about how nations should act.

(DPR) Nations always *do* act in ways intended to maximize their national interest.
(NPR) Nations always *should* act in ways intended to maximize their national interest.[3]

The realist arguments that we will consider are attempts to use descriptive political realism as a crucial part of the justification for normative political realism.

The first argument we will consider might be called the consequentialist argument for realism. According to this argument, a version of which has been defended by such influential analysts of foreign policy as the late Hans Morganthau, if nations do act to promote their national interest, they will produce more overall good than if they pursue moral goals. Hence, they ought to act in ways intended to maximize their national interest.

According to Morganthau's argument, if nations pursue their moral ideals in the international arena instead of realistically following their interests, their behavior will be unstable, unconstrained, and unpredictable. "What is good for the crusading country is by definition good for all mankind and if the rest of mankind refuses to accept such claims to universal recognition, it must be converted with fire and sword."[4] The apparent fanaticism of some versions of fundamentalist Islam, or imperialistic attempts to impose the conception of the good life shared by one culture on very different cultures in the name of "civilizing" them, might be examples of the kind of crusading moralism against which Morganthau and other realists have warned us. Indeed, some realists have condemned President George W. Bush's initiation of war with and subsequent occupation of Iraq on the grounds that it was based on a moralistic and unrealistic crusade to bring democracy to a land not ready to sustain it rather than based on U.S. national interests. On this view, moralism in international affairs amounts to a kind of moral fanaticism often leading to dangerous crusades.

On the other hand, the realists continue, if each state realistically calculates its own interests and restricts itself to their pursuit, its behavior becomes predictable, stable, and above all constrained. The kind of compromise that often is impossible on matters of deep moral difference becomes a matter of practical negotiation. Accordingly, peace, security, and toleration of national differences is best assured if every state avoids the pursuit of abstract moral ideals and pursues its own national interests instead. To summarize this argument, if states do act to promote their national interests, they will promote the overall best consequences as well. Therefore, states should always aim at maximizing self-interest.

In addition to this first consequentialist argument, realists often advance a second Hobbesian argument designed to show that it is morally permissible for states to promote their national interest, even when it might conflict with moral concerns. According to the Hobbesian argument, since descriptive political realism is true, international affairs closely resemble the state of nature as described by Hobbes. Just as individuals in the Hobbesian state of nature act egoistically in the pursuit of wealth and glory, so too do nations act egoistically in the pursuit of national interest. Even if all nations do not always act selfishly, it is much too risky to assume altruism on the part of any rival state since such an assumption can be suicidal. In other words, no nation can have any overriding reason to expect other nations to behave morally toward it. But then any nation that did act morally would be making itself vulnerable to predatory nations. As Morganthau maintains, "a foreign policy guided by universal moral principles . . . relegating the national interest to the background is under contemporary conditions . . . a policy of national suicide actual or potential."[5] Since morality does not require extreme self-sacrifice, although it may permit it, morality cannot require nations to sacrifice national interest to universal principles in a world where other nations are not prepared to do the same.

Are these arguments for realism defensible? While a thorough examination of realism requires more extended treatment than can be provided here, enough can be said to cast doubt on both the consequentialist and Hobbesian arguments.

A Critique of Realism

The consequentialist defense of realism amounts to the claim that better consequences will be promoted if nations act out of concern for national interest than if they act on moral principle. Realists who defend this argument, however, may have far too simplistic a view both of the concept of national interest and of the role morality might play in international affairs.

According to the consequentialist defense of realism, reliance on morality in world affairs will lead to dangerous and intolerant crusades in the name of ideals. Only reliance on the common standard of national interest will ensure predictability, restraint, and international stability. But at this stage of our inquiry, it probably is unnecessary to point out that the role of morality in world affairs need not be restricted to the kind of crusading moralism rightly rejected by the realists. As we have seen in our discussions in other chapters, moral inquiry need not be dogmatic, rigid, and intolerant. Willingness to compromise competing values, tolerance of differences, and sensitivity to the consequences of actions are themselves elements of a rational employment of morality in human affairs. It is far from clear that such a sensitive and rational morality will have the disastrous consequences predicted by realism if employed in the international arena.

Perhaps equally open to question is the assumption of the realists that the national interest constitutes a clear and objective standard for generating our own policies and predicting the behavior of other nations. We suggest that, on the contrary, the idea of national interest is subject to various interpretations and is as open to debate and misunderstanding as are the basic concepts of morality and ethics.

In particular, the realist's argument assumes that the national interest will be understood the same way by all observers regardless of their own normative commitments or ideological frameworks. Only if there is a common understanding of a nation's interest will all observers agree in their predictions about what the nation's self-interested behavior will be. Only if predictions are reliable in this way will the behavior of states seem stable and rational, preventing miscalculation. Imagine the damage if American policymakers based a prediction that a country that sponsors terrorism in the Middle East would not also employ similar forms of terrorism within the boundaries of the United States on a misunderstanding of how the terrorists perceived their interests. Our leaders might believe that continued use of terrorism is not in that group's interest, and let down their guard, when in fact the conception of group interest employed by the terrorists is very different from that postulated by American analysts. Similarly, suppose U.S. policymakers conclude that a "rogue state" will not sell weapons of mass destruction to terrorists because it would be vulnerable to retaliation by the United States but the rulers of the rogue state calculate that their national interest will be enhanced if they sell such weapons to terrorists because then the threat of terrorism will deter an invasion by the Americans.

In fact, as such examples suggest, the nature of a state's national interest often is debatable or contested. One sort of possible dispute is over consequences: if a nation acts in a certain way, what will happen? Even worse, different parties can have very different conceptions of what constitutes the national interest. Conceptions of the national interest can differ along a variety of dimensions. What is to count as the nation: a majority of its citizens, a set of institutions and laws, or a geographic territory? Is the nation's interest to be identified simply with aggrandizement of power, or might ideal elements also enter in? For example, is the United States' national interest necessarily enhanced by an increase in military strength even if that results in reduced respect for democratic institutions throughout the world? What of nations or groups who identify their causes with the will of God? Secular and religious accounts of national interest may differ radically in a great variety of ways.

Disaster in international affairs, then, can arise not only from crusading moralism but also from one state basing its own foreign policy upon mistaken assumptions about how other states see their national interest. The idea of national interest seems to be a contested one: proponents of different ideologies may well advocate different conceptions of the national interest. If so, the idea of national interest, rather than providing a clear, predictable, and neutral basis for the generation, explanation, and predication of policy, is itself at the center of debate over what policy should be.[6] As Charles Frankel, a philosopher and former official of the Department of State, has told us,

> A national interest is not a chart pinned to the wall from which one takes one's sense of direction. The heart of the decisionmaking process ... is not the finding of the best means to serve a national interest already perfectly known and understood. It is the determining of that interest itself: the reassessment of the nation's resources, needs, commitments, traditions and political and cultural horizons—in short, its calendar of values.[7]

In short, since the nature of the national interest is open to interpretation and debate, the assumption of the realists that it can serve as an ideologically neutral standard or a clear basis for justifying, explaining, and predicting the behavior of states seems mistaken.

What about the second argument proposed by the realists? Is the Hobbesian argument defensible? Do international affairs resemble Hobbes's state of nature in which states, rather than individuals, inhabit a lawless world governed only by the needs for survival and power? If so, what moral implications follow?

The claim that international affairs closely resemble Hobbes's state of nature is controversial and has frequently been attacked, for example by Charles Beitz in his book *Political Theory and International Relations*.[8] Beitz points to several important differences between the state of nature, as described by Hobbes, and international relations. In particular, he argues that for Hobbes, each individual in the state of nature is virtually self-sufficient, has a virtually equal capacity to kill any other individual, and has no grounds for reasonable expectation that other individuals would adhere to any set of common norms. However, in the modern world, states are increasingly economically interdependent, small or weak states normally do not represent serious threats to the greater powers, and general norms of international conduct, including respect for diplomatic personnel and fidelity to treaty, are generally observed. While these factors are not sufficient to show that the international arena is similar to a well-ordered domestic society, for there are important differences of degree there as well, they do cast doubt on the parallel with the "war of all against all" described by Hobbes.

Beitz's point, then, is that the international system does not closely resemble a Hobbesian state of nature, and that therefore descriptive political realism is false. However, even if international relations do resemble a Hobbesian state of nature more closely than writers such as Beitz would concede, the extreme conclusions of

211

the realists do not follow. That is, the premises that (1) no nation can count on other nations to act morally toward it, and (2) no nation is morally required to take extreme risks to its national interest do not entail (3) no moral requirements of any kind exist in international affairs. Rather, premises (1) and (2) establish at most that nations are not required to take severe risks, not that they are permitted to do anything at all which enhances their national interest to any degree. Similarly, individuals in Hobbes's state of nature may not be morally required to unilaterally disarm. It does not follow that they are permitted to torture, rape, mutilate, or otherwise victimize others without provocation merely for their own momentary gratification.

So far, the assumptions of the realist (a) that international affairs are a Hobbesian state of nature and (b) that if international affairs are a Hobbesian state of nature, then anything goes, have each been criticized. Equally open to criticism are the realist's assumptions about the nature of morality and about the nature of the national interest itself, assumptions that underlie the defense of realism in international affairs.

While we have not considered all possible defenses of political realism, we hope to have shown that since the two principal arguments for realism are open to serious objection, realism itself is far from being an obvious choice. Given our initial intuition that the Athenians violated the requirements of justice in warfare in their treatment of the Melians, the burden of proof would seem to be shifted to the realist. Accordingly, we will go on to discuss concrete moral issues in international affairs. Perhaps the most convincing refutation of realism, once its major defenses have been defused, is to show how morality might actually apply in the world arena. We will begin with a problem facing individuals as much as nations, the problem of famine and world hunger. What are our moral obligations to the severely disadvantaged in other lands?

WORLD HUNGER AND THE OBLIGATIONS OF THE AFFLUENT

The terrible plight of the world's most seriously disadvantaged people raises many issues for public policy. Among those issues are those having to do with the millions of victims of famine, near starvation, and infectious diseases such as AIDS, which is rampant in many underdeveloped countries throughout the globe (especially in areas of Africa). Consider the parents who watch their children slowly starve during the almost hopeless retreat along dusty roads from an area struck by famine. Consider the millions whose health is damaged, whose rational capacities may be impaired, because of inadequate diet. Think of the children born to mothers who are infected with HIV and who cannot afford drugs that control the virus that are widely available in the developed nations. What are the obligations of the more fortunate to alleviate such suffering?

Many of the issues raised by this question are empirical and conceptual as well as moral. For example, how extensive is world hunger? Such a question looks like a purely factual one, to be settled by empirical inquiry. However, it also raises an important conceptual issue. How is "hunger" to be defined? By varying our criteria of hunger and starvation, we can come up with widely different figures as to the extent of world hunger.

It sometimes is charged that some nations and organizations try to minimize the problem by maintaining that serious starvation is not as widespread as many health organizations claim. On the other hand, some observers have argued that inflated figures hurt the poor. In a still relevant article published in 1976, Nick Eberstadt argued that

> Food relief and development projects for seventy million people, spread across ninety countries, are a manageable undertaking, and with some international cooperation could be attempted fairly easily. If, on the other hand, the number of starving were believed to be a billion, the task might seem unmanageable or hopeless and for the governments involved politically dangerous to boot.[9]

This point carries as least as much force today, when people in affluent countries may feel overwhelmed by the extent of the environmental, social, and economic problems facing the world. If a problem seems unmanageable, people may do nothing to resolve it.

As we will see, empirical and conceptual disagreement over the nature and extent of world hunger has implications for the moral analysis of the issue. What are the moral obligations of the more advantaged nations and peoples of the world in light of world hunger? At least one writer, biologist Garrett Hardin, has argued that the more advantaged not only have no obligation to help, but may well be morally required not to help. Let us begin by considering his views.

Lifeboat Ethics and the Tragedy of the Commons

Hardin uses two analogies, that of lifeboat ethics and that of the tragedy of the commons, to make his case. Hardin begins by asking us to imagine that after a shipwreck, we sit with fifty other people in a fairly well-provisioned lifeboat. We find our boat surrounded by one hundred other survivors, treading water and asking for provisions. Since "they can all be seen as 'our brothers,' we could take them all into the boat, making a total of one hundred fifty in a boat designed for sixty. The boat swamps, everyone drowns. Complete justice, complete catastrophe."[10] Perhaps we could at least let an additional ten people into the boat, for after all its carrying capacity is sixty. Hardin replies that "If we do let an extra ten into the lifeboat, we will have lost our 'safety factor,' an engineering principle of critical importance."[11] Our own security would have been thrown into great danger.

213

The analogy to world hunger is fairly clear. If those of us in the affluent countries rescue the starving, we will all be swamped as world population grows and more and more people continue to need our aid. Those rescued will reproduce, so by saving some starving people now, we will be responsible for even more starving people later, until we are all overwhelmed by needs far too extensive to be met at all. By limiting suffering now, we would have produced even more suffering later. Aid would make the situation drastically worse, not better.

Hardin's argument is reinforced by the example of the tragedy of the commons. "If a pasture becomes a commons open to all, the right of each to use it may not be matched by a corresponding responsibility to protect it. . . . The considerate herdsman who refrains from overloading the commons suffers more than a selfish one who says his needs are greater."[12]

In short, everyone has an incentive to overload the commons. If I refrain from overloading, I will be exploited by those with no scruples. Since everyone reasons the same way and no one wants to pointlessly sacrifice his or her welfare, everyone overloads and the commons is eventually destroyed. Similarly, the simple provision of aid, as if it came from a global commons, will simply encourage more and more irresponsible behavior on the part of the recipients, until the global commons is exhausted and we are all reduced to the level of the severely disadvantaged.

Assessment of Hardin's Position

Are Hardin's arguments decisive? Should we apply his lifeboat ethic to world hunger? What are the real implications of the tragedy of the commons? Let us consider Hardin's position in some depth.

Unfortunately for his perspective, Hardin's position rests on some very debatable factual and moral assumptions. For one thing, Hardin makes the empirical assumptions that if aid is given to disadvantaged nations so as to minimize or prevent starvation, population will increase, and if population increases, the standard of living will fall still further. Each of these assumptions faces serious difficulties.

Thus, even if aid is given to a developing country to prevent starvation, it can be accompanied by education about and support for birth control. Aid does not have to be all of one type. Indeed, aid might be given only to those countries that are willing to implement birth control policies, or at least such states may be given priority in receipt of aid. (Such a selective policy might seem objectionable on humanitarian grounds, but one might want to go halfway with Hardin here and reply that one should give aid only where it actually will do some good.)

Perhaps of greater importance, there is evidence that indicates that when a developing nation becomes better off, its rate of population growth tends to decrease.[13] This may be because children are considered a resource in a poor nation; they bring in income and care for parents in old age. In a poor country, it pays to have many children since only a few will survive to maturity. However, as the country becomes more affluent, a higher percentage of children survive, and the family tends to have resources that it might rather invest elsewhere than in child care. There is less incentive to have many children as a form of old-age insurance. The better off the developing country becomes, the less its population may grow.

Finally, even if population in developing nations does grow, it does not necessarily imply that the standard of living will fall. Highly populated Japan, as well as the Benelux countries, illustrate the point that efficient use of human capital can produce a high standard of living along with high population density.

Hardin, of course, might reply correctly that while his empirical assumptions are not self-evident, neither are those of his opponents. Perhaps provision of aid will only generate more problems. Even a lowered rate of population growth in some developing nations may not be enough to help so long as the absolute size of the population grows. Be that as it may, it is important to see that Hardin's predictions are controversial and should not be taken as self-evident.

His moral assumptions are highly controversial as well. The moral theory upon which his argument seems to be based is a version of utilitarianism. It is because the alleged consequences of famine relief would be bad that Hardin rejects such aid. However, if, as we have argued, natural or human rights constrain the pursuit of utility, appeal to utilitarian consequences does not settle the case, particularly when Hardin's own predictions about the probable consequences of providing aid are open to question.

Thus, some proponents of an approach to morality that makes rights and justice more fundamental than utility may question whether those on the lifeboat—the citizens of the more affluent states—have any right to be there. Are their secure places the result of exploitation of the less affluent nations through colonialism, or just the result of the luck of being born in the right place at the right time? In either case, the fact that some are fortunate enough to be in the well-provisioned lifeboats does not mean they are morally entitled to be there.

A more moderate critic might acknowledge either that many of those in the developed nations do have rights to their position (rights they have either earned or legitimately inherited) or at least that it is not wrong for them to be there. For example, the right to liberty may protect us against great interference with our lives, even if it is in part a result of moral luck that we have enough to eat and someone born in Somalia does not. (Similarly, even if through accidents of birth I have healthy kidneys and you do not, it does not follow either that it is wrong for me to have healthy kidneys or that you can appropriate my kidneys without consent; you are blocked by my right to personal liberty.) However, the moderate critic will still want to argue that the idea of positive rights to a minimal welfare floor, which we have defended in chapter 3, supports claims of the starving. If there is a natural right to a minimally decent standard of living, the affluent will be morally obligated to make some contribution, even across national boundaries.

Is this kind of approach any more defensible than Hardin's? Let us go on to consider an argument for the view that the affluent of the world have stringent moral obligations to help relieve world hunger.

The Case for Sacrifice

Peter Singer, an Australian philosopher who has taught for many years in America, most recently at Princeton, and who has written on a wide variety of social issues, has argued that individuals in the developed nations have extensive and demanding obligations to relieve starvation. Although Singer has reformulated and to some degree moderated his position over time, we will discuss a particularly demanding early formulation of his view. After examining it, we can then consider whether a more moderate position is defensible.

In the demanding version of his argument, Singer argues from the following assumptions:

1. Suffering and death from lack of food, shelter, and medical care are bad.
2. If it is in our power to prevent something bad from happening, without thereby sacrificing something of comparable moral importance, we ought morally to do it.[14]

Given these assumptions, Singer maintains that since starvation clearly is bad, then we ought to give as much as we can to prevent it, up to the point where deprivation would cost us more than what we give up would benefit the recipient. Premise (2) does not merely require that we make some donation to famine relief but, on Singer's understanding of "comparability," requires us to give to the point of marginal utility—where further giving would hurt us more than it would help the recipients.

In fact, it is a major part of Singer's argument that we should not think of donations to famine relief as a kind of charity. Given our present way of thinking, donations to famine relief are regarded as admirable but optional. The individual who fails to give normally is not thought to have committed a wrong. But Singer's point is that our present way of thinking on the matter is mistaken; it is wrong to fail to give to relieve suffering up to the point of marginal utility. In particular, it is wrong to spend money on luxuries while children starve.

It might be objected that the fact that many of the world's starving live far away and are citizens of other countries blunts our obligation, but Singer would deny this. After all, suppose I could save a child drowning in a nearby swimming pool by throwing her a life raft and save a child in an underdeveloped country by mailing a check for an amount I do not need. Why should the difference in proximity make a difference to the force of my obligation in either case?

Let us accept this point, at least for now, and consider assumption (2), which states that if it is within our power to prevent something bad from happening without thereby sacrificing something of comparable moral importance, we ought to do it. How is this principle to be defended?

Singer defends the principle in part by appealing to example. Thus, he points out that "if I am walking past a shallow pond and see a child drowning . . . I ought to wade in and pull the child out" even if this means getting my new clothes muddy in the process.[15] However, this example actually does not support premise (2) since the sacrifice involved is relatively minor. It does not establish an obligation to sacrifice something significant let alone an obligation of the affluent to reduce themselves to near poverty to rescue the starving. To support (2), Singer would have to show that the rescuer has an obligation to risk his or her life, or at least something of great importance, to save the child. Since it is far from clear that such heroic action is morally required, Singer cannot defend (2) by only appeal to the example of the drowning child.

Perhaps (2) can be defended instead by appeal to the more general principle of impartiality. If everyone is to count as a fundamental moral equal of everyone else, we have no basis for favoring our own welfare over that of other people. If each counts for one and only one, preventing X from suffering a certain evil is morally required so long as the cost to me is less, even if only slightly less, than the evil I prevent by sacrificing my own interests. Otherwise, I am favoring myself and violating the principle of impartiality.

Looked at in this way, however, (2) looks suspiciously like a variant of utilitarianism, which might be called negative utilitarianism. Unlike standard utilitarianism, it does not require us to promote the good of others. But it does require us to aggregate the avoidance of evil so as to minimize total bad consequences of our acts or practices. If so, it is open to a number of the objections against utilitarianism that we discussed in chapter 2.

In particular, Singer's negative utilitarianism seems to leave little room for individuals to live their own lives, carry out their own projects, and develop in ways they choose for themselves. Rather, it requires individuals to sacrifice control over the direction of their lives, so long as by doing so they (perhaps only minimally) reduce the suffering of others. While there may indeed be a duty to alleviate suffering, it is questionable whether the duty is as demanding as Singer's argument suggests. The degree of sacrifice Singer requires reduces workers virtually to natural resources for the alleviation of suffering. Moreover, the alleged duty to relieve suffering may be virtually endless; no matter how much suffering any one person alleviates, there will still be more to alleviate the next day. We doubt that the demands of morality can be so demanding that people need to become virtual saints in order to simply do their duty.

Second, Singer's approach at least suggests that many people in affluent countries simply are selfish, spending money on unneeded luxuries when the money could better be spent in reducing the total suffering found in our world. While this picture may sometimes apply to all of us, we suggest it often is overdrawn. For example, if parents decide to save money to pay for their children's college education, it is far from clear that such action is either selfish or immoral. Similarly, working adults may save rather than give to famine relief to plan for retirement, so that they will not become dependent on others. They may also enjoy life by taking a vacation after hard work or make life more pleasant for children and grandchildren. Singer may be correct to say that mere proximity does not change our moral obligations to rescue suffering people in distant lands but our own commitments, such as commitments to family, friends, neighbors, and perhaps fellow citizens, may conflict with and sometimes override our obligations to make heavy sacrifices to rescue strangers.

A proponent of Singer's view might reply that our criticisms of (2) rest on a question that begs appeal to the intuitions of our readers. People in our culture, the critic might maintain, have been brought up to think of morality as relatively undemanding, as a set of constraints protecting individual liberty but not requiring much of the individual. Utilitarianism, however, attempts to reform this traditional moral perspective. A more demanding morality, the critic maintains, is more appropriate in a world where suffering is so frequent. To reject utilitarianism on the grounds that it is too demanding is to beg the question since the rejection is based on appeal to traditional moral intuitions, the very intuitions that the utilitarian urges us to reject.

This last-ditch utilitarian defense is a thoughtful one, but we suggest that it does not carry the day. For one thing, utilitarianism itself sometimes is defended by appeal to the intuition that we ought to be benevolent toward others. Perhaps more important, if utilitarianism implies that individual autonomy and the capacity for persons to live their own lives are not significant, and that our special relationships with others do not create moral commitments of their own, it is hard to see how either individual freedom or the significance of human relationships can be accommodated within a utilitarian framework.

Finally, if morality is made so demanding that people psychologically cannot live up to it, or are called upon to sacrifice virtually all their nonmoral goals on the altar of moral goodness, morality will come to be seen only as an abstract ideal with no real bearing on human life. The strains of commitment of adherence to a strict utilitarian morality may be too great—a point Singer himself has acknowledged in more recent writings.[16]

An interesting distinction, made by Brian Barry, between first- and second-order impartiality may be useful here.[17] First-order impartiality requires us to be impartial in all our everyday transactions with others. Interpreted strictly, it requires, such as, that parents show no preference for their own children in virtually any context, for example, in deciding whose children to play with. Singer apparently relies on this conception of first-order impartiality, which leaves little if any room for special relationships with others and the network of obligations and rights such relationships generate. However, the requirement that we should always be impartial in the first-order sense seems unjustifiable precisely because it has such unacceptable consequences. Barry suggests plausibly that instead, justice requires only second-order impartiality: the idea that the basic rules and principles of justice should be those that rational people could accept from an impartial perspective. Perhaps one of the rules that could be accepted would allow all parents to save for their own children's college education (rather than be committed to paying equally for the education of all children) or pay special attention to their own children's activities. If so, parents need not be morally required to sacrifice virtually all their savings for famine relief, any more than they would be morally required to play equally with all children, giving little special weight to their own families. More generally, Singer overlooks the claim that our special relationships with specific persons may block obligations to strangers from even arising. Maybe, as Singer asserts, distance makes no difference to our moral duty, but friendship and family might.

In any case, if, as we have argued, respect for the individual as a choosing, autonomous person is itself a fundamental moral value, a utilitarian ethic of world hunger which does not take such a value into consideration is open to the charge of swallowing up the person in the long-term pursuit of a better world. While, as we will argue, some sacrifice is required in a world where great suffering cries out for alleviation, it is doubtful that the more advantaged individual should be morally required to live virtually as a mere means for the alleviation of suffering, as Singer's variant of utilitarianism seems to require.

It also is worth noting that Singer's position, like that of Hardin, rests on factual assumptions about world hunger. In particular, his discussion seems to at least suggest that world hunger can best be dealt with by individual self-sacrifice on the part of the better off. If, as recent studies suggest, world hunger is paradoxically not due to severe food shortages but rather to the maldistribution of an adequate food supply, the best long-term solution may well involve political action at the state level designed to bring about institutional change in developing countries.[18] While this does not eliminate the need for interim help by individuals, it does call into question the assumption that we can make others better off only by making ourselves collectively worse off. It is at least arguable, although perhaps self-serving, to maintain that the Western nations need to remain affluent in order to contribute to an expanding world economy and in order to retain the influence needed to promote reform in the distribution of food in the developing world. Of course, this presupposes that people in the West have the alleviation of suffering among distant peoples as one of their moral priorities. Singer's work surely has played a significant role in bringing this priority to the forefront of the minds of many of his readers, even if his own proposed solution remains controversial.

World Hunger and Human Rights

Our discussion suggests that a position on world hunger more demanding than Hardin's but not quite so demanding as Singer's might be worth consideration. In particular, if people have the human right to a minimally decent standard of living, that right, since it is a human right and not a conventional one, applies across national boundaries. On the other hand, if people also possess human rights to liberty, and exercise those rights as members of social organizations, they acquire special obligations within those institutions: obligations to children, spouses, coworkers, and fellow citizens. Those obligations may frequently conflict with obligations to aid those in other lands. Moreover, as autonomous persons, it is far from clear that we are obligated to totally sacrifice our own life plan in order to benefit others, although it might well be especially praiseworthy should we choose to do so.

Singer has suggested that those who find his premise requiring sacrifice to nearly the point of marginal utility too stringent may want to replace it with the more moderate version (2'):

> (2') If it is in our power to prevent something very bad from happening without thereby sacrificing anything else morally significant, we ought, morally, to do it.

(2') differs from the more demanding (2) in that it allows a wider range of excuses for noncompliance; we may violate (2) only in order to preserve something of comparable worth but may violate (2') to preserve a morally significant but not necessarily comparable goal. The trouble with (2'), however, is that it seems empty without some specification of just what has moral significance.

Perhaps a more profitable route would be to approach the issue of global distribution from the perspective of theories of justice, which we already have examined. Indeed, although Rawls himself addressed issues of global justice only briefly in *A Theory of Justice* (1971), commentators have tried to apply his theory to global distributive issues. This seems a natural extension to many, since it appears arbitrary to restrict the veil of ignorance to those living in a particular society. Why not extend Rawls's veil of ignorance so that the parties in the Original Position are ignorant of their citizenship? Rawls himself addressed these issues later in his career in his 1993 Amnesty International lecture entitled "The Law of Peoples" later published in book form.[19]

However, applying Rawls's theory to international affairs raises complex issues of its own. Should the parties to the global original position be conceived of as representatives of states or as individuals who must decide whether or not to even have a system of nation-states? The former proposal suggests that distributive issues may revolve around states while the latter suggests, at least to its proponents, a focus on the worst-off group of individuals, Rawls himself focuses on different "peoples" at different levels of respect for basic rights, including at the lowest levels of outlaw states and tyrannies. A second issue concerns whether the global original position is meant to apply directly to the actual world or is intended to derive an ideal agreement that would be arrived at by just states or at least states that, even if they are not liberal democracies, by and large respect basic human rights of their citizens. Of course, an even more fundamental issue is whether broad principles of justice, as opposed to narrower humanitarian obligations to help relieve extreme suffering, apply across national boundaries in the first place.[20]

Debate over Rawls's version of global justice has focused around whether it is sufficiently sensitive to redistributive concerns. Rawls himself seems to have focused primarily on international order, where parties to the global original position represent states and primarily are concerned with establishing such rules of international justice as nonaggression and national sovereignty. Critics, who tend to favor an original position of individuals rather than representatives of peoples, charge that in view of the vast global disparities between the rich and the poor, the Rawlsian approach can and should be applied to distributive issues. Some, for example, have proposed a global tax that would redistribute funds from the rich to the poor nations.[21]

Let us consider one proposal for a global tax on natural resources, based partially on Rawlsian concerns about the "natural lottery" that distributes such goods around the world in an apparently arbitrary way. We will also discuss briefly the recent initiative, sponsored by the United Nations, with the support and participation of many world leaders, known as the Millennium Project.

NATURAL RESOURCES AND GLOBAL JUSTICE

Many of the world's less developed nations have maintained in the United Nations and in other international forums that a new international economic order, designed to more equally distribute the world's wealth, ought to be implemented. On their view, the current unequal distribution of wealth and resources between the developed nations and the Third World is inequitable and unjust. International treaties, including the proposed Law of the Sea Treaty, rejected by the United States in 1982, contain provisions calling for a shift of resources toward the underdeveloped nations and the more recent Millennium Project (the Millennium Declaration was signed at the U.N. Millennium Summit in 2000) encompasses initiatives to accomplish similar goals. According to advocates of global redistributive justice, the gap between the rich and the poor surely should be of at least as much concern internationally as within domestic society.

Although the general topic of global justice extends far beyond claims to natural resources, entitlements to natural resources are a central area of concern. Should a nation that lies on rich oil deposits or fertile fields have an absolute and exclusive claim to the fruits of what may be nothing more than good luck? Should natural resources that lie outside national boundaries, such as mineral deposits in Antarctica, in the depths of the sea, or in outer space, be regarded as the exclusive property of the discoverers, or should they be regarded as part of a global commons, the common heritage of mankind? After all, resource-rich nations may have enormous advantages over resource-poor ones. An individual born into a resource-rich country may, through an accident of birth, have a far longer, healthier, and more interesting life than an individual born into a resource-poor nation. Is such a situation fair or equitable?

In this section, we will explore two influential positions on ownership of natural resources. During the discussion, it will be important to keep in mind the distinction between natural resources that lie within national boundaries and those that do not, since different principles may apply in each case.

Locke and Libertarian Entitlements

Libertarianism, as understood here and discussed in chapter 4, is the political philosophy that holds that rights to liberty are fundamental and therefore it always is impermissible to interfere with personal liberty, except to protect liberty itself (or perhaps to compensate those whose liberty has been wrongly violated). For libertarians, the liberty to appropriate and exchange property is a particularly important one. But how does property get appropriated in the first place? An answer to that question might shed important light on claims to ownership of natural resources.

Many libertarians rely on a theory of appropriation proposed by John Locke, whose views we discussed in chapter 3. According to Locke, as long as we are in the state of nature, we are entitled to our body and what we produce with our body through our labor. Accordingly, we can appropriate property by mixing our labor with it. Owners of justly appropriated property can freely exchange it among themselves through the market, or can voluntarily transfer entitlements by giving gifts.

If we view international affairs as something like a Lockean state of nature, with nations having rights logically parallel to those of individuals in Locke's theory, then nations can be regarded as being entitled to control resources just as individual persons have control over their bodies. Moreover, states or other collective entities, such as corporations, can appropriate resources lying outside their own national boundaries by mixing their labor (or that of their agents) with it. For example, an American mining consortium can come to own mineral deposits on the deep sea bed through deep sea mining. On this view, since it is the corporation that has invested the resources, technology, and labor into deep sea mining, it acquires an entitlement to the minerals at the mining site.

This position is a libertarian one, since entitlements to resources arise from individuals or collectives exercising their liberty over their bodies. Libertarians point out that if we could not collectively or individually appropriate property through our free actions, our liberty to control our lives would be significantly restricted. In addition, such free appropriation also may enhance efficiency, since it rewards the productive and the enterprising.

A Critique of Libertarian Entitlements

Since the libertarian entitlement theory has been examined in chapter 4, the discussion here will focus on its application to appropriation of natural resources rather than on its overall validity. To begin with, even adherents of the Lockean theory of appropriation sometimes will admit that it is vague at crucial points. How much labor must be invested in resources before one can claim them? Why, as Robert Nozick asks, doesn't the laborer lose his labor rather than gain property? For example, if you grew a tomato, made tomato juice from it, and mixed the juice with the Atlantic Ocean, you would lose your tomato juice rather than acquire the Atlantic.[22] Finally, how broad is your entitlement? Thus, if you come to own a valuable resource, do you have a right to use it in ways that may harm your neighbors? For example, can you pollute at will simply because your mining operation is on your property? What are the limitations on Lockean entitlements generated by the rights of others?

These are general difficulties with the Lockean theory of acquisition. It is important to see that they count just as much against collective acquisition of property by a socialist state as against individualist acquisition by members of a capitalist one so long as either is defended on Lockean grounds.

Clearly, there is a problem, although not necessarily an unsolvable one, of explaining how property can be justly appropriated in the first place.[23] Rather than deal at length with the general problem, which might be resolved by revision of the Lockean approach, or by a more broad-based appeal either to the utility of various rules for acquiring property or to their relevance for preservation of individual freedom, we will consider in depth a particular argument against full appropriation of natural resources. Proponents of this argument maintain that even if the Lockean or some other individualistic approach to appropriation of other kinds of property is correct, none of these approaches apply to natural resources.

Resource Egalitarianism and the Geologic Lottery

Resource egalitarianism is the view that natural resources are the common heritage of mankind and that everyone in the world has a prima facie or presumptively equal claim to benefit from their development. As so defined, resource egalitarianism contradicts the libertarian view, since it denies that natural resources can be fully owned and totally controlled by the appropriators.

The first argument for resource egalitarianism that we will consider is based upon the "geologic lottery." That is, the resource egalitarian can argue that the location of natural resources throughout the globe is a matter of moral luck. The Saudis have done nothing to deserve the huge oil deposits in their territories, nor have Americans done anything to deserve the mineral deposits or fertile soil found within the continental United States. Location of resources is the result of a geologic lottery for which no human is responsible. Since no one is responsible for the location of natural resources, no one can claim to deserve control of them. Therefore, they must be regarded as the common heritage of mankind, to be developed and used for the benefit of all.

According to writers such as Charles Beitz, such a position would be endorsed from a global version of Rawls's original position: an initial situation in which the veil of ignorance (see chapter 4) is extended to cover knowledge of citizenship.

> The fact that someone happens to be located advantageously with respect to natural resources does not provide a reason why he or she should be entitled to exclude others from the benefits that might be derived from them. Therefore, the parties would think that resources (or the benefits derived from them) should be subject to redistribution under a resource redistribution principle.[24]

Moreover, Beitz maintains that such an argument is more defensible than Rawls's similar treatment of natural abilities and talents since "unlike talents, resources are not naturally attached to persons. . . . Thus, while we might feel that the possession of our talents confers a right to control and benefit from their use, we feel differently about resources."[25] Beitz also might have added that talents and skills are often developed through hard work, while resources just happen to be located in resource-rich nations. The citizens of such fortunate countries did not do anything to determine the initial distribution of natural resources. Hence, we cannot be said to deserve the natural resources we control even if, against Rawls, we can make claims of desert based on our own development of our talents.

Critique of the Lottery Argument

Is the lottery argument decisive? Before it is accepted, at least three kinds of objections need to be considered. First, it is important to be clear about exactly what the lottery argument establishes. Properly understood, it does not establish that ownership of or entitlement to natural resources is either morally or conceptually inappropriate. Rather, what it shows, at most, is that claims to entitlement or ownership cannot be based on personal or collective desert. However, if, for example, ownership is conceived of as a set of rules that promote utility if generally observed, or as a means of implementing the right to liberty, the appeal to the geologic lottery is beside the point. Property may also be thought of in other ways. For example, it may be understood as a buffer between the individual and others, offering a zone of protection for privacy and freedom. The lottery argument applies most directly against Lockean or desert theories of property; the degree to which it might apply to other approaches is more controversial.

Even ignoring this point, the lottery argument is open to further objection. In particular, it does not deal with the distinction between *actual* and *potential* resources.

It is true that no one is responsible for the distribution of potential resources around the globe. No human, for example, placed huge oil deposits in the Middle East. However, oil deposits become an actual resource only given a technology that can utilize them. Given a less advanced technology than now exists, or a much more advanced one, today's valuable oil supplies might be virtually worthless.

What is the significance of the distinction between actual and potential resources? Although no one is responsible for the initial distribution of potential resources, persons and collectivities such as nations can be responsible for turning potential into actual resources. An individual, by inventing a new technology, or a state, by supporting an enlightened policy with respect to science and education, can be responsible for the development of the technology that most efficiently utilizes the available resources. Thus, whether the lottery argument has force in particular instances depends on the facts at hand.[26]

This point has special application to natural resources found outside national boundaries, such as mineral deposits lying in the deep sea bed or in outer space. The ability to mine and develop such resources depends upon a complex combination of policies influencing technological development, education, and basic research in the sciences—precisely the kinds of things for which individuals and groups can plausibly claim credit.

It is open to the proponent of the lottery argument to reply that no one deserves the good luck to be born into the kind of society that makes efficient use of its human capital. Once this move is taken, however, we seem to be back with the more general argument that no one deserves individual talents and capacities. For if a society's development is at least in part due to such factors, and if people have the right to pass on at least some of those benefits to their descendants and to their fellow citizens, then even if one does not deserve to be born into an advantaged position, one may be entitled to some (although perhaps not all) of the inherited initial advantages anyway. So unless the proponent of the lottery argument is willing to extend it from geology to the individual level, an extension which writers such as Beitz try to avoid (perhaps because of the disadvantages pointed out in chapter 4), the appeal to the geologic lottery cannot be used as a general tool to undermine all claims of entitlement or ownership to natural resources (although in specific cases, this appeal may show that benefits from natural resources are undeserved). However, this does not mean that the idea of a global resource tax is illegitimate but only that it is not fully supported by the lottery argument.

RESOURCE EGALITARIANISM AND HUMAN RIGHTS

We have seen so far that there are difficulties both with an unrestricted Lockean entitlement approach to natural resources and with the view that special claims to natural resources based on desert never are justified because all such claims must be based on pure luck. Perhaps a view combining the best elements of resource egalitarianism and a libertarian entitlement theory might be worth considering.

While we are not able to present a full theory of how global justice might bear upon appropriation of natural resources, the account of natural or human rights sketched earlier does have implications in this area which may be worth consideration. The ground of such rights is the basic idea that humans are owed respect and concern as rational, autonomous creatures. This idea involves acknowledging the worth of human liberty, including the freedom to join and act as members of groups or institutions formed to secure goals that cannot be secured by individuals acting alone. Nations and corporations may at least sometimes constitute such groups. While there is a real problem as to whether unjust or oppressive nations, those that violate the fundamental rights of their citizens as free and autonomous beings, should have the same rights and status as reasonably just ones, the liberty of individuals to participate in collectives is the ground for collective claims over natural resources.

Thus, if the function of government is to protect the rights and interests of its citizens, subject to moral constraints of not violating the rights of others, and this requires territorial integrity, nations have at least a prima facie right to control who has access to resources within territories. Similarly, if nations or corporations take risks to develop resources lying in previously inaccessible areas outside national boundaries, they may have claims to ownership, or at least claims to a reasonable profit based upon desert or upon compensation for investment (and the risks which go along with it).

However, none of this implies that such resources ought to be under the absolute control of the developer or the host nation. This is because in addition to negative rights, other individuals have positive rights to a minimally decent standard of living. Even if a nation has a duty to put the crucial interests of its citizens first, this does not imply that it can totally ignore the human rights of others, especially when respect for the rights of distant peoples does not affect fundamental interests of its own citizens. Thus, in our view, the affluent nations, and their citizens, are under an obligation to make *reasonable* contributions to an overall scheme of global justice designed to ultimately create a global welfare floor below which no citizen of the world will be allowed to fall. This case becomes stronger if we acknowledge a minimal version of the lottery argument: that citizens of resource-rich nations do not deserve *all* the benefits that accrue from their good fortune even if, as we have argued, desert and entitlement claims to natural resources may have some grounding. While such a global welfare floor is at present utopian, even if conceived of as a compromise between opposing views, we suggest that there is an obligation to take *reasonable* steps, in light of other pressing obligations and needs, to help make it a reality.

One possible way of doing so is expecting those collectivities—nations or corporations—that develop resources lying outside national boundaries to pay an international tax on profits for such an end. Ideally, the demands of justice, while not so demanding as to unduly limit most individuals' life plans, do apply across national boundaries. While this might not amount to a global difference principle, requiring the worst-off to be made as well-off as possible, it might require transfers of some significance to implement a global welfare floor.

The United Nations Millennium Project, in which world leaders have pledged to provide funds to achieve feasible goals, such as eradication of extreme hunger, promotion of gender equity, reduction of child mortality, and improvement of maternal health, may well be a significant step toward achievement of a global welfare floor.[27] Contributions come from individuals (such as philanthropist George Soros, who gave fifty million dollars in 2006) and from corporations, as well as from nations. Yearly reports assess actual progress toward meeting these goals. While some of the problems we mentioned may apply to this initiative, such as the question of whether the project might inadvertently empower oppressive regimes, it seems to be a reasonable effort that may make a significant dent in world poverty—a task that is of the highest moral priority.

The Ideal and the Actual in International Affairs

The developed nations have received much criticism, not only from less developed countries but also from many of their own concerned citizens, for not providing sufficient nonmilitary aid to less developed areas of the globe. It has been charged that less than one percent of the U.S. gross national product is devoted to such aid. Critics state that this is a shockingly low total, and their point has force even if one adds past U.S. efforts that the critics sometimes ignore, including contributions to such international organizations as the World Bank.

While we share the view that an increase in such nonmilitary aid is warranted—and warranted on grounds of global justice rather than charity—we do note that there is a difficulty in jumping too quickly from premises about what justice ideally requires to conclusions about actual policy. In particular, if global justice is based on individualistic concerns, as it is in our account of natural rights, or on an attempt to apply Rawls's theory to international affairs, it is unclear just how it applies in a world of states. That is, global justice as so conceived justifies distributive principles for individuals, but actual distribution in the real world is among states. The problem, of course, is that unjust states may use any wealth they receive for unjust purposes rather than applying it to alleviating the plight of individuals.

Thus, consider the Law of the Sea Treaty, which in part would have regulated the development of undersea resources, and which was rejected by the United States in 1982 in spite of acceptance by virtually all the other nations of the globe. This treaty called for some redistribution of the benefits of deep sea mining to less developed nations. The United States' rejection, based in part on professed adherence by the administration of President Ronald Reagan to a Lockean entitlement theory (and perhaps also on economic self-interest), was criticized by those at home and abroad who viewed the deep sea bed as a global commons to be developed for the benefit of all.

Although these criticisms have some merit, the Law of the Sea Treaty was at best an imperfect instrument of global justice. In particular, it did not require either that recipient countries be internally just or that they use redistributed benefits in just ways. Indeed, given the sorry record of many states, some of the benefits almost surely would have been used for unjust purposes. It is arguable that the United States should have signed the treaty, although reasons other than those of global justice (such as the need for a stable international arena) seem most compelling. Given the defects of the entitlement theory, the treaty surely was rejected for the wrong reasons. Nevertheless, in view of the distinction between the actual and the ideal, it is doubtful that acceptance of the treaty was truly required by considerations of global justice.[28] This is so because there was little assurance that the redistributed funds would have been used for just purposes. Perhaps the Millennium Project, which is directly targeted at aspects of world poverty, will fare better in this regard.

In view of these considerations, an enlightened foreign policy would have as one of its principal aims a negative one. We should not act so as to violate or contribute to violation of rights abroad. Thus, we can try to avoid economic policies that exploit others and we can refrain from supporting dictatorships that grossly violate human rights. We can also take reasonable steps, in view of the realities, to implement positive rights. Surely we can and should do far more in this area than we are doing at present.

Nevertheless, as we have seen, rights can conflict. Although we should be suspicious of politicians who use the contested concept of national interest to justify any policy, however questionable, international realities may force unpleasant choices upon us. For example, should we continue support for a repressive but friendly dictatorship if the alternative may be its replacement by an at least equally repressive and hostile opposition?

Philosophy alone cannot settle such hard cases. Neither can ideal theory by itself. For example, although it may be debatable whether parties to an ideal hypothetical social contract among individuals would ever establish a system of nation-states, it is undeniable that we currently live in such a world order. Even if that world order differs in important ways from ideal justice, it does not follow that we can ignore an actual obligation to our own country, especially if it meets at least minimal standards of social justice. (Similarly, even if an ideal world would not include the family as we know it, it does not follow that we can simply ignore our familial duties in the real world.)[29]

Thus, what is required for just social policy in nonideal conditions, in addition to philosophical theory, is thorough knowledge of the facts and wise judgment concerning different policy alternatives. Nevertheless, moral principle and moral philosophy are not irrelevant to international affairs. While the concrete application of moral principles to international affairs raises many difficulties, over which good and reasonable people may disagree, such moral and philosophical principles do set constraints to which any justifiable foreign policy must conform.

CONCLUSION

In this chapter, we have argued that morality does play a role in foreign affairs. That role is not one of oversimplified moralism, rightly criticized by the realists, but of consideration of complex and often competing moral factors. Thus, in the area of international distributive justice, our discussion suggests that there are obligations on the more affluent nations, and their citizens, to promote an economically just global order, although the extent of these obligations is limited by the rights and deserts of their own citizens, and by the unfortunate realities of governance in many of the nations of the Third World.

The arguments for such a view may range from humanitarian ones in global emergencies, such as that following the 2005 Tsunami in Southeast Asia, to requirements of global justice, whether derived from a hypothetical global social contract or more directly, as we recommend, from the perspective of human rights.

Moral issues in international affairs are not restricted to distributive ones however. Unfortunately, the major cause of human suffering that arises in international affairs probably is war. Is war itself subject to moral analysis and constraints? We will consider issues raised by war, including issues of terrorism as well as humanitarian intervention, in the next chapter. What we have seen so far, however, is that while there is considerable debate over their extent and force, neither our duties nor our ethical concerns should stop at the water's edge.

NOTES

1. Thomas Hobbes, *Thucydides*, ed. Richard Slatter (New Brunswick, NJ: Rutgers University Press, 1975), 379.
2. Hobbes, *Thucydides*, 385.
3. The difference between descriptive and normative realism, and the use made of the former to justify the latter, was first pointed out to us by Robert Holmes.
4. Hans Morganthau, *In Defense of the National Interest* (New York: Knopf, 1951), 37.
5. Morganthau, *In Defense of the National Interest*, 35.
6. This argument is developed in Robert L. Simon, "A Limited Defense of the National Interest," in *Values and Value Theory in 20th Century America: Essays in Honor of Elizabeth*

Flower, ed. Murray G. Murphey and Ivar Berg (Philadelphia: Temple University Press, 1988), 195–214.

7. Charles Frankel, "Morality and U.S. Foreign Policy," *Headline Series* no. 224 (1975): 52.

8. Charles Beitz, *Political Theory and International Relations* (Princeton, NJ: Princeton University Press, 1979), esp. 27–66.

9. Nick Eberstadt, "Myths of the Food Crisis," *The New York Review of Books*, February 19, 1976, reprinted in *Moral Problems*, ed. James Rachels (New York: Harper & Row, 1979), 299.

10. Garrett Hardin, "Lifeboat Ethics: The Case Against Helping the Poor," in *Moral Problems*, ed. James Rachels, 280. Originally published in *Psychology Today*, 1974.

11. Hardin, "Lifeboat Ethics," 280.

12. Hardin, "Lifeboat Ethics," 282.

13. See, for example, William W. Murdoch and Allan Oaten, "Population and Food: Metaphors and Reality," *Bioscience*, September 9, 1975, reprinted in *Social Ethics: Morality and Social Policy*, ed. Thomas A. Mappes and Jane S. Zembaty (New York: McGraw-Hill, 1982), 372–79.

14. Peter Singer, "Famine, Affluence and Morality," *Philosophy and Public Affairs* 1, no. 3 (1972).

15. Singer, "Famine, Affluence and Morality," 231. This example has been discussed by Brian Barry in his essay "Humanity and Justice in Global Perspective," in *Ethics, Economics and the Law*, ed. J. Roland Pennock and John W. Chapman, Nomos 24 (New York: New York University Press, 1982), 221–25. Some of Barry's comments resemble the lines of our own criticism in the text, although we do not know if this sort of objection was precisely what Barry had in mind or if he would endorse it. In any case, we are indebted to his discussion of the example.

16. See, for example, Peter Singer, *Practical Ethics* (New York: Cambridge University Press, 1980), 180–81, where Singer acknowledges that the issue of how much can be reasonably demanded of others is more complex than indicated in "Famine, Affluence, and Morality." For his most recent views on a variety of issues involving globalization see *Singer's One World: The Ethics of Globalization* (New Haven, CT: Yale University Press, 2002).

17. See Brian Barry, *Justice as Impartiality* (New York: Oxford University Press, 1995), chaps. 8 and 9.

18. See Amartya K. Sen, *Poverty and Famines: An Essay on Entitlement and Deprivation* (New York: Oxford University Press, 1981) for a defense of the thesis that inadequate food supply in the famine-stricken country is not the principal cause of famine. In addition both Sen and Martha Nussbaum have provided a theory of development based on what they call the capabilities approach. See Amartya Sen, *Development as Freedom* (New York: Anchor Books 1999) and Martha C. Nussbaum, *Women and Human Development: The Capabilities Approach* (New York: Cambridge University Press, 2000).

19. John Rawls, *The Law of Peoples* (Cambridge, MA: Harvard University Press, 1999). Rawls's brief discussion of international justice in *A Theory of Justice* (Cambridge, MA: Harvard University Press, 1971) is found on 378ff.

20. For an argument that principles of justice do not apply globally, see Thomas Nagel, "The Problem of Global Justice," *Philosophy and Public Affairs* 33, no. 2 (2005): 113–47. For criticism, see Joshua Cohen and Charles Sable, "Extra Republican Nulla Justita?" *Philosophy and Public Affairs* 34, no. 2 (2006): 146–75; A. J. Julius, "Nagel's Atlas," *Philosophy and Public Affairs* 34, no. 2 (2006): 176–92.

21. For example, see Thomas Pogge, "An Egalitarian Law of Peoples," *Philosophy and Public Affairs* 23, no. 3 (1994): 195–224.

22. Robert Nozick, *Anarchy, State and Utopia* (New York: Basic Books, 1974). The tomato juice example is discussed on p. 175.

23. For discussion of philosophical arguments concerning the justification of property, see Lawrence C. Becker, *Property Rights* (Boston: Routledge & Kegan Paul, 1977). See also Becker's article "Property," in volume 2 of *The Encyclopedia of Ethics*, ed. Lawrence C. Becker and Charlotte B. Becker (New York: Garland Publishing, Inc., 1992), 1023–26.

24. Beitz, *Political Theory and International Relations*, 138.

25. Beitz, *Political Theory and International Relations*, 139.

26. Critics might object that even if our conceptual distinction between actual and potential resources is a good one, it does not show that actual states in the real world own the resources within their boundaries since they may not have done anything to convert the potential into the actual. The resources, so to speak, may have just fallen into their lap.

27. For information, go to http://www.un.org/millenniumgoals/ (26 October 2006) and http://www.millenniumcampaign.org/site/pp.asp?c=grKVL2NLE&b=185455 (26 October 2006).

28. For a related assessment of resource egalitarianism and libertarianism, some of which appears in the present discussion, see Robert L. Simon, "Troubled Waters: Global Justice and Ocean Resources," in *Earthbound*, ed. Tom Regan (New York: Random House, 1984), 179–213.

29. For discussion of how the distinction between the ideal and the actual might bear on issues of morality and international affairs, see Robert L. Simon, "Global Justice and the Authority of States," *The Monist* 66, no. 4 (1983): 557–72.

QUESTIONS FOR FURTHER STUDY

1. What is political realism about international affairs? How would you distinguish normative from descriptive realism?
2. What do you think is the strongest argument for political realism? What do you think is the strongest criticism of it? Is the criticism successful? Defend your view.
3. Explain Garrett Hardin's criticism of the view that the people of the affluent nations have duties to reduce global suffering by sending aid to the starving throughout the world. Is his position justified? Defend your evaluation of it.
4. Explain Peter Singer's argument that the people of the affluent nations should act to reduce global suffering by sending aid to the starving throughout the world and are wrong if they do not send such aid. What does Singer mean by the claim that giving should be to the point of declining marginal utility?
5. What do you think is the strongest criticism of the more demanding version of Singer's position (requiring giving to the point of declining marginal utility)? Is it successful? Would you support a more moderate version of Singer's requirement? How might such a moderate requirement best be formulated? Defend your position.

6. If an American expedition to a previously unexplored (and uninhabited) planet were to discover valuable minerals there, would there be an obligation to share some of the profits of developing that mineral deposit with the people of less developed countries? Why or why not? What are the principal arguments you would have to consider in arriving at a position?

7. Do you think the idea of a Rawlsian global original position is helpful in considering what might be the requirements of global justice? If not, why not? If so, would the parties to the original position be individuals, representatives of existing states, representatives of ideally just states, or some other alternative? Develop a brief account of a global original position and indicate what principles of justice, if any, might emerge from it.

8. Do the more fortunate of the world have some obligation or moral duty to reduce suffering throughout the globe? Defend your view.

SUGGESTED READINGS

Books

Aiken, William, and Hugh LaFollette, eds. *World Hunger and Moral Obligation.* Englewood Cliffs, NJ: Prentice-Hall, 1977.

Beitz, Charles. *Political Theory and International Relations.* Princeton, NJ: Princeton University Press, 1979.

Brown, Peter, and Douglas Maclean, eds. *Human Rights and U.S. Foreign Policy.* Lexington, MA: Heath, 1979.

Hare, J. E., and Carey B. Joynt. *Ethics and International Affairs.* New York: St. Martin's, 1982.

Hoffman, Stanley. *Duties Beyond Borders: On the Limits and Possibilities of Ethical International Politics.* Syracuse, NY: Syracuse University Press, 1981.

Jones, Charles. *Global Justice: Defending Cosmopolitanism.* New York: Oxford University Press, 1999.

Nardin, Terry. *Law, Morality and the Relations of States.* Princeton, NJ: Princeton University Press, 1983.

Nussbaum, Martha C. *Women and Human Development: The Capabilities Approach.* New York: Cambridge University Press, 2000.

Rawls, John. *The Law of Peoples.* Cambridge, MA: Harvard University Press, 1999.

Sen, Amartya. *Development as Freedom.* New York: Anchor Books, 1999.

Shue, Henry. *Basic Rights: Subsistence, Affluence and U.S. Foreign Policy.* Princeton, NJ: Princeton University Press, 1980.

Singer, Peter. *One World: The Ethics of Globalization.* New Haven, CT: Yale University Press, 2002.

Articles

Crisp, Roger, and Dale Jamieson. "Egalitarianism and a Global Resources Tax: Pogge on Rawls," in *The Idea of Political Liberalism*, ed. Victoria Davion and Clark Wolf. Lanham, MD: Rowman & Littlefield, 2000, 90–101.

Miller, Richard W. "Beneficence, Duty, and Distance." *Philosophy and Public Affairs* 32, no. 4 (2004): 357–83.

Nagel, Thomas. "The Problem of Global Justice." *Philosophy and Public Affairs* 33, no. 2 (2005): 113–47.

Pogge, Thomas. "An Egalitarian Law of Peoples." *Philosophy and Public Affairs* 23, no. 3 (1994): 195–224.

Risse, Mathias. "How Does the Global Order Harm the Poor?" *Philosophy and Public Affairs* 33, no. 4 (2005): 348–76.

9

WAR, MORALITY,
AND TERRORISM

War is one of the great scourges of human existence. It results not only in the death and maiming of combatants and suffering for those who love them but also in suffering for civilians brought about as a result of war, either through unintended consequences of military action, through intentional attacks on civilians and innocents, or as a result of disease and starvation, which so often accompany war. Nuclear war has the potential to end human life. Thus, it seems fitting not only to agree with the scripture that "Blessed are the peacemakers" but also to wonder if the resort to war can ever be morally permissible or justified.

Those sympathetic to political realism, the doctrine discussed in the previous chapter, which claims that morality does not apply to international affairs, may suggest that "all is fair in love and war." However, we have seen that there are strong reasons for rejecting realism. How then might morality apply to war? Is all war immoral? Can there be just wars, as when one country resists aggression by another? Is it always wrong to take military action that results in the death of civilians? What if the death of civilians is unintended, a kind of "collateral damage?" What is terrorism? Can terrorism ever be morally justified? In this chapter, we will explore such issues and try to arrive at some defensible responses.

PACIFISM: PHILOSOPHICAL AND PRACTICAL

One argument against the possibility of a morally permissible or just war maintains that war involves violence intended to harm others and that the use of such violence is always wrong. The view that the use of violence, in the sense of force intended to injure, kill, or otherwise harm others, is always wrong will be called philosophical pacifism. Pacifism as a philosophy of life is deeply committed to nonviolence regardless of the context. It should be distinguished from what we will call practical or pragmatic pacifism, which is defended as the morally best response to aggression in particular contexts, particularly as an alternative to modern war, and so is to be distinguished from a universal adherence to nonviolence regardless of circumstances.[1] We believe the historically most successful pacifist policies, such as Gandhi's nonviolent resistance to the British colonial occupation of India and Martin Luther King Jr.'s tactics in the American civil rights movement, fit best under the rubric of practical or pragmatic pacifism.

A full evaluation of philosophical pacifism would take us far beyond the topic of this chapter, the morality of war, so we will not examine it exhaustively here. There are two problems it faces that are worth noting, however.

The first is that sometimes the failure to use violence can result in significantly more harm to others than its use in self-defense or to protect the weak. Suppose a sniper is about to fire an automatic weapon at a large group of elementary school children in a playground and the only way the police can prevent the massacre is to shoot the sniper before he fires. If the justification of philosophical pacifism is that it prevents the suffering caused by violence, that justification would seem not to apply when the use of violence would itself minimize suffering in a particular context.

Philosophical pacifists might reply that their position is not one justified by its consequences; rather there is an absolute duty not to commit violence. In our sniper example, it would be the sniper who, according to the philosophical pacifist, is morally responsible for the death of the children while the police would not be guilty of wrongdoing by refusing to shoot the sniper, even if in not doing so some children would die. This leads to the second difficulty, however. If one accepts our view that the principle function of the state is to protect its citizens, particularly by protecting their human rights, then the agents of the state, such as the police, have a duty to shoot the sniper if that is the only or clearly most effective way to save the children. In such circumstances, it would be wrong for them not to do so.

Practical pacifists might agree with the above criticisms of broad philosophical pacifism but argue nevertheless that there is a case for a kind of pacifism that when conjoined with a commitment to nonviolent resistance is claimed to present a morally favored alternative to the destructiveness of modern war. Modern war, because of the increasing destructiveness of the weapons used to fight it, including weapons of mass destruction such as biological, chemical, and nuclear weapons, is especially difficult to justify in almost any circumstances and so it is understandable that forms of pacifism might be defended pragmatically as superior to it both morally and tactically.

So practical or pragmatic pacifism differs from philosophical pacifism first in that it is contextual. It does not argue that violence in all circumstances is unjustified but rather that violence as employed in modern warfare is unjustified. Secondly, practical pacifism does not maintain that no form of resistance to aggression by other nations is allowed; rather the practical pacifist (along with some philosophical pacifists) defends the effectiveness of nonviolent forms of resistance including civil disobedience, economic boycotts, general strikes, and other forms of noncooperation with the aggressor. As Harvard philosopher Michael Walzer, the author of the influential study *Just and Unjust Wars*, points out,

> Non-violence de-escalates the conflict and diminishes its criminality. By adopting the methods of disobedience, non-cooperation, boycott, and general strike, the citizens of the invaded country transform aggressive war into a political struggle. They treat the aggressor in effect as a domestic tyrant or usurper, and they turn his soldiers into policemen.[2]

After all, what benefit is there for a country that occupies another land if the occupied population shuts down its industry, refuses to cooperate, and resists the occupation in effective nonviolent ways?

Defenders of this position point to its success when employed by Gandhi against the British colonial rule of India and by Martin Luther King Jr. in the civil rights movement in the United States. Indeed, this position has an important moral point in its favor over and above the consequentialist claim that it avoids the destructiveness of modern war. In many of its forms, nonviolence appeals to the humanity and moral values of the oppressors by asking them whether they will commit violence against and even kill unarmed nonviolent resistors. It treats the oppressors as moral agents who are asked to examine their consciences while also putting pressure, for example, economic pressure, on them to listen carefully indeed to what their consciences tell them.

Some may doubt whether massive passive resistance to an invading army is practical. Can we really expect masses of civilians to resist in the ways required? We do not regard such doubts as unreasonable, although defenders of practical pacifism do have a response. As one such proponent, Robert Holmes, maintains:

> Military action cannot, in other words, hope to succeed without armies, guns, money, and equipment. By the same token, non-violence cannot be imagined to succeed when the basic conditions necessary for its success are similarly absent. These may well include . . . a degree of discipline and training on the parts of tens of thousands comparable to that required in the military; and it will require extensive background research into techniques of non-violence against various forms of aggression.[3]

In other words, if a nation invested as much in preparation for nonviolent resistance as it presently does for military preparedness, nonviolence might be as effective a response to aggression as military force, and involve far less destruction, suffering, and death.

We agree that the case for practical or pragmatic pacifism deserves far more attention than it has received in the general culture and that it might be an appropriate response to military aggression in some contexts. It certainly is a morally far more defensible form of response to perceived injustice (whether real or not) than suicide bombings directed against civilians in restaurants, at weddings or religious services, or in their homes and offices. Nevertheless, we also think it faces serious difficulties, the most important of which we will indicate below.

First, passive nonviolent resistance may well be effective when directed against a population that shares fundamental liberal values with the protesters, such as the British, who even at the height of their imperial power also had reverence for human life and dignity, and who eventually respected the drive for liberty; and perhaps the bulk of the American population, who could not stomach the brutality directed at civil rights protesters, and who had an underlying faith in human moral equality. It is far less clear, however, that such tactics would be effective against ruthless fanatical enemies, such as the Nazis or Stalin. Would nonviolent protests continue effectively if leaders were assassinated, their families threatened with torture and death, or protesters massacred? Of course, many protesters may have the great courage needed to carry on even in such dire circumstances, but surely there is room for doubt about whether sufficient masses of people would or could reasonably be expected to carry on in the face of ruthless suppression. Practical pacifists might reply, however, by pointing to the heroic actions of many brave Danes during Nazi occupation of Denmark who nonviolently protected Jewish Danes from the Nazis. Their critics, though, may question whether such resistance would have continued effectively had the Nazis been able to turn the full attention of the more ruthless elements of their forces to it.

Second, passive resistance and nonviolence, as well as war, can cause severe harm to innocents. For example, economic boycotts and general strikes may prevent food and medicine from getting to those vulnerable persons who desperately need them.[4] Moreover, reprisals for resistance may be violent and lead to the death of many, including children who are killed to take the heart out of the opposition. Finally, even if in the long run, nonviolent resistance would have worked even against a Hitler-led Nazi invasion of the United States, millions more may have become victims of the extended Holocaust that almost certainly would have continued if not for the force of arms used by the Allies in World War II.[5] Thus, whether passive resistance and nonviolence would be effective in reducing overall harm may be debatable in many contexts, especially if one construes "harm" to involve not only death but also loss of freedom and violation of other fundamental human rights.

Finally, even if practical pacifism when conjoined with nonviolent resistance is an important alternative to war, as we agree it is, it does not follow that resort to war, particularly as a response to military aggression by an enemy, always is morally impermissible. These two points are separate ones and the latter, the impermissibility of war, does not follow from the premise that sometimes (or even usually) other methods of resistance to aggression may be preferable. Accordingly, we need to explore the issue of whether the resort to war can ever be morally justified. A case for the moral permissibility of some wars has been made by the approach known as the theory of "just war," which we will examine in the next section.

JUST WAR THEORY AND ITS CRITICS

The theory (or more accurately theories) of just war maintain that sometimes resort to war is morally permissible. The just war tradition has many roots, including the work of Christian theologians and philosophers such as Augustine and Aquinas, as well as Jewish and Muslim scholars, although many of the latter seem to have focused on *jihad* or just conditions (although not necessarily violent ones) for spreading Islam throughout the world. The idea of just war was developed by philosophers in the scholastic and jurist tradition, including Hugo Grotius (1583–1645), Samuel Pufendorf (1632–1704), and Emerich de Vattel (1714–1767). Considerable interest in just war theory also developed during the twentieth century as a result of World War II, the Nuremberg trials of Nazi war criminals, debates about the morality of the Vietnam War and, most recently, discussion concerning the invasion of Iraq by the United States and its allies in 2003. In what follows, rather than presenting a comprehensive account of the different versions of just war theory, we will try to assess some of the main principles that have been central to the just war tradition.

Jus ad Bellum and *Jus in Bello*

Just war theorists have distinguished two issues: the justice of going to war in the first place and principles for carrying out a war justly, once it already is initiated. For a war to be started justly (*jus ad bellum*), it must have a just cause. That is, the reasons for going to war must be morally justifiable. Clearly, the desire to conquer another country or exploit its people would not be just reasons. However, resisting an invasion or protecting one's people from exploitation or domination would be allowable reasons for resisting an attack. So the primary and perhaps the only reason legitimating the resort to war would be resistance to aggression. (Some versions of the theory also allow war by one state to protect another from aggression by a third state or to punish the aggressor for attacking a weaker neighbor. Still others may allow intervention for humanitarian purposes, for example, to prevent mass slaughter or "ethnic cleansing," as in the case of the NATO intervention in the Balkans under the leadership of President Clinton.)

Some theorists have thought of international affairs as something like a Lockean state of nature where states are much like persons in Locke's theory (see chapter 3), with fundamental rights to self-protection. Just as it would be wrong to attack an individual person in Locke's state of nature because of the basic human rights to life and liberty, so states in the international state of nature have a similar right not to be attacked or to be victims of aggression. Some just war theorist, including John Rawls in his extension of his theory to international affairs, try to apply the contract model to international ethics and argue that the rules of war are what would emerge from a fair and rational social contract among states, peoples, or their representatives.[6]

We have no objection to the contractual approach as long as the analogy between persons and states is not taken too far. On liberal theory, including our own, states have value because they protect individuals, safeguard their rights, and meet human needs, so it is individuals, not states, that are of primary value. But this raises two issues about resistance to aggression as a legitimate justification for war. First, do unjust or oppressive states, those that do not protect the rights of their citizens but exploit or oppress the population instead, have rights to resist aggression? Second, what is aggression? For example, is a humanitarian intervention designed to protect a minority within a state from genocide or "ethnic cleansing" aggression?

The question of the rights of unjust states, such as oppressive dictatorships, is a vexing one. If we understand the rules of war as what representatives of states would agree to under ideal contractual conditions (say from behind the veil of ignorance, so they would not know which states they represented) should seriously unjust states be represented? From the perspective of rights theory, do states that violate the fundamental human rights of their people have the same standing as reasonably just or even minimally decent states?

One position compatible with liberal theory is to deny that such states have legitimacy and as a consequence also deny that they deserve the same protection from attack as liberal democracies. That does not mean that imperialistic or purely aggressive wars against such states are justified but that humanitarian intervention designed to protect the human rights of the inhabitants sometimes might be permissible (or even required) under appropriate circumstances.

Perhaps surprisingly, a somewhat different position has been taken by perhaps the most important liberal theorist, John Rawls, in his *The Law of Peoples*. In that essay, Rawls denies that only liberal democracies possess full legitimacy and adds that what he calls well-ordered hierarchical societies also deserve the protections against armed attack that apply to liberal democracies.[7] Such societies are organized around a theory of the good, such as a religious conception of the good life, rather than leaving choices about the good life to their citizens. An Islamic state might be such a well-ordered hierarchy. Rawls suggests such states have legitimacy and so are protected against armed intervention if they also satisfy certain conditions. Among the most important of these are that such a state must itself not be an aggressor (it must be nonexpansionist), and it must recognize a certain subset of human rights, including allowing freedom of worship for those who do not subscribe to the state religion, and allowing some minimal but real avenues for dissent and criticism within the internal hierarchical order.

However, we are reluctant to fully endorse Rawls's position on this point. Would it allow protection, for example, to a regime such as that of the Taliban, with its oppression of women and harsh penalties for religious transgression, or to a state based on the caste system in which a person's place in society was largely or entirely determined by the caste of his or her parents? We agree that armed intervention to change such a system often is dangerous and unwise, but that is more because such interventions are likely to have horrible consequences if not embarked on wisely with extensive understanding of the culture involved than because of any rights of hierarchical regimes themselves. However, if the people in the society support the kind of regime at issue, even if their support is not based on what liberal democrats would regard as critical inquiry and rational evaluation of relevant alternative ways of life, they may have rights as individuals to continue their way of life rather than having democracy forced down their throat.

Hence, we would be wary of regarding such states as fair game for armed intervention, although we would not rule it out in extreme cases where such states also support external aggression (as was the case with Taliban in Afghanistan providing a refuge for bin Laden to launch the 9/11 attacks on America) or are committing gross atrocities among their own people such as the ethnic cleansing in the Balkans and the more recent massacres in Rwanda and in regions of the Sudan. This suggests that a presumption of noninterference and protection against aggression should apply to some hierarchical states, but that presumption becomes weaker and hence easier to override the more oppressively such states behave toward their own people or other states.

To return to the main principle of the justice of war, a war is just only if it has a just cause. The principal and perhaps only just cause is resistance to aggression or attack, although we would also add as just causes the protection of a weaker state against aggression, even if the protector state has not itself been attacked, punishment of aggressors, and in limited contexts humanitarian intervention to protect against gross and systematic violations of human rights. "Aggression" is not to be understood simply as firing the first shot but as creating an imminent threat of attack that it would be unreasonable to interpret in any other way. Thus, a preemptive strike against an army massed on one's borders and clearly preparing to strike would be a legitimate act of self-defense rather than aggression even if it involved the first shots fired in a war.[8]

Two other principles of the justice of war also are important. The first is that of last resort. This does not mean that a state must exhaust every logically possible option before defending itself but rather that it must exhaust reasonable alternatives, such as appeal to international organizations and diplomacy or economic pressures against the aggressor, before resorting to force. States are not required by a justifiable theory of just war either to commit suicide or to place themselves in positions of untenable risk before defending themselves by force of arms but are obligated to take other steps to avoid the horrors of war. Thus, a not unreasonable criticism of the U.S. invasion of Iraq in 2003 is that the Bush administration did not give U.N. inspectors sufficient time to find the alleged weapons of mass destruction that were a principal justification for launching the war in the first place (although it also should be acknowledged that relatively few observers at the time doubted that Iraq had such weapons hidden away).

The second principle is that of proportionality. The good to be accomplished by the war must outweigh the evil of the war itself, or at least the resort to war must be the clear lesser of two evils. While this principle, as with the other principles of just war theory, requires interpretation and judgment in its application, it is far from empty. We will say more about this principle in connection with the theory of justice in war to which we now turn, but it along with the requirements of just cause and last resort at least appear to set significant limits on the circumstances in which resort to war is even allowable in the first place.

Just war theory sets limits not only on the allowable reasons for going to war but also on the way war may be conducted. That is, even if a nation's reasons for going to war justify its decision, the war is just only if it is conducted properly.

However, some who recognize the need for a moral justification for going to war in the first place may question whether moral rules apply to the process of warfare itself. Thus, a view that enjoys a degree of popularity is that one should go to war reluctantly and only for good cause, but once in it, one should do what it takes to win, whatever that is.

Note that even such a view restricts allowable actions in war to what is necessary to win. Thus, a gratuitous massacre of civilians, including children, would not be justified in such a view since it would not be required in order to achieve victory. Indeed, on a strict version of such a view, the indiscriminate bombing of German cities such as Dresden by the Allies during World War II, which resulted in thousands and thousands of civilian casualties, was almost certainly unnecessary to achieve victory over the Nazis (although it may have played some role in shortening the war), and so is morally suspect even from the point of view of the "do what it takes to win" theory.

However, just war theorists quite properly in our view either reject the "do what it takes to win" approach or at least modify it significantly. There are at least two sorts of arguments that justify their critique of such an approach. First, if all individuals are centers of moral value, possessors of human rights, proper concern must be shown for their protection. Noncombatants are not threats to the military force of the other side and hence their rights must be of foremost concern. Second, from a utilitarian perspective, the best consequences are achieved if death, suffering, and injury are kept to a minimum. Thus, from a rule utilitarian perspective, nations should be under moral pressure to follow rules or principles that when generally observed minimize the evils resulting from war. Accordingly, most theories of just war include some version or other of the two following principles, which can be justified by their role in protecting noncombatants and in reducing the overall suffering produced by war.

Suppose that using a great deal of force in a given area would promote victory but roughly the same military benefits could be achieved by use of less force, involving less chance of injury to noncombatants. Just war theorists would argue that the second approach is justified and the first is not. Indeed, since the goal can be achieved by use of the lesser force, the use of unnecessary additional force, resulting in greater risk to noncombatants, would be similar to the massacre referred to above. This leads to what has been called the principle of proportionality, which, roughly stated, requires using no more force than necessary to achieve military objectives and limits the degree of force that may be used to what is proportional to the significance of the objective for the overall war effort.

The second principle sets limits on who may be attacked and determines who is immune from attack. This is why deliberate attacks on innocent civilians, such as the suicide bombing of people at weddings and restaurants, causes such widespread revulsion and condemnation. The individuals who are killed or maimed are not involved in military activities and therefore are not legitimate targets. War should involve the military forces of the opposing sides, not those who can be regarded as innocent civilians. This leads to the principle of discrimination.

Difficulties arise, however, when attempts are made to formulate this principle more precisely. For example, should it be formulated to prohibit attacks on *innocents*, or on *civilians* and *noncombatants*? It is tempting to think in terms of innocents but we suspect that formulation is not satisfactory. After all, an opposing soldier in the aggressor's army arguably may be innocent (he was drafted against his will and his family will be executed if he does not fight) while a civilian accountant working for a hospital may not be so innocent if she donates all her money to the aggressor's cause and spends her spare time giving fiery speeches in support of the government's policy. Surely the soldier is not immune from attack, since he represents a threat to the forces of the defender, and the accountant is not a legitimate target in spite of her support for the cause of the aggressor. In addition, as Barbara MacKinnon points out, "the danger of using the term 'innocents' in place of 'noncombatants' is that it also allows some to say that no one living in a certain country is immune because they are all supporters of their country and so not innocent."[9]

Unfortunately, it is not so easy to specify just who is a noncombatant. Clearly children, hospital workers, and teachers are not but what about farmers since the military would have no food if not for their efforts or factory workers who are engaged in producing weapons for the armed forces? While we doubt if there is any precise line that can sharply distinguish combatants from noncombatants, we suggest that combatants are those either actively engaged in the war through the military or directly involved in support. Thus, in our view, the factory worker making munitions would be a combatant but regarding the farmers as combatants, especially if they are producing food for the general population, some of which happens to be bought by the military, is much more problematic.[10] In the remainder of this chapter, we will adopt the combatant vs. noncombatant distinction, but those who are committed to the innocent vs. noninnocent distinction may substitute that instead (and for convenience, we often will include it as an alternate formulation).

The principle of discrimination, however, does not absolutely prohibit injury to noncombatants but rather prohibits making them direct targets of attack. That is, noncombatants should not be *intentionally* targeted. However, one of the terrible consequences of war, especially modern war with its incredibly destructive weapons, is that such persons are injured, maimed, and killed through what has come to be called "collateral damage." This, in turn, leads to the criticism that just war theory, in spite of its well-intentioned attempt to interject moral limitations on the practice of war, is a moral failure, and that war, at least it its modern form, cannot be just after all. Can just war theory be defended in light of this criticism and other related objections?

Two Criticisms of the Theory of Just War

While theoretical attempts to show that at least some wars can be just have a distinguished history and have been influential on the practice of war itself, there also are powerful criticisms of the entire just war tradition. We will focus on two such criticisms: the alleged vagueness or indeterminacy of the principles employed in the theory and the criticism, just mentioned, that the discrimination principle cannot be satisfied under conditions of modern warfare.

According to the first objection, just war theory employs such notions as "aggression," "last resort," "innocent" or "noncombatant," and "proportionality." Critics of the just war tradition argue, however, that these expressions can be interpreted differently by different sides to a conflict. Each side can claim that the other was the aggressor. For example, which of the following count as aggression: armed invasion, an economic boycott that imposes suffering on the citizens of the targeted nation, stationing troops and bases in areas surrounding another country, threatening another country with force if it develops its military capacities, or not directly acting against another nation but sending funds to nongovernmental (terrorist) groups that attack the other nation's civilian population? If we count all of these as aggression, NATO, and especially the United States, committed aggression against the old Soviet Union by encircling it with a ring of bases (the famous "containment" policy), the United States is an aggressor against Iran and North Korea by attempting to halt those countries' alleged attempts to develop nuclear weapons, and the all too numerous countries who support terrorist groups are aggressors against the targets of the terrorists. Similar points can be made about the requirements of proportionality and last resort. For example, there is considerable disagreement among Americans about whether even the emergence of a genuine democracy in Iraq would be a sufficient good to outweigh the deaths of American soldiers and Iraqi civilians that the war in Iraq entailed and over whether President Bush followed the principle of last resort when he ordered the invasion of Iraq even when U.N. inspectors seemed to be making progress in investigating whether Iraq actually possessed weapons of mass destruction.

The criticism of indeterminacy of the principles of just war theory clearly has some force. We ourselves noted the difficulty of drawing any clear and distinct line between combatants and noncombatants. However, it is also true that the mere existence of borderline cases does not destroy important distinctions. As the eighteenth-century English literary figure Dr. Samuel Johnson pointed out, the existence of twilight does not mean there is no difference between night and day.[11] Similarly, there seem to be clear cases of aggression, such as Nazi invasion of Poland in 1939 and Saddam Hussein's invasion of Kuwait in 1990. Other cases may be less clear. Sometimes different sides may each have a partial justification for their interpretation. However, some interpretations just are not defensible. Children cannot plausibly be regarded as combatants, and publishing an insulting cartoon cannot plausibly justify the use of violence in which innocents may be harmed, even if publishing the cartoon while within the rights of the publisher is subject to moral criticism and protest nonetheless.[12]

More broadly, any set of general principles raises questions of interpretation, and often can be appealed to on behalf of opposing sides. We have seen that there are different conceptions of justice for example, some of which are quite sophisticated. It does not follow that justice is a useless concept or that reasoned argument cannot sort out the different conceptions and distinguish more reasonable from less reasonable views in many contexts. Thus, the critics of just war theory need to show more than that the principles the theory employs are not perfectly precise or that they admit of borderline cases. Rather, they need to show that the principles are nearly vacuous—that they can be used by opposing sides, with equal or nearly equal plausibility, in all or most realistic contexts. Otherwise, the objection of vagueness does not raise any special difficulties for just war theory that it does not also raise for all other theories that reply on principles.

In considering the objection of vagueness, we also need to think about the justification for employing just war theory in the first place. If we think of just war theory as an attempt to lay down principles that enable us to almost mechanically classify all wars as clear cases of either just or unjust conflicts, we agree that the theory is a failure. Applications of the principles to actual cases often will be messy and controversial. Usually, there will be no substitute for analysis of the facts of each case, and it will prove impossible to draw perfect lines or make distinctions that all reasonable people will immediately accept.

However, that a theory is not perfect in this sense does not imply it is useless or lacks value. Similarly, just because there is no perfect place to draw the line between drivers old enough to drive responsibly and those who are not, an imperfect line still may be valuable. We all agree that we don't want five-year-olds driving and we also don't want the frail elderly driving. But whether we set the line for obtaining a driver's license at sixteen, seventeen, eighteen, or nineteen may be debatable and often controversial. Still, even if there proves no perfect place to draw the line, it is better to have an imperfect line than none at all.

Suppose we consider just war theory not as an attempt to provide a precise set of standards that allow us to neatly distinguish wars into two sharp categories, just and unjust. Suppose the moral justification of the theory is less philosophically ambitious but of great practical and ethical significance nonetheless. We suggest there are two closely related justifications of practical import that support just war theory. First, even if its principles are open to interpretation, they do put the burden of proof on countries to justify their activities by making a case for compliance. In other words, they create a set of expectations that nations are expected to live by, or be exposed to extensive (sometimes worldwide) criticism if they do not. This is likely to reduce the suffering and violation of the rights of innocents or noncombatants that war entails. In other words, the first justification is that just war principles, when regarded as the norms of international behavior, reduce the horror and suffering of war.

Thus, U.S. military codes prohibit soldiers from engaging in immoral acts, such as deliberately harming civilians, during war. American soldiers were prosecuted and punished, for example, for the My Lai massacre during the Vietnam War, and if a massacre took place in Haditha in Iraq in 2005, then if the perpetrators are found guilty, they will be punished as well. In fact, American soldiers are supposed to refuse orders requiring gross violations of ethical requirements in war; since the Nuremberg trials of Nazi war criminals following World War II, the defense that "I was just following orders" is unacceptable.

Of course, even well-trained troops may violate fundamental moral rules under the pressure of war, especially if they see their comrades killed and, as during an insurgency, find it difficult to distinguish noncombatants from disguised enemy fighters. But while such conditions may reduce the culpability of individual soldiers, surely we want rules in place that prohibit killing of, for example, children and the aged, who are not involved in the fighting. (If we do not endorse such rules, then, as we will see, we have destroyed the moral basis for condemning terrorist attacks against American civilians, as in the attacks on the World Trade Center on 9/11.)

The first defense of just war theory against the charge of vagueness and indeterminacy, then, is that even though the principles of the theory are subject to interpretation and debate, having them in place serves the consequentialist function of protecting the human rights of noncombatants and reducing the overall evils of war. Once again, an imperfect line is better than no line at all.

The second defense relies on the value of impartiality. That is, no one wants our own noncombatants to be targeted or our soldiers tortured by an enemy who violates the rules of war. But impartiality prohibits us from making arbitrary exceptions just for our own side. If we are to be consistent with the values we apply elsewhere (for example, as developed in earlier chapters of this book), we need to apply the rules to all sides, unless there are morally relevant reasons for making exceptions.

Critics may object that the indeterminacy we have been worrying about will apply when it comes to making exceptions. The U.S. policy during the Afghan war of holding enemy combatants (accused hard-core members of Al Qaeda) indefinitely in prison at Guantanamo, Cuba, has been supported by the Bush administration on the grounds that the detainees were not soldiers but terrorists who would again engage in terrorist activities if simply released. However, this practice has led to widespread criticism throughout the world and undoubtedly has caused a loss of support and respect for the United States and the Bush administration. Indeed, in June of 2006, the U.S. Supreme Court ruled in a 5–3 decision that the policy of allowing such prisoners to be tried only in special military courts in which the rights of the defendant were significantly limited violated not only laws regulating military trials (the Uniform Code of Military Justice guarantees basic rights to defendants such as providing access to the evidence against them so that they have a fair opportunity to present a defense) but also the Geneva Convention. So while it may sometimes be controversial just when exceptions to established principles are justifiable, the principles set the burden of proof. Often, a relatively broad consensus will emerge on both the moral and practical political implications of overriding established principles of justice in war.

Of course, not all exceptions will be equally controversial. Thus, in the hypothetical case of a terrorist who has planted a nuclear weapon in a major American city, there is a case for torture if that is the only way to get the location of the weapon and disarm it before it detonates, perhaps killing millions of people. However, by too easily suspending or overriding presumptively justified principles, we not only reduce their power to limit the evils of war (the consequentialist argument) but also adopt a position that clashes with what we ourselves would endorse from an impartial point of view and so undermine our very own fundamental values.[13]

However, even if the indeterminacy objection to just war theory is itself not decisive, a second objection may be. What makes this objection so powerful is that it appeals to a value fundamental to liberal democratic societies, and indeed to our own defense of human rights in this book. According to the objection, war, or at least modern war with its powerful weapons of destruction, inevitably results in the killing of noncombatants (or innocents, if one regards the innocent vs. noninnocent distinction as crucial). Since the killing of noncombatants is prohibited by the discrimination principle, the just war theory itself rules out modern war as unjust. How can it ever be right to kill hundreds, perhaps many thousands of children, old people, bystanders, and even those civilians on the enemy side who may have opposed the war? How can that be done in the name of justice? Surely, if anything is morally prohibited, it is the killing of such people, ignoring their fundamental right not to be harmed, in the pursuit of a military goal. Indeed, aren't these victims simply being used as mere means to an end, reducing their humanity to merely instrumental value, much as some have accused the utilitarians of doing in sacrificing the few for the benefit of the many?

This objection indeed is a powerful one. We suggest it is at least partially successful in that it places a heavy burden of proof on those who would justify war. But is the burden of proof impossible to meet? Surely, for example, the Allied resistance to the Nazis in World War II was just; without such resistance the Holocaust would have continued and a Nazi empire might have dominated much of the world for generations. But if some wars are just, such as war efforts of the Allies in World War II, that suggests that just war theorists have responses to their critics worth our consideration.

There are a number of responses that might be made to the criticism that modern war is unjust due to its very nature since it involves the killing of noncombatants (or innocents). We shall consider two such replies: first, that it is only the *intentional* killing of noncombatants (innocents) that is prohibited and second that under specified conditions, the killing of noncombatants is the lesser evil.

The first response rests on the distinction long discussed by ethicists, particularly among theorists influenced by the teaching of Catholicism and especially the writings of the medieval philosopher-theologian Thomas Aquinas, between the intended consequences of an action and those consequences that are foreseen or expected but not intended by the agent. In other words, actions often have double effects: the intended goal and byproducts that may have been anticipated but are not intended and may even be repugnant to the agent. For example, a professor who gives back papers to her class may intend that her critical comments provide the students with enough information to improve on the next assignment but may also foresee that some students will be made unhappy by their low grades. The professor does not intend to make the students unhappy, only to help them improve, but she may foresee that they will in fact be unhappy when they see their grades. Similarly, an athlete who performs a winning play in a game may foresee that his act may make the families of the losing players unhappy but that is not his intent. He only intends to meet the challenges of the sport and play his best.

This commonsense distinction between intended and merely foreseen consequences of our actions is the basis of the principle of double effect—a principle that may rescue just war theory from its critics. Although different theorists formulate the principle somewhat differently, the main idea, when applied to modern war, is that we are prohibited from intentionally killing or targeting noncombatants (or innocents) but that it is not always wrong if such people are killed as the foreseen but *unintended* consequence of otherwise legitimate military action. In addition, theorists generally require at least that the intended target of the action is legitimate, for example, enemy soldiers or munitions factories, that the agent neither intends the harm to noncombatants nor requires it as a means to his military ends, and that the good results outweigh the evil consequences of the act (proportionality principle).[14]

Should we accept the principle of double effect? One problem that critics find with it is that it seems easy to manipulate so as to justify almost any action. Couldn't a religious fanatic attempting to blow up a school building filled with children claim that his intent is only to carry out the will of God (who is thought to want changes in U.S. policy) and that while he foresees the death of the children, he certainly doesn't intend to kill them?

However, we suggest this objection fails on two counts. After all, any principle can be manipulated by the cynical. Some could even claim (preposterously) that taking money from the poor and giving it to the rich satisfies Rawls's difference principle, perhaps by toughening up the worst-off group and making them more self-reliant. But just because a claim can be made doesn't mean the claim has any shred of plausibility. In the case of the religious fanatic and the school, not only is there no plausible evidence that God does want the school blown up, but there is also no plausible evidence that doing so will change U.S. policy. Moreover, the fanatic is not conforming to but actually *violating* double effect by using the children

WAR, MORALITY, AND TERRORISM

as a means to his political end. Double effect requires that the harm to noncombatants be a side effect of the use of force, not the means through which the goal of using force is accomplished.[15]

However, a second objection to double effect has considerable force. As Walzer puts it,

> What difference does it make whether civilian deaths are a direct or an indirect effect of my actions? It can hardly matter to the dead civilians, and if I know in advance that I am likely to kill so many innocent people and go ahead anyway, how can I be blameless?[16]

In other words, the distinction between intended consequences of our actions and ones we do not intend but foresee lacks the moral significance attributed to it by advocates of double effect. Robert Holmes supports this criticism with the following example.

> Or suppose two pilots fly over a military target surrounded by schools, hospitals, and recreation areas. Both have orders to destroy the military target. But one drops his bombs intending to destroy the target even though he knows that in the process he will kill innocent persons, the other does so intending as well to kill those persons. They perform virtually identical acts. But the one act, according to double effects, is permissible, the other impermissible.[17]

Holmes is asking us to consider whether the alleged difference between the two acts lacks moral weight or significance. If the two acts are "virtually identical," we would be inconsistent if we evaluate them differently.[18]

But are the acts virtually identical? After all, we distinguish the acts of murder (for example, premeditated killing for personal profit) from accidental killing (for example, you are cleaning what you think is an unloaded gun which goes off and kills a bystander) in part by considering the intention of the agent. Both are acts of killing, but only one is murder because only one is intended and planned. Similarly, one might argue that there is a substantial moral difference between the acts of the two pilots as only one intends to kill noncombatants.

However, such a reply may not be decisive since we often identify acts apart from the intentions of the agent.[19] Thus, two baseball players may each perform the act of hitting a home run even though one intends to go for the fences and the other intends to strike out (he has been bribed to throw the game) but hits the ball accidentally while taking a wild swing with his eyes closed.

So what should we conclude about double effect? This principle has been and will continue to be hotly debated. We ourselves have doubts about whether a case for it can be made plausibly enough to rescue just war theory from the charge that modern war violates the discrimination principle.

However, a more promising approach that basically involves conjoining double effect with other principles has been suggested by Michael Walzer and seems to us to have more promise than an appeal to double effect in isolation. This approach might be called a pluralistic modification of double effect.

Our question is whether just war theory can be justified in the face of the objection that modern war almost inevitably involves the killing of noncombatants or innocents and so violates its own principle of discrimination. Perhaps not if we take a totally absolutist line and maintain that even the single killing of an innocent or noncombatant is prohibited by morality.[20] But what if we take a less absolutist line and consider a modified and perhaps more justifiable version of double effect?

One suggestion is that if we conjoin a number of requirements, a plural test so to speak, some wars, such as the defense against the Nazis in World War II and some other wars of self-defense, can be justified. Michael Walzer develops this idea as follows.

> Simply not to intend the death of civilians is too easy. . . . What we look for in such cases is some sign of a positive commitment to save civilian lives. . . . And if saving civilian lives means risking soldiers' lives, the risk must be accepted. But there is a limit to the risks that we require. . . . We can only ask soldiers to minimize the dangers they impose.[21]

As we understand this proposal, Walzer is conjoining the doctrine of double effect to other conditions. In particular, we must think of an intention not just as a private mental state but as manifested in public action designed to minimize civilian casualties. Thus, nations might spend much of their wealth designing more and more precise weapons and those fighting the war might be asked to take *reasonable* risks to avoid harming noncombatants. For example, soldiers engaged in house-to-house fighting in a city might try to give warning to civilians to evacuate the area, avoid calling in indiscriminate air or artillery strikes, and take care to distinguish enemy fighters from noncombatants. (This may be extremely difficult while fighting an insurgency where the enemy attempts to blend in with the general population, but often in such cases it is the insurgents through their tactics and not the organized military that is endangering civilians and who must bear much of the blame for harm to noncombatants.) Finally, the condition of *proportionality* must be satisfied. The good to come of the action, or the evil averted by it, must significantly outweigh the harm.

Such a defense of just war theory will remain controversial. We suggest that while the modified or pluralistic version of double effect suggested by Walzer is undoubtedly open to objections we have not considered here, it is a reasonable attempt to satisfy the goals of just war theory that we identified earlier. That is, the principles of just war theory, perhaps as modified above, if generally observed would reduce the terrible suffering engendered by war and allow for greater preservation of human rights than would otherwise be the case. The theory is not philosophically airtight and should continue to be the subject of critical examination, but we suggest that in spite of its flaws, it is defensible from a human rights perspective.

Such a conclusion perhaps depends on the intuition, which we share, that at least some wars are just wars or at least justifiable ones. The paradigmatic modern case is World War II. Not all philosophers agree, however, that even the war against the Axis powers (Hitler's Germany, Tojo's Japan, and Mussolini's Italy) was morally acceptable. For example, Robert Holmes points out that while military force did stop Hitler, it was unsuccessful in ending fascism and racism, or the continuing threat of nuclear war. Douglas Lackey, another philosopher sympathetic to pragmatic pacifism, questions whether the 6.5 million deaths he attributes to the Allies in World War II (total deaths are estimated to exceed 30 million) were worth the benefits. Lackey concedes that many deaths would have followed an Axis conquest if the Allies had not fought back (or if the United States had stayed out of the war) but questions whether Japan or Germany would have invaded America. Even if they had, although a Nazi victory

> would have had morally frightful results . . . killing six and one-half million people is also morally frightful and preventing one moral wrong does not obviously outweigh committing the other. . . . Antiwar pacifists speak on behalf of the enemy dead, and on behalf of those millions who would have lived if the war had not been fought. On this silent constituency, they rest their moral case.[22]

While we agree that the case for pragmatic or practical pacifism deserves extended consideration, we do not find the sort of reasoning outlined above convincing. Holmes, we suggest, may be asking too much by saying World War II was not successful because it did not end fascism, racism, and the possibility of nuclear war. (Isn't this something like saying that antibiotics are unsuccessful because they do not cure cancer?) Surely, what World War II did achieve was significant. For one thing, consider the possibly millions more lives of Jews and other "non-Aryan" minorities that might have been lost if the Holocaust had continued as well as the massive human rights violations that rule by the Nazis or related fascist parties would have entailed.[23]

We also point out that the citizens of many states, particularly but not only in liberal democracies, have rights to live under their own governments and not to be conquered by others. Lackey is quite right to emphasize the cost of war in human lives in World War II was devastating and horrific. But we suggest that the costs of not fighting back also are enormous and justify the widely held belief that the Allied cause in World War II was just.[24] In Walzer's words, "Nazism was an ultimate threat to everything decent in our lives, an ideology and a practice of domination so murderous, so degrading even to those who might survive, that the consequences of its final victory were literally beyond calculation, immeasurably awful."[25]

We conclude, then, that a presumptive case can be made for some versions of just war theory, and that while the theory itself remains debatable, the reasons for supporting it outweigh the force of the criticisms. This does not mean that war should ever be embarked on except in the gravest circumstances but rather that, in special circumstances, some wars may be just or at least justified and that the horror involved in fighting them can be reduced by promoting general adherence to the principles of the theory and by identifying and punishing violators.

BRIEF COMMENTS ON NUCLEAR DETERRENCE AND WEAPONS OF MASS DESTRUCTION

Could a massive nuclear exchange between two superpowers ever be justified? During the Cold War, before the breakup of the Soviet Union, both the Soviet Union and the United States had vast arsenals of nuclear weapons targeted on each other's military installations and major population centers. Many of these weapons are still possessed by Russia and the United States and still are targeting major population centers. The possibility of a nuclear exchange during the Cold War perhaps was highest during the Cuban missile crisis when American president John F. Kennedy blockaded Cuba after the Soviet Union inserted missiles with nuclear capabilities there. Today, perhaps a greater threat lies not in massive nuclear strikes by superpowers but in smaller attacks by "rogue states" or use of nuclear weapons by terrorist groups. But the large powers, in spite of some significant reductions, still possess huge nuclear arsenals capable of devastating the earth.

It is hard even to imagine circumstances in which a full nuclear exchange between superpowers could ever be justified. Such an exchange would devastate the earth, perhaps making human life impossible. Innocents and noncombatants from all countries, not just the warring states, would be killed or suffer the effects of radiation. The principle of discrimination would be grossly violated.

However, it does not follow that the only morally acceptable option is unilateral nuclear disarmament or surrender in case of a nuclear threat or nuclear blackmail. Even if a full nuclear strike, even one in retaliation for a first strike by an enemy, is immoral, it does not follow that employment of the *threat* of nuclear retaliation is also immoral.[26] In any case, the leaders of the world's major nuclear superpowers, the United States and the old Soviet Union, believed they could best avoid a nuclear holocaust by threatening retaliation for a first strike thereby creating a balance of terror through mutually assured destruction (given the perhaps appropriate acronym of MAD).

There is considerable disagreement among students of military strategy and the ethics of war over whether even the threat of massive retaliation is morally permissible. Can it be moral to threaten to exterminate millions and millions of children? Utilitarians may calculate as follows:

Nuclear war may be a worse disaster than enemy domination and . . . the probability
of unilateral nuclear disarmament leading to enemy domination is greater than the

probability of nuclear deterrence leading to war. If so, the choice between nuclear deterrence and unilateral nuclear disarmament is a choice between a less probable risk of a greater disaster and a more probable risk of a lesser disaster.[27]

While some (but not all) utilitarians might defend the threat of massive nuclear retaliation as the lesser of the two evils, others (including some rule utilitarians) who assign priority to human rights, justice, and the sanctity of innocent life would disagree.

What about a so-called "counterforce" strategy where nuclear weapons are aimed at military targets rather than population centers? However, because the effects of nuclear weapons are so widespread and long-lasting, including with some kinds of weapons radiation damage to the land that can last many years (even decades or in extreme cases centuries), even the counterforce strategy involves extensive harm to noncombatants or innocents. It is doubtful, therefore, if the counterforce strategy could satisfy the proportionality principle. Moreover, some strategists have argued it raises the probability of a first strike since one side might hope to knock out in one quick blow the other side's ability to retaliate. Thus, the attempt to limit civilian casualties by targeting the enemy's military with nuclear weapons could make nuclear war between superpowers more likely and endanger civilians even more than the original doctrine of mutually assured destruction.[28]

Clearly, the best alternative is mutual nuclear disarmament by the superpowers or, if that cannot be achieved, vast reduction in their nuclear arsenals, coupled with a policy of nonproliferation of nuclear weapons to other states. Unfortunately, while there have been reductions in the nuclear arsenals of the United States and Russia, their remaining nuclear capacity remains huge while countries such as China, India, and Pakistan have become nuclear powers.[29] Indeed, in 2007, nations widely regarded as dangerous, such as Iran, are developing the capacity to build and launch nuclear weapons or, as in the case of North Korea, actually testing them.

The issues raised by all of these considerations are complex and call as much for political solutions as philosophical guidelines. While we find any first use of nuclear weapons to be morally prohibited because of their indiscriminate effects on noncombatants and also fail to see how massive nuclear retaliation could be justified, we suggest that preservation of some nuclear weapons by the liberal democracies as deterrents to their use by others may be the lesser of the evils available to us. The main goal of the liberal democracies, however, should be to develop through political action in the international community effective strategies of nonproliferation so as to keep these weapons of mass destruction out of the hands of those most likely to use them or threaten others with nuclear blackmail.

Perhaps, however, the greatest military threat to civilians in the liberal democracies is not from organized armed forces of an enemy state but from various terrorist groups. But what is terrorism and how is it to be morally evaluated?

THE MORAL EVALUATION OF TERRORISM

While the 9/11 attacks on the World Trade Center and Pentagon horrified Americans, aroused the sympathy of most of the world, and led to the War on Terror, terrorism has been around for a long time. Among relatively more recent acts characterized as terrorism might be included bombings of civilians carried out by the Irish Republican Army, the murder of Israeli athletes at the 1972 Munich Olympics, the bombing of the Murrah Federal Building in Oklahoma City in 1995 by homegrown American Timothy McVeigh, the explosion on and destruction of Pan American Flight 103 over Lockerbie, Scotland, in 1988 by agents with Libyan connections, and the devastating explosions in 2005 and 2006 on trains in London, Madrid, and Bombay. Although Al Qaeda or loosely connected Islamist sympathizers have been tied to many recent terrorist acts, such groups hardly have a monopoly on terrorism, which also has been associated with a variety of different groups and causes throughout the world.

But while there may be clear cases of terrorism, there is much debate on what counts as terrorism or how "terrorism" is to be defined, what acts fall under that heading, and whether terrorism is always wrong. Some regard the term "terrorism" as almost vacuous, used only to condemn those with whom we disagree, as when it is claimed that "one person's terrorist is another's freedom fighter." Others condemn terrorism but exclude what they call resistance movements from that heading, and so deny that, for example, a bombing of a café in Israel filled with teenagers, families, and the elderly is really terrorism rather than a legitimate response to perceived injustice. Let us see if we can sort out some of these issues and arrive at a moral assessment of terrorism.

What Is Terrorism?

How then should "terrorism" be defined? One would think that since we can identify terrorist acts, it should be easy to say what it is about such acts that makes them examples of terrorism. However, that is not the case. How terrorism should be defined in fact is quite controversial.

For example, we think it desirable that any characterization or definition of terrorism beg as few moral issues as possible. Thus, to take a crude example, it is not useful to define terrorism as "the wrongful use of violence to achieve undesirable political aims" because then people who disagree over when the use of violence is wrongful and when political aims are undesirable will also be unable to agree on just which acts fall under the heading of terrorism. What we want is an account of terrorism that makes it relatively easy to identify so that we can then morally evaluate it. It does no good merely to stipulate that terrorism is wrong by definition, because those who would defend certain acts as morally legitimate simply would then refuse to classify them as terrorism. (Perhaps this is why some Arab governments and other supporters of the Palestinians refuse to call bombings of Israeli noncombatants by Hamas or other such groups "terrorist": since they regard resistance as legitimate, such acts are not wrong according to their definition and hence are not terrorist acts in the first place.)

Secondly, a definition of terrorism should neither be too broad nor too narrow. But this requirement is difficult to satisfy. Was the bombing of the U.S.S. *Cole* in a harbor in Yemen in 2000 terrorist because it was carried out in peacetime during a routine visit to an allegedly friendly port, or was it a military action since the *Cole* was a naval warship and hence in the eyes of the bombers a legitimate target of attack? Was the German bombing of civilian areas of London and the Allied mass bombing of Dresden terrorist, since they seemed at least partially intended to target noncombatants in hope of terrorizing the civilian population and ending the war, or were they acts carried out by an organized uniformed military, and so, even if morally wrong, not examples of terrorism at all? What about campaigns of political assassination directed against leaders of an opposing state or party who are deemed responsible for its allegedly unjust policies? (Assassination of leaders was a tactic employed by anarchist movements in Europe during the nineteenth century.)[30]

In what follows, we will employ "terrorism" in a narrow sense that clearly covers cases such as the Oklahoma City bombing, the 9/11 attacks, and the bombings in London and Madrid of railroads and mass transit systems, as well as state-sponsored terrorism such as mass bombings designed to terrorize civilian populations. As we will use the term, "terrorism" refers to the organized or planned use of indiscriminate violence in order to achieve political aims by terrorizing a population or disrupting its normal life through fear and destruction. However, we are sympathetic to attempts to expand the definition to include politically motivated assassination, the use of violence against property for political reasons ("ecoterrorism"), and the use of violence against military personnel when they are not functioning as combatants, for example, the attack on the U.S.S. *Cole* or the blowing up of a bar or restaurant frequented by troops in peacetime.[31]

Both the narrower and broader characterization, while they may contain a presumption against the morality of terrorism, since it involves indiscriminate violence, do not entail or stipulate by definition that terrorism always is wrong. Perhaps the presumption can be defeated by showing the targets are not innocent or not noncombatants, or by appeal to proportionality. Thus philosopher Gabriel Palmer-Fernandez points out that there is considerable disagreement over the morality of what seem to be terrorist actions by the antislavery militant John Brown before the Civil War, including the hacking to death of a father and two sons at the Doyle farm in 1856.[32] Whether Brown's actions were justified, all things considered, is to be determined by argument, not by the way we have suggested terrorism be defined.

Nevertheless, it is difficult to see how most terrorist attacks, including the 9/11 attacks on the World Trade Center, the London, Madrid, and Bombay bombings of railroads, suicide bombings in Israel, and those directed against Iraqi civilians (including groups of children) can be morally defended. We need to consider the case against such acts, explain why the burden of proof that must be met if terrorism is to be justified is so high, and then consider some of the arguments that have been suggested on behalf of terrorism as a tactic that might be used by the weak against the strong.

The grave moral problem with many acts of terrorism is their violation of three major principles of just war theory—namely, last resort, proportionality, and discrimination. The violation of the crucial principle of discrimination is most important since protection of noncombatants or innocents is a fundamental requirement of conducting a war justly. Yet terrorism in paradigmatic cases, such as the 9/11 attacks, the bombing of trains in London in 2005, the 1995 Oklahoma City bombing, and the destruction in 1988 of Pan American Flight 103, all seem to target the very sort of individual that the principle of discrimination prohibits us from intentionally attacking. In other words, the only way to defend these acts is to abandon just war theory. But if just war theory is surrendered, the only options are practical pacifism, which we respect but which faces the objections outlined previously, or to acknowledge that anything goes in war, a position we have found reason to categorically reject. If all actions were allowed in war, there would be no basis for condemning the targeting of civilians in mass bombing campaigns, let alone the atrocities carried out in China by Japanese soldiers during World War II, or the My Lai massacre committed by American troops in Vietnam. But if those acts are rightly subject to the severest moral criticism, the kind of paradigmatic terrorist acts we are considering, which target noncombatants or civilians, must be evaluated as equally heinous.

Excuses for Terrorism

But is there a justification that the terrorists might provide that would show that at least some of the paradigmatic terrorist acts we are considering do have a moral justification after all? For one thing, terrorists could deny that their victims are truly innocent, or truly noncombatants. Thus, Islamic terrorists might argue that all Israelis are legitimate targets because they participate in a state that oppresses the Palestinians. Apologists for Al Qaeda can maintain that many of those in the World Trade Center during the 9/11 attacks were movers and shakers in the American economy, an economy that allegedly exploits many people in the Third World. Perhaps this is what the then–University of Colorado professor Ward Churchill meant in his claim (which ignited a national controversy) that many of the 9/11 victims were "little Eichmanns," referring to the manager of the Nazi death camps who treated their operation as a business, suppressing the moral horror of what was involved.[33] While Churchill exempted many of the victims (as building staff, police, and fire and other rescue officers) from his critique, his remarks suggest that the attackers might have regarded many of the victims as "complicit" in injustices they believe are caused around the world by America's pursuit of economic interest. Although we find Churchill's use of the "little Eichmanns" expression not only grossly offensive but also misguided and wrong, and his discussion of these issues often simplistic and inaccurate, we need to consider whether terrorists can argue with any degree of plausibility that their victims are not truly innocent or not truly noncombatants.

In fact, the defense that the victims of terrorism are complicit in some sense and so not truly protected by the principle of discrimination runs into major objections. First, the kind of destruction involved in the paradigmatic cases of terrorism we are considering is far too broad to be covered by this excuse. Were the many Syracuse University students on Pan American Flight 103, to say nothing of the children onboard or the flight crew, somehow complicit in American policy and so legitimate targets? What of the children in a day care center and the office workers killed in the Oklahoma City bombing? Or the janitors, flight crews, airplane passengers, and rescue workers killed on 9/11? To say that such people are complicit and so not protected by the principle of discrimination is to construe the principle so narrowly that virtually no one is covered (including those the terrorists themselves argue are victims of injustice).

Second, even if some victims are involved in what the terrorists regard as an unjust practice, it is one thing for them to be held responsible by some legitimate judicial body that observes procedural justice and quite another for them to be executed without any due process or chance to present a defense. Moreover, there are degrees of complicity, and it would take a very high level of involvement indeed to warrant infliction of the death penalty, even if one believes the activity at issue contributed somewhat to injustice (which itself is a highly debatable claim). Is it even remotely plausible to say that someone who works in a New York brokerage house is a central participant in the American economic machine and so deserves to be executed without due process or any finding of degree of involvement?[34]

Third, suppose for the sake of argument that it is questionable whether the economic and political influence of the liberal democracies throughout the world has been beneficial or harmful on balance. Whether the ordinary people who have been victims of terrorist attacks in the West have been involved in greater injustice than what would be involved in the kind of theocracy that many Islamic fundamentalists support, to say nothing of the ideals of neo-Nazis and white supremacist groups active in Europe and the United States, is extremely doubtful. Indeed, those fundamentalist Islamic regimes currently or recently in power, such as in Iran and the Taliban in Afghanistan, have abused power, subordinated women and even denied them access to basic education (in Afghanistan), stifled dissent and democratic opposition (in Iran), and imposed religious values on those who do not share them. Such forces can hardly claim to be warriors for social justice.

What if the terrorists reply that they reject what they may regard as primarily Western liberal ideals of social justice and instead see themselves as warriors for a conception of the good—a religious conception derived from their version of holy writ? We have seen, however (see the discussion in chapter 3), that liberal ideals and principles have their basis in reasoned argument and sometimes arise from sources that are not Western. They deserve our respect because of the justification that can be provided for them, which is neither parochial nor ethnocentric. Moreover, the terrorists and their supporters also appeal to such values when they denounce the injustices allegedly committed by those they oppose, and so they cannot claim to entirely reject the values cited by their critics.

Finally, claims that a cause, however violent, is sanctioned by God, and that the enemy are infidels who stand in the way of God's plan, can be made from many conflicting religious perspectives. While anyone can claim to alone speak for God, such claims cannot be verified in the arena of public discourse, and appeal to them alone can only lead to brutal religious wars with no compromise allowed or quarter given. At some point, people must ask whether they prefer the destruction involved in the search for religious dominance or the kind of peaceful resolution of disagreements promoted by reasonable discourse in the liberal state.

Our paradigmatic cases of terrorism violate the principle of discrimination. How does the principle of proportionality bear upon the paradigmatic cases of terrorism we have considered? Proportionality requires us to balance the positive and negative consequences of acts of terror rather than assess whether lines prohibiting certain acts, such as targeting noncombatants, have been crossed. As we have seen in our discussion of utilitarianism in chapter 2, this kind of balancing is notoriously hard to do in difficult cases and often involves controversial hypothetical judgments of the form, "If act X had not taken place, then consequence Y rather than Z would have taken place." The truth of such counterfactuals is notoriously difficult to assess.

Having said that, it is difficult to identify cases where indiscriminate violence of the kind associated with recent terrorism has led to significant successes for the terrorists' cause. What benefits have emerged from the murder of Israeli athletes at the Munich Olympics, the death of the passengers on Pan Am Flight 103, or the 9/11 attacks? Attacks on trains in Spain, for which Al Qaeda apparently was responsible, did lead to the withdrawal of Spanish troops from the American-led coalition in Iraq but had little effect on the war itself. Indeed, in the case of Palestinian terrorism, such acts of violence surely have created a backlash that has hurt the cause of the Palestinians far more than it has helped. Not only has such terrorism caused suffering by its victims and their families but it also has created distrust that makes future peace settlements much more difficult to establish than might otherwise have been the case. Given that terrorist acts are prima facie violations of the principle of discrimination, and given that there are few if any recent examples of successful outcomes brought about by terrorism, the burden of proof falls heavily upon the perpetrators of terrorist acts to show that proportionality is satisfied. (Terrorists might argue that what many throughout the world perceive as an American overreaction to 9/11, especially the invasion of Iraq, has led to the isolation of America and so helped the terrorists' cause. However, this claim is doubtful since it is highly debatable how permanent or deep that alleged isolation may be, or whether it actually helps the theocratic goals of the attackers, as opposed to simply fueling anti-American sentiment. Moreover, even if true, such a defense presupposes just what liberal democrats should deny—namely, that the cause of the terrorists is a just one.)

The principle of last resort also applies to terrorism. Even if, contrary to fact, recent paradigmatic cases of terrorism "work," could the goals have been accomplished in other, less harmful ways? For example, would the Palestinian cause have been helped more by an educational campaign conducted in the United States and Israel, stressing moral values and the desire for peace and cooperation, perhaps coupled with some of the techniques of nonviolent passive resistance suggested by the practical pacifists, than by blowing up civilians, often including non-Israelis and even fellow Arabs caught in the crossfire, in Israeli buses and cafés?

This point also undercuts the claim that terrorists have no other way to promote their cause since they cannot defeat their more powerful opponents, such as the United States, in open military conflicts. Political campaigns, nonviolent resistance, and making a moral case to relevant groups are also alternatives. It is true, however, that those fighting internally against a dictatorial tyranny may not have normal avenues of political expression open to them, but it also is far from clear that indiscriminately targeting civilians who are not responsible for oppression by the state is either an effective or a morally allowable means of overthrowing the regime in power. Michael Walzer suggests that there might be exceptions in supreme moral emergencies, such as stopping genocide. We agree, since our point is not that terrorism by its nature is always wrong or is always morally prohibited, but rather that the burden of proof against it is extremely high, and that contemporary paradigmatic forms of terrorism do not meet that burden, or even come close. As Walzer puts it, recent terrorism "has not been a means of avoiding disaster but of reaching for political success."[35]

We conclude then that there is a heavy burden of proof that anyone who would attempt to morally justify terrorism must meet. We see no reason to believe that contemporary terrorists can meet this burden. However, some who have sympathy for causes that the terrorists may support, such as a Palestinian state, or withdrawal of U.S. support for undemocratic regimes in various parts of the world, may maintain that our treatment is not evenhanded. According to such criticism, we condemn injustice by the terrorists but not by America.

In response, it is important to note that the principles of just war apply to all sides. For example, they apply as much to the terrorism practiced by right-wing death squads in various Latin American countries that murdered thousands of people in an allegedly anticommunist campaign carried out during much of the last thirty years of the twentieth century as to Timothy McVeigh or to Al Qaeda. They also apply to the behavior of countries such as the United States and its allies whenever violations occur. In fact, without such principles, we would lose much of the moral basis for criticizing our own behavior and that of our friends when it is wrong.

However, we also maintain that there is an enormous difference between military forces that seek to minimize the horrors of war by taking significant steps to limits casualties to noncombatants and who punish violations of the rules of war when they occur, and those who directly and indiscriminately target civilians. Wrongdoing in war can and does take place on all sides but not all wrongdoing is of equal seriousness or morally equivalent.

IRAQ AND THE DOCTRINE OF PREVENTIVE WAR

The invasion of Iraq in 2003 led by the United States, joined by Britain and smaller forces from other countries, sometimes called "the coalition of the willing" by the administration of President George W. Bush, raises a test case for the issues we have been discussing. Is the war in Iraq a just war, or if not just, perhaps justifiable in some broader sense? In the brief discussion that follows, we cannot explore this issue exhaustively so we will try to avoid taking a partisan stance. However, we will suggest questions that might help clarify the issues and offer a tentative conclusion.

Several justifications for American military action against Iraq were proposed by the Bush administration and other supporters of the war. These arguments are designed to show that the war had a just cause. According to the legalist justification, as it has been called, the United States and its allies were enforcing various U.N. resolutions with which the regime of Iraqi dictator Saddam Hussein allegedly had not complied. According to a second line of argument, the invasion would topple a brutal regime and replace it with democracy and so was justifiable on humanitarian grounds. Indeed, the introduction of democracy in Iraq, it was hoped, would serve as an example to accelerate the growth of democracy in the Middle East, a region noted for its autocratic regimes. According to the third argument, the war was justified to prevent Iraq from developing weapons of mass destruction and perhaps transferring them to terrorists who might use them against the United States and its friends.

The legalist argument rests primarily on U.N. Security Council Resolution 1441 (2002), which found Iraq to be in violation of previous Security Council resolutions and threatened "serious consequences" for continued failure to cooperate. One of the most important of these earlier resolutions was Resolution 687, which established formal conditions for the end of hostilities after the first Gulf War and Operation Desert Storm, the military operation that drove Iraqi forces out of Kuwait. Resolution 687, among other conditions, required Iraq to destroy its chemical and biological weapons and ballistic missiles and to accept and cooperate with U.N. inspections designed to verify compliance.

Even if the legalist argument is sound, and it is controversial among legal scholars, our focus is on the moral questions it raises.[36] Even if the United States and the "coalition of the willing" had a legal justification for the invasion of Iraq, was the principle of last resort satisfied? Many critics of the war, including many of those who were allies of the United States during Desert Storm, thought U.N. inspection teams, under the direction of Hans Blix, were making progress in verifying whether or not Iraq possessed weapons of mass destruction, and that international pressure had resulted in greater Iraqi cooperation, however grudging. Second, should the effort to enforce the U.N. resolutions have been more multilateral, involving cooperation of many more countries? Should the United States have acted in ways many of its strongest allies disapproved of, thereby alienating an enormous number of people throughout the world? In other words, even if we assume that the legalist argument is sound, was the decision to enforce the U.N. resolutions through an invasion of Iraq either wise or morally appropriate given the issue of last resort and the strong opposition of many of our closest friends in the international community? On the other hand, is there a moral case for enforcement in that if U.N. resolutions are not enforced, they will not be taken seriously, and international law, vital for preserving peace, will be weakened in the long run?[37]

What about the second argument, that the invasion was designed to depose a vicious dictator, Saddam Hussein, and introduce democracy into Iraq? This in turn might help spread democracy through the Middle East, where, with the exception of Israel, no states come close to conforming to the norms of democratic governance.

Overthrowing a brutal tyranny and replacing it with democracy and respect for human rights certainly are worthy goals that, in our view, have the *potential* to justify military action on humanitarian grounds. However, in our brief discussion of humanitarian intervention earlier in this chapter, we also pointed out that the details of such actions can be very messy and that careful planning and execution are required for such an intervention to be successful.

This suggests at least the following questions: Was the invasion of Iraq planned wisely and were contingencies anticipated? For example, were sufficient numbers of troops employed? Donald Rumsfeld, secretary of defense under President Bush and presumably the planner of the war, has been extensively criticized for disregarding prewar advice from the military about troop levels. Is this just Monday morning quarterbacking or legitimate criticism?[38] Was the degree of antipathy between Sunni and Shia in Iraq anticipated and planned for? Was the Bush administration caught off-guard by the strength of the Iraqi insurgency and the potential for civil war (Hobbes's state of nature?) between rival religious groups in Iraq? Moreover, to return to the issue raised by the legalist paradigm, even if there was a case for humanitarian intervention in Iraq, was the United States justified in acting with only the support of Britain and relatively few other states in opposition to much of the international community? (Take into account, however, that if virtually unanimous support is required, it can almost never be attained, and hence needed humanitarian interventions never could take place.)

Finally, consider the argument that probably resonated most forcefully with the American people. This might be called the argument for preventive war—namely, that the war was justified to stop the Iraqi regime from developing weapons of mass destruction and transferring them to terrorist groups that might use them against U.S. population centers. One can surely understand why such concerns might have strongly influenced Americans in the wake of the 9/11 attacks.

The Bush administration's rationale for what has come to be called preventive war has been advanced in a number of documents and speeches. The core idea is that the United States should be able to "stop rogue states and their terrorist clients before they are able to threaten or use weapons of mass destruction against the United States and our allies and friends." This implies that action can be legitimate "against such emerging threats before they are fully formed."[39]

This idea of a justified *preventive* war differs from the idea of *preemption* discussed above. Remember that just war theorists do not require that the aggressor actually fire the first shot; a preemptive strike by the defenders may be justified when attack is imminent. However, a preventive war is different since it involves a military attack to prevent a threat from developing in the first place, presumably well before it becomes imminent.

While the concern with rogue states that might make weapons of mass destruction available to terrorists, or use them themselves, is a real one, the doctrine of preventive war raises serious questions. In particular, does it make it too easy to go to war?[40] Would it justify an attack on our apparent ally Pakistan, whose scientists may have already transferred knowledge of how to make nuclear weapons to countries like Iran and North Korea? What about those states themselves? Moreover, how close to imminent must a threat be to justify going to war under this doctrine? The answer to each of these questions is far from clear, but the dangers of going to war too easily are apparent in the difficulties facing the United States in Iraq after the overthrow of Saddam Hussein.

Advocates of the doctrine might respond to the above questions by arguing that of course the doctrine must be applied judiciously. It does not imply that any threat justifies resort to war, just that a state *may* go to war in self-defense when it justifiably believes a threat involving weapons of mass destruction, while not imminent, is real. The problem, however, is that national leaders often may not decide judiciously and may be influenced by a variety of political, ideological, and economic interests. Was the decision to invade Iraq in 2003 unduly influenced by the apparently mistaken belief that Americans would be welcomed with open arms by Iraqis and that liberal democracy could rather easily be imported into Middle Eastern states where supporters of liberal values seem to be in the minority or, as in Iran, where adherents of liberal democracy may be quite numerous among the young but are relatively powerless in the face of theocratic oppression?

We suggest that while the theory of preventive war to prevent a future, but not imminent attack, with weapons of mass destruction should not be totally rejected, it only has application in the most extreme cases, and faces an especially heavy burden of proof. This is in large part because since the threat is not imminent, it is extremely doubtful that the principle of last resort can be satisfied, but also because the doctrine is so vague that it would justify war in far too many cases to be acceptable.[41]

Did the U.S. invasion of Iraq have a just cause? Our brief summary of the issues requires further development, but we believe that many of the questions we have raised, when explored in extended discussion, lack a satisfactory answer. While reasonable people will disagree about that point for some time, we point out that the burden of proof should be on those who make war, not on those who question the decision. This is in part because of the suffering produced by war, the difficulty of applying the principle of discrimination under conditions of modern war, and the high degree of likelihood of plans going awry under "the fog of war."

In expressing doubts about whether the Iraq war had a just cause, we do not mean to say that the war was one of aggression or that U.S. leaders had malevolent motives. On the contrary, the three defenses of going to war that we have examined might in some circumstances justify military action. However, we, along with many other Americans, question whether the resort to war was too quick (that the principle of last resort was violated), whether grave miscalculations were made about the ease of the transition from the regime of Saddam Hussein to democracy, resulting in a disproportionate loss of life and suffering, and whether the doctrine of preventive war was applied without sufficient evidence of a near imminent risk of spread of weapons of mass destruction.

Critics of such a view might respond that if a U.S. president had to wait for undeniable evidence of a future nuclear or biochemical threat, it might well be too late to prevent an attack. But that is to respond to a straw man. Critics of the war surely have a point when they ask not for undeniable evidence but for at least convincing evidence, and even more, the existence of a thoughtful plan to win the peace, such as, a plan for bringing rival groups in Iraq together to prevent the kind of insurgency that those familiar with the hostility between rival factions in Iraq feared.

We also think it is important to distinguish between support for our troops and criticism of the political decisions that lead to war. Failure to engage in the latter process makes it more likely that mistakes will be made again in the future and undermines the democratic process of discussion and debate through which our views are tested and justified. For example, did the U.S. policy of not according full rights under the Geneva Convention to prisoners suspected of being terrorists pave the way for the abuse of prisoners by American troops at Abu Ghraib, an event that probably turned a large proportion of the Iraqi population against the Americans following the largely welcome overthrow of Saddam? On the other hand, much of the responsibility for deaths of noncombatants in Iraq surely falls on the insurgency, many of whose leaders show virtual contempt for the principle of discrimination and engage in barbaric acts (including beheadings) that surely admit of no moral justification whatsoever.[42]

To summarize our view, we suggest that the application of the principles discussed in this chapter will, after extended discussion, fail to show that the Iraq war was a just war. Again, we emphasize that this does not mean it was a war of aggression or was badly motivated. But we believe more extended discussion will support the view that the war was neither embarked upon nor carried out wisely. Although there is danger of second-guessing decisions that may have appeared reasonable at the time (such as the belief that Iraq possessed weapons of mass destruction), to the extent that the decision of going to war was not thoroughly debated and rival views given due consideration, the process of decisionmaking not only was flawed but also may have been incompatible with the requirements of deliberative democracy.[43] We invite our readers to pursue this issue more thoroughly and determine for themselves whether a more exhaustive inquiry supports our view.

CONCLUSION

In this chapter, we have explored the theory of just war and have contrasted it with various versions of pacifism, particularly the view that we call practical or pragmatic pacifism. Our conclusion was that the theory of just war is defensible, not because it provides a clear and sharp line between just wars and unjust wars but because its principles create a burden of proof that those who go to war are obliged to meet.[44] This burden makes it more likely that human rights will be protected than otherwise and may limit the suffering caused by war to less than would otherwise be the case.

In a sense, then, our defense of the theory of just war is in part consequentialist and pragmatic (although not entirely utilitarian) because we believe a judicious application of the doctrine is best for protection of human rights. We claim, moreover, that paradigmatic instances of modern terrorism are immoral, largely because of their total disregard of the principle of discrimination.

We understand that our view is subject to some significant criticisms, particularly the responses that the principles of just war are so vague as to be too easily manipulated by each side to a conflict and that the major nations, as well as terrorist groups, also violate the principle of discrimination. (Note that these two objections may be in conflict; if the principle of nondiscrimination is so vague as to be useless, we cannot be sure that major nations violate it to a significant extent. Our critics cannot have it both ways.) We hope, of course, that discussion of these issues will support our conclusions but hope even more that reflection on the issues we have raised makes people more conscious of the moral issues raised by war and shows how difficult it is to actually justify the resort to war. In our view, while there can, in principle, be just wars, war should be entered into not only with the greatest reluctance and as a last resort, but only after extended skeptical debate over the proposed justifications for action.[44]

NOTES

1. We borrow the term "pragmatic pacifism" from Rick Werner, professor of philosophy at Hamilton College, who is developing an important defense of such a position, although

the characterization may first have been employed by Richard Wasserstrom. An important version of such a view also is defended forcefully by philosopher Robert Holmes in his book *On War and Morality* (Princeton, NJ: Princeton University Press, 1989), especially pp. 260–94. As indicated in the text, we would group the writings and tactics of Gandhi and Martin Luther King Jr. under the rubric of this form of pacifism because of their endorsement of forms of passive or nonviolent resistance although we understand that King himself may have been committed to a broad philosophical form of nonviolence in virtually all contexts. See for example King's famous and widely reprinted "Letter from the Birmingham Jail," a classic defense of the use of civil disobedience as a nonviolent tactic of resistance.

2. Michael Walzer, *Just and Unjust Wars*, third ed. (New York: Basic Books, 2000), 330. (The first edition was published in 1977.)

3. Holmes, *On War and Morality*, 276.

4. Thus, before the second Iraq War, leftist critics of U.N. sanctions pointed to the harm resulting to Iraqi children caused by lack of food and medicine. (It turns out that such deficiencies may have been due more to corruption by Iraqi ruler Saddam Hussein, who diverted funds intended for food and health care to the construction of his palaces, and to corruption within the U.N. aid programs themselves.)

5. In his discussion, Holmes points out that military force did stop Hitler but was unsuccessful in ending fascism and racism or the continuing threat of nuclear war. We suggest such remarks fail to give appropriate weight to the perhaps millions of lives saved by Allied force of, which that surely would have been lost if the Holocaust had continued and spread, and to mass violation of human rights if Nazism had triumphed. For discussion, see Holmes, *On War and Morality*, 277–78.

6. Thus, one could extend Rawls's original position to international affairs and think of the rules of just war as what it would be fair for representatives of different states to agree upon if behind a veil of ignorance that obscured from them the knowledge of which particular state they represented as well as knowledge of any of its characteristics. Rawls's work in this area in found in his *The Law of Peoples* (Cambridge: Harvard University Press, 1999).

7. Rawls, *Law of Peoples*, pp. 62–68. For critical discussion to which we are indebted, see Alan Buchanan, "Justice, Legitimacy, and Human Rights," in *The Idea of a Political Liberalism*, ed. Victoria Davion and Clark Wolff (Lanham, MD: Rowman & Littlefield, 2000), 73–89.

8. A classic case would be the Israeli preemptive attack in 1967 against massed Egyptian forces that were, Israel regarded (reasonably in our view), preparing for an assault on the Jewish state. For discussion, see Walzer, *Just and Unjust Wars*, 82–85.

9. Barbara MacKinnon, *Ethics: Theory and Contemporary Issues*, fourth ed. (Belmont, CA: Thomson-Wadsworth, 2004), 436. The example of the "innocent" soldier and the not so innocent civilian are also employed by MacKinnon and are familiar figures in the literature on the principle of discrimination.

10. Rather than attempting to draw a line, our suggestion would be to use what might be called a sliding scale to help distinguish combatants from noncombatants. That is, the less direct the role of the individual in the war effort, the greater the justification needed for subjecting that individual to attack.

11. Quoted by G. E. M. Anscombe in "War and Murder," in *Nuclear Weapons: A Catholic Response*, ed. Walter Stein (New York: Merlin Press, 1961), reprinted in MacKinnon, *Ethics: Theory and Contemporary Issues*, 452.

12. As noted in chapter 3, one may have a right to act in a particular way yet exercise that right foolishly or even in an unjustifiable manner. The right to freedom of speech, for example, may protect our entitlement to give an unreflective speech that distorts or ignores important evidence, but we may be unjustified in exercising our right in such a careless and irresponsible way.

13. We agree that there is no sharp line determining when the benefits of violating a principle are so great as to justify overriding it. Our point, however, is that the principle puts a heavy burden of proof on those who would suspend it to show that their activities are justified.

14. The principle of double effect is widely discussed by philosophers and military theorists who write on ethics and war. For discussion that we have found especially helpful, see Walzer, *Just and Unjust Wars*, esp. 153–59; and Holmes, *On War and Morality*, 193–213. For an overview of the issues, see William David Solomon, "Double Effect," in *Encyclopedia of Ethics*, ed. Lawrence C. Becker and Charlotte B. Becker (New York: Routledge, 2001), 418–20. Our discussion also was stimulated by the critical discussion of double effect expressed by Hamilton student Kristen Sherry in her senior thesis of 2006.

15. This requirement is not arbitrary or ad hoc. After all, the point of double effect is to rule out the targeting of noncombatants or innocents, or at least make such targeting presumptively wrong. But to use the death of such persons as a means to one's objective is in a highly intuitive sense to target them and intend their death.

16. Walzer, *Just and Unjust Wars*, 153.

17. Holmes, *On War and Morality*, 197.

18. Remember that it is a requirement of moral reasoning (the requirement of consistency) that relevantly similar acts must be evaluated similarly.

19. This is the sort of response made by Holmes, *On War and Morality*, 197.

20. Perhaps Paul Ramsey is the most influential thinker who uses double effect to reconcile the theory of just war with an absolute prohibition against killing innocents or noncombatants. See for example his *Nuclear Weapons and Christian Conscience* (Durham, NC: Lily Endowment in Christianity and Politics, Duke University, 1961).

21. Walzer, *Just and Unjust Wars*, 155–56.

22. Douglas Lackey, *The Ethics of War and Peace* (Englewood Cliffs, NJ: Prentice-Hall, 1989). The quotation in the text is from a reprinted excerpt from Lackey's "Pacifism" in James E. White, *Contemporary Moral Problems* (Belmont, CA: Thomson-Wadsworth, 2006), 492–93.

23. Holmes might reply by pointing to the heroic actions of many courageous Danes during Nazi occupation of Denmark who nonviolently protected Jewish Danes from the Nazis. We question, however, whether such resistance would have continued effectively had the Nazis been able to turn the full attention of the more ruthless elements of their forces to it.

24. Although the cause of the Allies was just, this does not mean that the way the war was fought was just in every respect. Thus, the indiscriminate bombing of some German cities, such as Dresden, and the dropping of two atomic bombs on Japan were, at the very least, morally questionable.

25. Walzer, *Just and Unjust Wars*, 253.

26. Can there be a justification for massive nuclear retaliation after one's own nation already has been destroyed, killing millions and millions of innocent civilians, almost all of whom may bear no responsibility for the original strike?

27. Gregory S. Kavka, "Nuclear Ethics," in *Encyclopedia of Ethics*, ed. Lawrence C. Becker and Charlotte B. Becker (New York: Routledge, 2001), 1248.

28. Similar problems have been raised about the missile defense systems (Strategic Defense Initiative) proposed by the administrations of Ronald Reagan and George W. Bush. These systems are designed to launch missiles (or even employ lasers from space satellites) that would destroy nuclear warheads on enemy missiles while in flight. Critics charge that even if such defense systems can be made to work they are destabilizing. If each superpower possessed such a system, one might be tempted to strike first in the hope of destroying enough of its opponent's nuclear capacity so as to survive a retaliatory strike by shooting down many of the enemy's missiles while in flight. Moreover, even an effective defense system might be flooded by dummy warheads, and so rendered unable to distinguish true nuclear missiles from the fakes.

Many strategists who continue to support the Strategic Defense Initiative acknowledge these difficulties and admit it cannot stop a massive launch by an enemy. However, they argue it could be effective against smaller strikes of perhaps one or two missiles from "rogue states" or terrorists.

29. Israel also is widely believed to have an effective nuclear capacity.

30. Some of these points are raised by Gabriel Palmer-Fernandez in his paper "Terrorism, Innocence, and Justice," *Philosophy & Public Policy Quarterly* 25, no. 3 (2005): 22–27.

31. For a broader definition, see Gabriel Palmer-Fernandez, "Terrorism, Innocence, and Justice," 24. For an example of a narrower definition, see R. G. Frey and Christopher Morris, *Terrorism and Justice* (New York: Cambridge University Press, 1991), 1–5.

32. Palmer-Fernandez, "Terrorism, Innocence, and Justice," 22.

33. Ward Churchill, "Some People Push Back: On the Justice of Roosting Chickens," *Pockets of Resistance*, September 2001, available at multiple websites including www.darknight-press.org (6 July 2006).

34. Note that whether U.S. interests, including corporations, have contributed significantly to injustice elsewhere in the world is a separate issue from whether the people working in the World Trade Center were legitimate targets. Our point is that regardless of one's response to the first question, the 9/11 attacks were clear violations of the discrimination principle.

35. Michael Walzer, *Arguing About War* (New Haven, CT: Yale University Press, 1994), 54. See also *Just and Unjust Wars*, esp. 251–55.

36. An influential statement of the legalist position is presented by law professor John Yoo in his article "International Law and the War in Iraq," *The American Journal of International Law* 97, no. 3 (2003): 563–76. However, David Luban points out that there "is a credible legal argument that legitimate wars of law enforcement must be authorized" by specific U.N. action and thus "no unilateral war can ever be a war of law enforcement." David Luban, "Preventive War," *Philosophy and Public Affairs* 32, no. 2 (2004): 212n.

37. Indeed, it might be argued that failure to enforce Security Council Resolution 1559, which required that Hizbollah withdraw from southern Lebanon and create a demilitarized buffer zone between it and Israel, contributed significantly to the Israeli incursion into Lebanon in July 2006 and the ensuing destruction. If the international community does not enforce such resolutions, countries that are threatened may well react militarily. (Hizbollah was widely reported to have imported thousands of rocket launchers and missiles aimed at Israel into the supposedly "demilitarized" buffer zone with no significant reaction from

the United Nations. These weapons were used against Israeli population centers during the 2006 incursion.)

38. Prior to the U.S. invasion of Iraq, the U.S. Army chief of staff, General Shinseki, recommended much higher troop levels than were eventually decided upon and was severely criticized by the Pentagon's civilian leaders for saying so. U.S. Ambassador Paul Bremer, the Bush administration's chief administrator in Iraq immediately following the defeat of Saddam's regime, also later criticized troop levels as being too low to establish security and ensure a peaceful transition to a new government.

39. *National Security Strategy of the United States of America* (2002) at http://www.whitehouse.gov/nsc/nss9.html. Quoted by Luban, "Preventive War," 208.

40. This point is a central one in Luban's discussion, "Preventive War."

41. Here, we follow the general conclusion of Luban's thoughtful paper, "Preventive War," but would reject his restriction that only the state being threatened may resort to a preventive attack because only that state is acting in self-defense. Suppose, for example, that state X learns that state Y plans to develop a nuclear weapon that it plans to use against state Z. Suppose Z is incapable of defending itself. We suggest that under some conditions, X might justifiably wage a preventive war against Y to protect Z.

42. We also have sympathy for the view, however, that the security situation in Iraq might have been much better, and the insurgency might as a result never have achieved great strength, if the United States had sent enough troops to provide safety for Iraqi inhabitants. In fact, in 2006, seven retired generals called for Secretary of Defense Donald Rumsfeld to resign because of what they consider his grave miscalculations in his plan for the war.

43. Indeed, critics have argued not only that the debate was less than thorough but also that the Bush administration tried to stifle or discredit critics, such as former defense analyst Richard Clarke, who claimed the administration not only was uninterested in considering the case against war but "cooked the books" to concoct a stronger case for war than actually existed.

44. In fact, we question the standard division of wars into two categories, "just" and "unjust." A third category, perhaps "unjustified" war, might be added to distinguish wars of aggression and expansion from wars that may have not unreasonable rationales but that are entered into unwisely, without due regard for how difficulties might undermine conformity to the principles of just war, and that are carried out with strategic ineptness.

45. We understand that sometimes immediate response is called for and that not all war plans can be debated in public—secrecy sometimes can be a legitimate concern—but the overall general principles that might justify going to war, as well as likely contingencies that might raise the issue of military responses, usually can be debated in advance.

QUESTIONS FOR FURTHER STUDY

1. Distinguish between philosophical and practical (pragmatic) pacifism. What do you think is a major argument for each and a major criticism of each? Is either view justified? Defend your view.
2. What sorts of reasons, if any, do you think can justify the resort to war? Defend your view by assessing possible criticisms of it.

3. How would you assess the claim that once a country is in a war, it should do anything necessary to win? Defend your view by considering a major objection to it.

4. Distinguish between a rights-based and a utilitarian justification of principles of just war theory. Is either approach defensible? Do you believe the approach of just war theorists is justifiable given criticisms of the theory? Defend your view.

5. Do you believe that modern war is sometimes just (or at least justifiable) given its destructiveness and the likelihood of violations of the discrimination principle? Defend your view by considering criticisms of it.

6. Do you think massive nuclear retaliation against the civilian centers of a country that has launched a massive first nuclear strike can be morally justified? What about the threat of retaliation as a device to prevent a first strike? Defend your view.

7. Is who counts as a terrorist purely a matter of opinion or is there some relatively objective or defensible way of distinguishing terrorists from others who engage in violence (or for distinguishing terrorist acts from other acts of violence)?

8. Under what circumstances, if any, do you think the resort to terrorism as characterized in this chapter might be justified? Defend your view.

9. Suppose country X is developing a nuclear weapons program and has a history of selling military intelligence to groups your country considers terrorists and who have actually carried out acts of terrorism against your country in the past. Do you think a preventive attack on the nuclear facilities of country X can be morally justified well before the nuclear weapons program becomes operational? What factors should you take into account in arriving at a decision? What moral considerations apply? Defend your view.

SUGGESTED READINGS

Books

Frey, R. G., and Christopher Morris. *Terrorism and Justice.* New York: Cambridge University Press, 1991.

Holmes, Robert. *On War and Morality.* Princeton, NJ: Princeton University Press, 1989.

Kavka, Gregory S. *Moral Paradoxes of Nuclear Deterrence.* Cambridge: Cambridge University Press, 1987.

Lackey, Douglas. *The Ethics of War and Peace.* Englewood Cliffs, NJ: Prentice-Hall, 1989.

Rawls, John. *The Law of Peoples.* Cambridge, MA: Harvard University Press, 1999.

Reichberg, Gregory, Henrik Syse, and Endre Begby, eds. *The Ethics of War: Classic and Contemporary Readings.* Malden, MA: Blackwell, 2006.

Sterba, James P., ed. *The Ethics of War and Nuclear Deterrence.* Belmont, CA: Wadsworth, 1985.

CHAPTER 9

Walzer, Michael. *Just and Unjust Wars*, third ed. New York: Basic Books, 2000.
——. *Arguing About War*. New Haven, CT: Yale University Press, 2004.

Articles

Anscombe, G. E. M. "War and Murder," in *Nuclear Weapons: A Catholic Response*, ed. Walter Stein. New York: Merlin Press, 1961, widely reprinted.
Brandt, Richard B. "Utilitarianism and the Rules of War." *Philosophy and Public Affairs* 1, no. 2 (1973): 145–65.
Buchanan, Allen. "Institutionalizing the Just War." *Philosophy and Public Affairs* 34, no. 1 (2006): 2–38.
Hare, R. M. "Rules of War and Moral Reasoning." *Philosophy and Public Affairs* 1, no. 2 (1973): 166–81.
Kavka, Gregory S. "Nuclear Ethics," *Encyclopedia of Ethics*, ed. Lawrence C. Becker and Charlotte B. Becker. New York: Routledge, 2001, 1247–50.
Luban, David. "Preventive War." *Philosophy and Public Affairs* 32, no. 2 (2004): 207–48.
McMahan, Jeff. "The Ethics of Killing in War." *Ethics* 114 (2004): 693–733.
Nagel, Thomas. "War and Massacre." *Philosophy and Public Affairs* 1, no. 2 (1973): 123–44.
Palmer-Fernandez, Gabriel. "Terrorism, Innocence, and Justice." *Philosophy and Public Policy Quarterly* (formerly *Report from the Institute for Philosophy and Public Policy*) 25, no. 3 (2005): 22–27.
Solomon, William David. "Double Effect," in *Encyclopedia of Ethics*, ed. Lawrence C. Becker and Charlotte B. Becker. New York: Routledge, 2001, 418–20.

POSTSCRIPT

In *The Individual and the Political Order*, we have examined some of the central issues in political and social philosophy and have evaluated different approaches to them. We also have proposed and tried to defend what we regard as a liberal approach to these issues. Although there are many different versions of liberalism, fundamental liberal values that we have tried to incorporate in our approach include recognition of individuals as bearers of fundamental human rights, including entitlements of persons to develop their own conception of the good life rather than allowing the state to impose a conception of the good or a vision of community on its citizens.

We are less concerned, however, with whether readers adopt our own position than to have provided a reasonable account of it. In addition, we have tried to provide a fair account of the views of those with whom we disagree. Indeed, it is only by testing one set of views against others and by assessing the supporting arguments for each that our beliefs or yours can be justified at all.

We believe that much political debate throughout society, even on college campuses, has degenerated into either a kind of preaching to the converted, where we discuss issues only with those who already agree with us, or a kind of angry and often self-righteous series of diatribes, where the participants rarely engage with the reasoning (if any) offered by their opponents and often demonize the opposition or present opposing views in their worst light. We hope that by bringing out the strengths as well as weaknesses of different approaches to political philosophy we have helped demonstrate the value of genuine dialogue, in which differences are honestly aired and criticisms and objections faced and discussed in an attempt to find the best resolution.

As we have seen, particularly in chapter 7, a number of contemporary approaches to political theory, including some versions of feminism and postmodernism, have called into question uncritical acceptance of such notions as objectivity, impartiality, and reasonableness. While these challenges sometimes have made valuable contributions by questioning unexamined assumptions about what is objective, impartial, or reasonable, we need to be careful not to throw out the baby with the bath water. After all, an argument that objectivity, impartiality, and reasonableness are mere illusions must itself make some sort of claim to be objective, unbiased, and reasonable. If it is none of those, why should we even take it seriously, let alone accept it? Of course, though, there is room for debate about how notions of objectivity, impartiality, and reasonableness are best understood.

Above all, we hope to have shown that reasoned evaluation of arguments not only can help us identify those positions that are indefensible because they involve gross violation of well-supported fundamental moral principles but also can help us make progress on difficult social and political issues where conflicting arguments are each sufficiently strong to appeal to reasonable people of good will. Often, we need to make judgments between conflicting views although there may be some support for each of the competing sides. All too often, people faced with difficult political and social issues react by throwing up their hands. "Who is to say who is right?" is one typical response of those paralyzed by complexity. Many others react with a dogmatic adherence to their own beliefs or to those of some unquestioned authority figure, regardless of possible criticisms of their own views or the reasons supporting conflicting viewpoints. Reasoned discussion of the issues provides an alternative both to dogmatism and to moral paralysis by analysis. We hope that *The Individual and the Political Order* helps to show that the alternative of reasoned discourse is feasible, of the highest importance to society, and intellectually stimulating as well.

INDEX

individual: liberal notion of, 187–89; as a product of culture (society), 23, 187–88; rational development of 158–59

inequality 195; of income or wealth, 1, 64–65, 87–88, 91, 96, 98, 221, 228; in the Lockean state of nature, 62, 64–65, 222

Johnson, Samuel, 244

justice, 4, 6, 12, 25, 38–39, 43, 54, 70, 83–84, 88, 90, 99–100, 156–57, 161, 185, 196–98, 200, 202, 213, 219, 221, 227–28, 245, 253; global, 220–21, 226–29; historical (end state) vs. nonhistorical principles of, 91; liberal theory of, 100–01; patterned principles of 91; Rawls's theory of, 84–89, 91, 184–87, 190, 220–21; Rawls's two principles of, 86–88, 91; procedural, 84–86, 88–89, 99–100, 177, 190; socialist principle of, 98; Walzer's theory of, 189

Justinian, 54–55

Kantianism, 196–97

Kennedy, John F., 252

King, Martin Luther Jr., 21, 144, 236–37

Kohlberg, Lawrence, 196

Kymlicka, Will, 193–94

labor, 61–62, 92, 95–97, 99, 222–23; division of, 95–97

Lackey, Douglas, 251

law of nature, 15, 43, 54, 62. *See also* natural law

Law of the Sea Treaty, 221, 227–28

Lenin, 98

liberalism, 22–23; welfare, 24

libertarianism (libertarians), 6, 24, 69, 89, 92–94, 110, 125, 141, 222–23, 226

liberty, 4–5, 23, 38, 56, 61, 68–69, 86, 90, 105, 110, 114, 116, 120, 123, 128, 130, 184, 192, 222–23, 226 ; concept of, 106–08, 110–11; negative, 107–10, 141,; positive, 107–10, 164,; priority of, 141–42, 145; vs. equality, 89, 93, 141,; vs. security, 142–46. *See also* freedom

lifeboat ethics, 213–15

Lincoln, Abraham, 190

Locke, John, 19, 23, 59–65, 71, 78, 92, 101, 141, 153, 162, 174–75, 222; criticisms of, 64–65, 223

luck, 100, 215, 221, 225–26; moral, 94, 215, 224

Lyons, David, 46

MacCallum, Gerald, 110n10

MacIntyre, Alasdair, 183

MacKinnon, Barbara, 243

Madison, James, 153, 159

majority voting, 39, 63, 142, 154, 162, 168–69, 200

Mandela, Nelson, 76

Marx, Karl, 84, 89, 95–99; criticisms of 98–99; theory of justice, 95–98

Matusa, Mari, 136

McVeigh, Timothy, 254, 259

merit, 83–84, 88, 100; as a criterion of justice 83–84, 189

Mill, John Stuart, 35–40, 42, 106–7, 111–13, 116, 123, 127–30, 134, 141, 156–59, 185; harm principle, 112–16, 122–24, 126–27; justification for democracy, 157–59

minimum standard of living. *See* welfare floor

moral relativism, 3, 71, 170–71

morality: and war, 2, 6, 207; enforcement of, 116–20, 122, 134; in international affairs, 207–9, 229

Morganthau, Hans, 208–9

Moore, G. E., 38

national interest, 207–10, 212, 228; concept of, 210–11

natural law, 54–57, 59–63. *See also* law of nature

natural resources, 223–27; as an issue of justice, 221–26

Nazis, 51, 56, 238, 242, 244, 246–47, 250–51, 256

need, 83–84, 93, 99, 214; as a criterion of justice, 83–84, 98–99, 189

nihilism, 3

Nixon, Richard, 144

Noddings, Nel, 196

social contract theory, 30, 59, 61, 63–65,
85, 88–89, 162, 174–76, 228–29; tacit
consent in, 175–76
Socrates, 57
Soros, George, 227
special interests, 29
speech, 109, 127, 130–31, 134–40, 200–1;
codes, 131–40, 146,; free, 5, 105, 111,
116, 135, 154, 171–72; hate, 5–6, 105,
115, 131–36, 140, 146
Stalin, Joseph, 238
state, 220–21, 239–41; as protector of
human rights, 58, 63, 66, 68–70, 78, 174,
177–78, 191, ; 239; as an adjudicator of
rights conflicts, 78, 174, 178, 199; civic
republican view of, 191–92; function of
14, 17, 20, 24–25, 29, 52, 59, 63, 100, 174,
191, 202; legitimacy of, 5, 14–25; the
neutral, 22–25; utilitarian justification
of, 25, 39; welfare, 67, 69, 110
state of nature, 14–16, 18–20, 60, 92, 211;
Hobbesian, 209, 211–12, 261; Lockean,
60–63, 222, 239
Stephens, James Fitzjames, 113, 117, 128
Stoics, 54–55, 60
suicide: prevention of, 123–5

Taliban, 202, 240–41
Taylor, Charles, 183, 188, 193
terrorism (terrorists), 143, 145–46, 157, 210,
229, 235, 246, 254–59, 261–62, 264;
definition of, 253–56; excuses for, 256–59
Thompson, Dennis, 167
Thoreau, Henry David, 12
Thucydides, 207–8
tolerance (toleration), 5, 170, 184, 190, 194,
210

United Nations, 66, 260–61; Declaration of
Human Rights, 59, 66, 76; Millennium
Project, 221, 227
utilitarian: justification of democracy,
155–59; justification of the state, 48
utilitarianism, 29, 33–34, 56, 71, 100,
127–30, 196, 215, 217–19, 242, 247, 252,
258, 264; act distinguished from rule,
36–38, 41–43, 46, 129, 156; Bentham's
30–36; criticisms of 32–35, 38–47, 56,
58, 217–19; economic theory of, 39–40;
ideal, 39; Mill's, 35–40, 128–30;
negative, 217

Vattel, Emerich de, 239
veil of ignorance (ignorance principle),
85–89, 99–100, 175, 177, 184, 198, 220,
224

Walzer, Michael, 183, 189, 236, 249,
250–51, 259
war, 146, 207, 229, 235, 238, 240–43, 245,
248, 252, 260–264; of all against all, 14,
16, 18, 20, 60, 160, 185, 211; just, 9, 143,
212, 235, 238–47, 250–51, 263–64;
nuclear, 235, 251–53; preventive 9,
260–262
Warren, Earl, 145
Washington, George, 158
Wasserstrom, Richard, 53, 73
welfare floor, 92–93
Will, George, 23
Williams, Bernard, 43–44, 74
Williams, Melissa, 167
Wolff, Robert Paul, 12n3, 20–21, 161

Young, Iris Marion, 101, 183, 197–202

ABOUT THE AUTHORS

Norman E. Bowie is the Elmer L. Andersen Chair in Corporate Responsibility at the University of Minnesota. He is the author or editor of fifteen books and over seventy-five scholarly articles in business ethics, political philosophy, and related fields. His most recent book is *Management Ethics* and his most recent edited book is *Blackwell Guide to Business Ethics*. His authoritative coedited text *Ethical Theory and Business* is in its seventh edition and the eighth edition is in press. He is currently associate editor of *Business Ethics Quarterly*. He is on the editorial board of the *Academy of Management Review*. He has held a position as Dixons Professor of Business Ethics and Social Responsibility at the London Business School and been a fellow at Harvard's Program in Ethics and the Professions. He is a founding member of the Society for Business Ethics and served as it president in 1988. He is past president of the American Society for Value Inquiry and in 1997 received the James Wilbur Award for extraordinary contributions to the appreciation and advancement of human values. He served as executive director of the American Philosophical Association from 1972 to 1977.

Robert L. Simon is the Marjorie and Robert W. McEwen Professor of Philosophy at Hamilton College. He is the author of *Fair Play*, *Values and Sport*, and *Neutrality and the Academic Ethic* as well as many articles in ethics, political philosophy, and philosophy of sport. He also is the editor of *The Blackwell Guide to Social and Political Philosophy*. He has held fellowships from the National Endowment for the Humanities, the American Council of Learned Societies, the National Humanities Center, and the Center for Advanced Study in the Behavioral Sciences. He combines his interest in philosophy and sport by having served as president of the International Association for the Philosophy of Sport and as golf coach at Hamilton. In 2007, he was named to the advisory and editorial board of the NCAA's new initiative, the Scholarly Colloquium on Intercollegiate Sports, which encourages research in a variety of disciplines on college sports.